EXPLORATIONS IN GIFTEDNESS

This book is a scholarly overview of modern concepts, definitions, and theories of intellectual giftedness, and of past and current developments in the field of gifted education. The authors consider, in some detail, the roles of intelligence, creativity, and wisdom in giftedness and the interaction between culture and giftedness, as well as how giftedness can be understood in terms of a construct of developing expertise. The authors also review and discuss a set of key studies that address the issues of identification and education of children with intellectual gifts. This volume may be used as a summary overview of the field for educators, psychologists, social workers, and other professionals who serve intellectually gifted children and their families.

Robert J. Sternberg is provost and senior vice president and professor of psychology and education at Oklahoma State University as well as honorary professor of psychology at the University of Heidelberg. Prior to coming to Oklahoma State, he was dean of the School of Arts and Sciences at Tufts University. Sternberg is president of the International Association for Cognitive Education and Psychology and president-elect of the Federation of Associations of Behavioral and Brain Sciences. Sternberg's PhD is from Stanford, and he has 11 honorary degrees. He is the author of about 1,200 publications and has held more than $20 million in grants. He is the recipient of approximately two dozen professional awards.

Linda Jarvin is an associate research professor in the Department of Education at Tufts University and director of its Center for Enhancing Learning and Teaching (CELT). She received her PhD in cognitive psychology and individual differences from the University of Paris V (France) and her postdoctoral training at Yale University. She has extensive experience with curriculum planning and development, designing and implementing professional development opportunities for K–12 teachers and college professors, and facilitating programmatic evaluation plans.

Elena L. Grigorenko is associate professor of child studies, psychology, and epidemiology and public health at Yale University and adjunct professor of psychology at Columbia University and Moscow State University, Russia. She received her PhD in general psychology from Moscow State University, Russia, in 1990, and her PhD in developmental psychology and genetics from Yale University in 1996. Grigorenko has published more than 250 peer-reviewed articles, book chapters, and books. She has received multiple professional awards for her work. Her research has been funded by the NIH, NSF, DOE, USAID, Cure Autism Now, Foundation for Child Development, American Psychological Foundation, and other federal and private sponsoring organizations.

Explorations in Giftedness

Robert J. Sternberg
Oklahoma State University

Linda Jarvin
Tufts University

Elena L. Grigorenko
Yale University

CAMBRIDGE
UNIVERSITY PRESS

KH

CAMBRIDGE UNIVERSITY PRESS
Cambridge, New York, Melbourne, Madrid, Cape Town, Singapore,
São Paulo, Delhi, Dubai, Tokyo, Mexico City

Cambridge University Press
32 Avenue of the Americas, New York, NY 10013-2473, USA

www.cambridge.org
Information on this title: www.cambridge.org/9780521740098

First published 2011

Printed in the United States of America

A catalog record for this publication is available from the British Library.

Library of Congress Cataloging in Publication data
Sternberg, Robert J.
Explorations in giftedness / Robert J. Sternberg, Linda Jarvin, Elena L.
Grigorenko.
    p.   cm.
Includes bibliographical references and index.
ISBN 978-0-521-51854-3 (hardback) – ISBN 978-0-521-74009-8 (pbk.)
1. Gifted children.   I. Jarvin, Linda.   II. Grigorenko, Elena L.   III. Title.
LC3993.S84   2010
371.95–dc22   2010029220

ISBN 978-0-521-51854-3 Hardback
ISBN 978-0-521-74009-8 Paperback

10/4/11

This book is dedicated to our dear friend and colleague Joseph Renzulli of the University of Connecticut, who, perhaps more than anyone else, has changed both the way we conceive of giftedness and the nature of gifted education itself.

CONTENTS

PREFACE

William James and William James Sidis represent almost opposite ends of a continuum. William James was a gifted youngster who was to become one of the leading philosophers and psychologists of his generation. Some consider him to be the greatest American psychologist of all time. William James Sidis was a gifted youngster who flamed out early in life and, after an extraordinary start, became bitter, let his health go, and died at an early age. James is remembered as a gifted adult who started off as a gifted youngster. Sidis never reached the glory of his namesake and is remembered as a classic example of a bright flame that was extinguished early.

What is it that leads some gifted youngsters to become gifted adults and others not to make the transition from being a gifted youngster to being a gifted adult? What leads individuals to make transitions in the kinds of developing expertise that lead society to label these individuals as gifted, not only from childhood to adulthood but from one stage of childhood to another stage of childhood or from one stage of adulthood to another stage of adulthood? More specifically, what leads individuals from some ethnic groups to be identified as gifted more frequently than individuals from other ethnic groups?

Is it possible that some of the children not being identified as gifted have the gifts and talents to be major contributors to their fields, and that some of the children being identified have lesser talents? In particular, is it possible that underserved minority students have the abilities to excel in their careers, but never get the chance to display these talents because the educational system does not recognize their gifts? Consider three key problems of giftedness dealt with in this book.

First, consider the issue of *identification*. One of the goals of gifted education is to identify those who are most likely to make important contributions, of whatever kind, to society. From this point of view, we need to understand what giftedness is and what transitions in giftedness are over the life span in order to understand which children truly have the most potential to develop the kinds of expertise needed to make important contributions, and which are more likely to flame out and thus be less likely to develop the needed expertise and to make such contributions. Without such understanding, we may be identifying as gifted individuals those who have a lesser potential contribution to make. They may, for example, be good in taking tests, but contribute little to the world. We may be failing especially to identify under-served minority children who could excel in careers, but whose excellence is not shown in the conventional assessments used for identification.

Second, consider the issue of *instruction*. To the extent that giftedness is in part a matter of developing expertise, educators may be able to help young children develop the kinds of expertise that will lead to long-term contributions if they can determine just what types of expertise these are. Educators cannot adequately decide on how and what to teach if they are not clear as to what kinds of expertise they are trying to develop through their instruction. A further important issue is that underserved minority children often may best learn in ways that do not correspond well to the ways in which traditional instruction is delivered, so that these children do not have the opportunity to fulfill their potential to excel. Instruction needs to match identification to ensure that students identified as gifted are taught in a way that helps them capitalize on strengths and compensate for or correct weaknesses.

Third, consider the issue of *evaluation*. Samples of children's performance – homework assignments, examinations, essays, projects, and the like – should be evaluated in terms of the kinds of expertise that are important to develop. Such evaluation thus requires identifying what kinds of expertise are important. Otherwise, we may end up evaluating children on the wrong criteria and rewarding the wrong children (as well as adults). Essentially, these are criteria that are viewed as mattering in school but not later in careers, or even earlier in school but not later in a school career. The evaluation must match the identification and instruction. Underserved minority children may make it through the identification and instruction processes, but unless the evaluations of achievement match what they have learned, they will not get credit for their achievements.

Thus, the objective of the research we have done has been to discover the bases for identification, instruction, and evaluation that warrant successful transitions in giftedness across developmental levels and that, in particular, do justice to members of underrepresented minorities. The problem is how to capitalize on the talent of the nation's youngsters, our most precious resource as a nation. Currently, traditional memory and analytical abilities are stressed in the identification of children for gifted education programs. However, our research has suggested that creative and practical skills are as important as, if not more important than, analytical skills to success in life. We have found that even individuals who are analytically and creatively gifted will not necessarily possess the abilities to excel as adults. For example, they may be able to produce creative artwork but not know how to get it exhibited, or write creative stories but not know how to get them published, or have creative entrepreneurial ideas but not know how to get them funded, or compose creative musical arrangements but not know how to get them performed. They may fail in later transitions of giftedness because they are ineffective at promoting their ideas.

This book aims to bring together some of the enduring themes and most significant work on gifted and talented identification and education of Robert J. Sternberg and his collaborators at the Center for the Psychology of Abilities, Competencies, and Expertise (PACE), a center originally at Yale University and then at Tufts University. This book represents an overview of roughly a dozen years of research in the United States and abroad. We are grateful to all the collaborators we have had over the years, and in addition to the PACE team members listed below, we wish to acknowledge the contributions of Li-fang Zhang, an occasional visiting Fellow at the PACE Center, who collaborated in our work on the "pentagonal theory of giftedness" described in Chapter 1. Rena Subotnik contributed to the work on music and giftedness. Lee Coffin and Tzur Karelitz played important roles in our work at Tufts. Joseph Renzulli, director of the National Research Center for Giftedness/Talent, has been an invaluable colleague and friend over the many years we were involved in the National Center, the senior author as associate director.

We are very grateful to all the PACE members who were involved in this effort, and wish to thank (in alphabetical order)

Damian Birney, Mark Bluemling, Derrick Carpenter, Hillary Chart, Tona Donlon, Niamh Doyle, Sarah Duman, Nancy Fredine, Carol Gordon, Lesley Hart, Jonna Kwiatkowski, Donna Macomber, Nefeli Misuraca, Erik Moga, Alexei Nelayev, Tina Newman, Paul O'Keefe, Carolyn Parish, Judi Randi, Morgen Reynolds, Robyn Rissman, Emma Seppala, Gregory Snortheim, Steven Stemler, Olga Stepanossova, and Mei Tan.

The work reflected in this book and the book's preparation were supported by several grants: Grants REC-9979843, REC-0710915, and REC-0633952 from the National Science Foundation; the College Board and Educational

Testing Services (ETS) through Contract PO # 0000004411; Grant Award # 31-1992-701 from the United States Department of Education, Institute for Educational Sciences (as administered by the Temple University Laboratory for Student Success); Grant R206R950001 under the Javits Act Program as administered by the Office of Educational Research and Improvement, U.S. Department of Education; and a grant from the W. T. Grant Foundation. Grantees undertaking such projects are encouraged to express freely their professional judgment. This book, therefore, does not necessarily represent the position or policies of the National Science Foundation, the College Board, Educational Testing Services, the United States Department of Education, or the W. T. Grant Foundation and no official endorsement should be inferred.

RJS, LJ, ELG
June 2010

1

What Is Giftedness?

The Montgomery County, Maryland, public schools decided in December of 2008 to scrap the gifted label (De Vise, 2008; Stabley, 2008). According to school officials, erasing the label does not matter because gifted instruction is still available – to all students. Not all parents have been pleased with this decision: "If Montgomery school officials don't 'give these kids a name, they can ignore the real fact they exist,' Lori White Wasserman, a parent, wrote on an e-mail list for advocates of gifted instruction in the county" (quoted in De Vise, 2008).

The school officials had reasons for their decision. How good the reasons were is a matter of debate.

First, Montgomery County is a district in which, according to De Vise (2008), most if not all parents think their children are above average. One is reminded of Garrison Keillor's mythical Lake Wobegon, where all the children are above average (Garrison Keillor quotes, 2009). So some parents were apparently offended when their children were not identified as gifted.

Second, Montgomery County is among those school districts that are extremely competitive. Its schools are nationally, and perhaps internationally, famous and students work very hard to compete in a pressured atmosphere. Dropping the "gifted" label is one effort to decrease the competition and the marks of separation among the students in the district.

Third, Montgomery's philosophy appears to be that all children should receive the quality of education traditionally reserved for the gifted. If all children receive basically the same instruction, then it is not clear what value there is to labeling children differentially. The labels then might be seen as serving no clear educational purpose, other than to label!

Do we need a label of "gifted"? What does "gifted" really mean? Why is a child who scores in the top 1% on the Wechsler Intelligence Scale for Children much more likely to be labeled as gifted than a child whose

100-meter sprinting time places her in the top 1% of her age cohort? Why is a physicist who is considered #1 in the country by his or her peers or another panel of judges considered gifted, whereas the bank robber who is #1 on the FBI's most-wanted list is not?

In one culture, the gifted individual might be viewed as a hunter; in another culture, as a drummer; and in a third, as a student. The first two cultures might not even have any type of formal schooling, whereas the third one might not provide much opportunity for the development of hunting skills. So we need some basis for specifying how we identify gifted individuals.

THE PENTAGONAL THEORY FOR IDENTIFYING THE GIFTED

We have proposed that giftedness can be understood in terms of five criteria. We have referred to this as the "pentagonal" theory of giftedness (Sternberg, 1993; Sternberg & Zhang, 1995).

The Excellence Criterion

The excellence criterion states that the individual is *superior in some dimension or set of dimensions relative to peers.* To be gifted, one has to be extremely good at something – in psychological terminology, high in a judged dimension or dimensions. How high is "extremely high" may vary from one context to another, but the gifted person is always perceived to be abundant in something, whether it be creativity, wisdom, or another skill or construct. In the present view, excellence relative to peers is a necessary condition for an individual to be labeled as gifted, but not a sufficient one.

The qualification "relative to peers" is necessary because the designation of excellence depends upon the skills of those against whom one is judged. A 10-year-old's raw score on an intelligence test might convert into a very high score relative to age peers but would seem unexceptional relative to children 5 years older. Similarly, a musical performance that would be exceptional for an 8-year-old taking weekly music lessons at school might be quite undistinguished for an 8-year-old who has been trained at a specialized music school since age 4.

There are those who would like to dispense with the "gifted" label. Some of the educators in Montgomery County seem to be among them. To the extent their argument is that all children deserve an excellent education, we agree. But to the extent that the argument implies there are not individual differences in excellence of the students, we disagree. There are individual differences in almost everything – height, weight, body build, musical skills, and athletic skills. What, exactly, do such individual differences imply?

First, the existence of individual differences says nothing about modifiability. Most individual differences are modifiable (Sternberg, 1997a). Gifted education does not imply that students are stuck at a particular level of performance. All students, including gifted ones, can improve in their levels of skills and knowledge.

Second, as students learn, patterns of individual differences change (Sternberg & Grigorenko, 2001a, 2002a). So if one does gifted identification, one has to realize that who is identified as gifted may change as a function of the kinds of tasks presented and the kinds of situations in which they are presented. The people who are the best hunters are not necessarily the best mathematicians, and vice versa. But no one has yet found a way to eliminate individual differences.

Third, there is intraindividual variability as well as interindividual variability. The people who look smart at one age or skill level might be different from those who look smarter at a different age or skill level. For example, the champion mathematician of the sixth-grade arithmetic class may flame out when he or she reaches trigonometry. Similarly, the ace in trigonometry may be much less adept in constructing complex mathematical proofs.

Finally, excellence will exist whether we have a word for it or not. We can get rid of the "gifted" label, but giftedness will continue to exist whether we label it or not. In anti-utopian novels, such as Orwell's *1984* or Clarke's *The City and the Stars*, politicians may try to homogenize the masses. But people will differ despite the efforts of politicians, educators, or anyone else. They will also have different educational needs. Changing how language is used will not change the differential needs with which students come to the classroom.

The Rarity Criterion

The rarity criterion states that to be labeled as gifted, an individual must possess a *high level of an attribute that is rare relative to peers*. The rarity criterion is needed to supplement the excellence criterion because a person may show an abundance of a given attribute, but if a high evaluation of that attribute is not judged to be rare, the person is not viewed as gifted. Suppose we give a test of mastery of the basics of the English language to a class of college seniors at a good university. They should all score very high on the test because all are proficient in the basics of English. But even if all received perfect scores, we would not say they are all therefore gifted. Thus, one may display excellence, but unless such excellence is rare, one is not likely to be viewed as gifted.

The senior author once heard a talk in which the speaker said that, were it not for bad schooling, everyone would have an IQ over 180. It is not clear what he meant, as IQs are assigned on the basis of statistical deviations from the average score, and if people's performances increased, the average IQ would still be 100. Indeed, Flynn (1987) found that people's performances, at least on IQ tests, increased through much of the 20th century. Test publishers just kept redefining what they meant by an IQ of 100, so that the level of performance needed to reach this score increased.

The point is that even if mean levels increase, there will still be people who perform at high (as well as low) levels that are relatively rare. Their educational needs will be different from the needs of those who perform at more typical levels in their cohort. Anyone who has ever sat through a class bored stiff because the material was much too easy (or frustrated because the material was much too hard) knows this fact. So the level of absolute performance that is labeled as "gifted" may change from one time to another; but the fact that some few people will do much better than others will not change.

Grade inflation is, in a way, a refusal to acknowledge that there will always be differences, whatever they mean. Grade inflation may genuinely reflect a difference in the quality of students over time – perhaps they are getting better. It probably also reflects an abrogation of the responsibility of teachers to recognize that, whatever the mean, individual differences will still exist. But if we were to give everyone A's or to assign everyone an IQ of 180 or above, we still would not dispense with the fact that gifted performance represents the top of one or more distributions, wherever those distributions may be at a given time or place.

The Productivity Criterion

The productivity criterion states that *the dimension(s) along which the individual is evaluated as superior must lead to, or potentially lead to, productivity.* Consider the contestants in a beauty contest. Why must they answer questions about issues of the day rather than rely solely on their appearance? In fact, appearance is probably the major determinant in the contest, so why is it not sufficient? Despite the fact that the contest is about beauty, beauty in itself is not perceived as productive or potentially productive. Each contestant needs to demonstrate that she can do something. In contrast, the contestant in a scientific competition is not judged on other dimensions, such as personal appearance, because the scientific work itself – the basis of the contest – is viewed as productive.

The productivity criterion generates disagreements over exactly who should be labeled as gifted. Some, for example, believe that a high score on an intelligence test is not sufficient grounds for labeling a person as gifted. These people see the tests as meaningless (e.g., Gardner, 1983) because the high-scoring person has not shown that he or she can do anything. Others view getting a high score on the test as doing something in and of itself. At worst, the high score shows the person's potential for productivity.

In childhood, of course, it is possible to be labeled as gifted without having been productive. In fact, children are typically judged largely on potential rather than actual productivity. As people get older, however, the relative weights of potential and actualized potential change, and emphasis is placed on actual productivity. Any number of gifted children become adults whom people do not think of as exceptional. Renzulli (1986) has referred to such adults as "school-house gifted."

People who do not realize their potential through some kind of productive work may still be labeled as gifted, but with qualifications. They may be called gifted individuals whose gifts somehow failed to actualize themselves. To earn the label "gifted" without qualification, a person must accomplish something.

In this book, we argue that there is good reason to think about productivity, or at the very least, potential productivity, as a criterion for giftedness. Simply receiving high scores on an IQ test trivializes what it means to be gifted. If one looks at organizations that accept only people with high IQs, one will find in those organizations some people who are contributing something meaningful to the world, and others whose sole claim to fame in their lives may be their IQ test scores. We shall argue here that such a claim – to be gifted solely on the basis of IQ – is a small one indeed: Truly to be gifted, you need to be productively intelligent, not just intelligent in some abstracted sense that makes no contact with the world outside the IQ test.

The Demonstrability Criterion

The demonstrability criterion states that the *superiority of the individual on the dimension(s) that determine giftedness must be demonstrable through one or more tests that are valid assessments.* The individual needs to be able to demonstrate, in one way or another, that he or she really has the abilities or achievements that led to the judgment of giftedness. Simply claiming giftedness is not enough. Thus, a person who scores poorly on all measures used in assessment and who is unable to demonstrate in any compelling alternative way that he or she does indeed have special abilities will not be viewed as gifted.

The assessment instrument(s) used, however, must be valid. Validity means that each instrument is shown to measure what it is supposed to measure. If, for example, a child presents a high score on a new intelligence test that requires only that the child dot i's, the results are unlikely to be valid. Dotting i's is not an acceptable measure of intelligence. Or suppose that a job candidate gives a persuasive talk, suggesting unusual gifts both in research and in presentation. But when asked about the content of the talk, he is unable to answer even the simplest of questions. Gradually, members of the audience conclude that the job candidate was somehow programmed, probably by his graduate advisor. In fact, he has no idea of what he was talking about. The job talk then would be invalid as a measure of the candidate because it did not actually reflect his gifts (or lack thereof), but rather, his advisor's.

The validity issue has become extremely important in recent years in the identification of intellectually gifted schoolchildren. In the past, many schools were content to use standardized intelligence tests, and perhaps grades in school and scores on achievement tests, as sole bases for identifying children as intellectually gifted. As the focus of testing has shifted more and more toward an emphasis on performance – and product-based assessment – however, some have questioned the sufficiency of the traditional measures (e.g., Gardner, 1983; Renzulli, 1986) as sole bases for ascertaining giftedness. Someone who would have been labeled as gifted under traditional measures might not now be so labeled. The implicit theory – folk conception – of giftedness may not have changed, but what is considered valid as a demonstration of giftedness may have.

The Value Criterion

The value criterion states that for a person to be labeled as gifted, *the person must show superior performance in one or more dimensions that is valued for that person by his or her society*. The value criterion restricts the label of giftedness to those who have attributes that are valued as relevant to giftedness. The individual who is #1 on the FBI's most wanted list might be superior in one or more dimensions, rare in his ability to perform certain malevolent acts, and able to demonstrate his skills upon demand. He may even be highly productive, if in a criminal way. But because what he is so good at is not valued by society at large, he is not likely to be labeled as gifted by the American populace. Still, it is quite possible that he would be labeled as gifted by other bank robbers; the pentagonal theory allows that what is prized as a basis for giftedness may differ from one culture, or even subculture, to another.

Who is qualified to judge giftedness, anyway? Anyone can judge, although not all implicit theories are good ones. The pentagonal theory allows us to say that people of another place or time have erred in their evaluations of a person's gifts. If we do so, it is true that we are claiming a privileged position with regard to the identification of someone as gifted. We are arguing that our values are right because those of certain others were wrong, or because these others did not have access to information we now have. In either of these cases, we are claiming the privilege of being in a superior position to judge. What we must realize, of course, is that others may do the same with respect to us in some other time or place. They may view our criteria as quaint, obscure, or just wrong.

Implicit theories by nature are relativistic; there is never any guarantee that people's personal values will match across time and space. But implicit theories provide the best practical form or structure by which to identify the gifted. For a judgment to occur according to strict standards, one needs to add content to implicit theories.

The value criterion is the one about which our society has been least reflective. Many schools still use today the same bases for assigning the label of "gifted" that were being used a century ago. But the skills that are relevant to gifted performance may well have changed. For example, arithmetic-computation skill was more important in 1960 than in 2010, because in 2010 calculators and computers are available that were not available in 1960. Certainly our own skill in measuring giftedness has changed, although that change is not always recognized in educational practice. In Chapter 2, we will present a model that we believe is useful in capturing the attributes relevant for identifying gifted individuals in today's world.

TESTING THE PENTAGONAL THEORY

The pentagonal theory was intended to capture people's implicit theories, or folk conceptions, of what giftedness means. Does it? We conducted a study to determine whether the pentagonal theory did indeed capture people's implicit theories of giftedness (Sternberg & Zhang, 1995). College students as well as parents of gifted children were given descriptions of children. Each description gave six pieces of information about a child. Then the participants were asked to judge whether (a) they would identify the described student as gifted and whether (b) they thought the school would identify the described student as gifted. The descriptions were based on hypothetical students and hypothetical tests. In the example below, for instance, Bernadine is fictional and the Bader Creativity Test is fictional. Here is a sample item:

1. Bernadine's score on the Bader Creativity Test was good.
2. This score was in the top 20% of her school.
3. The Bader Creativity Test has been found to be accurate in predicting gifted performance for 40% of students.
4. The school considers the Bader Creativity Test to be a mediocre measure of giftedness.
5. Bernadine submitted four independent projects.
6. The school believes that independent projects are an excellent measure of giftedness.

Descriptions were the same for boys and girls, with only the names changed. Thus, for example, for half the students, "Bernadine" was "Seth." There were 60 descriptions in all, presented in three different orders across participants to minimize order effects.

Of course, not all items involved the Bader Creativity Test. In fact, each item involved a different test. Although the names of the tests were different, only six constructs were involved, balanced equally across items: creativity, intelligence (e.g., the Hunter Intelligence Test), social skills (e.g., the Perkins Social-Skills Test), motivation (e.g., the Bradley Motivation Test), and achievement (e.g., the Swanson Achievement Test).

The results were quite straightforward for both samples. Using a statistical technique called multiple regression, we found that all of the criteria mattered for both the individual's judgment and the school's judgment except demonstrability, which mattered only for self-judgments but not assessed judgments of the schools. That is, the participants thought demonstrability mattered but were not convinced that schools would. But from the standpoint of the individual's judgment, all five criteria did, in fact, matter.

IMPLICATIONS OF THE PENTAGONAL THEORY

Consider some of the implications of the pentagonal theory for questions that one might ask in the field of gifted education.

1. What percentage of children should be identified as gifted?

We have been asked this question many times, as though there is a single right answer. Of course, there is not. But the pentagonal theory helps us address this question by separating two often confounded concepts that ought to be distinguished: excellence and rarity.

Our use of norm-based measurement (in which measures are based on comparisons of one individual's performance with that of other individuals), which practically equates excellence and rarity, leads to confusion. All of us who have taught know that one year we may have an excellent class, in which many or even most of the students perform at a very high level, and another year we may have a weak class in which few people perform well. Criterion-based measurement (in which measures are based on performance relative to some external standard, regardless of how other students perform) helps us avoid confounding excellence with rarity. We need to think in criterion-based terms to answer the question regarding the "right" percentage to be identified.

One way of using the pentagonal theory is to suggest that we identify as gifted that percentage of students whose performance on some set of standards meets a present criterion of excellence and for whom we have the resources to provide special services. We thereby acknowledge that our limitations in identification reflect not only students' abilities but also our ability to serve such students. We need to consider excellence independently of rarity and to realize that we seek out rarity in part because of our inability to serve all students who may truly have very impressive potentials.

Historically, percentages have been chosen and then treated as though they are somehow nonarbitrary. But there is no one percentage that is truly a cutoff for giftedness. Indeed, it is not even clear what it would mean to have such a percentage.

2. What constructs or measures should we use to identify the gifted?

The pentagonal theory makes clear that there is no one right construct or measure, or even set of constructs or measures that we ought to use. Rather than simply doing what we do because it has always been done that way, we need to take responsibility for stating explicitly just what it is that we value and why. If we care about the potential of an individual to contribute to himself/herself, others, and society in a productive way, then we need to justify why the measures we use will help identify such potentially productive individuals.

Programming for the gifted can pass through various stages of sophistication. The least metacognitively (self-) aware formulators of programs for the gifted simply use whatever measures have been used in the past to identify the gifted in a way that is almost wholly lacking in reflection and self-awareness. Call them Stage I programmers. Stage II programmers, somewhat more aware of modern theories, may latch onto a particular theory of giftedness and use that, citing the theorist as their authority. These programmers have considered some alternatives. Stage III programmers are still more metacognitively aware and will be able to defend why they use a particular set of traditional techniques not clearly based in any theory. But the most thoughtful programmers, those of Stage IV, will not simply latch onto whatever happens to be around, with or without justification, but rather, will have a conception of what it is that they value and will then seek a theory or a combination of theories to help realize the system of values. Stage IV programmers realize that the use of an explicit theory (conventional theory formulated by experts) to help identify the gifted automatically makes a statement not only about the constructs with which the theory or theories deal (such as intelligence or creativity) but also about what is valued by those who will make identification decisions. In Stage IV, you first decide what you are looking for and then decide how to find it. Too often in the past, identification of the gifted has failed adequately to grapple with the question of "what are we looking for?"

3. What kind of educational program is ideal for gifted children?

Debates about the best program for gifted children take on a different character when viewed from the standpoint of the pentagonal theory. There is no one right answer to the question of what kind of program is best. Rather, we again need to ask ourselves what we value – best for what? If we value rapid learning and believe that rapid learners will be in an enhanced position to contribute to our society, then acceleration makes sense. If we believe that what matters is the depth or care students take in probing into what they learn, enrichment will be preferable. If both are prized, we might use a combination. Whatever we do, we should ensure that the values expressed in the instructional program are the same as those expressed in the identification program. If we select for rapid learners, we ought to teach in kind. Once we clarify what we value, we should then act accordingly. The reason that debates about how to teach the gifted go on indefinitely is that there is no one right answer.

In conclusion, the pentagonal theory provides a basis for understanding how people assign the label of "giftedness" to some individuals but not others. It suggests a framework supporting such judgments. Explicit theories of abilities, formulated by experts, fill in the rest.

DO WE STILL NEED A LABEL OF "GIFTEDNESS"?

We believe that the "gifted" label serves a value function in society. But we are skeptical with regard to the way the label is typically used. In particular, we do not believe it appropriate to label someone as gifted merely on the basis of IQ, or of IQ and achievement-test scores.

The problem with traditional labeling is that it is very much oriented toward only one aspect of giftedness, namely, the academic side. Academic skills are certainly important, especially during the school years, when children are largely evaluated in terms of their academic accomplishments. But are these skills the only ones or even the primary ones that will matter later in life? After the school years, few people will be taking either IQ or achievement tests, and the ability to get grades, unless it is transformed into something else, will not matter a great deal for future life outcomes. People will need to be able to adapt to rapidly changing environments; to work as parts of teams; to resolve conflicts with their peers, spouses, and children; and to maintain their health to the extent they can. Will academic skills still matter? Sure. People need to read prescription and nutritional labels, evaluate claims of advertisers and politicians, and make sense of their finances. But academic skills are only part of what leads to the realization of gifted potential. In this book, we consider many other skills as well.

MYTHS ABOUT GIFTEDNESS

The fall 2009 issue of *Gifted Child Quarterly*, a premier journal in the field of giftedness, carried a set of articles on myths in gifted education. We end this introductory chapter summarizing this list of myths, naming the researchers who have identified the myths, and then correcting the myths. We cannot do full justice to the ideas of the researchers and urge interested readers to consult the original articles for more details. Their ideas represent our own position quite well, so we present these ideas as an entrée into the rest of the book. We have combined some of the myths in the original issue of the journal when they overlapped, and we take responsibility for rewording some of the myths as they were originally presented.

1. The gifted and talented consist of one single and relatively homogeneous group over time (Reis & Renzulli, 2009a).

Correction: Giftedness is not one thing and what constitutes giftedness can change over time.

2. Giftedness equals high IQ in roughly the top 3% to 5% of the population (Borland, 2009b).

Correction: Giftedness does not inhere just in IQ, and there is no arbitrary percentage of the population that a priori constitutes the gifted segment of that population. What we mean by "giftedness" is a social construction, so it can vary from one time and place to another.

3. There is a single "silver bullet" in identification (Callahan, 2009; Friedman-Nimz, 2009; Worrell, 2009).

Correction: There is no set of assessment procedures that everyone today or ever will unanimously agree upon as the "right" set of procedures for identification of the gifted. Further, there is no one test score that tells us all we need to know about giftedness; we need multiple criteria.

4. Creativity cannot be measured (Treffinger, 2009).

Correction: There are various measures of creativity. Although none is perfect, they can give us at least some reading of individuals' creative skills.

5. There is one right way to teach gifted children (Hertzberg-Davis, 2009; Kaplan, 2009; Sisk, 2009).

Correction: Instruction to gifted children needs to be differentiated – it needs to recognize that different gifted children have different ways in which they learn. Curriculum needs to be differentiated.

6. Gifted education can be "patched on" to regular instruction – that is, it can be done as an add-on to regular curriculum (Adams, 2009; Tomlinson, 2009).

Correction: Gifted instruction needs to be systematically planned for and delivered.

7. Gifted services need relatively little attention because the learners are advanced anyway and almost anything will work (Gentry, 2009; S. Moon, 2009; Robinson, 2009; VanTassel-Baska, 2009).

Correction: Preparing quality programs for the gifted is at least as arduous as preparing other kinds of instructional programs because the needs of gifted learners are complex and diverse. The gifted program needs to fit into a comprehensive range of special-education services.

8. High-stakes tests can be counted on to assess the achievements of gifted children (T. Moon, 2009).

Correction: High-stakes tests are limited in what they measure and, taken alone, provide an inadequate assessment of the accomplishments of gifted learners.

9. The social and emotional needs of gifted learners are pretty much the same as those of other children their age (Peterson, 2009).

Correction: Gifted learners have their own special set of socioemotional challenges, some of them deriving from the very gifts that enable them to excel.

10. Advanced Placement (AP) college-level courses provide an adequate way for gifted high school children to be challenged (Gallagher, 2009).

Correction: AP courses often do not provide sufficient means for gifted students to engage fully their gifts and talents, especially their creative ones.

So these are some myths. What can we say more affirmatively about gifted education? Please read on to find out!

2

Theories of Giftedness

Theories of giftedness are diverse. In this chapter, we shall cover some of the main theories, as reviewed in major works on conceptions of giftedness (Renzulli, Gubbins, McMillen, Eckert, & Little, 2009; Sternberg & Davidson, 1986, 2005; see also Phillipson & McCann, 2007).

NO CONCEPTION

It is odd and might even seem oxymoronic to think of no conception of giftedness as a conception of giftedness. But Borland (2005, 2009a) has argued that gifted education would proceed better if we all viewed giftedness as a "chimera" (p. 2). Borland suggests that we dispense with a concept of giftedness for several reasons.

First, Borland asserts, giftedness is a social construct anyway, and one of doubtful validity. There is no absolute, definitive standard for what makes a person gifted. Societies construct their own conception of what they mean by giftedness. And, according to Borland, we all would be better off if they dispensed with the construct. Borland asserts that such a construct is of relatively recent invention. According to him, "there were no 'gifted' children in the 19th century" (p. 3).

We do not agree with this assertion. In the first place, the origins of mental testing date back to the ancient Chinese (Thomason & Qiong, 2008). They used tests, among other things, for selecting civil servants. Sir Francis Galton was writing about individuals of extreme gifts in the 1800s, and he is today considered one of the founders of the modern giftedness movement (Galton, 1869). Moreover, whether the term *gifted* was used or not, the concept certainly existed. Great painters such as Michelangelo or DaVinci, great musicians such as Bach and Beethoven, and great scientists such as

Galileo and Newton have always been seen as different from ordinary people, who never could have equaled their accomplishments.

Borland further argues against a point by Gallagher (1996), namely, that if "gifted child" is a social construct, so is "opera singer" and "baseball player" and we would not want to claim that there is no such thing as an opera singer or a baseball player. Borland points out that we could not have opera without opera singers or baseball without baseball players, but we could have schools without gifted students. That is true. But perhaps a better analogy is whether we could have "schools for the gifted" without gifted students. There the answer is no. Certainly we could have schools. In the same way, we could have opera and baseball without gifted opera singers and gifted baseball players, but the world would be a very different place without the gifted performers, not only in opera and baseball, but in every field. If everyone sang and played baseball the way we, the authors of this book, do these things, the world would be the poorer for it!

Second, according to Borland, educational practices based on the notion of particular children who are gifted have not been effective. Borland cites sources, generally from 20 or more years ago, arguing that there is little evidence for the effectiveness of gifted education. If, however, one were to pick up issues of major publications in giftedness – *Gifted Child Quarterly, Roeper Review, High Ability Studies* – one would find numerous studies suggesting that gifted education *is* effective. One would especially hope that some progress has been made in the past 20+ years, although, perhaps, more work needs to be done. But we believe that relying on such reviews as Slavin (1990), whether old or new, is fraught with challenges. Things have changed a lot in the more than 20 years since 1990.

Gifted education as we know it today is of relatively recent invention. True, there have long been special schools for special students. Harvard and Yale date back to early in the country's history and were always intended for individuals of gifts, although conceptions of what such gifts are have changed. Suppose that someone were to have looked at the effects of medical interventions for heart attacks in the early 1900s or even as late as the mid-20th century. Interventions and preventive measures were far less advanced than they are today. But there is a much longer history of dealing with heart problems than there has been of taking gifted education seriously. Even if something has not yet been tremendously successful, this does not mean that further efforts will not be. In the United States, the average life span increased from 49 years to 77 years from 1900 to 1998 (Aging and lifespan, n.d.) and was 78 in 2005 (Average life span at birth by race and sex, 1930–2005, n.d.). As time goes on, our ability to improve our services increases and past levels of success do not necessarily predict future ones, especially when there are discontinuous gains, such as the discovery of penicillin as an antibiotic or, for that matter, of new ways of teaching gifted students.

Third, Borland argues, having a notion of giftedness exacerbates what are already inequitably distributed educational resources. This comment strikes us as surprising, given that the proportion of special-education funding spent on gifted students, at least in the United States, is less than 1% of the total special-education budget. But if one looks at educational programming, state by state, district by district, there can be little doubt that when funds get scarce, gifted programming is among the first kinds of programming to fall by the wayside. Regardless of the percentage, philosophically, some people will always feel that any percentage spent on special programming for gifted students is too large.

We are not among those who are philosophically opposed to gifted programming. In a highly competitive globalized world, those nations that do not do well by their gifted students put themselves at risk for falling behind. Countries differ widely in their contributions to literature, science, art, music, and other fields. Some countries today, for example, make great strides in scientific research; others make few strides at all. Can there be much doubt that education for the gifted children in these countries will make a difference in the ability of the children to contribute great work in their chosen field of endeavor? To make outstanding scientific contributions, for example, one needs a powerful education in the science of one's choosing and related sciences. One also needs to gain the experience of doing cutting-edge research. Such experience is not to be had from a middle-of-the-road education. So is it a waste of resources to provide to those who can most advance society the best education possible that recognizes their talents? We think not. And any able student who has ever spent a year or more bored in mathematics classes that were way below his or her level is likely, we believe, to agree. Gifted education, we believe, is not "at odds with education in a democracy," any more than is special education for those with intellectual disabilities. Would we then say that if gifted education is at odds with democracy, so is any kind of special education? Rather, a democracy should provide equal opportunity to everyone, recognizing that not everyone can avail himself or herself equally well of every opportunity presented.

In the end, Borland suggests that we "dispense with the concept of giftedness . . . and focus instead on the goal of differentiating curricula and instruction for all of the diverse students in our schools" (pp. 12–13). But we believe that Borland has set up a false dichotomy here. We certainly endorse the concept of providing differentiated education according to children's needs and desires. But that does not mean that we need to dispense with the notion that some children are gifted, or at the very least, more gifted than others. It may mean that we need to dispense with the notion that there is one fixed population that is "gifted" and another that is not. We heartily agree that such a concept, based upon a single measure such as IQ, is outmoded. But as we will see, giftedness has become a more complex and, we believe, sophisticated construct in recent years, and so we can keep the notion and still have a more differentiated notion of both gifts and talents, on the one hand, and instruction for those with these gifts and talents, on the other.

IQ AND RELATED CONSTRUCTS

Historically, IQ has played a very important role in conceptions of giftedness and identification of those alleged to be gifted. This approach formed the basis for the classic Terman study (Terman, 1925; Terman & Oden, 1959). It still underlies a number of conceptions (e.g., Gallagher & Courtright, 1986; Robinson, 2005).

Related constructs, such as SAT scores, also are used widely in conceptualizing and identifying the gifted (Brody & Stanley, 2005; Stanley & Benbow, 1986). In these cases, scores closely akin to *g*, or general intellectual ability, are used to assess giftedness. Such scores have proven useful in selecting students for accelerated experiences, such as in mathematics.

It is not hard to understand why measures of IQ and related measures have played such a major role in conceptions and identification procedures. Even today, outside some theory books, psychometric *g* or IQ continues to be the leading indicator for identification in many, if not most, gifted programs. Why would psychometrically based constructs play such a major role in identification?

There are several reasons. We will refer here to IQ but equally might refer to psychometric *g* or scores on similar tests such as the SAT or ACT.

1. IQ can be quantified. It helps, in identification, to have a number that distinguishes those who make it from those who do not.

Tests yield quantified, seemingly precise measures of students' abilities. Consumers have been taken with their apparent precision of measurement. The problem is that the actual validity of the tests comes nowhere near the tests' appearance of validity. From the standpoint of decision making, in general, it is much easier to make a decision relying heavily on numbers than to make one relying heavily on seemingly subjective data, such as teachers' letters of recommendation or lists of extracurricular activities. Skilled admissions officers, therefore, take into account the subjective as well as the objective factors, recognizing the need for a holistic evaluation of each applicant. They resist the temptation to do their job the easy way – by the numbers.

Anyone is susceptible to overinterpreting numbers. Some years ago the senior author of this book was giving a talk to an audience of people who drilled for oil. The audience was interested in selecting people who would be skilled in predicting where oil was to be found. As he was talking about our work, someone in the audience raised his hand and made a curious point. This person said that their company had the same problem with clients that we had with admissions. Clients would often prefer them to drill for oil in places where there were quantitative indices indicating the likelihood of oil, even if the quantitative indices were known to be of poor validity. They would prefer to go with quantitative rather than superior qualitative information, simply because it was associated with numbers. And they got a lot of dry holes.

2. The tests by which IQ is quantified are objective, or at least, reasonably so.

There is a story many people know: A man is looking in the dark for keys that he has lost. The only light is a nearby street lamp, and even it is fairly dim. A policeman walks by and notices the man searching the ground.

"What are you doing?" asks the policeman.

"I am searching for my keys," answers the man.

"I will help you look," replies the policeman.

They look and look but the keys do not turn up.

"Are you sure you lost your keys here?" asks the policeman.

"No, I lost them over there," says the man, pointing to a location rather far from where they are looking.

"Why, then, are you looking for your keys here?" queries the policeman.

"Because the light is better here."

This apocryphal story describes, in our minds, a problem with modern-day cognitive testing and much other assessment. People assess the skills that are easiest to assess. In fairness, the keys are not all somewhere else. We believe that IQ, or g, or related constructs provide some of the keys. Perhaps the keys scattered when they dropped! But they are only some of the keys. However, measuring other qualities, such as motivation, creativity, resilience, and passion is much harder, and so testers may tend to eschew trying to measure these constructs, especially in high-stakes testing situations. They may conclude that the constructs are mushy, rather than that earlier attempts to measure them have sometimes been mushy.

These other qualities often do not lend themselves to so-called objective measurement. In our own experience, objective tests intended to measure creativity usually end up instead measuring something close to the *g* construct, even though that is not what was intended. Other kinds of assessments need to be devised, as discussed later in this book.

3. IQ has familiarity. Those who run gifted programs know what IQ is and, for the most part, feel comfortable with it.

Familiarity is obviously an advantage, at some level. But the danger of familiarity is that it may lead to entrenchment – to a failure to do something new because one falls into a rut with something old. Although the surface structure of tests has changed, the deep structure has changed little or not at all.

The familiarity of IQ as a basis for identifying gifted children is a practical plus but familiarity cuts both ways. If we always do what is familiar and comfortable to us, then we will never progress beyond where we are. We need to respect the old, but also try the new. The technology of intelligence assessment has not changed a great deal in the last hundred years. In comparison, other technologies such as of computation (e.g., numerical computation via computers), entertainment (e.g., DVDs), and word processing (e.g., word processing via computers) have changed enormously. Perhaps it is time for us to allow ourselves to be a bit more uncomfortable and try things that are new – if not instead of IQ, then in addition to it.

In fairness, most contemporary gifted programs do use additional means for identification. But others rely exclusively on IQ, perhaps because it better lends itself to cutoffs. The problem is that such cutoffs end up being largely arbitrary. Suppose a program has an IQ cutoff of 130. Could anyone in good conscience argue that an IQ of, say, 129 is really worse than an IQ of 130? Given measurement error and other kinds of errors, no one plausibly could make such a claim.

When computers first became practical for home use, many people understandably held back. They were unfamiliar with the technology and were not sure that it would really buy them anything over the calculating machines and typewriters they had been using. As each successive event has occurred in computing technology, there have been those who embrace the leading edge and those who hold back. The same has been true of other technologies as well, such as music delivery. The senior author of this book still buys CDs. Not many of his friends do! So we must watch that our comfort with an old and comfortable technology does not lead us into a rut from which we just cannot get out.

4. IQ has a history of perceived successful use in identifying the gifted (Gallagher & Courtright, 1986; Robinson, 2005; Terman, 1925; Terman & Merrill, 1937, 1973).

We agree that IQ has been successfully used in the past for gifted identification and we believe that the data overwhelmingly show that IQ-related skills are correlated with many kinds of success (see Sternberg & Kaufman, in press). At the same time, the correlations tend to be modest to moderate. They are at a level that suggests that IQ is part of what matters for different kinds of success but is not all that matters. There are reasonable indications that other aspects of intelligence matter as well (Cantor & Kihlstrom, 1987; Gardner, 2006; Mayer, Salovey, & Caruso, 2000; Wagner, 2000). These other kinds of, or aspects of, intelligence are not as well validated as IQ or *g*. At the same time, as a field, we have probably reached the limit of what IQ or *g* is going to tell us so that it makes sense to explore new measures to see whether they might reveal other aspects of individuals that conventional psychometric measures do not reveal, and thus could augment traditional tests.

5. IQ can be reliably measured. It shows high reliability both with respect to internal consistency of tests and with respect to test-retest consistency.

Reliability is necessary but not sufficient in an assessment for identification of the gifted. It tells us that an attribute can be measured consistently, but for that matter, it is likely that finger-tapping speed can be measured consistently, or nose length, and yet neither of these would probably be viewed as appropriate measures for gifted identification. If the other kinds or aspects of intelligence mentioned above cannot be assessed reliably, then they are not ready for prime time in gifted identification. But if we, as a field, do not invest resources in exploring them, we will not learn whether reliable measurement is possible. Early IQ tests are not as reliable as the tests are today. Reliability often can be improved with refinement of measures.

Reliability, however, can be a double-edged sword. Consider two major types in turn.

Internal-consistency reliability is a desired property of psychometric tests. The higher the internal-consistency reliability of a test, the greater is the extent to which the test measures just a single construct. To the extent that the performances one attempts to predict via psychometric tests are complex, a homogeneous test may not capture all the variation that one ideally would hope to capture. If intelligence is indeed multifaceted, moreover, very high reliability may mask the various facets, as it can occur only when a single facet is being measured.

Test-retest reliability is also typically desired in psychometric tests. This kind of reliability assesses the extent to which a test measures the same thing across time. If people's scores correlate highly across time, then the test has high test-retest reliability.

If one views high test-retest reliability as a positive property of a psychometric test, then one views it as a negative if the test scores are not correlated over time. But to the extent that intelligence is modifiable, one might expect correlations over time to be moderate or even somewhat modest. Thus insisting on high test-retest reliability might lead publishers to produce tests that contain item types that are least susceptible to modifiability in their performance.

6. IQ predicts school performance moderately well. For all the complaints one might have, this correlation has been shown again and again.

We agree that IQ is a reasonable predictor of school performance. But then, other kinds of measures also have showed promise (e.g., Gardner, Feldman, Krechevsky, & Chen, 1998; Mayer, Brackett, & Salovey, 2004; Sternberg & the Rainbow Project Collaborators, 2006; Williams et al., 2002). So the question is whether assessments can be brought to a point where giftedness could be assessed in a multidimensional way that goes beyond IQ. We do not see other types of assessments as incompatible with, but rather as complementary to, more traditional assessments. As we will see below, many researchers believe that such complementation can be obtained.

7. IQ correlates with life performance as well, as Terman found and others have found since him. It predicts things as diverse as later health, longevity, and job success (Deary, Whalley, & Starr, 2008).

As noted above, we agree that IQ predicts many things and our thesis is not that IQ should be replaced, but rather, that it should be supplemented.

It makes sense that IQ should predict many things. People who are more analytical in their behavior are less likely to do stupid things. For example, prior to committing a crime, they are more likely carefully to evaluate the consequences if they are caught. They are also more likely to evaluate the consequences of failing to take prescription medicine or of performing up to a high standard in their jobs.

There may be other kinds of measures that would supplement IQ and provide even higher prediction. One such measure is conscientiousness, which has been found to predict job-related behavior in addition to cognitive ability (Postlethwaite, Robbins, Rickerson, & McKinniss, 2009). It would seem likely that there are other measures that would further supplement conscientiousness in enhancing prediction to real-life performances.

8. Measures of IQ exist that can be given to people of virtually all ages, down even to infancy and up through old age.

IQ is different from other indices in that there are measures for such a large variety of ages. For other kinds of assessments to reach the point where they are potentially as useful as IQ, even as supplementary measures, their age ranges will have to be extended.

9. Measures of IQ exist that have been normed across countries and cultures.

The cross-cultural norming of IQ tests is a big plus. Yet it is perhaps not as big a plus as it seems. In Chapter 8 we discuss issues of culture and giftedness. One can give a test to anyone in any culture and get some kind of a score. The question is what the score means. Our discussion in Chapter 8 argues that although one does get scores across cultures, the scores do not necessarily mean the same thing across cultures. One needs to have caution in interpreting these scores.

10. IQ tests have, to many people, face validity, because they measure the same skills that are required for school success.

The face validity of IQ test items depends somewhat on the population that is being targeted. The face validity may seem greater to people of more academic education who are familiar with the kinds of tasks required for successful completion of IQ tests than to people of less academic education who have many competencies, but not necessarily those measured by the tests. McClelland (1973) suggested that we test for competence rather than IQ because, he believed, there were many kinds of competencies relevant to success that IQ did not tap. Many investigators still feel the same way.

11. IQ testing can be done in a reasonably cost-effective way, especially if a first screening is done by group testing and follow-up individual testing, if done at all, is done only on those who scored well on the group tests.

To our knowledge, there are no supplemental measures that have the cost-effectiveness of conventional intelligence tests, with the possible exception of personality tests based on the five-factor model of personality (McCrae & Costa, 1997). Future measures will thus have a cost-effectiveness barrier to overcome. Yet, without the research to determine whether such measures can be made cost-effective, we will never get such measures.

12. IQ tests have been very extensively researched, so their various kinds of properties are fairly well known.

Other kinds of tests have also been fairly extensively researched, such as the five-factor tests mentioned earlier as well as some creativity tests (Plucker & Makel, in press), such as the Torrance Tests of Creative Thinking (Torrance & Wu, 1981). Tests of a broader spectrum of abilities also have some research behind them as well (e.g., Sternberg & the Rainbow Project Collaborators, 2006).

13. There is a fairly broad selection of tests that can be used so schools and other organizations doing gifted identification have a choice of measures and also can confirm results of one measure with another measure.

The breadth of selection is obviously a plus. However, this breadth is a little like the breadth one has in choosing among various General Motors cars. Although there are many models, they differ little under the skin.

14. IQ tests can be adapted to special populations, such as those with various kinds of physical and mental disabilities.

The tests are adaptable to special populations. The biggest problem is interpreting the results for these special populations. For example, consider populations with reading disability. How can a test interpreter really know their IQ? One option is to give an exclusively nonverbal test. The problem is that IQ also has a verbal component, so the interpreter is learning perhaps their level of fluid g (flexible thinking in the face of novel problems) but not their level of crystallized g (general information that can be used to solve problems) – and not their full IQ. Another option is to give verbal tests with a more generous time limit. But then it is difficult to compare their scores with the scores of people who were timed. One can of course compare the numbers, but one will know that the numbers did not mean the same thing as the two groups did not operate under the same constraints. Another option is to give exactly the same tests with the same time limits but then the students with reading disabilities did not have a fair shake at showing their intelligence because the reading disability will have interfered with their being able to show what they can do. None of this is to say that it is a totally hopeless task, but the difficulties are nontrivial.

15. IQ tests are promoted and sometimes hyped by publishers with substantial resources.

There are likely other reasons that IQ tests have been used so often in gifted identification, but these reasons should make clear that the decision to use IQ tests is one that is based in historical precedent and psychometric validation. It is easy to find fault with IQ, and indeed, we (Sternberg, 1985a, 1997a) and many others (e.g., Gardner, 2006; Renzulli, 2005) have done so. But it is important to take into account the large number of reasons, including but not limited to the 15 cited above, that IQ has played such a large role in gifted identification over many years.

So, in conclusion, IQ has much going for it as a model for identifying the gifted, but there is at least some evidence that supplementing it would make sense.

IQ PLUS OTHER QUALITIES

The third model is of IQ plus other qualities. This is the model that has probably received the most attention. Several authors have proposed models of this kind, and here we review the main ones.

Renzulli

One of the best-known models of giftedness is the Renzulli model (Reis & Renzulli, in press; Renzulli, 1984, 2005, 2009). Renzulli argues that there are two kinds of giftedness, which he has referred to as *schoolhouse giftedness* and *creative-productive giftedness*. The former kind results in good grades and test scores. It is the kind of giftedness most visible to teachers. It is also typically the kind of giftedness that gets students identified as "gifted." IQ is a primary although not exclusive basis of schoolhouse giftedness. For example, someone could have a high IQ but not realize it in school achievement, in which case it is possible the individual would not be identified by the school as gifted. Creative-productive giftedness is the kind of giftedness shown by adults when they compose music, do works of art, write novels, design scientific experiments, come up with new advertising campaigns, create new management structures, and so on. Although this kind of giftedness is more obvious in adults, it can be found in children, primarily through project work in which the children have a chance to create a product. In adults, schoolhouse giftedness is less visible because adults typically do not need to memorize or do the kinds of tasks that directly lead to high scores on tests or high grades.

A problem, according to Renzulli, is that in adulthood, people will be viewed as gifted primarily as a result of their creative-productive giftedness, whereas in childhood they will be viewed as gifted primarily as a result of their schoolhouse giftedness. Because the two kinds of giftedness do not necessarily correspond, people may fail to be identified as gifted as children, but they will later prove to be gifted as adults, and vice versa.

Renzulli has also proposed a "three-ring" conception of giftedness, according to which giftedness occurs at the intersection of above-average ability, task commitment, and creativity. In this model, giftedness is not a function just of an extraordinary IQ. Someone could have an extraordinary IQ but not be labeled as gifted because of lower task commitment or creativity. Or someone could be identified as gifted with an above-average but not spectacular level of IQ because of high levels of creativity and task commitment. In his more recent work (e.g., Renzulli, 2005), referred to by the somewhat unusual name of "Operation Houndstooth," Renzulli has augmented his model and pointed out the importance of broader traits, such as optimism, courage, romance with a topic or discipline, sensitivity to human concerns, physical/mental energy, and vision/sense of destiny.

Renzulli (2009) has presented a theory of different kinds of knowledge that can be taught to gifted students, or really, to students in general: knowledge about facts, about conventions, about trends and sequences, about classifications and categories, about criteria, about principles and generalizations, and about theories and structures. Reis and Renzulli (2009b) have suggested that there are three types of enriched instruction that can help gifted children. Type I enrichment, general exploratory activities, is intended to stimulate new interests in gifted children. Type II enrichment, group training activities, involves development of critical and creative thinking and of learning-to-learn skills. Type III enrichment, individual and small group investigation of real problems, develops higher level creative and research skills.

Tannenbaum

Tannenbaum (1986) proposed what he referred to as a "psychosocial approach" to giftedness. Tannenbaum was particularly interested in the question of how society decides what to label as "giftedness." He proposed that there are four different kinds of talents.

Scarcity talents are talents that are in short supply. These talents are ones such as Jonas Salk used to discover the polio vaccine or Abraham Lincoln demonstrated in his political and statesmanship skills. *Surplus talents* are ones that elevate people's sensibilities and sensitivities. These would be the talents shown by Michelangelo or Dante. Although it would seem as though there is a value judgment implicit in the use of the terms *scarcity* and *surplus*, Tannenbaum claims that he does not intend to create one. Scarcity talents are ones that help society find the answer to a pressing need (such as to kill germs). Surplus talents are ones that help elevate society but do not address the same kind of pressing need, according to Tannenbaum. *Quota talents* are ones that have a limited market, so being identified as gifted in them is possible only if one falls within a quota. For example, society needs only so many physicians, engineers, lawyers, and business executives. One has to be good enough to fall into the quotas society creates. These quotas may differ across time and space. For example, lawyers become less needed when there are fewer business deals, or engineers when less societal money is being expended on new technologies. Finally, *anomalous talents* are ones that are not easily defined – such as those that make it into the *Guinness Book of World Records*. Tannenbaum gives as examples speed reading, mastery of large amounts of trivia, and trapeze artistry.

Taking into account this taxonomy, Tannenbaum (1986) defines giftedness in children as the children's "potential for becoming critically acclaimed performers or exemplary producers of ideas in spheres of activity that enhance the moral, physical, emotional, social, intellectual, or aesthetic life of humanity" (p. 33). In terms of Renzulli's theory, then, Tannenbaum is speaking of creative-productive giftedness rather than schoolhouse giftedness.

Sternberg and Zhang

Sternberg (1993) and Sternberg and Zhang (1995) have proposed a "pentagonal implicit theory of giftedness," described in detail in the previous chapter. To summarize, according to this theory, giftedness has five aspects and for a person to be labeled as gifted, the person must satisfy all five aspects.

The first criterion is the *excellence criterion*. This criterion states that gifted individuals are superior to their peers in some dimension or set of dimensions. The second criterion is the *rarity criterion*. For individuals to be labeled as gifted, they must show a high level of an attribute that is rare among their peers. The third criterion is the *productivity criterion*. This criterion states that the dimension(s) along which the individual is evaluated as superior must lead or potentially lead to productivity. The fourth criterion is the *demonstrability criterion*. This criterion states that an individual's superiority in the dimension or dimensions that determine giftedness must be demonstrable through one or more tests or valid assessments. The fifth criterion is the *value criterion*. For a person to be labeled as gifted, that person must show superior performance on a dimension that is valued by his or her society. The value criterion restricts the label of giftedness to those with attributes that are viewed as relevant to giftedness. The individual at the top of the police's most-wanted list might be superior in one or more dimensions, possessing a rare ability to perform malevolent acts and be able to demonstrate the skill upon demand. The individual may be highly productive in a criminal way. But he or she will not be labeled as gifted. Some of Tannenbaum's anomalous talents, on this view, will not merit a label of giftedness.

Feldhusen

Feldhusen (1986, 2005) studied highly gifted adults and suggested that gifted individuals show a number of signs, starting early in their lives:

1. Early mastery of knowledge or techniques in a field or art form.
2. Signs of high-level intelligence, reasoning ability, or memory in early childhood.
3. High-energy level, drive, commitment or devotion to study or work as a young person.
4. Intense independence, preference for working alone, individualism.
5. A sense (self-concept) of creative power and an internal locus of control.
6. Stimulated by association with other gifted youth or adults.
7. Heightened reactions to details, patterns, and/or other phenomena in the physical world.
8. Profit from access to accelerated artistic or intellectual experiences. (p. 115)

Feldhusen boiled these characteristics down, in part, to high levels of creativity, knowledge or information, motivation, self-concept, general intelligence, and special talents.

Haensly, Reynolds, and Nash

An interesting point of view has been proposed by Haensly, Reynolds, and Nash (1986), who have suggested that giftedness is quite a complex construct. In particular, they have suggested that gifted people (a) see possibilities that others fail to see, (b) act upon those possibilities in an extraordinary way or with the help of an extraordinary set of skills, (c) maintain sufficient intensity to overcome the obstacles that inevitably get in their way, (d) produce a response, whether physical or material, and (e) share the outcome of the process with society in a meaningful way (p. 132). They further suggest that in gifted people, there is an extraordinary *coalescence* of abilities that are directed in response to some setting. The quality or worth of that response is determined in large part by the *context* in which they live. Gifted people often encounter *conflict* with past ways of doing things and seek to impose their own ways. And they display *commitment* to the solution of the problems on which they are working.

Csikszentmihalyi

Csikszentmihalyi (Csikszentmihalyi, 1996; Csikszentmihalyi & Robinson, 1986), like Haensly and her collaborators (1986), has emphasized the importance of context in giftedness. He believes that "talent cannot be observed except against the background of well-specified cultural expectations" (Csikszentmihalyi & Robinson, 1986). Giftedness is not a personal trait but rather an interaction between an individual and the environment. Someone who has the innate talent to be an exceptional writer will not become one in a preliterate society, and someone who could be an exceptional musician will not be in a society that has a religious prohibition against music, as do some societies today. Csikszentmihalyi also suggests that talent cannot be a stable trait, because people's capacity for action changes over the course of their life span as the cultural demands for performance change.

An example of Csikszentmihalyi's point can be found in popular musicians. Most of them have relatively short careers. For every Barbara Streisand, who has had a wonderfully long career, there is a Barry Manilow or a Johnny Mathis who has a brief period of creative musicianship and then spends much of the rest of his or her life singing songs from that brief period, such as in Las Vegas. The problem is that the formula that works for them typically works only for a short period of time. So one might hear Barry Manilow or the Bangles on the radio today, but what one hears is likely to be from the relatively short period when the singer or group had some kind of affordance with the popular audience.

The same generalization applies in other kinds of careers as well. For example, scientists generally have a period of maximum productivity, after which the novelty of their contributions seems to decrease (Simonton, 1988b, 1994). There may be many reasons for their decline in productivity and contribution, but one of them is almost certainly that, as time goes on, the match between what they have to offer and what their field seeks decreases.

Csikszentmihalyi (1996) has distinguished between the domain and the field. The domain is the scope of inquiry in which one works. For example, one might work in music, or mathematics, or literature. The field is the social organization of the domain. What the field requires of the domain changes over time, and the match between what a contributor has to offer and what the field wants changes over time. Relatively few gifted individuals are able fully to change with it over long periods of time. Rather, they become out of date.

As Feldman (1986; Feldman with Goldsmith, 1991) has pointed out, gifted individuals move through the stages or levels of a domain. People move with greater or lesser success. Some people may successfully navigate the demands of the elementary-school years and be gifted at this point, and then fail to meet the demands of secondary school. Others may be brilliant undergraduates but find themselves flummoxed when, in graduate school, they need to contribute their own creative ideas. But even those who are creative early in their careers may find that the field changes and, in some degree, leaves them behind; others are recognized as creative only later because what they have to offer matches what the field requires later, but not earlier. Csikszentmihalyi's point is that people are not stably gifted but rather gifted to the degree that they are labeled as such at various points in their lives and careers.

Winner

Winner (Von Károlyi & Winner, 2005; Winner, 1996) has views related to those of Haensly and Csikszentmihalyi. Winner has suggested that gifted children stand out from other children in four crucial ways.

The first way is that they operate on a different timetable. They often show a level of precocity that other children do not show. They grasp knowledge more quickly and at a deeper level than do other children. Winner agrees with Ericsson, Krampe, and Tesch-Roemer (1993) that deliberate practice is an important element of giftedness, but she takes serious issue with their view that deliberate practice is sufficient. Rather, she claims that the motivation for deliberate practice derives in large part from innate abilities.

The second way in which gifted children differ is their having a different drive. Highly gifted children are driven by what Winner refers to as a "rage to master" material in their domain of giftedness. They are practically indefatigable in learning what they need to know later to make a contribution to that field.

The third way is that they march to the beat of a different drummer. They do things earlier, better, and faster than do many other children. Often, they solve problems in qualitatively different ways.

Finally, they feel different. They are aware that they are different from others and feel that they are treated differently. Such feelings can be positive but also can lead to feelings of exclusion and rejection.

Gruber

Howard Gruber was one of the leading figures of his day in the field of creativity, and arguably, *the* leading figure. His biography of Darwin (Gruber, 1981) is considered one of the premier works illustrating his "evolving systems" conception of creativity, according to which creative people construct over the course of their careers a set of projects, one emerging out of another, that is successively larger in scope and that addresses fundamental questions the creative people formulate and set out to answer.

According to Gruber (1986), creatively gifted individuals share certain attributes. One is their willingness to invest the time they need to think about the projects that interest them. Gruber believed that the stereotype that gifted people have "aha" insights was false. On the contrary, Gruber showed that their ideas work themselves out slowly and gradually over time. These people are willing to invest the large amounts of time needed for this evolution to take place. Gruber also pointed out that there is no one creative trajectory. People like Galton (1869) and Roe (1953) were preoccupied with precocity. But not all gifted adults were precocious. Gruber cites Freud as an example of someone who showed no particular early precocity.

For Gruber, what is special about the gifted is a kind of self-mobilization and feeling of specialness. Gruber (1986) quotes Paracelsus, the Renaissance scientist and occultist, as summarizing this concept: "'I am different, let this not upset you'" (p. 258). The truly gifted tend to feel this way. The development of their self-concept then involves at least three elements. First, they have a grasp of the disparity between the actual and the possible. They are visionaries who see, as more real, the possible than the actual. Second, they have a sense of special mission. They will commit tremendous energy to the realization of their projects. Third, they have a high level of aspiration and a great sense of daring (Gruber, 1986, p. 259).

Gruber's view is quite disparate from the high-IQ view but not necessarily disjoint with it. There may be people who have these high aspirations but who lack the intelligence to realize them. The gifted have these aspirations and also the ability to make them come true.

Gardner

Gardner's (1983, 2006) view of multiple intelligences is covered in Chapter 4, and hence is not elaborated upon here. Rather, what we emphasize here is Gardner's views of the crystallizing experience (Walters & Gardner, 1986). Walters and Gardner have argued that many of the most gifted adults have had some experience in their childhood that essentially set the course of their lives. For example, the authors point to Evariste Galois, a great French mathematician who lived only 20 years before being killed in a duel. He came across a geometry book that excited his interest in mathematics and set the course of his short life. Composer Claude Debussy, they point out, was uninterested in musical composition until he had a teacher who excited his passion.

The notion of a crystallizing experience is important to the study of giftedness because it suggests that traditional notions of gifted education may, at some level, miss the point. Acceleration is not likely to provide such a crystallizing experience, and enrichment may not provide it either. This view suggests the importance of providing gifted students with a very wide variety of exciting experiences – perhaps Renzulli's Type III enrichment mentioned earlier – and thereby helping them to have the crystallizing experience that will set them on a course to potential greatness.

Gagné

Francois Gagné (2000, 2005) has proposed what he refers to as the DMGT model, standing for Differentiated Model of Giftedness and Talent. The model proposes that giftedness has six components, divided into two sets of three. The first set of components describes what Gagné refers to as the "core" of the talent-development process and the second set to the catalysts that either promote or inhibit the development of giftedness.

Gagné's model is somewhat complex. Gagné has suggested that there are four kinds of natural abilities (NAT) that contribute to giftedness. They are intellectual, creative, socioaffective, and sensorimotor. A gifted artist might excel especially in creative talents, a gifted basketball player in sensorimotor talents. A gifted politician might excel in socioaffective talents and a gifted lawyer in intellectual talents. Affecting the display of these talents is an element of chance (CH) – who your parents are, where you grow up, when you grow up, and what opportunities you are provided with. These natural abilities feed into a developmental process (LP) that has catalytic intrapersonal (IC) and environmental (EC) aspects. If you cannot manage your talents or if you throw them away then you will experience negative catalytic effects. If you make the most of those talents and apply yourself, you will experience positive catalytic effects. Similarly, the environment will greatly affect your opportunities to develop your abilities. Finally, these natural abilities as affected by catalysts will lead to systematically developed skills or talents (SYSDEV), such as those in the academic, artistic, business, and sports domains. Abilities, then, are what you are born with and talents are what you develop as a result of the interaction of the abilities with the catalysts.

Gagné's model is especially important because it recognizes the dynamic nature of the development of giftedness. Rather than merely listing attributes of gifted persons, the model explicitly shows how the attributes interact in the dynamic development of gifts into talents.

VanTassel-Baska

Whereas the theorists we have considered have generally emphasized domain-general qualities that apply across gifted children, VanTassel-Baska (1998, 2005) has emphasized the domain-specific aspects of giftedness. In particular, she has defined giftedness as "the manifestation of general intelligence in a specific domain of human functioning at a level significantly beyond the norm such as to show promise for original contributions to a field of endeavor" (p. 359). In this view, giftedness occurs in one or more domains rather than being just a general propensity. Lots of people may have the general propensity, but unless it manifests itself in one or more specific domains, it remains unrealized potential, not giftedness. VanTassel-Baska further believes that giftedness is multidimensional, that it is affected by both genetic and environmental factors, that it should be taken into account in developing school curriculum, that it helps identify those who can profit from advanced work, and that ability must be coupled with focused effort for a person to attain success.

In this chapter, we have reviewed various approaches to giftedness, clustered within three main categories: (a) no conceptual framework; (b) IQ-based framework; and (c) more-than-IQ-skill based framework. We briefly exemplified each of these approaches, focusing primarily on the theories that engage other-than-IQ conceptions of giftedness. In the next chapter, we elaborate especially on our own views.

3

WICS as a Model of Giftedness

When schools identify children as gifted in one or more domains, they often focus on what the children know about the domain (school achievement) and the children's ability to learn about that domain more rapidly or more thoroughly than do other individuals (school aptitudes). But gifted adults are usually identified in terms of the leadership roles they take in their fields, not in terms of how quickly they learned about their fields. For example, Mozart was a leading composer in the sense that other musicians came to follow his mode of composition, and musicians came to play his music; Picasso's style as an artist has been imitated by many followers, and other followers have simply admired that style. Great political leaders compare their leadership style to that of greater leaders, such as Lincoln or Roosevelt.

The goal of this chapter is to argue that giftedness is, in large part, a function of *creativity* in generating ideas, *analytical intelligence* in evaluating the quality of these ideas, *practical intelligence* in implementing the ideas and convincing others to value and follow the ideas, and *wisdom* to ensure that the decisions and their implementation are for the common good of all stakeholders. The model is referred to as WICS – *w*isdom, *i*ntelligence, *c*reativity, *s*ynthesized – although the order of elements in the acronym is intended only to make it pronounceable (Sternberg, 2003c, 2003d, 2005c, 2005d).

Creativity, intelligence, and wisdom are not merely innate. Although these attributes may be partially heritable, heritability is distinct from modifiability (Sternberg & Grigorenko, 1999a). People can develop their creativity, intelligence, and wisdom. Thus, one is not "born" gifted. Rather, giftedness in wisdom, intelligence, and creativity is, to some extent, a form of developing competency and expertise (Sternberg, 1998a, 1999a, 2003b, 2005c, 2005d, 2006a) whereby genes interact with environment, as discussed

34

in Chapter 4. The environment strongly influences the extent to which we are able to utilize and develop whatever genetic potentials we have (Grigorenko & Sternberg, 2001b; Sternberg & Arroyo, 2006; Sternberg & Grigorenko, 1997b, 2001b).

Giftedness involves both skills and attitudes. The skills are developing competencies and expertise. The attitudes are with respect to how one employs the skills one has developed.

This view of giftedness contrasts with many traditional views. Some traditional models of giftedness stress identification of "fixed" traits or behaviors that make people gifted; other models instead emphasize the interaction between internal attributes and situations (Sternberg & Davidson, 1986, 2005).

In general, one might say that there are three received views of the nature of giftedness, as discussed in detail in the previous chapter. The first is that giftedness is a superfluous or outdated concept (Borland, 2003, 2005). On this view, giftedness is a social invention that serves to create divisions in society that have no constructive purpose. Indeed, it creates divisions where they should not be. The techniques that have been developed for gifted education can and should be used for all education, and then would be advantageous for all children.

A second view is that giftedness is measured well by traditional assessments, whether IQ tests, SATs, or other conventional measures of g-based abilities. For example, the late Julian Stanley and his collaborators (Benbow, Lubinski, & Suchy, 1996; Brody & Stanley, 2005; Stanley & Brody, 2001) have made extensive use of the SAT and related tests in their talent searches, identifying children as gifted based on their SAT scores. Robinson (2005) and Gallagher (2000) have been major supporters as well of traditional psychometric approaches to the assessment of giftedness. The basic idea in their view is that, when all is said and done, traditional tests tell us most of what we need to know for assessing who is gifted.

A third view is that conventional tests are largely incomplete – that they measure some of what is relevant to giftedness, but not all of it and, in most cases, not even most of it (Feldhusen, 2005; Freeman, 2005; Gardner, 1983; Gordon & Bridglall, 2005; Mönks & Katzko, 2005; Reis, 2005; Renzulli, 1977, 1986, 2005; Runco, 2005). These models differ in their details (see Chapter 2). For example, Renzulli emphasizes the importance of above-average ability, creativity, and task commitment in his model. Gardner (1983, 1999a, 1999b) emphasizes the importance of eight multiple intelligences: linguistic, logical-mathematical, spatial, musical, bodily-kinesthetic, naturalist, intrapersonal, and interpersonal. The model presented in this chapter is of this third kind, emphasizing skills including but also going beyond intelligence as measured by conventional tests.

The chapter considers the elements of creativity, intelligence, and wisdom, in that order, because it represents the order in which the elements often are initially used. As gifted performance evolves, however, the elements become interactive and so order becomes less relevant. The chapter then considers how the concepts can be employed in teaching and assessment, and finally, how they can be employed in identifying the gifted.

CREATIVITY

Creativity refers to the skills and attitudes needed for generating ideas and products that are (a) relatively novel, (b) high in quality, and (c) appropriate to the task at hand. Creativity is important for giftedness because it is the component whereby one generates the ideas that will influence others.

Creative Giftedness as a Confluence of Skills and Attitudes

A confluence model of creativity (Sternberg & Lubart, 1995, 1996) suggests that creative people show a variety of characteristics. These characteristics represent not innate abilities but largely decisions (Sternberg, 2000a). In other words, to a large extent, people decide to be creative.

Creativity is greatly attitudinal, as Thomas Edison recognized when he referred to his inventions as 99% perspiration and 1% inspiration. Being creatively gifted is hard work!

What are the elements of the creative attitude (Kaufman & Sternberg, 2006; Sternberg, 1999b)? Keep in mind that few people have all of these elements. They need only enough of them to translate their potential gifts into actualized ones.

1. Problem Redefinition

Creative individuals do not define a problem the way everyone else does, simply because everyone else defines the problem that way. They decide on the exact nature of the problem using their own judgment. Most important, they are willing to defy the crowd in defining a problem differently from the way others do (Sternberg, 2002b; Sternberg & Lubart, 1995). Gifted individuals are more willing to redefine problems and better able to do so. For example, the Founding Fathers originally conceived of the problem of an oppressive British government as one of how to minimize the burdens imposed by the British monarchy. Finding that they were unable to alleviate this burden sufficiently, they redefined the problem as one of how to shake off the monarchy entirely.

2. Problem Analysis

Creative individuals are willing to analyze whether their solution to the problem is the best one possible. Gifted individuals are more willing to analyze their own decisions, and better see their strengths and weaknesses. They recognize that they are not always right and that not all their work is their best work, and they are self-critical in analyzing the quality of their own work.

3. Selling a Solution

Creative individuals come to realize that creative ideas do not sell themselves; rather, creators have to decide to sell their ideas, and then decide to put in the effort to do so. Gifted individuals are better salespeople. They persuade others of the value of their ideas and to follow those ideas. They thus need to be able to articulate the value of their ideas in a clear and persuasive way. It is worth noting how different this skill is from that required to do well on an IQ test. The Picassos, Darwins, Lincolns, and Gandhis of the world have worked hard to develop their ability to sell their ideas. People who are gifted with respect to IQ may not have developed this skill at all.

Not all gifted people are good salespeople for their ideas, of course. Some, such as Van Gogh, become famous only after their death. Others, such as Jean Piaget, become famous only after others interpret their ideas and present them in a way that communicates these ideas to the public better than did the original creator. Luck plays a large role: Will one find that communicator? Will there be a receptive audience in a given time or place? And mostly, will one ever have the opportunity to present one's ideas to others in the first place?

4. Recognizing How Knowledge Can Both Help and Hinder Creative Thinking

Creative people realize that knowledge can hinder as well as facilitate creative thinking (see also Frensch & Sternberg, 1989; Sternberg, 1985a). Sometimes people become entrenched and susceptible to tunnel vision, letting their expertise hinder rather than facilitate their exercise of their giftedness. Gifted people are more likely to recognize their own susceptibility to entrenchment and take steps to battle against it, such as seeking able advisors, new ideas from novices, and so forth.

5. *Willingness to Take Sensible Risks*
Creative people recognize that they must decide to take sensible risks, which can lead them to success but also can lead them, from time to time, to fail (Lubart & Sternberg, 1995). Gifted people are more willing to take large risks and to fail as often as necessary to accomplish their long-term goals.

6. *Willingness to Surmount Obstacles*
Creative people are willing to surmount the obstacles that confront anyone who decides to defy the crowd. Such obstacles result when those who accept paradigms confront those who do not (Kuhn, 1970; Sternberg & Lubart, 1995). All gifted people encounter obstacles. Curiously, gifted people are particularly susceptible to obstacles, because they often want to move followers more quickly and farther than the followers might be ready to move. So the gifted person needs great resilience to accomplish his or her goals.

7. *Belief in One's Ability to Accomplish the Task at Hand*
Creative people believe in their ability to get the job done. This belief is sometimes referred to as self-efficacy (Bandura, 1996). Gifted people believe in themselves and their ideas – not necessarily in the value of every single idea, but in the value of their overall strategy for their contributions.

8. *Willingness to Tolerate Ambiguity*
Creative people recognize that there may be long periods of uncertainty during which they cannot be certain they are doing the right thing or that what they are doing will have the outcome they hope for. The more gifted the people, the greater is the ambiguity, because these people try to generate new ideas that can create transformational change for others as well as themselves.

9. *Willingness to Find Extrinsic Rewards for the Things One Is Intrinsically Motivated to Do*
Creative people almost always are intrinsically motivated for the work they do (Amabile, 1983, 1996). Creative people find environments in which they receive extrinsic rewards for the things they like to do anyway. Gifted children remain gifted as adults if they love what they do.

10. *Continuing to Grow Intellectually Rather Than to Stagnate*
Creative people avoid, to the extent possible, getting stuck in their patterns
of thought. Their thinking evolves as they accumulate experience and expertise. They learn from experience rather than simply letting its lessons pass
them by. Lifelong gifted people do not flame out as time passes. Rather, they
adapt to changing circumstances.

Types of Creative Ideas

The creative ideas gifted people propose can be of different types (Sternberg,
1999b; Sternberg, Kaufman, & Pretz, 2002). Consider each type of gifted
contribution in turn (Sternberg, Kaufman, & Pretz, 2003).

Conceptual Replication
This type of idea is an attempt to show that a field or organization is in the
right place at the right time. The individual therefore attempts to maintain it
in that place. The view of the person is that the field or organization is where
it needs to be. The person's role is to keep it there. The replicative thinker
metaphorically pedals in place, as with a stationary bicycle. This type of
thinking is only minimally creative – it is a limiting case. The creativity is in
dealing with applying a past model to an ever-changing environment.

Replicative thinking is likely to be most successful during time periods
of relative stability, both in terms of consumer demands and in terms of
competitive threats. In times of flux, the kind of thinking that worked before
may not work again, and an organization or paradigm of thinking may lose
preeminence by selecting a thought-leader who is a replicative thinker.

Redefinition
This type of thinking is an attempt to show that a field or organization is
in the right place, but not for the reason(s) that others, including previous
thinkers, think it is. The current status of the field or organization thus is
seen from a different point of view. Redefiners often end up taking credit for
ideas of others because they find a better reason to implement the others'
ideas, or say they do. This type of thinking is, on average, only slightly
more creative than replicative thinking. The creativity is in realizing how to
redefine what previous thinkers did.

Forward Incrementation
This type of thinking is an attempt to lead a field or an organization forward in the direction it already is going. Most creative thinking is probably

forward incrementation. In such thinking, one takes the helm with the idea of advancing the creative program of the person one has succeeded. The promise is of progress through continuity. Creativity through forward incrementation is probably the kind that is most easily recognized and appreciated as creativity. Because it extends existing notions, it is seen as creative. Because it does not threaten the assumptions of such notions, it is not rejected as useless or even harmful. Forward incrementations tend to be successful when times are changing in relatively predictable and incremental ways. The times thus match the thinking. When times change unpredictably, those following this strategy may find that it no longer works.

Advance Forward Incrementation

This type of thinking is an attempt to move a paradigm or an organization forward in the direction it is already going, but by moving beyond where others are ready for it to go. One moves the paradigm or organization ahead at a very fast clip. Advance forward incrementations usually are not successful at the time they are attempted because people in fields and organizations are not ready to go where the thinker wants them to go. Or significant portions of them may not wish to go to that point, in which case people form an organized and sometimes successful source of resistance.

Redirection

This type of thinking is an attempt to redirect an organization, field, or product line from where it is headed toward a different direction. The gifted individual decides that the direction in which the field or organization currently is moving is less than adaptive and so redirects the organization elsewhere. Redirective thinkers need to match to environmental circumstances to succeed. If they do not have the luck to have matching environmental circumstances, their best intentions may go awry.

Reconstruction/Redirection

This type of creative thinking is an attempt to move a field or an organization or a product line back to where it once was (a reconstruction of the past) so that it may move onward from that point, but in a direction different from the one it took originally. Reconstruction/redirection tends to be successful when an organization had strong leadership, then gets a weak leader who takes the organization in the wrong direction. The reconstruction/redirection becomes an attempt to return to a safe, or at least more nearly secure, harbor.

Reinitiation

This type of thinking is an attempt to move a field, organization, or product line to a different as yet unreached starting point and then to move from that point. Reinitiation is appropriate when a field or an organization must either entirely transform itself, or die.

Synthesis

In this type of creative thinking, the creator integrates two ideas that previously were seen as unrelated or even as opposed. What formerly were viewed as distinct ideas now are viewed as related and capable of being unified. Integration is a key means by which progress is attained in the sciences. It represents neither an acceptance nor a rejection of existing paradigms, but rather, a merger of them. Sometimes, syntheses occur across disciplines.

What holds these kinds of creative thinking together is that they represent various forms of "propulsion" through a conceptual space. In other words, a creative thinker wishes to move his or her followers from one point to another. In replication, the limiting case of creativity, the thinker does not move at all in the space. In redefinition, the leader stays in the same place but redefines the location (or axes pinpointing the location). In forward incrementation, the thinker moves the organization or field forward in the conceptual space in the direction the organization already is going. In redirection, the thinker moves the organization in a new direction in the space. In reconstruction/redirection, the thinker moves backward in the space in the direction from which the organization or field came, and then redirects from a point already passed at an earlier time. In reinitiation, the thinker changes both the starting point and direction in the space. And in synthesis, the thinker essentially "adds" vectors in the space – combining the vector in which his or her field or organization is moving with that in which another organization is moving to synthesize their movements.

Various forms of creative contributions engender different kinds of creative thinking. In particular, some creative thinkers transform the nature of an organization or field, whereas others do not. At a given time, in a given place, transformation may or may not be called for. So transformation is not necessarily needed. But the creative thinkers who tend to be remembered over the course of history are probably, in most cases, those who transform ways of thinking.

One might ask whether gifted thinkers are more likely to show one or another form of creativity. For example, are gifted thought leaders more likely to be reinitiators than to be replicators? Probably, on average, gifted thought leaders are more likely to adopt leadership styles that involve challenging existing paradigms. But two important points must be kept in mind.

First, the various types of creativity refer to kinds of novelty, not quality. Creativity, however, involves quality as well as novelty. One can have a very novel idea that is nevertheless not good. For example, terrorists destroyed the World Trade Center using passenger-filled airplanes. That was a novel idea, perhaps, but not a good idea. It lacked all the qualities of wisdom (to be discussed below). So even if the idea was a redirection of terrorism, it was not the act of a gifted person in the sense of the WICS model. Stalin, perhaps, can be called "ingenious" in his methods for maintaining the reins of power, but he was not a gifted leader in the sense of WICS because of his lack of wisdom. Hence, it is always important that there is a balance of creativity, intelligence, and wisdom. Merely being a reinitiator, for example, does not make one a gifted thinker.

Second, even the more mundane forms of creativity can lead someone to be labeled as gifted. As an example, violin makers have been trying for centuries to replicate the sound of a Stradivarius violin, without much luck. If a violin maker succeeded, he would be considered gifted indeed. If a gifted individual were able to replicate within a society some of the creativity of the Renaissance in art, literature, and science, he or she might be considered to be quite gifted. So the type of creativity does not necessarily speak to whether a person is gifted. Even more modest types of creativity can result in gifted performance.

Our research on creativity (Lubart & Sternberg, 1995; Sternberg & Lubart, 1995) has yielded several conclusions. First, creativity often involves defying the crowd, or as we have put it, buying low and selling high in the world of ideas. Creative people are good investors: They do what needs to be done, rather than just what other people or polls tell them to do. Second, creativity is relatively domain specific. Third, creativity is weakly related to traditional intelligence, but certainly is not the same thing as academic intelligence. In general, it appears that there is a threshold of IQ for creativity, but it is probably about 120 or even lower (see review in Sternberg & O'Hara, 2000). So let's next consider the role of intelligence in giftedness.

INTELLIGENCE

Intelligence would seem to be important to giftedness, but how important? Intelligence, as conceived of here, is not just intelligence in its conventional narrow sense – some kind of general factor (*g*) (Demetriou, 2002; Jensen, 1998, 2002; Spearman, 1927; see essays in Sternberg, 2000b; Sternberg & Grigorenko, 2002b) or as IQ (Binet & Simon, 1905; Kaufman, 2000; Wechsler, 1939), but rather, in terms of the theory of successful intelligence (Sternberg, 1997a, 1999c, 2002b). Successful intelligence is defined as the skills and attitudes needed to succeed in life, given one's own conception of success, within one's sociocultural environment. Successfully intelligent people balance adaptation to, shaping of, and selection of environments by capitalizing on strengths and compensating for or correcting weaknesses. Here we focus on successful intelligence and in the next chapter we will review different theoretical models of intelligence, including implicit models.

Gifted individuals, in this view, are not necessarily good at everything. Rather, they know their own strengths and weaknesses. They make the most of the strengths and find ways to deal with the weaknesses. Two particular aspects of the theory of successful intelligence are especially relevant. These are academic and practical intelligence (see also Neisser, 1979).

It is clear how intelligence would have aspects of skill. But how would it have aspects of an attitude? The main way is through the decision to apply it. Many gifted people know better, but do so anyway. Their minds tell them what they should be doing, but their motives – for power, for fame, for money, for sex, or whatever – lead them in different directions. Gifted people may fail in their endeavors not because they are not smart enough, but because they choose not to use the intelligence they have.

Academic Intelligence

Academic intelligence refers to the memory and analytical skills and attitudes that in combination largely constitute the conventional notion of intelligence – the skills and attitudes needed to recall and recognize but also to analyze, evaluate, and judge information.

The literature on giftedness is in large part a literature on academic intelligence (see, e.g., essays in Sternberg & Davidson, 1986). Certainly academic intelligence is important to giftedness and to gifted leadership. But there are many people who have been gifted intellectually who have not become gifted leaders. They lacked the other qualities of WICS.

The academic skills and attitudes matter for giftedness, because gifted individuals need to be able to retrieve information that is relevant to leadership decisions (memory) and to analyze and evaluate different courses of action, whether proposed by themselves or by others (analysis).

The longtime primary emphasis on *academic* intelligence (IQ) in the literature relating intelligence to giftedness has perhaps been unfortunate. Indeed, recent theorists have been emphasizing other aspects of intelligence, such as emotional intelligence (e.g., Caruso, Mayer, & Salovey, 2002; Goleman, 1998a, 1998b) or multiple intelligences (Gardner, 1995), in their theories. In the WICS model, the emphasis is on practical intelligence (Hedlund et al., 2003; Sternberg et al., 2000; Sternberg & Hedlund, 2002), which has a somewhat different focus from emotional intelligence. Practical intelligence is a part of successful intelligence. Practical intelligence is a core component of giftedness and thus will receive special attention here.

Practical Intelligence

Practical intelligence is the set of skills and attitudes to solve everyday problems by utilizing knowledge gained from experience to purposefully adapt to, shape, and select environments. It thus involves changing oneself to suit the environment (adaptation), changing the environment to suit oneself (shaping), or finding a new environment within which to work (selection). One uses these skills to (a) manage oneself, (b) manage others, and (c) manage tasks.

Different combinations of intellectual skills engender different types of giftedness. Gifted people vary in their memory skills, analytical skills, and practical skills. A gifted individual who is particularly strong in memory skills but not in the other kinds of skills may have vast amounts of knowledge at his or her disposal, but be unable to use it effectively. A gifted individual who is particularly strong in analytical skills as well as memory skills may be able to retrieve information and analyze it effectively but may be unable to convince others that his or her analysis is correct. A gifted individual who is strong in memory, analytical, and practical skills is most likely to be effective in influencing others. But, of course, there are gifted people who are strong in practical skills but not in memory and analytical skills (Sternberg, 1997a; Sternberg et al., 2000). In conventional terms, they are "shrewd" but not "smart." They may be effective or even gifted in getting others to go along with them, but they may end up leading these others down garden paths.

Gifted individuals ideally need to be high in practical intelligence. Their creativity may help them generate wonderful ideas, but it will not ensure that they can implement the ideas or convince others to follow the ideas. Many creative individuals have ended up frustrated because they have been unable to convince others to follow on their ideas. As noted earlier, such individuals are fortunate when they can compensate for their weakness in selling ideas by having others who sell the ideas for them. Many analytically intelligent individuals have been frustrated because they could analyze ideas well but not persuade others of the value of their ideas.

Sternberg and his colleagues (Hedlund et al., 2003; Sternberg et al., 2000; Sternberg & Wagner, 1993; Sternberg, Wagner, & Okagaki, 1993; Sternberg, Wagner, Williams, & Horvath, 1995; Wagner & Sternberg, 1985; Wagner, 1987) have taken a tacit-knowledge-based approach to understanding practical intelligence. Individuals draw on a broad base of knowledge in solving practical problems, some of which is acquired through formal training and some of which is derived from personal experience. Much of the knowledge associated with successful problem solving can be characterized as tacit. It is knowledge that may not be openly expressed or stated; thus individuals must acquire such knowledge through their own experiences. Furthermore, although people's actions may reflect their knowledge, they may find it difficult to articulate what they know. For their own contributions, what matters is not so much what tacit knowledge they can articulate but rather, how much of this knowledge they can apply. However, to serve as effective mentors, it helps greatly if they can articulate as well as act on this knowledge.

The main findings (reviewed in Sternberg et al., 2000) from tacit-knowledge research are that (a) tacit knowledge tends to increase with experience; (b) it correlates minimally and sometimes not at all with scores on tests of academic intelligence; (c) it does not correlate with personality; (d) it predicts job performance significantly; and (e) it provides significant incremental prediction over conventional academic-intelligence measures.

Relative Importance of Different Aspects of Intelligence and Creativity Over Time

We undertook a study to see how different attributes of the WICS model (e.g., creativity, academic intelligence, and practical intelligence) contribute to an individual's being identified as gifted in different stages of life. Transitions in the nature of developing expertise that lead to a label of giftedness can be studied longitudinally (i.e., the same participants studied over time) or cross-sectionally (i.e., participants at different stages of life studied at the same time). We chose a cross-sectional design for the main study for three reasons (Subotnik & Arnold, 1993). First, longitudinal studies often have high dropout rates over time, with the more successful individuals (in terms of whatever the study is measuring) more likely to remain in the study and

TABLE 3.1. *Categories of Student Participants*

| | | Giftedness "label" | | |
		Highly gifted	Gifted	Not identified as gifted
Age	Pre-k students	Verbal	Verbal	Verbal
	(ages 3–5)	Quantitative	Quantitative	Quantitative
	Middle-school students	Verbal	Verbal	Verbal
	(grades 5–6)	Quantitative	Quantitative	Quantitative
	Secondary-school students	Verbal	Verbal	Verbal
	(grades 11–12)	Quantitative	Quantitative	Quantitative
	College students	Verbal*	Verbal*	Verbal*
		Quantitative**	Quantitative**	Quantitative**

* Majors in English/English Literature.
** Majors in Mathematics.

thus bias the results as the sample size progressively diminishes. Second, longitudinal studies of the kind we would need would require half a century to complete, and we could not assure the availability of personnel over that period of time to complete the work adequately – nor did we believe that the problem of the research should wait that long to be addressed. Third, the realities of research funding render it problematic to maintain funding over such a long period of time. We decided, however, to complement the large cross-sectional study with a smaller longitudinal sample.

There were two groups of participants: individuals who were evaluators (teachers, parents, college/university professors/instructors), and individuals who were evaluated (students). The members of the first group of participants filled out questionnaires and were interviewed regarding the characteristics of highly gifted, gifted but not highly gifted, and nongifted individuals in their area of endeavor. The second class of participants was assessed for their potentials and demonstrated levels of performance.

Evaluated participants (and their corresponding evaluators) consisted of three samples of individuals in each of four cohorts, as summarized in Table 3.1. It was not possible adequately to study children with all kinds of gifts in all areas of specialization, and these specializations needed to be defined broadly enough to allow us to find adequate samples yet narrowly enough to ensure that there was at least some homogeneity in the gifts that were being studied within an area. We therefore chose two areas of giftedness that can be studied at each of the life epochs described above. These two areas, loosely representing aspects of the humanities and sciences, were

(a) verbally oriented (reading/writing) performance (we use the letter V to signify this group) and (b) quantitatively oriented (mathematical/scientific) performance (we use the letter Q to signify this group). We chose these areas because (a) both are important to society; (b) they are the two areas that seem to be valued most by schools; (c) they are the two broad areas most frequently assessed by conventional standardized tests of abilities and achievement; (d) various objective and subjective measures for these are readily available; and (e) giftedness in both is often recognized fairly early (in contrast, say, to giftedness in sculpture, which often is not recognized until later).

Within each group, we sampled for minority groups, including African American and subgroups of Hispanic underserved minority students, and in addition to seeking representation from diverse ethnic groups we recruited in schools representing a wide range of (a) geographical locations, (b) urban versus suburban status, and (c) socioeconomic makeup.

In both the cross-sectional and longitudinal studies, the main independent variables were the results of the measures assessing the skills of evaluated individuals within the confluence framework (for confluence models, see also Chapter 5).

Specifically, we assessed evaluator and student participants with the measures outlined in Table 3.2..

What did we learn about the relative importance of different factors (academic intelligence, practical intelligence, creativity and other factors) for the different age groups, and, by inference, over time?

We hypothesized that creative and practical abilities will be of increasing importance to giftedness, with increasing age and across domains; in contrast, the importance of analytical abilities will be retained across ages but will decrease relative to that of creative and practical abilities. The data collected indicate (a) it is difficult to distinguish analytical, practical, and creative abilities from each other at the earliest life stages (pre-k and elementary school), but (b) by middle school they can be well distinguished, and, in line with our hypothesis, we see a decrease in the importance of analytical skills versus practical and creative skills from grade 5 to grade 8. (c) At the high school level we see an increase in the importance of creative skills. (d) Yet, at the college level all three types of abilities distinguish gifted from nongifted students. Thus, although our general hypotheses with regard to the increasing importance of creative and practical skills across the life span have been confirmed, there is a substantial amount of developmental fluctuation that deserves further investigation.

TABLE 3.2. *Assessment Instruments*

Type of factor (Academic intelligence, Practical Intelligence, Creativity, or Other)	Measure	Teachers	Parents	Pre-k	Middle school	High school	College
O	Demographic information	X	X		X	X	X
O	Student's/parents' educational style	X	X		X	X	X
O	Teaching style						
O	Teacher rating scale of child's actual behavior (Harter, 1985a)	X	X				
A, C, P	Analytical, creative, and practical ability ratings	X	X				
O (motivation)	Subject preferences				X	X	X
O (motivation)	Student future goals				X	X	X
A	Bracken School Readiness Assessment (Bracken, 2002)			X			
A	Comprehensive Assessment of Spoken Language (CASL; Carrow-Woolfolk, 2001)			X			
A	Concept About Print (CAP; Clay, 2002)			X			
A	Pre-CTOPP (Comprehensive Test of Phonological Processing; Lonigan et al., 2002)			X			
A	Wechsler Preschool and Primary Scale of Intelligence – III (Wechsler, 2002)			X			
A	Woodcock-Johnson III (WJ-III; Woodcock et al., 2001)			X			
A	Culture Fair Intelligence Test (Cattell & Cattell, 1973)				X	X	X
A	Mill Hill Vocabulary Scale (Raven et al., 1992)				X	X	X
P	School/College Life Questionnaire (Sternberg et al., 2006)				X	X	X

Code	Measure						
C	Creative Story (Sternberg et al., 2006)					X	X
C	Creative Collage Task (Amabile, 1982; Sternberg et al., 2006)					X	X
O (personality)	Adjective Check List (Gough & Heilbrun, 1983)	X	X			X	X
A, C, P	Sternberg Triarchic Abilities Test (STAT; Sternberg et al., 1996)	X	X			X	X
P	Thinking Style Questionnaire (Grigorenko & Sternberg, 1995; Sternberg, 1997)	X	X			X	
O	Potential Success Factors Questionnaire (Sternberg & Grigorenko, 2007)	X	X			X	
O (motivation)	Achievement Motivation Questionnaire (Elliot & McGregor, 2001)		X			X	
O (self concept)	Implicit Theories of Intelligence Scale (Dweck, 1999)	X	X			X	
O (self perception)	Self-Perception Profile (Harter 1985b, 1986)		X			X	
A	Standardized achievement test scores (GPA, ACT, SAT, GRE as applicable)	X	X			X	X
A	Academic and nonacademic awards		X				X
O	Teacher's views on giftedness	X	X			X	X

We also hypothesized that the importance of the legislative thinking style – a desire to do things one's own way, which is associated with creativity – would increase with age in tandem with the importance of creative giftedness. We expected the importance of the executive style – a desire to be told what to do – would be associated with memory learning and would decrease with age. As per our hypothesis, we noted that the relative importance of the legislative thinking style versus an executive thinking style increases when tracking middle school students from fifth through eighth grade.

WISDOM

A gifted individual can have all of the above skills and attitudes and still lack an additional quality that, arguably, is the most important quality a gifted person can have, but perhaps, also the rarest. This additional quality is wisdom (see also Baltes & Staudinger, 2000). Wisdom is viewed here in terms of a proposed balance theory of wisdom (Sternberg, 1998b), according to which an individual is wise to the extent he or she uses successful intelligence, creativity, and knowledge as moderated by positive ethical values, to (a) seek to reach a common good, (b) by balancing intrapersonal (one's own), interpersonal (others'), and extrapersonal (organizational/institutional/spiritual) interests, (c) over the short and long term, to (d) adapt to, shape, and select environments. Wisdom is in large part a decision to use one's intelligence, creativity, and knowledge for a common good.

Wise people do not look out just for their own interests, nor do they ignore these interests. Rather, they skillfully balance interests of varying kinds, including their own, those of their stakeholders, and those of the organization for which they are responsible. They also recognize that they need to align the interests of their group or organization with those of other groups or organizations because no group operates within a vacuum. Wise individuals realize that what may appear to be a prudent course of action over the short term does not necessarily appear so over the long term. Giftedness in wisdom is a matter of balance – skillful balance of the various interests and of the short and long terms in making decisions.

Gifted leaders who have been less than fully successful often have been so because they have ignored one or another set of interests. For example, Richard Nixon and Bill Clinton, in their respective cover-ups, not only failed to fulfill the interests of the country they led but also failed to fulfill their own interests. Their cover-ups ended up bogging down their administrations in scandals rather than allowing them to make the positive accomplishments they had hoped to make. Freud was a great leader in the fields of psychiatry and psychology, but his insistence that his followers (disciples) conform quite exactly to his own system of psychoanalysis led him to lose those disciples and the support they might have continued to lend to his efforts. He was an expert in interpersonal interests, but not as applied to his own life. Napoleon lost sight of the extrapersonal interests that would have been best for his own country. His disastrous invasion of Russia, which appears to have been motivated more by hubris than by France's need to have Russia in its empire, partially destroyed his reputation as a successful military leader and paved the way for his later downfall.

Gifted individuals can be intelligent in various ways and creative in various ways; it does not guarantee they are wise. Indeed, probably relatively few gifted individuals at any level are particularly wise. Yet the few individuals who are wise to the point of being gifted – perhaps Nelson Mandela, Martin Luther King, Jr., Mahatma Gandhi, Winston Churchill, Mother Teresa – leave an indelible mark on the people they lead and, potentially, on history. It is important to note that wise people, and especially wise leaders, are probably usually charismatic, but charismatic leaders are not necessarily wise, as Hitler, Stalin, and many other charismatic leaders have demonstrated over time.

Much of the empirical data on wisdom has been collected by Paul Baltes and his colleagues. Over a number of years, they (e.g., Baltes, Smith, & Staudinger, 1992; Baltes & Staudinger, 1993) have collected a wide range of data showing the relevance of wisdom for gifted performance. For example, Staudinger, Lopez, and Baltes (1997) found that measures of intelligence and personality as well as their interface overlap with but are nonidentical to measures of wisdom in terms of constructs measured; and Staudinger, Smith, and Baltes (1992) showed that leading human services professionals outperformed a control group on wisdom-related tasks. The professionals thought more contextually in terms of life pragmatics than did the control participants. Staudinger and her colleagues also showed that older adults performed as well on such tasks as did younger adults, and that older adults did better on such tasks if there was a match between their age and the age of the fictitious characters about whom they made judgments. Baltes, Staudinger, Maercker, and Smith (1995) found that older individuals in leadership positions who were nominated for their wisdom performed as well as did clinical psychologists on wisdom-related tasks. They also showed that up to the age of 80, older adults performed as well on such tasks as did younger adults. In a further set of studies, Staudinger and Baltes (1996) found that performance settings that were ecologically relevant to the lives of their participants and that provided for actual or "virtual" interaction of minds increased wisdom-related performance substantially. These results suggest that part of wise leadership is achieving a meeting of minds rather than merely imposing the view of the leader's mind on the minds of the followers.

SYNTHESIS

One of the most gifted individuals of the 20th century was Nelson Mandela. He transformed South Africa from a repressive Apartheid state into a model of modern democracy. It did not become a country without problems. But if one looks at the alternative model provided by Robert Mugabe in Zimbabwe, economically, politically, and morally a failed state, one can see how badly things could have gone.

What made Nelson Mandela so successful? He had the creativity to envision a transformation of South Africa from a state that deprived the large majority of its citizens of human rights to one that would embrace human rights for all, including the former oppressors. He had the analytical intelligence to evaluate his plan and to fine-tune it as it was implemented. He had the practical intelligence to implement the plan with great success and to persuade a very broad range of constituencies that his plan was a good one. Such persuasion was no mean feat, especially in largely preventing a massive exodus of white people and in convincing black people that reconciliation rather than retribution was the key to success in the new democratic state. And he had the wisdom to let go of the massive abuse of human rights to which he himself had been subjected in prison, and to propose a plan that was in the common good for all stakeholders.

Gifted leadership requires each of the elements of WICS. Without creativity, one cannot truly be a gifted leader. Leaders constantly confront novel tasks and situations. If they lack the creativity to deal with them effectively, they fail. Mugabe, in place of creating a new vision, essentially copied the model of divisive dictators such as Stalin, pitting one group against the other, and has presided over a state in radical decline on all measures of well-being. Without the application of a high level of intelligence, one cannot be a gifted leader. Any leader may have creative ideas, but ones that are either flawed from the outset or that fail in implementation. The leader needs the intelligence to distinguish good ideas from bad ones, and to ensure that followers follow rather than ignore or rebel against the leader. And without wisdom, a leader may choose a path that benefits his or her cronies, as in the case of Mugabe or Saddam Hussein, but few others. Gifted leadership requires WICS.

There probably is no model of giftedness that will totally capture all of the many facets – both internal and external to the individual – that make for a gifted person. The WICS model may come closer than some models, however, in capturing dimensions that are important. It is based upon the notion that a gifted individual, in the ideal, decides to synthesize wisdom, intelligence, and creativity. Gifted leadership requires such a synthesis.

A gifted leader needs exceptional creative skills and attitudes to come up with ideas; academic skills and attitudes to decide whether they are good ideas; practical skills and attitudes to make the ideas work and to convince others of the value of the ideas; and wisdom-based skills and attitudes to ensure that the ideas are in the service of the common good rather than just the good of the leader or perhaps some clique of family members or followers. A leader lacking in creativity will be unable to deal with novel and difficult situations, such as a new and unexpected source of hostility. A leader lacking in academic intelligence will not be able to decide whether his or her ideas are viable, and a leader lacking in practical intelligence will be unable to implement his or her ideas effectively. An unwise leader may succeed in implementing ideas but may end up implementing ideas that are contrary to the best interests of the people he or she leads.

We may look at WICS as a model just for adults, but that is not what it is at all. The WICS model suggests we need to broaden the way we conceive of giftedness in childhood. Giftedness is not just a matter of ability-test scores or of grades. The state of the world makes clear that what the nations of the world need most is *gifted leaders* – people who make a positive, meaningful, and enduring difference to the world – not just individuals who get good grades or good test scores, or who have the skills that will get them into elite colleges, which in turn will prepare them to make a lot of money. The United States is so individualistic that it is working against its own self-interests. We risk developing successive generations of self-interested gifted individuals who view their gifts primarily as a means to serve their own needs and desires. The country needs leaders, and WICS provides a model for developing leadership in its young.

4

Intelligence and Giftedness

In the previous chapter, we briefly discussed intelligence as it is conceived of in the WICS model. In this chapter, we consider the nature of intelligence in more detail and review different models of intelligence proposed over the years. What is intelligence and what does it predict? This chapter discusses the nature of intelligence and how it relates to giftedness. Intelligence is important not only because it is relevant to identification of the gifted, but also because it predicts their school and life achievement (Barnett, Rindermann, Williams, & Ceci, in press; Deary & Batty, in press; Mayer, in press). It also helps predict whether one's intelligence will remain potential or be developed into useful expertise (Ackerman, in press). The chapter is divided into several major parts: The first discusses people's conceptions of intelligence, also referred to as implicit theories of intelligence; the second presents a brief discussion of intelligence testing; the third offers a review of major approaches to understanding intelligence; the fourth discusses how intelligence can be improved; and the last part briefly draws some conclusions. The chapter does not discuss artificial intelligence and computer simulation, neural networks, or parallel distributed processing. Much more detail can be found in Sternberg (2000b) and Sternberg and Kaufman (in press; see especially Davidson & Kemp, in press). A good source for the history of theories and research on intelligence is Mackintosh (in press).

IMPLICIT THEORIES OF INTELLIGENCE

What do people believe intelligence to be? In 1921, when the editors of the *Journal of Educational Psychology* asked 14 famous psychologists that question, the responses varied but generally embraced two themes: Intelligence involves the capacity to learn from experience and the ability to adapt to the surrounding environment. Sixty-five years later, Sternberg and Detterman (1986) asked 24 cognitive psychologists with expertise in intelligence research the same question. They, too, underscored the importance of learning from experience and adapting to the environment. They also broadened the definition to emphasize the importance of metacognition – people's understanding and control of their own thinking processes. Contemporary experts also more heavily emphasized the role of culture, pointing out that what is considered intelligent in one culture may be considered stupid in another (Ang & Van Dyne, in press; Serpell, 2000; in Chapter 8, we provide a detailed review of the similarities and differences in implicit definitions of intelligence in different cultures).

Intelligence, then, is the capacity to learn from experience, using metacognitive processes to enhance learning, and the ability to adapt to the surrounding environment, which may require different adaptations within different social and cultural contexts. People gifted in intelligence thus excel in these attributes, are relatively rare with regard to the level of the attributes, and productively can demonstrate that they possess these attributes.

According to the *Oxford English Dictionary*, the word *intelligence* entered our language in about the 12th century. Today, we can look up intelligence in numerous dictionaries, but most of us still have our own implicit (unstated) ideas about what it means to be smart and even gifted; that is, we have our own implicit theories of intelligence. We use our implicit theories in many social situations, such as when we meet people or when we describe people we know as being very smart or not so smart. Within our implicit theories of intelligence, we also recognize that the word has different meanings in different contexts. A gifted salesperson may show a different kind of intelligence from that of a gifted neurosurgeon or a smart accountant, each of whom may show a different kind of intelligence from that of a smart choreographer, composer, athlete, or sculptor. We often use our implicit and context-relevant definitions of intelligence to make assessments of intelligence. Is your mechanic smart enough to find and fix the problem in your car? Is your physician smart enough to find and treat your health problem? Is a particular attractive person smart enough to hold your interest in a conversation? Western notions about intelligence are not always shared by other cultures (Sternberg & Kaufman, 1998). For example, the Western emphasis on speed of mental processing (Sternberg et al., 1981) is not shared in many cultures. Other cultures may even be suspicious of the quality of work that is done very quickly. Indeed, other cultures emphasize depth rather than speed of processing.

Also, in the West, some prominent theorists have pointed out the importance of depth of processing for full command of material (e.g., Craik & Lockhart, 1972). Even within the United States, many people have started viewing as important not only the cognitive aspects but also the emotional aspects of intelligence. Mayer, Salovey, and Caruso (2000, p. 396) defined emotional intelligence as "the ability to perceive and express emotion, assimilate emotion in thought, understand and reason with emotion, and regulate emotion in the self and others." There is good evidence for the existence of some kind of emotional intelligence (Ciarrochi, Forgas, & Mayer, 2001; Mayer & Salovey, 1997; Mayer, Salovey, & Caruso, 2000; Salovey & Sluyter, 1997), although the evidence is mixed (Davies, Stankov, & Roberts, 1998). A related concept is that of social intelligence, the ability to understand and interact with other people (Kihlstrom & Cantor, 2000). Research also shows that personality variables are related to intelligence (Ackerman, 1996).

Explicit definitions of intelligence frequently take on an assessment-oriented focus. In fact, some psychologists, dating back at least to Edwin Boring (1923), have defined intelligence as whatever it is that the tests measure. This definition, unfortunately, is circular and, moreover, what different tests of intelligence measure is not always the same. Different tests measure somewhat different constructs (Daniel, 1997, 2000; Embretson & McCollam, 2000; Kaufman, 2000; Kaufman & Lichtenberger, 1998), so it is not feasible to define intelligence by what tests test, as though they all measured the same thing. Although most cognitive psychologists do not go to that extreme, the tradition of attempting to understand intelligence by measuring various aspects of it has a long history (Brody, 2000).

INTELLIGENCE TESTING

History

Contemporary measurements of intelligence usually can be traced to one of two very different historical traditions. One tradition concentrated on lower level, psychophysical abilities (such as sensory acuity, physical strength, and motor coordination); the other focused on higher level, judgment abilities (which we traditionally describe as related to thinking).

Francis Galton (1822–1911) believed that intelligence is a function of psychophysical abilities, and for several years, Galton maintained a well-equipped laboratory where visitors could have themselves measured on a variety of psychophysical tests. These tests measured a broad range of psychophysical skills and sensitivities, such as weight discrimination (the ability to notice small differences in the weights of objects), pitch sensitivity (the ability to hear small differences between musical notes), and physical strength (Galton, 1883). Wissler (1901), one of the many enthusiastic followers of Galton, attempted to detect links among the assorted tests, which would unify the various dimensions of psychophysically based intelligence. Much to Wissler's dismay, no unifying association could be detected. Moreover, Wissler found that the psychophysical tests did not predict college grades. The psychophysical approach to assessing intelligence soon faded almost into oblivion, although it would reappear many years later.

An alternative to the psychophysical approach was developed by Alfred Binet (1857–1911). He and his collaborator, Theodore Simon, also attempted to assess intelligence, but their goal was much more practical. Binet had been asked to devise a procedure to distinguish normal from mentally retarded learners in an academic setting (Binet & Simon, 1916). In Binet's view, judgment, not psychophysical acuity, strength, or skill, is the key to intelligence. For Binet (Binet & Simon, 1916), intelligent thought – mental judgment – comprises three distinct elements: direction, adaptation, and criticism. The importance of direction and adaptation certainly fits with contemporary views of intelligence, and Binet's notion of criticism actually seems prescient, considering the current appreciation of metacognitive processes as a key aspect of intelligence. Binet viewed intelligence as a broad potpourri of cognitive and other abilities, and as highly modifiable.

Major Intelligence Scales

Lewis Terman of Stanford University built on Binet and Simon's work in Europe and constructed the earliest version of what has come to be called the Stanford-Binet Intelligence Scales (Roid, 2003; Terman & Merrill, 1937, 1973; Thorndike, Hagen, & Sattler, 1986). The most recent version (SB-V) yields five subscores: Fluid Reasoning, Knowledge, Quantitative Reasoning, Visual-Spatial Processing, and Working Memory. For years, the Stanford-Binet test was the standard for intelligence tests, and it is still widely used, as are the competing Wechsler scales (Wechsler, 1939, 2003).

The Wechsler tests traditionally yielded three scores – a verbal score, a performance score, and an overall score. The verbal score is based on tests such as vocabulary and verbal similarities, in which the test-taker has to say how two things are similar. The performance score is based on tests such as picture completion, which requires identification of a missing part in a picture of an object; and picture arrangement, which requires rearrangement of a scrambled set of cartoon-like pictures into an order that tells a coherent story. The overall score is a combination of the verbal and performance scores. The most recent edition of the Wechsler Intelligence Scale for Children (WISC-IV) yields four index scores: Verbal Comprehension (VCI), Perceptual Reasoning (PRI), Processing Speed (PSI), and Working Memory (WMI). The most recent version of the Wechsler Adult Intelligence Scale (WAIS-IV) yields the same index scores as the WISC-IV.

Although Wechsler clearly believed in the worth of attempting to measure intelligence, he did not limit his conception of intelligence to test scores. Wechsler believed that intelligence is not represented just by a test score or even by what we do in school. We use our intelligence not just in taking tests and in doing homework, but also in relating to people, in performing our jobs effectively, and in managing our lives in general.

PSYCHOMETRIC APPROACHES TO INTELLIGENCE

Psychologists interested in the structure of intelligence have relied on factor analysis as an indispensable tool for their research (Willis, Dumont, & Kaufman, in press). Factor analysis is a statistical method for separating a construct – intelligence in this case – into a number of hypothetical factors or abilities the researchers believe to form the basis of individual differences in test performance. The specific factors derived, of course, still depend on the specific questions being asked and the tasks being evaluated. Factor analysis is based on studies of correlation. The idea is that the more highly two tests are correlated, the more likely they are to measure the same thing. In research on intelligence, a factor analysis might involve these steps: (a) Give a large number of people several different tests of ability; (b) determine the correlations among all those tests; (c) statistically analyze those correlations to simplify them into a relatively small number of factors that summarize people's performance on the tests. The investigators in this area have generally agreed on and followed this procedure, yet the resulting factorial structures of intelligence have differed among theorists such as Spearman, Thurstone, Guilford, Cattell, Vernon, and Carroll.

Spearman: Theory of *g*

Charles Spearman is usually credited with inventing factor analysis (Spearman, 1927). Using factor-analytic studies, Spearman concluded that intelligence can be understood in terms of both a single general factor that pervades performance on all tests of mental ability and a set of specific factors, each of which is involved in performance on only a single type of mental ability test (e.g., arithmetic computations). In Spearman's view, the specific factors are of only casual interest because of their narrow applicability. To Spearman, the general factor, which he labeled "*g*," provides the key to understanding intelligence. Spearman believed *g* to be attributable to "mental energy." Many psychologists still believe Spearman's theory to be essentially correct (e.g., Jensen, 1998; see essays in Sternberg & Grigorenko, 2002b). The theory is useful in part because *g* accounts for a sizable, although not fixed, percentage of variance in school and job performance, usually somewhere between 5% and 40% (Jensen, 1998). Spearman (1923) provided a cognitive theory of intelligence. He suggested that intelligence comprises apprehension of experience (encoding of stimuli), eduction of relations (inference of relations), and eduction of correlates (application of what is learned). He therefore may have been the earliest serious cognitive theorist of intelligence.

If one accepts Spearman's theory, then a gifted person can be defined simply as one who excels in general intelligence. This simple definition historically has been among the most widely used. Individuals are given an intelligence test, usually an individually administered one, and an overall score is computed. If the score is over a certain threshold, the individual is labeled as gifted. In Lewis Terman's (1925) studies of giftedness, an IQ of 140 was generally used as the cutoff. Other studies have used other values.

There is no one score that inherently serves as a privileged cutoff. One of us recently served as a consultant to a school for gifted children for which there was an IQ cutoff – 130. When the consultant inquired why 130 was used, he was told that it was not the school that decided on 130 as the cutoff but the publisher of the test. This admissions officer truly believed that if someone scored 130 or above, he or she was gifted, and if the individual scored under 130, he or she was not. There is no magic cutoff, however. Someone using the Spearman model who wanted a cutoff would have to determine it on the basis of what percentage of students the school or school district was able to or wished to serve.

Thurstone: Primary Mental Abilities

In contrast to Spearman, Louis Thurstone (1887–1955) concluded (Thurstone, 1938) that the core of intelligence resides not in one single factor but in seven such factors, which he referred to as *primary mental abilities: verbal comprehension*, measured by vocabulary tests; *verbal fluency*, measured by time-limited tests requiring the test-taker to think of as many words as possible that begin with a given letter; *inductive reasoning*, measured by tests such as analogies and number-series completion tasks; *spatial visualization,* measured by tests requiring mental rotation of pictures of objects, *number,* measured by computation and simple mathematical problem-solving tests; *memory,* measured by picture and word-recall tests; and *perceptual speed,* measured by tests that require the test-taker to recognize small differences in pictures or to cross out a "each time it appears in a string" of varied letters.

Thurstone's model leaves one in a very different place in the identification of the gifted from Spearman's model. Here, one needs to decide how to combine multiple pieces of information, which arguably, are not equally valuable. For example, many school districts would view verbal comprehension as more valuable to identifying giftedness than they would perceptual speed.

There are several ways in which the Thurstone model might be operationalized. One would be to combine scores from the different factors on a more or less equal basis, perhaps into a composite IQ, and then set a cutoff, much as would be done with the Spearman model. Another would be to combine the test scores into a composite IQ but to differentially weight the factor scores. Yet another would be to use multiple cutoffs – to require that a person score above a certain level on all or some number of the factors for the person to be labeled as gifted. One might include all the scores in such a model, or just a subset of them. Finally, one might use some kind of mixed model, whereby one has to score very high perhaps on one or two factors, and then at least somewhat high on all or almost all of the remainder of the factors.

Guilford: Structure of Intellect

At the opposite extreme from Spearman's single *g*-factor model is J. P. Guilford's (1967, 1982, 1988) structure-of-intellect model, which includes up to 150 factors of the mind in one version of the theory. According to Guilford, intelligence can be understood in terms of a cube that represents the intersection of three dimensions – operations, contents, and products. Operations are simply mental processes, such as memory and evaluation (making judgments, such as determining whether a particular statement is a fact or opinion). Contents are the kinds of terms that appear in a problem, such as semantic (words) and visual (pictures). Products are the kinds of responses required, such as units (single words, numbers, or pictures), classes (hierarchies), and implications. Thus, Guilford's theory, like Spearman's, had an explicit cognitive component.

Guilford's theory is not so popular today because it has been shown statistically to be flawed (Horn & Knapp, 1973). But it has been used in gifted identification and so we should at least consider what its implications would be for such use. To obtain 150 different scores for each individual is simply not practical. Even if one were to obtain such a huge number of scores, it is unlikely that they would be reliable or even particularly discriminatively valid – that is, clearly differentiable from each other. So one would have to devise a model of identification that tests just some of the skills and then uses the scores thus obtained in a way similar to that for the Thurstonian factors. The disadvantage of the model is that one would not be able to know for sure how the individual would have fared had one been able to test more of the factors in the model.

Cattell, Vernon, and Carroll: Hierarchical Models

A more parsimonious way of handling a number of factors of the mind is through a hierarchical model of intelligence. One such model, developed by Raymond Cattell (1971), proposed that general intelligence comprises two major subfactors – fluid ability (speed and accuracy of abstract reasoning, especially for novel problems) and crystallized ability (accumulated knowledge and vocabulary). Subsumed within these two major subfactors are other, more specific factors. A similar view was proposed by Philip E. Vernon (1971), who made a general division between practical-mechanical and verbal-educational abilities.

More recently, John B. Carroll (1993) proposed a hierarchical model of intelligence based on his analysis of more than 460 data sets obtained between 1927 and 1987. His analysis encompasses more than 130,000 people from diverse walks of life and even countries of origin (although non–English-speaking countries are poorly represented among his data sets). The model Carroll proposed, based on his monumental undertaking, is a hierarchy comprising three strata – Stratum I, which includes many narrow, specific abilities (e.g., spelling ability, speed of reasoning); Stratum II, which includes various broad abilities (e.g., fluid intelligence, crystallized intelligence); and Stratum III, a single general intelligence, much like Spearman's *g*. In addition to fluid intelligence and crystallized intelligence, in the middle stratum Carroll included learning and memory processes, visual perception, auditory perception, facile production of ideas (similar to verbal fluency), and speed (which includes both sheer speed of response and speed of accurate response). Although Carroll did not break new ground, in that many of the abilities in his model have been mentioned in other theories, he did masterfully integrate a large and diverse factor-analytic literature, thereby giving great authority to his model.

In practice, the hierarchical models tend to lead to similar means of gifted identification as does the *g*-based model. The reason is that the factors are hierarchically arranged under, and hence are conceptually and statistically subordinate to, *g*. The tests one might use are more likely to be multifactorial. But in the end, they will yield an IQ or similar score, which is likely to serve as the basis for identification.

A FAMOUS APPLICATION OF THE PSYCHOMETRIC MODEL

Probably the best-known psychometric studies of gifted individuals were conducted by Lewis Terman. He conducted a *longitudinal study* that followed particular individuals over the course of their life spans (Terman, 1925; Terman & Oden, 1959). The study has continued since Terman's death. In his sample of the gifted, Terman included children from California under age 11 with IQs over 140, as well as children in the 11- to 14-year age bracket with slightly lower IQs. The mean IQ of the 643 research participants selected was 151. Only 22 of these participants had IQs lower than 140.

The accomplishments in later life of the selected group were extraordinary by any criterion. For example, 31 men were listed in *Who's Who in America*. There were numerous highly successful businessmen as well as individuals who were successful in other professions. The sex bias is obvious. Most of the women became homemakers, so it is impossible to make any meaningful comparison between the men (none of whom were reported to have become househusbands) and the women. As with all correlational data, it would be difficult to assign a causal role to IQ in accounting for the accomplishments of the successful individuals in the study. Many factors other than IQ could have contributed to the success of Terman's sample. Among the most important of them is familial socioeconomic status and the final educational level achieved by these individuals.

As discussed in Chapter 3, today, many, if not most, psychologists look to more than IQ to identify the intellectually gifted. Even those who see intelligence as the basis for giftedness tend to look beyond just IQ.

COGNITIVE APPROACHES TO INTELLIGENCE

Cognitive theorists are interested in studying how people (or other organisms; Zentall, 2000) mentally represent and process what they learn and know about the world. The ways in which various cognitive investigators study intelligence differ primarily in terms of the complexity of the processes being studied. Among the advocates of cognitive approaches have been Ted Nettelbeck, Arthur Jensen, Earl Hunt, Herbert Simon, and the senior author of this book, Robert Sternberg. Each of these researchers has considered both the speed and the accuracy of information processing to be important factors in intelligence. In addition to speed and accuracy of processing, Hunt considered verbal versus spatial skill, as well as attentional ability.

Inspection Time

Nettelbeck (e.g., 1987, in press; Nettelbeck & Lally, 1976; Nettelbeck & Rabbitt, 1992; see also Deary, 2000, 2002; Deary & Stough, 1996) suggested a speed-related indicator of intelligence, involving the encoding of visual information for brief storage in working memory. But what is critical in this view is not speed of response but rather the length of time a stimulus must be presented for the subject to be able to process that stimulus. The shorter the presentation length, the higher the score. The key variable is the length of time for the presentation of the target stimulus, not the speed of responding by pressing the button. Nettelbeck operationally defined inspection time as the length of time for presentation of the target stimulus after which the participant still responds with at least 90% success. Nettelbeck (1987) found that shorter inspection times correlate with higher scores on intelligence tests (e.g., various subscales of the Wechsler Adult Intelligence Scale – WAIS) among differing populations of participants. Other investigators have confirmed this finding (e.g., Deary & Stough, 1996).

The inspection-time focus gives a different perspective on giftedness from any of the psychometric foci. This view is of the gifted as superior processors of information. The gifted can look at a scene – in the case of inspection time a very simple one – and derive information from it very rapidly that a nongifted person would take longer to extract, probably less accurately. This kind of measure is unlikely to be used in schools because it is so remote from the requirements of school-based tasks.

Choice Reaction Time

Arthur Jensen (1979, 1998, 2002) emphasized a different aspect of information-processing speed; specifically, he proposed that intelligence can be understood in terms of speed of neuronal conduction. In other words, the smart person is someone whose neural circuits conduct information rapidly.

When Jensen proposed this notion, direct measures of neural-conduction velocity were not readily available, so he primarily studied a proposed proxy for measuring neural-processing speed – choice reaction time, the time it takes to select one answer from among several possibilities. For example, suppose that you were one of Jensen's participants. You might be seated in front of a set of lights on a board. When one of the lights flashed, you would be expected to extinguish it by pressing as rapidly as possible a button beneath the correct light. The experimenter would then measure your speed in performing this task. Jensen (1982b) found that participants with higher intelligence quotients (IQs) are faster than participants with lower IQs in their reaction time (RT), that is, the time between when a light comes on and the finger leaves the home (central) button. In some studies, participants with higher IQs also showed a faster movement time, the time between letting the finger leave the home button and hitting the button under the light. Based on such tasks, Reed and Jensen (1991, 1993) proposed that their findings might be attributable to increased central nerve-conduction velocity, although at present this proposal remains speculative.

Other researchers have suggested that various findings regarding choice RT may be influenced by the number of response alternatives and the visual-scanning requirements of Jensen's apparatus rather than being attributable to the speed of RT alone (Bors, MacLeod, & Forrin, 1993). In particular, Bors and colleagues found that manipulating the number of buttons and the size of the visual angle of the display could reduce the correlation between IQ and RT. Thus, the relation between reaction time and intelligence is unclear.

The choice RT view of giftedness is very similar to the lay conception of the very smart person as "quick." This individual can process information rapidly and hence appears to be "on the ball." The notion gives credence to intelligence tests that have strict time limits, with the idea that someone who cannot answer problems quickly, whatever the person's mental powers, is less able than someone who can provide quick responses. A risk of this approach is that it may reward impulsiveness as well as simply speed of processing. Another risk is that depth of processing will be ignored in favor of rapidity of processing.

Lexical Access Speed and Speed of Simultaneous Processing

Like Jensen, Earl Hunt (1978) suggested that intelligence be measured in terms of speed. However, Hunt was particularly interested in verbal intelligence and focused on lexical-access speed – the speed with which we can retrieve information about words (e.g., letter names) stored in our long-term memories. To measure this speed, Hunt proposed a letter-matching RT task (Posner & Mitchell, 1967). For example, suppose that you are one of Hunt's participants. You would be shown pairs of letters, such as "A A," "A a," or "A b." For each pair, you would be asked to indicate whether the letters constitute a match in name (e.g., "A a" match in name of letter of the alphabet but "A b" do not). You would also be given a simpler task, in which you would be asked to indicate whether the letters match physically (e.g., "A A" are physically identical, whereas "A a" are not). Hunt would be particularly interested in discerning the difference between your speed for the first set of tasks, involving name matching, and your speed for the second set, involving matching of physical characteristics. Hunt would consider the difference in your reaction time for each task to indicate a measure of your speed of lexical access. Thus, he would subtract from his equation the physical-match reaction time. For Hunt, the response time in indicating that "A A" is a physical match is unimportant. What interests him is a more complex reaction time – that for recognizing names of letters. He and his colleagues found that students with lower verbal ability take longer to gain access to lexical information than do students with higher verbal ability.

Earl Hunt and Marcy Lansman (1982) also studied people's ability to divide their attention as a function of intelligence. For example, suppose that you are asked to solve mathematical problems and simultaneously to listen for a tone and press a button as soon as you hear it. We can expect that you would both solve the math problems effectively and respond quickly to hearing the tone. According to Hunt and Lansman, one thing that makes people more intelligent is that they are better able to timeshare between two tasks and to perform both effectively. In sum, process timing theories attempt to account for differences in intelligence by appealing to differences in the speed of various forms of information processing; inspection time, choice RT, and lexical access timing all have been found to correlate with measures of intelligence. These findings suggest that higher intelligence may be related to the speed of various information-processing abilities, including encoding information more rapidly into working memory, accessing information in long-term memory more rapidly, and responding more rapidly.

The Hunt and Lansman view has interesting implications for the study of giftedness in that it suggests the importance of not just being able to process information but also of being able to ignore irrelevant information. People are constantly bombarded with informational noise of various kinds and, in this view, the smart ones screen out what is not potentially relevant to them.

The issue is more complicated than it seems because of the difficulty, at times, of knowing what eventually may be relevant. Creative people often are those who take in signals that to others might seem irrelevant. Something that seems irrelevant at one time may turn out later to be relevant after all. So it is very nontrivial to know exactly what one will need at some future time.

Why, in general, would more rapid encoding, retrieval, and responding be associated with higher intelligence test scores in the first place? Do rapid information processors learn more? Other research on learning in aged persons investigated whether there is a link between age-related slowing of information processing and (a) initial encoding and recall of information and (b) long-term retention (Nettelbeck et al., 1996; Bors & Forrin, 1995). The findings suggest that the relation between inspection time and intelligence may not be related to learning. In particular, Nettelbeck et al. found there is a difference between initial recall and actual long-term learning; whereas initial recall performance is mediated by processing speed (older, slower participants showed deficits), longer term retention of new information (preserved in older participants) is mediated by cognitive processes other than speed of processing, including rehearsal strategies. This implies speed of information processing may influence initial performance on recall and inspection time tasks, but speed is not related to long-term learning. Perhaps faster information processing aids participants in performance aspects of intelligence test tasks rather than contributing to actual learning and intelligence. Clearly, this area requires more research to determine how information-processing speed relates to intelligence.

Working Memory

Some work suggests that a critical component of intelligence may be working memory (Conway, Getz, Macnamara, & Engel, in press). Indeed, Kyllonen (2002) and Kyllonen and Christal (1990) have argued that intelligence may be little more than working memory! Daneman and Carpenter (1983) had participants read sets of passages and, after they had read the passages, try to remember the last word of each passage. Recall was highly correlated with verbal ability. Turner and Engle (1989) had participants perform a variety of working-memory tasks. In one task, for example, the participants saw a set of simple arithmetic problems, each of which was followed by a word or a digit. An example would be "Does $(3 \times 5) - 6 = 7$?" The participants saw sets of two to six such problems, and solved each one. After solving the problems in the set, they tried to recall the words that followed the problems. The number of words recalled was highly correlated with measured intelligence. It therefore appears that the ability to store and manipulate information in working memory may be an important aspect of intelligence, although probably not all there is to intelligence.

The Componential Theory and Complex Problem Solving

In our early work on intelligence, the senior author (Sternberg, 1977) began using cognitive approaches to study information processing in more complex tasks, such as analogies, series problems (e.g., completing a numerical or figural series), and syllogisms (Sternberg, 1977, 1983, 1985a). The goal was to find out just what made some people more intelligent processors of information than others. The idea was to take the kinds of tasks used on conventional intelligence tests and to isolate the components of intelligence – the mental processes used in performing these tasks, such as translating a sensory input into a mental representation, transforming one conceptual representation into another, or translating a conceptual representation into a motor output (Sternberg, 1982). Since then, many people have elaborated upon and expanded this basic approach (Lohman, 2000).

Componential analysis breaks down people's reaction times and error rates on these tasks in terms of the processes that make up the tasks. This kind of analysis revealed that people may solve analogies and similar tasks by using several component processes, including encoding the terms of the problem; inferring relations among at least some of the terms; mapping the inferred relations to other terms that would be presumed to show similar relations; and applying the previously inferred relations to the new situations. Consider the analogy, LAWYER : CLIENT :: DOCTOR : (a. PATIENT b. MEDICINE). To solve this analogy, you need to encode each term of the problem, which includes perceiving a term and retrieving information about it from memory. You then infer the relationship between lawyer and client – that the former provides professional services to the latter. You then map the relationship in the first half of the analogy to the second half of the analogy, noting that it will involve that same relationship. Finally, you apply that inferred relationship to generate the final term of the analogy, leading to the appropriate response of PATIENT. Studying these components of information processing reveals more than measuring mental speed alone.

When measuring speed alone, we found significant correlations between speed in executing these processes and performance on other, traditional intelligence tests. However, a more intriguing discovery is that participants who score higher on traditional intelligence tests take longer to encode the terms of the problem than do less intelligent participants, but they make up for the extra time by taking less time to perform the remaining components of the task. In general, more intelligent participants take longer during global planning – encoding the problem and formulating a general strategy for attacking the problem (or set of problems) – but they take less time for local planning – forming and implementing strategies for the details of the task (Sternberg, 1981). The advantage of spending more time on global planning is the increased likelihood that the resulting overall strategy will be correct. Thus, brighter people may take longer to do something than will less bright people when taking more time is advantageous. For example, the brighter person might spend more time researching and planning a term paper but less time in actually writing it. This same differential in time allocation has been shown in other tasks as well (e.g., in solving physics problems; Larkin et al., 1980; Sternberg, 1979, 1985a); that is, more intelligent people seem to spend more time planning for and encoding the problems they face but less time in the other components of task performance. This may relate to the previously mentioned metacognitive attribute many include in their notions of intelligence. The bottom line, then, is that intelligence may reside as much in how people allocate time as it does in the amount of time it takes them to do cognitive tasks.

In a similarly cognitive approach, Simon studied the information processing of people engaged in complex problem-solving situations, such as when playing chess and performing logical derivations (Newell & Simon, 1972; Simon, 1976). A simple, brief task might require the participant to view an arithmetic or geometric series, figure out the rule underlying the progression, and guess what numeral or geometric figure might come next – for example, more complex tasks might include some problem-solving tasks (e.g., the water jugs problems; see Estes, 1982). These problems were similar or identical to those used on intelligence tests.

Lohman and Lakin (in press) have reviewed the literature on modern reasoning-based approaches to intelligence. They have found that there is a strong correlation between reasoning and most tests of intelligence, in large part because intelligence tests rely so heavily on reasoning. They also have found that knowledge plays an important role in such correlations, especially for deductive reasoning.

BIOLOGICAL APPROACHES TO INTELLIGENCE

Although the human brain is clearly the organ responsible for human intelligence, early studies (e.g., those by Karl Lashley and others) seeking to find biological indices of intelligence and other aspects of mental processes were a resounding failure, despite great efforts. As tools for studying the brain have become more sophisticated, however, we are beginning to see the possibility of finding physiological indicators of intelligence. Some investigators (e.g., Matarazzo, 1992) believe that we will have clinically useful psychophysiological indices of intelligence very early in the current millennium, although widely applicable indices will be much longer in coming. In the meantime, the biological studies we now have are largely correlational, showing statistical associations between biological and psychometric or other measures of intelligence. The studies do not establish causal relations but they are very promising in showing areas of the brain associated with intelligent behavior (Haier, in press).

Brain Size

One line of research looks at the relationship of brain size to intelligence (see Jerison, 2000; Vernon et al., 2000). The evidence suggests that, for humans, there is a modest but significant statistical relationship between brain size and intelligence. It is difficult to know what to make of this relationship, however, because greater brain size may cause greater intelligence, greater intelligence may cause greater brain size, or both may depend on some third factor. Moreover, probably more important than the size of the brain is how efficiently it is used. On average, for example, men have larger brains than women, but women have better connections of the two hemispheres of the brain through the corpus callosum. So it is not clear which gender, on average, would be at an advantage, and probably neither would be. It is important to note that the relationship between brain size and intelligence does not hold across species (Jerison, 2000). Rather, what holds seems to be a relationship between intelligence and brain size relative to the rough general size of the organism.

Speed of Neural Conduction

Complex patterns of electrical activity in the brain, which are prompted by specific stimuli, appear to correlate with scores on IQ tests (Barrett & Eysenck, 1992). Several studies (e.g., McGarry-Roberts, Stelmack, & Campbell, 1992; Vernon & Mori, 1992) initially suggested that speed of conduction of neural impulses correlates with intelligence as measured by IQ tests. A follow-up study (Wickett & Vernon, 1994), however, failed to find a strong relation between neural-conduction velocity (as measured by neural-conduction speeds in a main nerve of the arm) and intelligence (as measured on the Multidimensional Aptitude Battery). Surprisingly, neural-conduction velocity appears to be a more powerful predictor of IQ scores for men than for women, so gender differences may account for some of the differences in the data (Wickett & Vernon, 1994). Additional studies on both males and females are needed.

Positron Emission Tomography and Functional
Magnetic Resonance Imaging

An alternative approach to studying the brain suggests that neural efficiency may be related to intelligence; such an approach is based on studies of how the brain metabolizes glucose (simple sugar required for brain activity) during mental activities. Richard Haier and colleagues (Haier et al., 1992) cited several other researchers who support their own findings that higher intelligence correlates with reduced levels of glucose metabolism during problem-solving tasks – that is, smarter brains consume less sugar (and hence expend less effort) than do less smart brains doing the same task. Furthermore, Haier and colleagues found that cerebral efficiency increases as a result of learning on a relatively complex task involving visuospatial manipulations (the computer game Tetris). As a result of practice, more intelligent participants show not only lower cerebral glucose metabolism overall but also more specifically localized metabolism of glucose. In most areas of their brains, smarter participants show less glucose metabolism, but in selected areas of their brains (believed to be important to the task at hand), they show higher levels of glucose metabolism. Thus, more intelligent participants may have learned how to use their brains more efficiently to focus their thought processes on a given task.

More recent research by Haier and colleagues suggests that the relationship between glucose metabolism and intelligence may be more complex (Haier et al., 1995; Larson et al., 1995). Whereas Haier's group (1995) confirmed the earlier findings of increased glucose metabolism in less smart participants (in this case, mildly retarded participants), the study by Larson et al. (1995) found, contrary to the earlier findings, that smarter participants had increased glucose metabolism relative to their average comparison group.

One problem with earlier studies is that the tasks used were not matched for difficulty level across groups of smart and average individuals. The Larson et al. study used tasks that were matched to the ability levels of the smarter and average participants and found that the smarter participants used more glucose. Moreover, the glucose metabolism was highest in the right brain hemisphere of the more intelligent participants performing the hard task – again suggesting selectivity of brain areas. What could be driving the increases in glucose metabolism? Currently, the key factor appears to be subjective task difficulty, with smarter participants in earlier studies simply finding the tasks too easy. Matching task difficulty to participants' abilities seems to indicate that smarter participants increase glucose metabolism when the task demands it. The preliminary findings in this area need to be investigated further before any conclusive answers are reached.

Some neuropsychological research (e.g., Dempster, 1991) suggests that performance on intelligence tests may not indicate a crucial aspect of intelligence – the ability to set goals, to plan how to meet them, and to execute those plans. Specifically, persons with lesions in the frontal lobe of the brain frequently perform quite well on standardized IQ tests, which require responses to questions within a highly structured situation but do not require much in the way of goal setting or planning. If intelligence involves the ability to learn from experience and to adapt to the surrounding environment, the ability to set goals and to design and implement plans cannot be ignored. An essential aspect of goal setting and planning is the ability to attend appropriately to relevant stimuli and to ignore or discount irrelevant stimuli.

EVOLUTIONARY THEORY

Some theorists have tried to understand intelligence in terms of how it has evolved over the eons (e.g., Bjorklund & Kipp, 2002; Bradshaw, 2002; Byrne, 2002; Calvin, 2002; Corballis, 2002; Cosmides & Tooby, 2002; Flanagan, Hardcastle, & Nahmias, 2002; Grossman & Kaufman, 2002; Pinker, 1997; see Gabora & Russon, in press, for a review). The basic idea in these models is that we are intelligent in the ways we are because it was important for our distant ancestors to acquire certain sets of skills. According to Cosmides and Tooby (2002), for example, we are particularly sensitive at detecting cheating because people in the past who were not sensitive to cheaters did not live to have children, or had fewer children. Evolutionary approaches stress the continuity of the nature of intelligence over long stretches of time, and in some theories, across species. However, during evolution, the frontal lobe increased in size, so it is difficult to know whether changes in intelligence are just a manifestation of physiological changes or the other way around.

CONTEXTUAL APPROACHES TO INTELLIGENCE

According to contextualists, intelligence cannot be understood outside its real-world context. The context of intelligence may be viewed at any level of analysis, focusing narrowly, on the home and family environment, or extending broadly, on entire cultures. Even cross-community differences have been correlated with differences in performance on intelligence tests; such context-related differences include those of rural versus urban communities, low versus high proportions of teenagers to adults within communities, and low versus high socioeconomic status of communities (see Coon, Carey, & Fulker, 1992). Contextualists are particularly intrigued by the effects of cultural context on intelligence. In fact, contextualists consider intelligence so inextricably linked to culture that they view intelligence as something that a culture creates to define the nature of adaptive performance in that culture, and to account for why some people perform better than others on the tasks that the culture happens to value (Sternberg, 1985b). Theorists who endorse this model study just how intelligence relates to the external world in which the model is being applied and evaluated. In general, definitions and theories of intelligence will more effectively encompass cultural diversity by broadening in scope. Before exploring some of the contextual theories of intelligence, we will look at what prompted psychologists to believe that culture might play a role in how we define and assess intelligence.

People in different cultures may have quite different ideas of what it means to be smart. One of the more interesting cross-cultural studies of intelligence was performed by Michael Cole and colleagues (Cole et al., 1971). These investigators asked adult members of the Kpelle tribe in Western Africa to sort concept terms. In Western culture, when adults are given a sorting task on an intelligence test, more intelligent people typically sort hierarchically. For example, they may sort names of different kinds of fish together, and then the word fish over that, with the name animal over fish and over birds, and so on. Less intelligent people typically sort functionally. They may sort fish with eat, for example, because we eat fish, or clothes with wear, because we wear clothes. The Kpelle sorted functionally – even after investigators unsuccessfully tried to get the Kpelle spontaneously to sort hierarchically. Finally, in desperation, one of the experimenters (Glick) asked a Kpelle to sort as a foolish person would sort. In response, the Kpelle quickly and easily sorted hierarchically. The Kpelle had been able to sort this way all along; they just hadn't done it because they viewed it as foolish – and they probably considered the researchers rather unintelligent for asking such stupid questions.

The Kpelle people are not the only ones who might question Western understandings of intelligence. In the Puluwat culture of the Pacific Ocean, for example, sailors navigate incredibly long distances, using none of the navigational aids that sailors from technologically advanced countries would need to get from one place to another (Gladwin, 1970). Were Puluwat sailors to devise intelligence tests for Americans, we might not seem very intelligent. Similarly, the highly skilled Puluwat sailors might not do well on American-crafted tests of intelligence. These and other observations have prompted quite a few theoreticians to recognize the importance of considering cultural context when assessing intelligence.

The preceding arguments may make it clear why it is so difficult to come up with a test that everyone would consider culture-fair – equally appropriate and fair for members of all cultures. If members of different cultures have different ideas of what it means to be intelligent, then the very behaviors that may be considered intelligent in one culture may be considered unintelligent in another. Take, for example, the concept of mental quickness. In mainstream U.S. culture, quickness is usually associated with intelligence. To say someone is "quick" is to say that the person is intelligent and, indeed, most group tests of intelligence are quite strictly timed. Even on individual tests of intelligence, the test-giver times some responses of the test-taker. Many information-processing theorists and even psychophysiological theorists focus on the study of intelligence as a function of mental speed.

In many other cultures of the world, however, people believe that more intelligent people do not rush into things. Even in our own culture, no one will view you as brilliant if you decide on a marital partner, a job, or a place to live in the 20 to 30 seconds you might normally have to solve an intelligence-test problem. Thus, given that there exist no perfectly culture-fair tests of intelligence, at least at present, how should we consider context when assessing and understanding intelligence?

Several researchers have suggested that providing culture-relevant tests is possible (e.g., Baltes, Dittmann-Kohli, & Dixon, 1984; Jenkins, 1979; Keating, 1984) – that is, tests that employ skills and knowledge that relate to the cultural experiences of the test-takers. Baltes and his colleagues, for example, designed tests measuring skill in dealing with the pragmatic aspects of everyday life. Designing culture-relevant tests requires creativity and effort but probably is not impossible. A study by Daniel Wagner (1978), for example, investigated memory abilities – one aspect of intelligence as our culture defines it – in our culture versus the Moroccan culture. Wagner found that level of recall depended on the content that was being remembered, with culture-relevant content being remembered more effectively than irrelevant content (e.g., compared with Westerners, Moroccan rug merchants were better able to recall complex visual patterns on black-and-white photos of Oriental rugs). Wagner further suggested that when tests are not designed to minimize the effects of cultural differences, the key to culture-specific differences in memory might be the knowledge and use of metamemory strategies, rather than actual structural differences in memory (e.g., memory span and rates of forgetting).

In Kenya, research has shown that rural Kenyan schoolchildren have substantial knowledge about natural herbal medicines they believe fight infection; Western children, of course, would not be able to identify any of these medicines (Sternberg et al., 2001a; Sternberg & Grigorenko, 1997a). In short, making a test culturally relevant appears to involve much more than just removing specific linguistic barriers to understanding. Stephen Ceci (Ceci & Roazzi, 1994) found similar context effects in children's and adults' performance on a variety of tasks. Ceci suggests that the social context (e.g., whether a task is considered masculine or feminine), the mental context (e.g., whether a visuospatial task involves buying a home or burgling it), and the physical context (e.g., whether a task is presented at the beach or in a laboratory) all affect performance. For example, 14-year-old boys performed poorly on a task when it was couched as a cupcake-baking task but performed well when it was framed as a battery-charging task (Ceci & Bronfenbrenner, 1985). Brazilian maids had no difficulty with proportional reasoning when hypothetically purchasing food but had great difficulty with it when hypothetically purchasing medicinal herbs (Schliemann & Magalhües, 1990). Brazilian children whose poverty had forced them to become street vendors showed no difficulty in performing complex arithmetic computations when selling things but had great difficulty performing similar calculations in a classroom (Carraher, Carraher, & Schliemann, 1985; also see discussion in Chapter 8). Thus, test performance may be affected by the context in which the test terms are presented.

SYSTEMS APPROACHES TO INTELLIGENCE

Gardner: Multiple Intelligences

Howard Gardner (Davis, Christodoulou, Seider, & Gardner, in press; Gardner, 1983, 1993) proposed a theory of multiple intelligences, in which intelligence is not just a single, unitary construct. Instead of speaking of multiple abilities that together constitute intelligence (e.g., Thurstone, 1938), Gardner (1999a) speaks of eight distinct intelligences that are relatively independent of each other. Each is a separate system of functioning, although these systems can interact to produce what we see as intelligent performance. In some respects, Gardner's theory sounds like a factorial one because it specifies several abilities that are construed to reflect intelligence of some sort. However, Gardner views each ability as a separate intelligence, not as a part of a single whole. Moreover, a crucial difference between Gardner's theory and factorial ones is in the sources of evidence Gardner used for identifying the eight intelligences. Gardner used converging operations, gathering evidence from multiple sources and types of data. Gardner's view of the mind is modular. A major task of existing and future research on intelligence is to isolate the portions of the brain responsible for each of the intelligences. Gardner has speculated regarding at least some of these locales, but hard evidence for the existence of these separate intelligences has yet to be produced. Furthermore, Nettelbeck and Young (1996) question the strict modularity of Gardner's theory. Specifically, the phenomenon of preserved specific cognitive functioning in autistic savants (persons with severe social and cognitive deficits, but with corresponding high ability in a narrow domain) as evidence for modular intelligences may not be justified. According to Nettelbeck and Young, the narrow long-term memory and specific aptitudes of savants is not really intelligent. As a result, there may be reason to question the intelligence of inflexible modules.

Sternberg: The Triarchic Theory of Successful Intelligence

Whereas Gardner emphasizes the separateness of the various aspects of intelligence, Sternberg (2003d) tends to emphasize the extent to which they work together in the triarchic theory of successful intelligence (Sternberg, 1985a, 1988b, 1996b, 1999c, 2005b), as discussed in the previous chapter. According to the triarchic (tri-, "three"; -archic, "governed") theory, intelligence comprises three aspects, dealing with the relation of intelligence (a) to the internal world of the person, (b) to experience, and (c) to the external world.

How Intelligence Relates to the Internal World
This part of the theory emphasizes the processing of information, which can be viewed in terms of three different kinds of components: (a) metacomponents – executive processes (i.e., metacognition) used to plan, monitor, and evaluate problem solving; (b) performance components – lower order processes used to implement the commands of the metacomponents; and (c) knowledge-acquisition components – the processes used to learn how to solve the problems in the first place. The components are highly interdependent.

How Intelligence Relates to Experience
The theory also considers how prior experience may interact with all three kinds of information-processing components. That is, each of us faces tasks and situations with which we have varying levels of experience, ranging from a completely novel task, with which we have no previous experience, to a completely familiar task, with which we have vast, extensive experience. As a task becomes increasingly familiar, many aspects of the task may become automatic, requiring us to make little conscious effort to determine what step to take next and how to implement that next step. A novel task makes demands on intelligence different from those of a task for which automatic procedures have been developed.

According to the triarchic theory, relatively novel tasks – such as visiting a foreign country, mastering a new subject, or acquiring a foreign language – demand more of a person's intelligence. In fact, a completely unfamiliar task may demand so much of the person as to be overwhelming.

How Intelligence Relates to the External World
The triarchic theory also proposes that the various components of intelligence are applied to experience to serve three functions in real-world contexts – adapting ourselves to our existing environments, shaping our existing environments to create new environments, and selecting new environments. According to the triarchic theory, people may apply their intelligence to many different kinds of problems. Some people may be more intelligent in the face of abstract, academic problems, for example, whereas others may be more intelligent in the face of concrete, practical problems. The theory does not define an intelligent person as someone who necessarily excels in all aspects of intelligence. Rather, intelligent persons know their own strengths and weaknesses and find ways in which to capitalize on their strengths and either to compensate for or to correct their weaknesses.

True Intelligence

Perkins (1995) proposed a theory of what he refers to as *true intelligence*, which he believes synthesizes classic views as well as new ones. According to Perkins, there are three basic aspects of intelligence – neural, experiential, and reflective. Concerning neural intelligence, Perkins believes that some people's neurological systems function better than do the neurological systems of others, running faster and with more precision. He mentions "more finely tuned voltages" and "more exquisitely adapted chemical catalysts" as well as a "better pattern of connectivity in the labyrinth of neurons"

(Perkins, 1995, p. 497), although it is not entirely clear what any of these terms mean. Perkins believes this aspect of intelligence to be largely genetically determined and unlearnable. This kind of intelligence seems to be somewhat similar to Cattell's (1971) idea of fluid intelligence.

The experiential aspect of intelligence is what one has learned from experience. It is the extent and organization of the knowledge base, and thus is similar to Cattell's (1971) notion of crystallized intelligence. The reflective aspect of intelligence refers to the role of strategies in memory and problem solving, and appears to be similar to the construct of metacognition or cognitive monitoring (Brown & DeLoache, 1978; Flavell, 1981).

No empirical test of the theory of true intelligence has been published, so it is difficult to evaluate the theory at this time. Like Gardner's (1983) theory, Perkins's theory is based on literature review, and as noted previously, such literature reviews often tend to be selective and then interpreted in a way that maximizes the fit of the theory to the available data.

The Bioecological Model of Intelligence

Ceci (1996) proposed a bioecological model of intelligence, according to which multiple cognitive potentials, context, and knowledge all are essential bases of individual differences in performance. Each of the multiple cognitive potentials enables relationships to be discovered, thoughts to be monitored, and knowledge to be acquired within a given domain. Although these potentials are biologically based, their development is closely linked to environmental context, and it is difficult, if not impossible, to cleanly separate biological from environmental contributions to intelligence. Moreover, abilities may express themselves very differently in different contexts. For example, children given essentially the same task in the context of a video game versus a laboratory cognitive task performed much better when the task was presented in the video game context.

The bioecological model appears in many ways to be more a framework than a theory. At some level, the theory must be right. Certainly, both biological and ecological factors contribute to the development and manifestation of intelligence. Perhaps what the theory needs most at this time are specific and clearly falsifiable predictions that would set it apart from other theories.

IMPROVING INTELLIGENCE

Although designers of artificial intelligence have made great strides in creating programs that simulate knowledge and skill acquisition, no existing program even approaches the ability of the human brain to enhance its own intelligence. Human intelligence is highly malleable and can be shaped and even increased through various kinds of interventions (Detterman & Sternberg, 1982; Grotzer & Perkins, 2000; Perkins & Grotzer, 1997; Sternberg et al., 1996; Sternberg et al., 1997; see Ritchhart & Perkins, 2005, Chap. 32, for a review of work on teaching thinking skills). Moreover, the malleability of intelligence has nothing to do with the extent to which intelligence has a genetic basis (Sternberg, 1997a). An attribute (such as height) can be partly or even largely genetically based and yet be environmentally malleable.

The Head Start program was initiated in the 1960s to provide preschoolers with an edge on intellectual abilities and accomplishments when they started school. Long-term follow-ups have indicated that by mid-adolescence, children who participated in the program were more than a grade ahead of matched controls who did not experience the program (Lazar & Darlington, 1982; Zigler & Berman, 1983). The children in the program also scored higher on a variety of tests of scholastic achievement, were less likely to need remedial attention, and were less likely to show behavioral problems. Although such measures are not truly measures of intelligence, they show strong positive correlations with intelligence tests.

An alternative to intellectual enrichment outside the home may be to provide an enriched home environment. A particularly successful project has been the Abecedarian Project, which showed that the cognitive skills and achievements of lower socioeconomic status children could be increased through carefully planned and executed interventions (Ramey & Ramey, 2000). Bradley and Caldwell (1984) found support for the importance of home environment with regard to the development of intelligence in young children. These researchers found that several factors in the early (preschool) home environment were correlated with high IQ scores – emotional and verbal responsivity of the primary caregiver and the caregiver's involvement with the child, avoidance of restriction and punishment, organization of the physical environment and activity schedule, provision of appropriate play materials, and opportunities for variety in daily stimulation. Further, Bradley and Caldwell found that these factors more effectively predicted IQ scores than did socioeconomic status or family-structure variables. It should be noted, however, that the Bradley-Caldwell study is correlational and therefore cannot be interpreted as indicating causality. Furthermore, their study pertained to preschool children, and children's IQ scores do not begin to predict adult IQ scores well until age 4. Moreover, before age 7, the scores are not very stable (Bloom, 1964). More recent work (e.g., Pianta & Egeland, 1994) suggested that factors such as maternal social support and interactive behavior may play a key role in the instability of scores on tests of intellectual ability between ages of 2 and 8. The Bradley and Caldwell data should not be taken to indicate that demographic variables have little effect on IQ scores. To the contrary, throughout history and across cultures, many groups of people have been assigned pariah status as inferior members of the social order. Across cultures, these disadvantaged groups (e.g., native Maoris vs. European New Zealanders) have shown differences in tests of intelligence and aptitude (Steele, 1990; Zeidner, 1990). Another example is provided by Ogbu (1986), who showed that such was the case of the Burakumin tanners in Japan, who, in 1871, were granted emancipation but not full acceptance into Japanese society. Despite their poor performance and underprivileged status in Japan, those who immigrate to America and are treated like other Japanese immigrants perform on IQ tests and in school achievement at a level comparable to that of their fellow Japanese Americans. Similar positive effects of integration were shown on the other side of the world. In Israel, the children of European Jews score much higher on IQ tests than do children of Arabic Jews – except when the children are reared on kibbutzim in which the children of all national ancestries are raised by specially trained caregivers, in a dwelling separate from their parents. When these children shared the same child-rearing environments, there were no national-ancestry-related differences in IQ.

Altogether, there is now abundant evidence that people's environments (e.g., Ceci, Nightingale, & Baker, 1992; Reed, 1993; Sternberg & Wagner, 1994; Wagner, 2000), their motivation (e.g., Collier, 1994; Sternberg & Ruzgis, 1994), and their training (e.g., Feuerstein, 1980; Sternberg, 1987) can profoundly affect their intellectual skills. Thus, the controversial claims made by Herrnstein and Murray (1994) in their book, *The Bell Curve*, regarding the futility of intervention programs, are unfounded when one considers the evidence in favor of the possibility of improving cognitive skills. Likewise, Herrnstein and Murray's appeal to "a genetic factor in cognitive ethnic differences" (Herrnstein & Murray, 1994, p. 270) falls apart in light of the direct evidence against such genetic differences (Sternberg, 1996a), and results from a misunderstanding of the heritability of traits in general. Heredity certainly plays a role in individual differences in intelligence (Loehlin, 2000; Loehlin, Horn, & Willerman, 1997; Plomin, 1997), as does the environment (Grigorenko, 2000, 2002; Mandelman & Grigorenko, in press; Sternberg & Grigorenko, 1999a; Wahlsten & Gottlieb, 1997).

Genetic inheritance may set some kind of upper limit on how intelligent a person may become. However, we now know that for any attribute that is partly genetic, there is a reaction range – that is, the attribute can be expressed in various ways within broad limits of possibilities. Thus, each person's intelligence can be developed further within this broad range of potential intelligence (Grigorenko, 2000). We have no reason to believe that people now reach their upper limits in the development of their intellectual skills. To the contrary, the evidence suggests that we can do quite a bit to help people become more intelligent (for further discussion of these issues, see Mayer, 2000, and Neisser et al., 1996).

Environmental as well as hereditary factors may contribute to retardation in intelligence (Grigorenko, 2000; Sternberg & Grigorenko, 1997b). Environmental influences before birth may cause permanent retardation, which may result from a mother's inadequate nutrition or ingestion of toxins such as alcohol during the infant's prenatal development (Grantham-McGregor, Ani, & Fernald, 2002; Mayes & Fahy, 2001; Olson, 1994), for example. Among the other environmental factors that can negatively impact intelligence are low social and economic status (Ogbu & Stern, 2001; Seifer, 2001), high levels of pollutants (Bellinger & Adams, 2001), inadequate care in the family or divorce (Fiese, 2001; Guidubaldi & Duckworth, 2001), infectious diseases (Alcock & Bundy, 2001), high levels of radiation (Grigorenko, 2001), and inadequate schooling (Christian, Bachnan, & Morrison, 2001). Physical trauma can injure the brain, causing mental retardation.

A puzzling question is whether more people are now becoming intellectually gifted. Flynn (1987; in press) has pointed out that, during the 20th century, raw scores on IQ tests rose roughly 3 points per decade. IQs did not rise because publishers kept renorming the tests. The obvious question is whether, over time, one could make the case that the number of people who are intellectually gifted is therefore increasing. Based on raw scores, the answer would be yes, but based on standard scores (IQs), the answer is no. From the standpoint of WICS, IQ is not identical to intelligence, so one could not answer this question merely on the basis of IQ.

In conclusion, many approaches have been taken to improve understanding of the nature of intelligence. Great progress has been made in elaborating the construct, but much less progress in converging upon either a definition or a universally accepted theory. Much of current debate revolves around trying to figure out what the construct is and how it relates to other constructs, such as learning, memory, and reasoning. Intelligence can be measured, to some extent, and it can be improved. Improvements are not likely to eliminate individual differences, however, because attempts to improve intelligence can help people at all levels and with diverse kinds of intelligence. No matter how high one's intelligence, there is always room for improvement; and no matter how low, there are always measures that can be taken to help raise it.

5

Creativity and Giftedness

As mentioned in Chapter 3, creativity is the ability to produce work that is novel (i.e., original, unexpected), high in quality, and appropriate (i.e., useful, meets task constraints) (Cropley & Cropley, in press; Lubart, 1994; Ochse, 1990; Sternberg, 1988b, 1999b; Sternberg & Lubart, 1995, 1996). Creativity is a topic of wide scope that is important at both the individual and societal levels for a wide range of task domains. At an individual level, creativity is relevant – for example, when one is solving problems in school (Beghetto, in press; Smith & Smith, in press), on the job (Puccio & Cabra, in press), and in daily life (Richards, in press). At a societal level, creativity can lead to new scientific findings, new movements in art, new inventions, and new social programs. The economic importance of creativity is clear because new products or services create jobs. Furthermore, individuals, organizations, and societies must adapt existing resources to changing task demands to remain competitive. The most important contributions to a society are generally made by those who are most creative (Simonton, in press). This chapter attempts to provide readers with a basic understanding of the literature on creativity. It first reviews alternative approaches to understanding creativity. Then it reviews alternative approaches to understanding kinds of creative work. Finally, it draws some conclusions. For a more thorough review of theories and perspectives on creativity, see Kaufman and Sternberg (in press) and especially Kozbelt, Beghetto, and Runco (in press).

Creativity is not just something exhibited by the greats, like Picasso, Tolstoy, and Einstein. Creativity is engaged when one copes with novelty in the environment, such as new financial status, a new significant other, or the birth of children. People need creativity when they must figure out how to live in a way different from the way they have lived before (Moran, in press). Creatively gifted people see beyond others in how to adjust to new ideas or circumstances. They may do so individually or as part of a group (Sawyer, in press).

Creativity may be viewed as taking place in the interaction between a person and the person's environment (Amabile, 1996; Csikszentmihalyi, 1996, 1999; Feldman, Csikszentmihalyi, & Gardner, 1994; Sternberg, 1985a; Sternberg & Lubart, 1995). According to this view, the essence of creativity cannot be captured just as an intrapersonal variable. Thus, we can characterize a person's cognitive processes as more or less creative (Finke, Ward, & Smith, 1992; Rubenson & Runco, 1992; Ward & Kolomyts, in press; Weisberg, 1986), or the person as having a more or less creative personality (Barron, 1988; Feist, 1999, in press). We further can describe the person as having a motivational pattern that is more or less typical of creative individuals (Hennessey & Amabile, 1988), or even as having background variables that more or less dispose that person to think creatively (Simonton, 1984, 1994). However, we cannot fully judge that person's creativity independent of the field and the temporal context in which the person works. For example, a contemporary artist might have thought processes, personality, motivation, and even background variables similar to those of Monet, but that artist, painting today in the style of Monet or of Impressionism in general, probably would not be judged as creative in the way Monet was. When artists, including Monet, experimented with Impressionism, their work showed a sharp deviation from painting styles of the past, and unless the contemporary artist introduced some new twist, he or she might be viewed as imitative rather than creative.

The importance of context is illustrated by the difference, in general, between creative discovery and rediscovery. For example, BACON and related programs of Langley, Simon, Bradshaw, and Zytkow (1987, see a more detailed description later in this chapter under "Cognitive Approaches") rediscover important scientific theorems that were judged to be creative discoveries in their time. The processes by which these discoveries are made via computer simulation are presumably not identical to those by which the original discoverers made their breakthroughs. One difference is that contemporary programmers can provide, in their programming of information into computer simulations, representations and particular organizations of data that may not have been available to the original creators. However, putting aside the question of whether the processes are the same, a rediscovery might be judged to be creative with respect to the rediscoverer, but it would not be judged creative with respect to the field at the time the rediscovery is made. Ramanujan, the famous Indian mathematician, made many such rediscoveries. A brilliant thinker, he did not have access in his early life to much of the recent literature on mathematics, and so unwittingly regenerated many discoveries that others had made before him.

Consider some of the main approaches to the study of creativity (based on Sternberg & Lubart, 1996). A more detailed description of the approaches can be found in Kaufman and Sternberg (in press).

MYSTICAL APPROACHES TO THE STUDY OF CREATIVITY

The study of creativity has always been tinged – some might say tainted – with associations to mystical beliefs. Perhaps the earliest accounts of creativity were based on divine intervention. The creative person was seen as an empty vessel that a divine being would fill with inspiration. The individual would then pour out the inspired ideas, forming an otherworldly product. In this vein, Plato argued that a poet is able to create only that which the Muse dictates, and even today, people sometimes refer to their own Muse as a source of inspiration. In Plato's view, one person might be inspired to create choral songs, another, epic poems (Rothenberg & Hausman, 1976). Often, mystical sources have been suggested in creators' introspective reports (Ghiselin, 1985). For example, Rudyard Kipling referred to the "Daemon" that lives in the writer's pen: "My Daemon was with me in the Jungle Books, Kim, and both Puck books, and good care I took to walk delicately, lest he should withdraw. . . . When your Daemon is in charge, do not think consciously. Drift, wait, and obey" (Kipling, 1985, p. 162).

The mystical approaches to the study of creativity have probably made it harder for scientists to be heard. Many people seem to believe, as they believe for love (see Sternberg, 1988a, 1988d), that creativity is something that just does not lend itself to scientific study because it is a more spiritual process. We believe it has been hard for scientific work to shake the deep-seated view of some that, somehow, scientists are treading where they should not.

The mystical approach does not shed much light on the nature of creative giftedness. Giftedness has often been seen in a kind of mystical way – as something that is a gift from God or divine providence or whatever mystical source people might choose to believe in. The problem with such a view of giftedness is that this view sheds no light on its nature, on how to assess it, or on how to develop it.

PRAGMATIC APPROACHES

Equally damaging for the scientific study of creativity, in our view, has been the takeover of the field, in the popular mind, by those who follow what might be referred to as a pragmatic approach. Such proponents have been concerned primarily with developing creativity, secondarily with understanding it, but almost not at all with testing the validity of their ideas about it. Perhaps foremost in this approach is Edward De Bono, whose work on *lateral thinking* – seeing things broadly and from varied viewpoints – as well as other aspects of creativity has had what appears to be considerable commercial success (e.g., De Bono, 1971, 1985, 1992). De Bono's concern is not with theory but with practice. Thus, for example, he suggests using a tool such as "Positive-Minus-Interesting" (PMI) to focus on the aspects of an idea that are pluses, minuses, and interesting. Or he suggests using the word "po," derived from hy*po*thesis, sup*po*se, *po*ssible, and *po*etry, to provoke rather than judge ideas. Another tool, that of "thinking hats," has individuals metaphorically wear different hats, such as a white hat for data-based thinking, a red hat for intuitive thinking, a black hat for critical thinking, and a green hat for generative thinking, in order to stimulate seeing things from different points of view.

De Bono is not alone in this enterprise. Osborn (1953), based on his experiences in advertising agencies, developed the technique of brainstorming to encourage people to solve problems creatively by seeking many possible solutions in an atmosphere that is constructive rather than critical and inhibitory. Gordon (1961) developed a method called synectics, which involves primarily seeing analogies, also for stimulating creative thinking.

Authors such as Adams (1974, 1986) and von Oech (1983) suggested that people often construct a series of false beliefs that interfere with creative functioning. For example, some people believe that there is only one right answer and that ambiguity must be avoided whenever possible. People can become creative by identifying and removing these mental blocks. Von Oech (1986) also suggested that to be creative we need to adopt the roles of explorer, artist, judge, and warrior to foster our creative productivity.

These approaches have had considerable public visibility, and they may well be useful. From our point of view as psychologists, however, most of these approaches lack any basis in serious psychological theory as well as serious empirical attempts to validate them. Of course, techniques can work in the absence of psychological theory or validation. However, the effect of such approaches is often to leave people associating a phenomenon with commercialization and to see it as less than a serious endeavor for psychological study.

Many of the interventions for gifted children have been based on a pragmatic approach. They have lacked any theory but have been viewed as things that work, for whatever reason. Some of the sources cited above have served as ways either to develop the creativity of the gifted or to make people gifted who otherwise might not perform at gifted levels.

THE PSYCHODYNAMIC APPROACH

The psychodynamic approach can be considered the first of the major 20th-century theoretical approaches to the study of creativity. Based on the idea that creativity arises from the tension between conscious reality and unconscious drives, Freud (1908/1959) proposed that writers and artists produce creative work as a way to express their unconscious desires in a publicly acceptable fashion. These unconscious desires may concern power, riches, fame, honor, or love (Vernon, 1970). Case studies of eminent creators, such as Leonardo da Vinci (Freud, 1910/1964), were used to support these ideas.

Later, the psychoanalytic approach introduced the concepts of adaptive regression and elaboration for creativity (Kris, 1952). *Adaptive regression,* the primary process, refers to the intrusion of unmodulated thoughts in consciousness. Unmodulated thoughts can occur during active problem solving but often occur during sleep, intoxication from drugs, fantasies or daydreams, or psychoses. *Elaboration,* the secondary process, refers to the reworking and transformation of primary process material through reality-oriented, ego-controlled thinking. Other theorists (e.g., Kubie, 1958) emphasized that the preconscious, which falls between conscious reality and the encrypted unconscious, is the true source of creativity because here thoughts are loose and vague but interpretable. In contrast to Freud, Kubie claimed that unconscious conflicts actually have a negative effect on creativity because they lead to fixated, repetitive thoughts. More recent work has recognized the importance of both primary and secondary processes (Noy, 1969; Rothenberg, 1979; Suler, 1980; Werner & Kaplan, 1963).

Although the psychodynamic approach may have offered some insights into creativity, psychodynamic theory was not at the center of the emerging scientific psychology. The early 20th-century schools of psychology, such as structuralism, functionalism, and behaviorism, devoted practically no resources at all to the study of creativity. The Gestaltists studied a portion of creativity – insight – but their study never went much beyond labeling, as opposed to characterizing the nature of insight. Further isolating creativity research, the psychodynamic approach and other early work on creativity relied on case studies of eminent creators. This methodology has been criticized historically because of the difficulty of measuring proposed theoretical constructs (e.g., primary process thought), and the amount of selection and interpretation that can occur in a case study (Weisberg, 1993). Although there is nothing a priori wrong with case study methods, the emerging scientific psychology valued controlled, experimental methods. Thus, both theoretical and methodological issues served to isolate the study of creativity from mainstream psychology.

PSYCHOMETRIC APPROACHES

When we think of creativity, eminent artists or scientists such as Michelangelo or Einstein immediately come to mind. However, these highly creative people are quite rare and difficult to study in the psychological laboratory. In his address to the American Psychological Association (APA), Guilford (1950) noted that the rarity of highly creative individuals and the difficulty of studying them in the laboratory had limited research on creativity. He proposed that creativity could be studied in everyday subjects using paper-and-pencil tasks. One of these was the Unusual Uses Test, in which an examinee thinks of as many uses for a common object (e.g., a brick) as possible. Many researchers adopted Guilford's suggestion, and "divergent thinking" tasks quickly became the main instruments for measuring creative thinking. The tests were a convenient way of comparing people on a standard "creativity" scale. Divergent thinking is still considered an important aspect of creativity (Runco, in press).

Building on Guilford's work, Torrance (1974) developed the Torrance Tests of Creative Thinking. These tests consist of several relatively simple verbal and figural tasks that involve divergent thinking plus other problem-solving skills. The tests can be scored for fluency (total number of relevant responses), flexibility (number of different categories of relevant responses), originality (statistical rarity of the responses), and elaboration (amount of detail in the responses). Some subtests from the Torrance battery include: (a) Asking questions: The examinee writes out all the questions he or she can think of, based on a drawing of a scene. (b) Product improvement: The examinee lists ways to change a toy monkey so children will have more fun playing with it. (c) Unusual uses: The examinee lists interesting and unusual uses of a cardboard box. (d) Circles: The examinee expands empty circles into different drawings and titles them.

A number of investigators have studied the relationship between creativity and intelligence, at least as measured by IQ. Three basic findings concerning creativity and conventional conceptions of intelligence are generally agreed upon (see, e.g., Barron & Harrington, 1981; Kim, Cramond, & VanTassel-Baska, in press; Lubart, 1994). First, creative people tend to show above-average IQs, often above 120 (see Renzulli, 1986). This figure is not a cutoff but rather a recognition that people with low or even average IQs do not seem to be well represented among the ranks of highly creative individuals. Cox's (1926) geniuses had an estimated average IQ of 165. Barron estimated the mean IQ of his creative writers to be 140 or higher, based on their scores on the Terman Concept Mastery Test (Barron, 1963, p. 242). It should be noted that the Concept Mastery Test is exclusively verbal and thus provides a somewhat skewed estimate of IQ. The other groups in the Institute for Personality Assessment (IPAR) studies, that is, mathematicians and research scientists, were also above average in intelligence. Anne Roe (1953, 1972), who did similarly thorough assessments of eminent scientists before the IPAR group was set up, estimated that IQs for her participants ranged between 121 and 194, depending on whether the IQ test was verbal, spatial, or mathematical.

Second, above an IQ of 120, IQ does not seem to matter as much to creativity as it does below 120. In other words, creativity may be more highly correlated with IQ below an IQ of 120, but only weakly or not at all correlated with it above an IQ of 120. (This relationship is often called the threshold theory, meaning that high levels of creativity are possible beyond a certain level of IQ but not below it.) In the architects study, in which the average IQ was 130 (significantly above average), the correlation between intelligence and creativity was −.08, not significantly different from zero (Barron, 1969, p. 42). However, in the military officer study, in which participants were of average intelligence, the correlation was .33 (Barron, 1963, p. 219). These results suggest that extremely highly creative people often have high IQs, but not necessarily that people with high IQs tend to be extremely creative (see also Getzels & Jackson, 1962). Some investigators (e.g., Simonton, 1994; Sternberg, 1996b) have suggested that very high IQ may actually interfere with creativity. Those who have very high IQs may be so highly rewarded for their IQ-like (analytical) skills that they fail to develop the creative potential within them, which may then remain latent.

Third, the correlation between IQ and creativity is variable, usually ranging from weak to moderate (Flescher, 1963; Getzels & Jackson, 1962; Guilford, 1967; Herr, Moore, & Hasen, 1965; Plucker & Makel, in press; Torrance, 1962; Wallach & Kogan, 1965; Yamamoto, 1964). The correlation depends in part on what aspects of creativity and intelligence are being measured, how they are being measured, and in what field the creativity is manifested. The role of intelligence is different in art and music, for instance, than in mathematics and science (McNemar, 1964). An obvious drawback to the tests used and assessments done by some researchers, such as asking for unusual uses of a paperclip, is the time and expense involved in administering them, as well as the subjective scoring of them. In contrast, Mednick (1962) produced a 30-item, objectively scored, 40-minute test of creative ability called the Remote Associates Test (RAT). The test is based on his theory that the creative thinking process is the forming of associative elements into new combinations. More remote associations, on this view, are more creative (Mednick, 1962). Because the ability to make these combinations and arrive at a creative solution necessarily depends on the existence of the combinations (i.e., the associative elements) in a person's knowledge base, and because the probability and speed of attainment of a creative solution are influenced by the organization of the person's associations, Mednick's theory suggests that creativity and intelligence are very related; they are overlapping sets. Moderate correlations of .55, .43, and .41 have been shown between the RAT and the WISC (Wechsler Intelligence Scale for Children), the SAT verbal, and the Lorge-Thorndike Verbal intelligence measures, respectively (Mednick & Andrews, 1967). Correlations with quantitative intelligence measures were lower ($r = .20, .34$), and correlations with other measures of creative performance have been more variable (Andrews, 1975).

This psychometric approach for measuring creativity had both positive and negative effects on the field. On the positive side, the tests facilitated research by providing a brief, easy to administer, objectively scorable assessment device. Furthermore, research was now possible with "everyday" people (i.e., noneminent samples). However, there were also some negative effects.

First, some researchers criticized brief paper-and-pencil tests as trivial, inadequate measures of creativity saying that larger productions, such as actual drawings or writing samples, should be used instead. Second, other critics suggested that no fluency, flexibility, originality, and elaboration scores captured the concept of creativity. In fact, the definition and criteria for creativity are a matter of ongoing debate, and relying on the objectively defined statistical rarity of a response with regard to all the responses of a subject population is only one of many options. Other possibilities include using the social consensus of judges (see Amabile, 1983).

Third, some researchers were less enchanted by the assumption that noneminent samples could shed light on eminent levels of creativity, which was the ultimate goal for many studies of creativity (e.g., Simonton, 1984, in press). Thus, a certain malaise developed and continues to accompany the paper-and-pencil assessment of creativity. Some psychologists, at least, avoided this measurement quagmire in favor of less problematic research topics.

The cognitive approach to creativity seeks understanding of the mental representations and processes underlying creative thought (see Lubart, 2000–2001). By studying, say, perception or memory, one would already be studying the bases of creativity; thus, the study of creativity would merely represent an extension, and perhaps not a very large one, of work that is already being done under another guise. For example, in the cognitive area, creativity was often subsumed under the study of intelligence. We do not argue with the idea that creativity and intelligence are related to each other (Lubart, 2003; Sternberg & O'Hara, 1999). However, the subsumption has often been so powerful that researchers such as Wallach and Kogan (1965), among others, had to write at length on why creativity and intelligence should be viewed as distinct entities. In more recent cognitive work, Weisberg (1986, 1988, 1993, 1999) has proposed that creativity involves essentially ordinary cognitive processes yielding extraordinary products. A similar point has been made by Perkins (1981). Weisberg attempted to show that the insights depend on subjects using conventional cognitive processes (e.g., analogical transfer) applied to knowledge already stored in memory. He did so through the use of case studies of eminent creators and laboratory research, such as studies with Duncker's (1945) candle problem. This problem requires participants to attach a candle to a wall using only objects available in a picture (candle, box of tacks, and book of matches). (Hint: You need melted candle wax.) Langley et al. (1987) made a similar claim about the ordinary nature of creative thinking.

As a concrete example of this approach, Weisberg and Alba (1981) had people solve the notorious nine-dot problem. In this problem, people are asked to connect nine dots, which are arranged in the shape of a square with three rows of three dots each, using no more than four straight lines, never arriving at a given dot twice, and never lifting their pencil from the page. The problem can be solved only if people allow their line segments to go outside the periphery of the dots. Typically, solution of this task had been viewed as hinging upon the insight that one had to go "outside the box." Weisberg and Alba showed that even when people were given the insight, they still had difficulty in solving the problem. In other words, whatever is required to solve the nine-dot problem, it is not just some kind of extraordinary insight.

There have been studies with both human subjects and computer simulations of creative thought. Approaches based on the study of human subjects are perhaps prototypically exemplified by the work of Finke, Ward, and Smith (1992) (see also contributions to Smith, Ward, & Finke, 1995; Sternberg & Davidson, 1994; Ward & Kolomyts, in press; Ward, Smith, & Finke, 1999). Finke and his colleagues have proposed what they call the *Geneplore model,* according to which there are two main processing phases in creative thought – a generative phase and an exploratory phase.

In the generative phase, an individual constructs mental representations referred to as preinventive structures, which have properties promoting creative discoveries. In the exploratory phase, these properties are used to come up with creative ideas. A number of mental processes may enter into these phases of creative invention, such as retrieval, association, synthesis, transformation, analogical transfer, and categorical reduction (i.e., mentally reducing objects or elements to more primitive categorical descriptions).

In a typical experimental test based on the model (Finke & Slayton, 1988), participants will be shown parts of objects, such as a circle, a cube, a parallelogram, and a cylinder. On a given trial, three parts will be named, and participants will be asked to imagine combining the parts to produce a practical object or device. For example, participants might imagine a tool, a weapon, or a piece of furniture. The objects thus produced are then rated by judges for their practicality and originality. Morrison and Wallace (2002) found that judged creativity on such a task correlated strongly with the individuals' perceived imagery vividness.

The senior author of this book has also conducted research on convergent creative thinking that required participants to think in unusual ways. Eighty individuals were presented with novel kinds of reasoning problems that had a single best answer. For example, they might be told that some objects are green and others blue, whereas still other objects might be grue, meaning green until the year 2000 and blue thereafter, or bleen, meaning blue until the year 2000 and green thereafter. Or they might be told of four kinds of people on the planet Kyron: blens, who are born young and die young; kwefs, who are born old and die old; balts, who are born young and die old; and prosses, who are born old and die young (Sternberg, 1981, 1982; Tetewsky & Sternberg, 1986). Participants' task was to predict future states from past states, given incomplete information. For example, if you are shown a picture of a large individual in an earlier year and a picture of the same individual as smaller in a subsequent year, what must the individual be (a pross). In another set of studies, 60 people were given more conventional kinds of inductive reasoning problems, such as analogies, series completions, and classifications. However, the problems had premises preceding them that were either conventional (dancers wear shoes) or novel (dancers eat shoes). The participants had to solve the problems as though the counterfactuals were true (Sternberg & Gastel, 1989a, 1989b).

In these studies, the researchers found that correlations with conventional kinds of tests depended on how novel or nonentrenched the conventional tests were. The more novel the items were, the higher were the correlations of our tests with scores on successively more novel conventional tests. Thus, the components isolated for relatively novel items would tend to correlate more highly with more unusual tests of fluid abilities than with tests of crystallized abilities. The researchers also found that when response times on the relatively novel problems were componentially analyzed, some components better measured the creative aspect of intelligence than did others. For example, in the "grue-bleen" task mentioned previously, the information processing component requiring people to switch from conventional green-blue thinking to grue-bleen thinking, and then back to green-blue thinking again, was a particularly good measure of the ability to cope with novelty.

Computer simulation approaches, reviewed by Boden (1992, 1999), have as their goal the production of creative thought by a computer in a manner that simulates what people do. Langley et al. (1987), for example, as mentioned in the introduction to this chapter, developed a set of programs that rediscover basic scientific laws. These computational models rely on heuristics – problem-solving guidelines – for searching a data set or conceptual space and finding hidden relationships between input variables. The initial program, called BACON, uses heuristics such as "if the value of two numeric terms increase together, consider their ratio" to search data for patterns. One of BACON's accomplishments has been to examine observational data on the orbits of planets available to Kepler and to rediscover Kepler's third law of planetary motion. This program is unlike creative functioning, however, in that the problems are given in structured form, whereas creative functioning is largely about figuring out what the problems are (see Runco, 1994). Further programs have extended the search heuristics, the ability to transform data sets, and the ability to reason with qualitative data and scientific concepts. There are also models concerning an artistic domain (see Locher, in press). For example, Johnson-Laird (1988) developed a jazz improvisation program in which novel deviations from the basic jazz chord sequences are guided by harmonic constraints (or tacit principles of jazz) and random choice when several allowable directions for the improvisation exist.

SOCIAL-PERSONALITY AND SOCIAL-COGNITIVE APPROACHES

Developing in parallel with the cognitive approach, work in the social-personality approach has focused on personality variables, motivational variables, and the sociocultural environment as sources of creativity. Researchers such as Amabile (1983), Barron (1968, 1969), Eysenck (1993), Gough (1979), MacKinnon (1965), and others noted that certain personality traits often characterize creative people. Through correlational studies and research contrasting high and low creative samples (at both eminent and everyday levels), a large set of potentially relevant traits has been identified (Barron & Harrington, 1981; Feist, 1999, in press). These traits include independence of judgment, self-confidence, attraction to complexity, aesthetic orientation, openness to experience, and risk taking. Proposals regarding self-actualization and creativity can also be considered within the personality tradition. According to Maslow (1968), boldness, courage, freedom, spontaneity, self-acceptance, and other traits lead a person to realize his or her full potential.

Rogers (1954) described the tendency toward self-actualization as having motivational force and being promoted by a supportive, evaluation-free environment. These ideas, however, seem at odds with the many studies that have linked creativity and mental illness (e.g., Kaufman, 2001a, 2001b; Kaufman & Baer, 2002; Ludwig, 1995). If full creative potential is truly linked with self-acceptance and other positive traits, then one would not expect to find so many eminent creative individuals to have such maladjusted and poor coping strategies (Kaufman, 2002; Kaufman & Sternberg, 2000).

Focusing on motivation for creativity, a number of theorists have hypothesized the relevance of intrinsic motivation (Amabile, 1983, 1996; Crutchfield, 1962; Golann, 1962), need for order (Barron, 1963), need for achievement (McClelland, Atkinson, Clark, & Lowell, 1953), and other motives. Amabile (1983, 1996; Hennessey & Amabile, 1988) and her colleagues conducted seminal research on intrinsic and extrinsic motivation. Studies using motivational training and other techniques have manipulated these motivations and observed effects on creative performance tasks, such as writing poems and making collages. Finally, the relevance of the social environment to creativity has also been an active area of research. At the societal level, Simonton (1984, 1988a, 1994, 1999, in press) conducted numerous studies in which eminent levels of creativity over large spans of time in diverse cultures have been statistically linked to environmental variables. These variables include, among others, cultural diversity, war, availability of role models, availability of resources (e.g., financial support), and number of competitors in a domain. Cross-cultural comparisons (e.g., Lubart, 1990) and anthropological case studies (e.g., Maduro, 1976; Silver, 1981) have demonstrated cultural variability in the expression of creativity. Moreover, they have shown that cultures differ simply in the amount that they value the creative enterprise.

The social-cognitive and social-personality approaches have each provided valuable insights into creativity. However, if you look for research that investigates both social-cognitive and social-personality variables at the same time, you would find only a handful of studies. The cognitive work on creativity has tended to ignore the personality and social system, and the social-personality approaches tended to have little or nothing to say about the mental representations and processes underlying creativity.

Looking beyond the field of psychology, Wehner, Csikszentmihalyi, and Magyari-Beck (1991) examined 100 more recent doctoral dissertations on creativity. They found a "parochial isolation" of the various studies concerning creativity. There were relevant dissertations from psychology, education, business, history, history of science, and other fields, such as sociology and political science. However, the different fields tended to use different terms and focus on different aspects of what seemed to be the same basic phenomenon. For example, business dissertations used the term *innovation* and tended to look at the organizational level, whereas psychology dissertations used the term *creativity* and looked at the level of the individual. Wehner, Csikszentmihalyi, and Magyari-Beck (1991) described the situation with creativity research in terms of the fable of the blind men and the elephant. "We touch different parts of the same beast and derive distorted pictures of the whole from what we know: 'The elephant is like a snake,' says the one who only holds its tail; 'The elephant is like a wall,' says the one who touches its flanks" (p. 270).

EVOLUTIONARY APPROACHES TO CREATIVITY

The evolutionary approach to creativity was instigated by Donald Campbell (1960), who suggested that the same kinds of mechanisms that have been applied to the study of the evolution of organisms could be applied to the evolution of ideas. This idea has been enthusiastically picked up by a number of investigators (Gabora & Kaufman, in press; Simonton, 1995, 1998, 1999). The basic idea underlying Simonton's approach is that there are two basic steps in the generation and propagation of creative ideas. The first is *blind variation*, by which the creator generates an idea without any real idea of whether the idea will be successful (selected for) in the world of ideas. Indeed, Dean Simonton (1996) argued that creators do not have the slightest idea as to which of their ideas will succeed. As a result, their best bet for producing lasting ideas is to go for a large quantity of ideas. The reason is that their hit rate remains relatively constant through their professional life span. In other words, they have a fixed proportion of ideas that will succeed. The more ideas they have in all, the more ideas they have that will achieve success. The second step is *selective retention*. In this step, the field in which the creator works either retains the idea for the future or lets it die out. Those ideas that are selectively retained are the ones that are judged to be novel and of value, that is, creative. This process, as well as blind generation, is described further by Cziko (1998).

Does an evolutionary model really adequately describe creativity? Robert Sternberg (1997a, 2003d) argued that it does not, and David Perkins (1998) also had doubts. Sternberg argued that it seems utterly implausible that great creators such as Mozart, Einstein, or Picasso were using nothing more than blind variation to come up with their ideas. Good creators, like experts of any kind, may or may not have more ideas than other people have, but they have better ideas, ones that are more likely to be selectively retained. The reason they are more likely to be selectively retained is that they were not produced in a blind fashion. This debate is by no means resolved, however, and is likely to continue into the future for some time to come. Perkins (1995, 1998) argued that the analogy between biological evolution and creativity is oversimplified. In particular (Perkins, 1998), biological evolution relies on massive parallel search for mutations (millions of bacteria, for example, are mutating every second), whereas humans do not.

At the same time, humans can do fairly extensive searches, such as when they seek out new antibiotics. Were it the case that an understanding of creativity required a multidisciplinary approach, the result of a unidisciplinary approach might be that we would view a part of the whole as the whole. At the same time, though, we would have an incomplete explanation of the phenomenon we are seeking to explain, leaving dissatisfied those who do not subscribe to the particular discipline doing the explaining. We believe that traditionally this has been the case for creativity. More recently, theorists have begun to develop confluence approaches to creativity, which we now discuss.

CONFLUENCE APPROACHES TO THE STUDY OF CREATIVITY

Many more recent works on creativity hypothesize that multiple components must converge for creativity to occur (Amabile, 1983; Csikszentmihalyi, 1988; Gardner, 1993; Gruber, 1989; Gruber & Wallace, 1999; Lubart, 1994, 1999; Lubart, Mouchiroud, Tordjman, & Zenasni, 2003; Mumford &

Gustafson, 1988; Perkins, 1981; Simonton, 1988b; Sternberg, 1985b; Sternberg & Lubart, 1991, 1995, 1996; Weisberg, 1993; Woodman & Schoenfeldt, 1989). Sternberg (1985b), for example, examined laypersons' and experts' conceptions of the creative person. People's implicit theories contain a combination of cognitive and personality elements, such as "connects ideas," "sees similarities and differences," "has flexibility," "has aesthetic taste," "is unorthodox," "is motivated," "is inquisitive," and "questions societal norms." At the level of explicit theories, Amabile (1983, 1996; Collins & Amabile, 1999) described creativity as the confluence of intrinsic motivation, domain-relevant knowledge and abilities, and creativity-relevant skills. The creativity-relevant skills include (a) a cognitive style that involves coping with complexities and breaking one's mental set during problem solving; (b) knowledge of heuristics for generating novel ideas, such as trying a counterintuitive approach; and (c) a work style characterized by concentrated effort, an ability to set aside problems, and high energy.

Gruber (1981, 1989) and Gruber and Davis (1988) proposed a developmental *evolving-systems model* for understanding creativity. A person's knowledge, purpose, and affect grow over time, amplify deviations that an individual encounters, and lead to creative products. Developmental changes in the knowledge system have been documented in cases such as Charles Darwin's thoughts on evolution. Purpose refers to a set of interrelated goals, which also develop and guide an individual's behavior. Finally, the affect or mood system notes the influence of joy or frustration on the projects undertaken.

Csikszentmihalyi (1988, 1996; Feldman, Csikszentmihalyi, & Gardner, 1994) took a different "systems" approach and highlighted the interaction of the individual, domain, and field. An individual draws upon information in a domain and transforms or extends it via cognitive processes, personality traits, and motivation. The field, consisting of people who control or influence a domain (e.g., art critics and gallery owners), evaluates and selects new ideas. The domain, a culturally defined symbol system such as alphabetic writing, mathematical notation, or musical notation, preserves and transmits creative products to other individuals and future generations. Gardner (1993; see also Policastro & Gardner, 1999) conducted case studies that suggest that the development of creative projects may stem from an anomaly within a system (e.g., tension between competing critics in a field) or moderate asynchronies between the individual, domain, and field (e.g., unusual individual talent for a domain). In particular, Gardner (1993) analyzed the lives of seven individuals who made highly creative contributions in the 20th century, with each specializing in one of the multiple intelligences

(Gardner, 1983): Sigmund Freud (intrapersonal), Albert Einstein (logical-mathematical), Pablo Picasso (spatial), Igor Stravinsky (musical), T. S. Eliot (linguistic), Martha Graham (bodily-kinesthetic), and Mohandas Gandhi (interpersonal). Charles Darwin would be an example of someone with extremely high naturalist intelligence. Gardner pointed out, however, that most of these individuals actually had strengths in more than one intelligence, and that they also had notable weaknesses in others (e.g., Freud's weaknesses may have been in spatial and musical intelligences).

Although creativity can be understood in terms of uses of the multiple intelligences to generate new and even revolutionary ideas, Gardner's (1993) analysis goes well beyond the intellectual. For example, Gardner pointed out two major themes in the behavior of these creative giants. First, they tended to have a matrix of support at the time of their creative breakthroughs. Second, they tended to drive a "Faustian bargain," whereby they gave up many of the pleasures people typically enjoy in life to attain extraordinary success in their careers. However, it is not clear that these attributes are intrinsic to creativity, per se; rather, they seem to be associated with those who have been driven to exploit their creative gifts in a way that leads them to attain eminence. Gardner (1993) further followed Csikszentmihalyi (1988, 1996) in distinguishing between the importance of the domain (the body of knowledge about a particular subject area) and the field (the context in which this body of knowledge is studied and elaborated, including the persons working with the domain [Baer, in press], such as critics, publishers, and other "gatekeepers"). Both are important to the development and, ultimately, the recognition of creativity.

A final confluence theory considered here is Sternberg and Lubart's (1991, 1995) *investment theory of creativity.* According to this theory, creative people are ones who are willing and able to "buy low and sell high" in the realm of ideas (see also Lubart & Runco, 1999; Rubenson & Runco, 1992, for use of concepts from economic theory). Buying low means pursuing ideas that are unknown or out of favor but that have growth potential. Often, when these ideas are first presented, they encounter resistance. The creative individual persists in the face of this resistance, and eventually sells high, moving on to the next new or unpopular idea.

Preliminary research within the investment framework has yielded support for this model (Lubart & Sternberg, 1995). This research has used tasks such as (a) writing short stories using unusual titles (e.g., "the octopus' sneakers"), (b) drawing pictures with unusual themes (e.g., "the earth from an insect's point of view"), (c) devising creative advertisements for boring products (e.g., cufflinks), and (d) solving unusual scientific problems (e.g., how could we tell if someone had been on the moon within the past month?). This research showed creative performance to be moderately domain specific and to be predicted by a combination of six distinct but interrelated resources: intellectual abilities, knowledge, styles of thinking, personality, motivation, and environment. Concerning the confluence of components, creativity is hypothesized to involve more than a simple sum of a person's level on each component. First, there may be thresholds for some components (e.g., knowledge), below which creativity is not possible regardless of the levels on other components. Second, partial compensation may occur in which a strength on one component (e.g., motivation) counteracts a weakness on another component (e.g., environment).

Third, interactions may also occur between components, such as intelligence and motivation, in which high levels on both components could multiplicatively enhance creativity. In general, confluence theories of creativity offer the possibility of accounting for diverse aspects of creativity (Lubart, 1994). For example, analyses of scientific and artistic achievements suggest that the median rated creativity of work in a domain tends to fall toward the lower end of the distribution and the upper – high creativity – tail extends quite far. This pattern can be explained through the need for multiple components of creativity to co-occur in order for the highest levels of creativity to be achieved. As another example, the partial domain specificity of creativity that is often observed can be explained through the mixture of some relatively domain-specific components for creativity, such as knowledge, and other more domain-general components, such as, perhaps, the personality trait of perseverance. Creativity, then, is largely something that people show in a particular domain.

ALTERNATE APPROACHES TO UNDERSTANDING KINDS OF CREATIVE CONTRIBUTIONS

Generally, we think of creative contributions as being of a single kind. However, a number of researchers on creativity have questioned this assumption. There are a number of ways of distinguishing among types of creative contributions. It is important to remember, though, that creative contributions can be viewed in different ways at different times. At a given time, the field can never be sure of whose work will withstand the judgments of the field over time (e.g., that of Mozart) and whose work will not (e.g., that of Salieri) (Therivel, 1999).

Theorists of creativity and related topics have recognized that there are different types of creative contributions (see reviews in Ochse, 1990;

Sternberg, 1988b; Weisberg, 1993). For example, Kuhn (1970) distinguished between normal and revolutionary science. Normal science expands upon or otherwise elaborates upon an already existing paradigm of scientific research, whereas revolutionary science proposes a new paradigm (see Dunbar & Fugelsang, 2005, Chap. 29). The same kind of distinction can be applied to the arts and letters.

Gardner (1993, 1994) also described different types of creative contributions individuals can make. They include (a) the solution of a well-defined problem, (b) the devising of an encompassing theory, (c) the creation of a "frozen work," (d) the performance of a ritualized work, and (e) a "high-stakes" performance. Each type of creativity has as its result a different kind of creative product.

Other bases for distinguishing among types of creative contributions also exist. For example, psychoeconomic models such as those of Rubenson and Runco (1992) and Sternberg and Lubart (1991, 1995, 1996) can distinguish different types of contributions in terms of the parameters of the models. In the Sternberg-Lubart model, contributions might differ in the extent to which they "defy the crowd" or in the extent to which they redefine how a field perceives a set of problems.

Simonton's (1997) model of creativity also proposes parameters of creativity, and various kinds of creative contributions might be seen as differing in terms of the extent to which they vary from other contributions and the extent to which they are selected for recognition by a field of endeavor (see also Campbell, 1960; Perkins, 1995; Simonton, 1997). However, in no case were these models intended explicitly to distinguish among types of creative contributions.

Maslow (1967) distinguished more generally between two types of creativity, which he referred to as primary and secondary. Primary creativity is the kind of creativity a person uses to become self-actualized – to find fulfillment in himself or herself and his or her life. Secondary creativity is the kind of creativity with which scholars in the field are more familiar – the kind that leads to creative achievements recognized by a field.

Ward, Smith, and Finke (1999) noted that there is evidence to favor the roles of both focusing (Bowers, Regehr, Balthazard, & Parker, 1990; Kaplan & Simon, 1990) and exploratory thinking (Bransford & Stein, 1984; Getzels & Csikszentmihalyi, 1976) on creative thinking. In focusing, one concentrates on pursuing a single problem-solving approach, whereas in exploratory thinking one considers many such approaches. A second distinction made by Ward and his colleagues is between domain specific (Clement, 1989; Langley et al., 1987; Perkins, 1981; Weisberg, 1986) and universal (Finke, 1990, 1995; Guilford, 1968; Koestler, 1964) creativity skills. Finally, Ward and his colleagues distinguish between unstructured (Bateson, 1979; Findlay & Lumsden, 1988; Johnson-Laird, 1988) and structured or systematic (Perkins, 1981; Ward, 1994; Weisberg, 1986) creativity, where the former is displayed in systems with relatively few rules, and the latter, in systems with many rules. There are tens of thousands of artists, musicians, writers, scientists, and inventors today. What makes some of them stand out from the rest? Why will some of them become distinguished contributors in the annals of their field and others be forgotten?

Although many variables may contribute to who stands out from the crowd, certainly creativity is one of them. The standouts are often those who are doing particularly creative work in their line of professional pursuit. Are these highly creative individuals simply doing more highly creative work than their less visible counterparts, or does the creativity of their work also differ in quality? One possibility is that creative contributors make different *decisions* regarding *how* to express their creativity.

Sternberg and colleagues developed a propulsion theory of creative contributions (Sternberg, 1999b; Sternberg, Kaufman, & Pretz, 2002) that addresses this issue of how people decide to invest their creative resources. The basic idea is that creativity can be of different kinds, depending on how it propels existing ideas forward. When developing creativity in children, we can foster different kinds of creativity, ranging from minor replications to major redirections in their thinking.

Creative contributions differ not only in their amounts but also in the types of creativity they represent. For example, both Sigmund Freud and Anna Freud were highly creative psychologists, but the nature of their contributions seems in some way or ways to have been different. Sigmund Freud proposed a radically new theory of human thought and motivation, and Anna Freud largely elaborated on and modified Sigmund Freud's theory. How do creative contributions differ in quality and not just in quantity of creativity?

The type of creativity exhibited in a creator's works can have at least as much of an effect on judgments about that person and his or her work as does the amount of creativity exhibited. In many instances, it may have more of an effect on these judgments. Given the importance of purpose, creative contributions must always be defined in some context. If the creativity of an individual is always judged in a context, then it will help to understand how the context interacts with how people are judged. In particular, what are the types of creative contributions a person can make within a given context? Most theories of creativity concentrate on attributes of the individual (see Sternberg, 1999b). However, to the extent that creativity is in the inter-action of person with context, we would also need to concentrate on the attributes of the individual and the individual's work relative to the environmental context.

This is what we attempted to do in a study of classical musicians and the skills and practical variables that come into play to gain visibility in the context of the U.S. classical music scene today (Subotnik & Jarvin, 2005; Subotnik, Jarvin, Moga, & Sternberg, 2003). We interviewed students at three top U.S. conservatories, their faculty, and gatekeepers (e.g., artistic directors at major classical music venues, critics in major newspapers, agents) about the various psychosocial variables that they believe contribute to success at different stages in an artist's career. Based on the data, we developed a model highlighting which variables matter most as a young musician progresses from abilities to competency, to expertise, and finally to scholarly productivity/artistry. While some variables, such as musicality, are consistently important, others are mediating variables, such as teachability, which matters much in the beginning of a career but is seen as less important with time as students are expected to differentiate themselves. An example of a mediating variable that increases in importance over time is the increasing ability to know one's strengths and weaknesses, and ultimately to capitalize on strengths.

In sum, creativity, which has often been viewed as beyond study, is any-thing but. Creativity can be understood about as well as any psychological construct if appropriate methods are brought to bear upon its investigations. The history of creativity theory and research is long and interesting. It represents a diversity of attempts to understand the phenomenon. More recently, scholars have recognized that creativity can be of multiple kinds and have tried to understand these different kinds. A full account of creativity would need to take into account not just differing amounts of creativity but also differing kinds. These kinds would include creativity that accepts current paradigms, creativity that rejects them, and creativity that synthesizes them into a new whole.

6

Wisdom and Giftedness

Wisdom is usually left out of accounts of giftedness, or at least, of childhood giftedness. But in an age where lack of wisdom seems to be responsible for wars, economic hardship, and societal stagnation, can a society really afford to leave wisdom out of the equation? And is wisdom only associated with older people?

By one account, aging is the key to wisdom – at some age, one somewhat mysteriously becomes wise. By a second account, one is becoming wiser with age, but slowly and incrementally; one is, on this account, building upon the life experiences one has had earlier that have bestowed upon one a steadily increasing supply of wisdom, one that is likely to increase until one's last days. By a third account, one is increasingly rapidly losing whatever wisdom one may have gained in one's life. And by a fourth account, one has lost whatever wisdom one may have had long ago.

We all have a considerable stake in which of these accounts is correct. The accounts range from suggesting that junior people should now come running to an older person for advice, to suggesting that they should now start running away from the older person just as fast as they can. Would that we had the wisdom to know for sure which account was correct. As it is, we only can present the evidence, offer our appraisal, and then let the reader, and the young people who depend on us, decide.

There almost certainly is no one trajectory of wisdom with age. In other words, age is not, in and of itself, a variable that is valid for indexing the development of wisdom. Age in itself always has been an "empty" independent variable. Rather, age is a proxy for other things, such as personal growth (Ryff, 1989; Staudinger, Dörner, & Mickler, 2003; Staudinger, Dörner, & Mickler, 2005), openness to experience (Kramer, 2000), or ability to learn from experience (Sternberg et al., 2000). In the case of wisdom, it has been, in large part, a proxy for experience. But experience does not create wisdom.

Rather, one's ability to profit from and utilize one's experience in a reflective and directed way is what determines how wisdom develops. Thus, using age as an independent variable can distract us from understanding the cognitive and other mechanisms involved in the development and decline of wisdom.

WHAT IS WISDOM?

Different approaches have been taken to figuring out what wisdom is (Staudinger & Glueck, in press; Sternberg & Jordan, 2005). Consider, in turn, philosophical, implicit-theoretical, and explicit-theoretical approaches to the nature of wisdom.

Philosophical Approaches

Philosophical approaches have been reviewed by Robinson (1990; see also Robinson, 1989, with regard to the Aristotelian approach in particular; Kupperman, 2005; Labouvie-Vief, 1990; Osbeck & Robinson, 2005, for further reviews). Robinson (1989; Osbeck & Robinson, 2005) notes that the study of wisdom has a history that long antedates psychological study, with the Platonic dialogues offering the first intensive Western analysis of the concept of wisdom. Robinson points out that, in these dialogues, there are three different senses of wisdom: wisdom as (a) *sophia*, which is found in those who seek a contemplative life in search of truth; (b) *phronesis*, which is the kind of practical wisdom shown by statesmen and legislators; and (c) *episteme*, which is found in those who understand things from a scientific point of view.

Aristotle distinguished between *phronesis*, the kind of practical wisdom mentioned above, and *theoretikes*, or theoretical knowledge devoted to truth. Robinson notes that according to Aristotle, a wise individual knows more than the material, efficient, or formal causes behind events. This individual also knows the final cause, or that for the sake of which the other kinds of causes apply.

Other philosophical conceptions of wisdom have followed up on the early Greek ones. Of course, it is not possible to review all of these conceptions here. But as an example, an early Christian view emphasized the importance of a life lived in pursuit of divine and absolute truth. To this day, most religions aim for wisdom through an understanding not just of the material world but also of the spiritual world and its relationship to the material world. Not all religions search for absolute truth, however. In some matters, it is not clear any such truth exists.

Implicit-Theoretical Approaches

Implicit-theoretical approaches to wisdom have in common the search for an understanding of people's folk conceptions of what wisdom is. Thus, the goal is not to provide a "psychologically true" account of wisdom but rather an account that is true with respect to people's beliefs, whether these beliefs are right or wrong.

Holliday and Chandler (1986) used an implicit-theories approach to understanding wisdom. Approximately 500 participants were studied across a series of experiments. The investigators were interested in determining whether the concept of wisdom could be understood as a prototype (Rosch, 1975) or central concept. Principal-components analysis of one of their studies revealed five underlying factors: exceptional understanding, judgment and communication skills, general competence, interpersonal skills, and social unobtrusiveness.

Sternberg (1985b, 1990b) has reported a series of studies investigating implicit theories of wisdom. In one study, 200 professors each of art, business, philosophy, and physics were asked to rate the characteristicness of each of the behaviors obtained in a prestudy from the corresponding population with respect to the professors' ideal conception of each of an ideally wise, intelligent, or creative individual in their occupation. Laypersons were also asked to provide these ratings but for a hypothetical ideal individual without regard to occupation. Correlations were computed across the three ratings. In each group except philosophy, the highest correlation was between wisdom and intelligence; in philosophy, the highest correlation was between intelligence and creativity. The correlations between wisdom and intelligence ratings ranged from .42 to .78 with a median of .68. For all groups, the lowest correlation was between wisdom and creativity. Correlations between wisdom and creativity ratings ranged from −.24 to .48 with a median of .27. The only negative correlation (−.24) was for ratings of professors of business.

In a second study, 40 college students were asked to sort three sets of 40 behaviors each into as many or as few piles as they wished. The 40 behaviors in each set were the top-rated wisdom, intelligence, and creativity behaviors from the previous study. The sortings then were each subjected to nonmetric multidimensional scaling. For wisdom, six components emerged: *reasoning ability, sagacity, learning from ideas and environment, judgment, expeditious use of information,* and *perspicacity.*

Examples of behaviors showing high loadings under each of these six components were "has the unique ability to look at a problem or situation and solve it," "has good problem-solving ability," and "has a logical mind" for *reasoning ability*; "displays concern for others," "considers advice," and "understands people through dealing with a variety of people" for *sagacity*; "attaches importance to ideas," "is perceptive," and "learns from other people's mistakes" for *learning from ideas and environment*; "acts within own physical and intellectual limitations," "is sensible," and "has good judgment at all times" for *judgment*; "is experienced," "seeks out information, especially details," "has age, maturity, or long experience" for *expeditious use of information*; and "has intuition," "can offer solutions that are on the side of right and truth," "is able to see through things – read between the lines" for *perspicacity*.

In this same study, components for intelligence were *practical problem-solving ability, verbal ability, intellectual balance and integration, goal orientation and attainment, contextual intelligence*, and *fluid thought*. Components for creativity were *nonentrenchment, integration and intellectuality, aesthetic taste and imagination, decisional skill and flexibility, perspicacity, drive for accomplishment and recognition, inquisitiveness*, and *intuition*.

In a third study, 50 adults were asked to rate descriptions of hypothetical individuals for intelligence, creativity, and wisdom. Correlations were computed between pairs of ratings of the hypothetical individuals' levels of the three traits. Correlations between the ratings were .94 for wisdom and intelligence, .62 for wisdom and creativity, and .69 for intelligence and creativity, again suggesting that wisdom and intelligence are highly correlated in people's implicit theories.

Yang (2001) studied wisdom among 616 Taiwanese Chinese people. She found four factors of wisdom: competencies and knowledge, benevolence and compassion, openness and profundity, and modesty and unobtrusiveness. Similar factors were obtained by Takayama (2002) in a study of implicit theories of wisdom among Japanese men and women of widely varying ages. The four factors that emerged were knowledge and education, understanding and judgment, sociability and interpersonal relationships, and an introspective attitude.

Takahashi and Bordia (2000) compared implicit theories of wisdom in American, Australian, Indian, and Japanese participants. They found identical factors for American and Australian groups. For them, the adjective *wise* was semantically most similar to *experienced* and *knowledgeable*. It was least similar to *discreet*. The ideal self, among this group, was characterized as knowledgeable and wise. In contrast, being aged and discreet were seen as quite undesirable. The Indian and Japanese adults, in contrast, viewed *wise* as semantically closest to *discreet*, followed by *aged* and *experienced*.

The Japanese saw being wise and discreet as most desirable, and being knowledgeable was seen as much less desirable. In all four cultural groups, being wise was seen as extremely desirable, but being aged was seen as being extremely undesirable. So none of the groups of young people wanted to be old!

Montgomery, Barber, and McKee (2002) asked older people to characterize wisdom in their lives. Six attributes emerged from their study. These attributes were giving guidance, having knowledge, having experience, having moral principles, and engaging in compassionate relationships. In a related study, Sowarka (1989) found that narratives of wise people emphasized their ability to solve problems through the use of novel and efficacious strategies.

Explicit-Theoretical Approaches

Explicit theories are constructions of (supposedly) expert theorists and researchers rather than of laypeople. In the study of wisdom, most explicit-theoretical approaches are based on constructs from the psychology of human development.

Some scholars define wisdom in ways that suggest it is a property of increasing maturity. Birren and Fisher (1990), for example, defined it as "the integration of the affective, conative, and cognitive aspects of human abilities in response to life's tasks and problems. Wisdom is a balance between the opposing valences of intense emotion and detachment, action and inaction, and knowledge and doubts. *It tends to increase with experience and therefore age but is not exclusively found in old age*" (Birren & Fisher, 1990, p. 326; italics added). In many views, some degree of age is, at best, a necessary but not sufficient condition for the development of wisdom.

Taranto (1989) offered another view of wisdom, based on a thorough review of the literature. She defined wisdom as the recognition and response of the individual to human limitation. A related view is that of McKee and Barber (1999), who defined wisdom as seeing through illusion. Brugman (2000) defined it as expertise in uncertainty. On this view, wisdom involves cognitive, affective, and behavioral components. Brugman believes that wisdom goes hand in hand with increasing doubt and uncertainty regarding the comprehensibility of reality.

Ardelt (2000a, 2000b) has proposed a somewhat more complex view. She has defined wisdom as involving three components: (a) the cognitive ability to see truth or reality as it actually is; (b) reflectivity, in becoming aware of and transcending one's subjectivity and projections; and (c) empathy and compassion for others. Kant, in the *Critique of Pure Reason*, took a different view, stating that people could not see truth or reality as it actually is but only as it is filtered by their senses.

The most extensive program of research has been that conducted by Baltes and his colleagues. For example, Baltes and Smith (1987, 1990) gave adult participants life-management problems, such as "A fourteen-year-old girl is pregnant. What should she (what should one) consider and do?" and "A fifteen-year-old girl wants to marry soon. What should she (what should one) consider and do?" Baltes and Smith tested a five-component model on participants' protocols in answering these and other questions, based on a notion of wisdom as expert knowledge about fundamental life matters (Smith & Baltes, 1990) or of wisdom as good judgment and advice in important but uncertain matters of life (Baltes & Staudinger, 1993). Wisdom is reflected in these five components: (a) rich factual knowledge (general and specific knowledge about the conditions of life and its variations), (b) rich procedural knowledge (general and specific knowledge about strategies of judgment and advice concerning matters of life), (c) life span contextualism (knowledge about the contexts of life and their temporal [developmental] relationships), (d) relativism (knowledge about differences in values, goals, and priorities), and (e) uncertainty (knowledge about the relative indeterminacy and unpredictability of life and ways to manage).

Three kinds of factors – general person factors, expertise-specific factors, and facilitative experiential contexts – are proposed to facilitate wise judgments. These factors are used in life planning, life management, and life review. An expert answer should reflect more of these components, whereas a novice answer should reflect fewer of them. The data collected to date generally have been supportive of the model.

Over time, Baltes and his colleagues (e.g., Baltes, Smith, & Staudinger, 1992; Baltes & Staudinger, 1993) collected a wide range of data showing the empirical utility of the proposed theoretical and measurement approaches to wisdom. For example, Staudinger, Lopez, and Baltes (1997) found that measures of intelligence and personality as well as their interface overlap with but are nonidentical to measures of wisdom in terms of constructs measured. Staudinger, Smith, and Baltes (1992) showed that human-services professionals outperformed a control group on wisdom-related tasks. In a further set of studies, Staudinger and Baltes (1996) found that performance settings that were ecologically relevant to the lives of their participants and that provided for actual or "virtual" interaction of minds increased wisdom-related performance substantially.

Sternberg (1990a, 1990b) also proposed an explicit theory, suggesting that the development of wisdom can be traced to six antecedent components: (a) knowledge, including an understanding of its presuppositions and meaning as well as its limitations; (b) processes, including an understanding of what problems should be solved automatically and what problems should not be so solved; (c) a judicial thinking style, characterized by the desire to judge and evaluate things in an in-depth way; (d) personality, including tolerance of ambiguity and of the role of obstacles in life; (e) motivation, especially the motivation to understand what is known and what it means; and (f) environmental context, involving an appreciation of the contextual factors in the environment that lead to various kinds of thoughts and actions.

Whereas that theory (Sternberg, 1990b) specified a set of *antecedents* of wisdom, the subsequent balance theory (Sternberg, 1998b) specifies the *processes* (balancing of interests and of responses to environmental contexts) in relation to the *goal* of wisdom (achievement of a common good). The first theory is incorporated into the balance theory as specifying antecedent sources of developmental and individual differences, as discussed later.

According to the balance theory, wisdom is the application of intelligence, creativity, and knowledge as mediated by positive ethical values toward the achievement of a common good through a balance among (a) intrapersonal, (b) interpersonal, and (c) extrapersonal interests, over the (a) short and (b) long terms, in order to achieve a balance among (a) adaptation to existing environments, (b) shaping of existing environments, and (c) selection of new environments (Sternberg, 1998b, 2000c, 2001b, 2003a; Sternberg & Lubart, 2001).

What kinds of considerations might be included under each of the three kinds of interests? Intrapersonal interests might include the desire to enhance one's popularity or prestige, to make more money, to learn more, to increase one's spiritual well-being, to increase one's power, and so forth. Interpersonal interests might be quite similar, except as they apply to other people rather than oneself. Extrapersonal interests might include contributing to the welfare of one's school, helping one's community, contributing to the well-being of one's country, or serving God, and so forth. Different people balance these interests in different ways. At one extreme, a malevolent dictator might emphasize his or her own personal power and wealth; at the other extreme, a saint might emphasize only serving others and God.

What constitutes appropriate balancing of interests, an appropriate response to the environment, and even the common good all hinge on values. Ethical values, therefore, are an integral part of wise thinking. The question arises as to "whose values"? Although different major religions and other widely accepted systems of values may differ in details, they seem to have in common certain universal values, such as respect for human life, honesty, sincerity, fairness, and enabling people to fulfill their potential. Of course, not every government or society has subscribed to such values. Hitler's Germany and Stalin's Russia blatantly did not, and most societies today only subscribe to them in some degree, but not fully.

On this view, people may be smart but not wise. People who are smart but not wise exhibit one or more of the following fallacies in thinking: (a) egocentrism – thinking that the whole world revolves around them; (b) omniscience – thinking they know everything; (c) omnipotence – thinking they can do whatever they want; (d) invulnerability – thinking they can get away with anything; (e) unrealistic optimism; and (f) ethical disengagement – believing ethics apply to others but not to themselves (Sternberg, 2002a, 2005b).

Some theorists have viewed wisdom in terms of postformal-operational thinking, thereby viewing wisdom as extending beyond the Piagetian stages of intelligence (Piaget, 1972). Wisdom thus might be a stage of thought beyond Piagetian formal operations. For example, some authors have argued that wise individuals are those who can think reflectively or dialectically, in the latter case with the individuals' realizing that truth is not always absolute but rather evolves in a historical context of theses, antitheses, and syntheses (e.g., Basseches, 1984a, 1984b; Kitchener, 1983, 1986; Kitchener & Brenner, 1990; Kitchener & Kitchener, 1981; Labouvie-Vief, 1980, 1982, 1990; Pascual-Leone, 1990; Riegel, 1973). Consider a very brief review of some specific dialectical approaches.

Kitchener and Brenner (1990) suggested that wisdom requires a synthesis of knowledge from opposing points of view. Similarly, Labouvie-Vief (1990) has emphasized the importance of a smooth and balanced dialogue between logical forms of processing and more subjective forms of processing. Pascual-Leone (1990) has argued for the importance of the dialectical integration of all aspects of a person's affect, cognition, conation (motivation), and life experience. Similarly, Orwoll and Perlmutter (1990) have emphasized the importance to wisdom of an integration of cognition with affect. Kramer (1990) has suggested the importance of the integration of relativistic and dialectical modes of thinking, affect, and reflection. And Birren and Fisher (1990), putting together a number of views of wisdom, have suggested as well the importance of the integration of cognitive, conative, and affective aspects of human abilities.

Other theorists have suggested the importance of knowing the limits of one's own extant knowledge and of then trying to go beyond it. For example,

Meacham (1990) has suggested that an important aspect of wisdom is an awareness of one's own fallibility and the knowledge of what one does and does not know. Kitchener and Brenner (1990) have also emphasized the importance of knowing the limitations of one's own knowledge. Arlin (1990) has linked wisdom to problem finding, the first step of which is the recognition that how one currently defines a problem may be inadequate. Arlin views problem finding as a possible stage of postformal operational thinking. Such a view is not necessarily inconsistent with the view of dialectical thinking as such a postformal-operational stage. Dialectical thinking and problem finding could represent distinct postformal-operational stages, or two manifestations of the same postformal-operational stage.

Although most developmental approaches to wisdom are ontogenetic, Csikszentmihalyi and Rathunde (1990) have taken a philogenetic or evolutionary approach, arguing that constructs such as wisdom must have been selected for over time, at least in a cultural sense. In other words, wise ideas should survive better over time than unwise ideas in a culture. The theorists define wisdom as having three basic dimensions of meaning: (a) that of a cognitive process, or a particular way of obtaining and processing information; (b) that of a virtue, or socially valued pattern of behavior; and (c) that of a good, or a personally desirable state or condition.

GENERALIZED VIEWS OF THE RELATIONSHIP
BETWEEN WISDOM AND AGE

Do people become more gifted in terms of their wisdom as they age? Although giftedness is often studied in children, wisdom may be something best studied in adults, and particularly, mature adults. There are five generalized views of the relationship of wisdom to age.

The first is what might be called the "received" view. It is the view with which many of us grow up. According to this view, wisdom develops in old age. Although old age may bring with it physical decline, it also brings with it a sort of spiritual awakening or reawakening that enables one to become wise.

A second view is what might be called the "fluid intelligence" view. This view has been advocated by Paul Baltes and his colleagues, among others (e.g., Baltes & Staudinger, 2000). This view tracks wisdom with fluid intelligence, so that wisdom is believed to show roughly the same pattern of incline and decline as fluid intelligence, or the ability to think flexibly in novel ways (Horn & Cattell, 1966). According to this theory, wisdom increases until early adulthood, and then levels off for a period of time. It then starts to decline in middle age or late middle age. At best, one may hold on to it in substantial measure until early old age (see Jordan, 2005; McAdams & de St. Aubin, 1992).

A third view is what might be called the "crystallized intelligence" view. This view holds that wisdom tracks like crystallized intelligence (Horn & Cattell, 1966; Schaie, 1996). According to this view, wisdom begins to increase relatively early in life and then continues to increase until old age, perhaps until 10 or so years before one's death, when disease processes might impair its continued growth (see Jordan, 2005; Sternberg, 1998b). According to this view, then, the development of wisdom increases well into the later years. There is some empirical evidence from longitudinal work to support this point of view (Hartman, 2000; Wink & Helson, 1997).

A fourth view is that wisdom tracks *both* fluid and crystallized intelligence (Birren & Svensson, 2005). This makes its pattern of development more complex than that of either kind of intelligence individually. According to this view, intelligence will increase until somewhere in the middle or later part of the adult life span, but then, as fluid abilities start to decline, the increase in crystallized abilities will not be enough to offset the decline in wisdom. So there will be decline somewhat earlier than the crystallized view alone would predict.

A fifth view is that wisdom actually declines monotonically with age (Meacham, 1990), starting early in life. There appears to be relatively little empirical evidence for this view, intriguing though it may be. However, there is empirical evidence that wisdom declines in very old age, say, for people, on average, over 75 (Baltes & Staudinger, 2000). Such decline appears to be related to declines in physical health.

The last point of view, that taken here, is that individual differences in the development of wisdom are so large that averages probably tell us little about how wisdom develops. It is not any kind of experience (i.e., crystallized intelligence) in itself that leads to wisdom, but rather the decision to use that experience in a reflective, action-oriented way that leads to a common good.

IMPLICIT THEORIES

Implicit Theories of Wisdom and Age?

Implicit theories of wisdom are people's conceptions of what wisdom is and how it develops. An excellent recent review of implicit theories of wisdom can be found in Bluck and Glück (2005). Most research on wisdom, unlike that on intelligence and creativity, has been in terms of implicit theories. Thus to understand the relationship between wisdom and giftedness, it helps to understand what people mean when they refer to a person as wise.

Carl Jung (1964) suggested that people have an archetype for wisdom that expresses itself in dreams. Regardless of the people's age, the archetype associates wisdom with age. He believed that women dream of a superior female figure, such as a priestess, sorceress, Earth mother, or goddess or nature of love. Men dream of a masculine initiator, a wise old man, a spirit of nature, or something similar (Jung, 1964; see also Birren & Svensson, 2005). So, for Jung, wisdom was clearly associated with maturity, if not old age.

Heckhausen, Dixon, and Baltes (1989) studied beliefs about the development of wisdom in adulthood. Participants were asked to rate characteristics, including "wise," in terms of the extent to which they believed each characteristic increased during adulthood. In a second study, participants were asked to rate the desirability of changes over life. In general, participants associated increasing age with undesirable changes. There were two exceptions to this trend, however: "dignified" and "wise." Both were viewed as increasing with age and as being desirable. Wisdom was believed to begin to increase around age 55, and to continue to increase except, perhaps, toward the very end of life.

Another way to study wisdom is to ask participants to nominate wise people. Paulhus, Wehr, Harms, and Strasser (2002) asked undergraduates to list the wisest people they could think of. The 15 top nominees were, in descending order, Gandhi, Confucius, Jesus Christ, Martin Luther King, Jr., Socrates, Mother Teresa, Solomon, Buddha, the Pope, Oprah Winfrey, Winston Churchill, the Dalai Lama, Ann Landers, Nelson Mandela, and Queen Elizabeth. One might expect that part of being listed would be a matter of one's fame. The authors also asked participants to list the most famous people they could think of. The only overlaps with regard to the top 15 were for Jesus Christ and Nelson Mandela. Most of the people listed are spiritual leaders in some sense, and most, but certainly not all, became famous for their wisdom in their later years.

In a related study, Perlmutter, Adams, Nyquist, and Kaplan (1988) examined people's conceptions of the relationship of wisdom to age. They found that 78% of the participants related wisdom to age. People nominated as wise in this study were, for the most part, over 50 years of age. Interestingly, perhaps, ages of nominees increased with ages of participants, suggesting that people of different ages drew on different cohorts. In another study,

Jason et al. (2001) reported that people nominated as wise had an average age of 60, a result similar to that found by Baltes, Staudinger, Maercker, and Smith (1995).

In a study by Knight and Parr (1999), participants were asked to judge the wisdom of people who were young, middle-aged, or old. Older individuals were generally rated as wiser than those of middle age or of younger age. Stange, Kunzmann, and Baltes (2003) also found that older participants were rated as wiser. But age was not the only factor related to wisdom. Listening behavior and good advice were also related to levels of wisdom. However, Hira and Faulkender (1997) found that gender also matters. Curiously, older men and younger women were judged to be significantly wiser than younger men and older women.

Clayton (1975), who was one of the first investigators to study wisdom empirically, examined conceptions of wisdom in people of different ages. She found that the concept of wisdom becomes more differentiated with age. There was no relationship between a participant's own age and his or her perception of his or her own level of wisdom.

In her work, Clayton (1975, 1976, 1982; Clayton & Birren, 1980) multi-dimensionally scaled ratings of pairs of words potentially related to wisdom for three samples of adults differing in age (younger, middle-aged, older). In her earliest study (Clayton, 1975), the terms that were scaled were ones such as *experienced, pragmatic, understanding,* and *knowledgeable.* In each study, participants were asked to rate similarities between all possible pairs of words. The main similarity in the results for the age cohorts for which the scalings were done was the elicitation of two consistent dimensions of wisdom, which Clayton referred to as an affective dimension and a reflec-tive dimension. There was also a suggestion of a dimension relating to age. The greatest difference among the age cohorts was that mental representa-tions of wisdom seemed to become more differentiated (i.e., to increase in dimensionality) with increases in the ages of the participants.

Clayton and Birren also found that the stimuli "aged" and "experienced" were located at a greater distance in the multidimensional space from "wise" in the older participants than in the younger participants. In other words, older participants were less likely to accept the idea that wisdom necessarily comes with old age than were younger participants. Moreover, Perlmutter et al. (1988) did not find that, with age, people's self-ratings of wisdom increased. In the Clayton and Birren study, for the older group, "under-standing" and "empathetic" were located closer to "wise" than they were for younger groups, suggesting somewhat different conceptions of wisdom with age.

Glück and her colleagues (2005) found age differences in implicit theories of wisdom. Describing life situations in which they had shown wisdom, adolescents most often spoke of situations in which they had provided empathy and support. Young adults most often spoke of situations in which they demonstrated self-determination and assertion. Older adults most often spoke of situations in which they demonstrated knowledge and flexibility.

EXPLICIT THEORIES

When Does Wisdom First Develop?

According to some accounts, Prince Siddhartha Gautama was born in India in 563 B.C. After living a privileged life, he left his home at age 29 to seek spiritual enlightenment (Birren & Svensson, 2005; Dyer, 1998). After becoming enlightened, he became known as the "Buddha." For the Buddha, the marked beginning on his journey toward wisdom thus began just short of the fourth decade of his life.

Not everyone becomes as revered as Prince Siddhartha did. But the story has a familiar ring. The tale, oft-repeated since early times, is of someone growing up and leading an unenlightened life, and then realizing it is time to change. The person studies or does whatever it takes to change, and then discovers spiritual or some other form of wisdom.

In psychology, Henry Murray, who was to become famous as the Harvard psychology professor who formulated the Thematic Apperception Test (TAT) as well as a theory of personality based upon motivational needs, grew up in a very highly privileged family in New York City (Robinson, 1992). According to Robinson (1992), in his early life, he distinguished himself mostly for his amiability and his skill in fitting into the upper-class milieu of Groton and then Harvard. He made captain of the crew team but was less than successful at it. A rather mediocre academic record as an undergraduate was no impediment during those times to admission to the best medical programs, and he was accepted both at Harvard and Columbia. Wanting to be near his family and the privilege associated with them, he chose Columbia. And there, in medical school, he underwent a transformation that was to change his life. He became seriously interested in medical and later psychological research and became a leading contributor to the burgeoning field of psychology. At just a tad earlier than the age at which Siddhartha underwent his transformation, Henry Murray underwent his own.

Erik Erikson (1950), a premier psychological theorist, believed that wisdom is associated with age, but he marked the development of wisdom as the result of success in dealing with his eighth and last stage of psychosocial development, "ego integrity versus despair." He was not stating that wisdom could not begin to develop earlier but rather that it was in the final stage of life development that one through the natural course of things either successfully met a life challenge and became wise, or one failed to meet the challenge and did not. In effect, dealing with the certain and imminent prospect of one's own death leads either to integrity or despair.

Following up on the Eriksonian tradition, Takahashi and Overton (2005) have argued that wisdom is a relatively late-emerging form of understanding that integrates cognitive and affective elements. They believe it emerges dialectically from earlier analytic and synthetic skills, but that it integrates these skills into a broader framework.

Earlier, several dialectical theories of wisdom were discussed under the umbrella of neo-Piagetianism. These theories view wisdom as first developing in the postformal-operational years – that is, after the age of 11 or 12 (e.g., Labouvie-Vief, 1990; Riegel, 1973). These theories usually have traced the development of wisdom most distinctly to the college years, or early adulthood – roughly 18 to 24 years of age. Thus, they view wisdom as starting quite a bit earlier than the "received" view of wisdom commencing in old age.

A similar view is taken by Richardson and Pasupathi (2005; see also Pasupathi, Staudinger, & Baltes, 2001), who argue that critical building blocks of wisdom are gained during adolescence and early adulthood. Indeed, the building blocks of wisdom may be laid down even earlier than adolescence (Csikszentmihalyi & Nakamura, 2005). First, the cognitive abilities needed for wisdom initially develop around adolescence, such as self-reflective thinking and breadth of knowledge. Second, adolescents form an imaginary audience that allows them to step outside themselves and to see others as the others see them (Lapsley & Murphy, 1985), although perhaps with more self-preoccupation than would be experienced by those others. Third, adolescents become more cognizant of the meanings of their own autobiographical experiences. When adults are asked to remember events from earlier in their lives, there is a *reminiscence bump* with respect to events of adolescence and very early adulthood (Rubin & Schulkind, 1997). The events of these periods are formative and provide a basis for the development of wisdom.

Another model, the Berlin model developed by Baltes and colleagues discussed earlier (see also Kunzmann & Baltes, 2005), views wisdom as requiring a great deal of knowledge, contextualism, and value relativism and tolerance. This view, too, suggests the development of wisdom starting earlier than late adulthood.

What Is the Trajectory of Wisdom Throughout the Adult Life Span?

Brugman (2000) reviewed six empirical studies that addressed the question of what trajectory wisdom takes with age. He concluded that wisdom does not, on average, increase in later life. Indeed, he concluded that "one needs to be old and wise to see that wisdom does not come with age" (p. 115). Staudinger (1999) has made a similar claim, namely, that wisdom shows no growth between 20 and 75 years of age. Similarly, others have claimed that whereas adolescents show increases in wisdom development (see also Anderson, 1998; Paspupathi et al., 2001), adults after the age of 24 rarely do.

In the Berlin model, the development of wisdom plateaus, for most people, toward the end of the college years – in the early 20s. Age is not seen as key in this model (Staudinger, Maciel, Smith, & Baltes, 1998). Rather, other factors, such as social intelligence, openness to experience, and exposure to positive role models are the important variables, and age is, at best, a proxy variable for other things.

Labouvie-Vief and her colleagues (1989) have suggested that emotional control and emotional understanding – what Mayer, Salovey, and Caruso (2000) refer to as emotional intelligence – increase with age. Middle-aged and older adults express their emotional states in more sophisticated language than do younger people and are less likely to have difficulty in regulating their emotions (see also Blanchard-Fields, 1986; Carstensen, 1995; Takahashi & Overton, 2005).

Kramer et al. (1992) have argued that older adults outperform younger ones in wisdom-related tasks. Hui and Yee (1994) studied middle-aged (mean 45 years) and older adults (mean 70 years) in both American and Japanese communities. They found that older adults generally performed better on wisdom measures, regardless of gender or cultural background. These findings thus suggest that wisdom increases in the later years.

Birren and Svensson (2005) consider the possibility that the lessening respect for the elderly and lessening ascription of wisdom to the elderly in Western society may have a basis in reality. The world is changing very rapidly, both in terms of technology and social/cultural customs. The rate of change perhaps was slower in other times and may still be slower in other places. In times in which the world in which one grows old is pretty much the same as the world in which one first became old, the wisdom one accumulated throughout one's life span might put one at a considerable advantage over others. But in a time of rapid change, one's wisdom may become out of date, applying to a world that no longer exists. So it may be that in rapidly changing societies, the experience of the elderly actually is worth less, and hence they are valued less (Csikszentmihalyi & Nakamura, 2005).

Work in the Berlin paradigm suggests that the development of wisdom levels off around the age of 24 or even as early as 20 (Smith & Baltes, 1990; Smith, Staudinger, & Baltes, 1994; Staudinger, Smith, & Baltes, 1992). But older adults are as likely as younger ones to reach the highest scores in the groups that have been tested with regard to wise thinking (Smith & Baltes, 1990). So although the mean may not increase over the adult life span, the maxima may (Baltes et al., 1995; Baltes & Staudinger, 2000). Older clinical psychologists score higher than younger people in fields other than clinical psychology on wisdom-related measures, but no higher than younger clinical psychologists on such measures (Smith & Baltes, 1990; Smith et al., 1994).

Staudinger, Smith, and Baltes (1992) showed that older adults performed as well on such tasks as did younger adults, and that older adults did better on such tasks if there was a match between their age and the age of the fictitious characters about whom they made judgments. Baltes, Staudinger, Maercker, and Smith (1995) found that older individuals nominated for their wisdom performed as well as did clinical psychologists on wisdom-related tasks. They also showed that up to the age of 80, older adults performed as well on such tasks as did younger adults.

The type of task may also affect wisdom-related performance. In life-planning tasks, but not life-review tasks, dealing with a problem relevant to one's own age provides no advantage in dealing with problems in a wise way (Baltes et al., 1995; Smith & Baltes, 1990; Smith et al., 1994). Life review may improve simply because one has had, in one's later years, more years to review and gain perspective. Individual differences also play a role. Pasupathi and Staudinger (2001) found that for adults who performed at above-median levels on a task of moral reasoning, age was positively associated with wisdom. But there was no relation for individuals at below-median levels of moral reasoning.

As mentioned earlier, work in the Berlin paradigm has found that interaction with other people – what the investigators refer to as *interactive minds* – improves wisdom-related thinking (Staudinger & Baltes, 1996). Because older people often become increasingly isolated as a function of the design of our society, their ability to think wisely may decrease not just as a function of decreases in skills but also of decreases in ability to interact with others (Jordan, 2005).

Is Wisdom Beneficial?

There is evidence that wisdom does lead to higher degrees of subjective well-being (SWB) in older adults, holding constant other variables (Ardelt, 1997). Similarly, Takahashi and Overton (2005) have suggested that wisdom brings an internal sense of reward by helping people better to appreciate the subjective meaning in their lives. Hui and Yee (1994) found that wisdom and life satisfaction are positively correlated in older adults. Although older adults experienced losses, these losses helped them better appreciate what they had and gave them new insights into their lives and what they meant. This in turn increased their satisfaction with their lives.

A different view is that of Baltes (1997). Baltes has proposed that wise people may experience what he refers to as *constructive melancholy*. People who are wise, in this view, see the sadness as well as the joy in the complex events of life.

The view of Baltes and his colleagues is also different from that of traditional thinkers, such as Erikson (1959), who believe that wisdom involves some degree of emotional distance and detachment. The traditional psychoanalytical view of the therapist, for example, emphasizes the importance of keeping one's emotional distance from the patients one advises lest one get caught up in their problems and thereby become unable to help the patients overcome these problems. In the Berlin view, wisdom inheres not in detachment but in sympathizing and empathizing with fellow human beings in the crises that beset them (Kunzmann & Baltes, 2005). Hence, wisdom may bring with it at least as much sadness as joy. People who do good work and apply their wisdom to it may see that others, in contrast, use their intelligence for less positive ends, which may lead to sadness (Solomon, Marshall, & Gardner, 2005).

Another factor that may work against wisdom leading to happiness is the presence of negative stereotypes about aging (e.g., Levy, Slade, Kunkel, & Kasl, 2002). To the extent that people have negative stereotypes, they may find sadness in thinking about their own age-related status and hence feel the sadness invoked by these stereotypes joining whatever sadness the wisdom of aging may bring. Actual decreases in physical health may also lead to such sadness (Jordan, 2005).

What Can Be Concluded from This Review?

First, there is far from any universally accepted view of the relationship of wisdom to age. Views on this relationship are all over the place, ranging from wisdom decreasing with age, to increasing with age, to remaining largely stable with age, at least after a certain threshold (such as the early 20s or so).

Second, empirical data also reveal contradictory results. There seems to be a consensus that wisdom drops off in later old age at the point that mental health declines. Beyond that, results have been varied. So the data do not conclusively support any single position.

Third, there are almost certainly widespread individual differences in the trajectory of wisdom. These individual differences may account for at least part of the differences in results that have been obtained. These differences mirror differences that have been shown in the development of fluid and crystallized abilities. Moreover, people differ in personality attributes that are relevant for the development of wisdom, such as openness to experience and reflectivity. So there probably is no one trajectory that applies to everyone.

Fourth, much seems to depend on the circumstances in which people live. People who are isolated, deprived of meaningful interactions with others, or isolated from developing their knowledge-based skills may be at risk for failing to develop wisdom. Probably, at least some of the control of the development of wisdom lies in situational rather than personal variables.

Fifth, differences in results may depend in part upon the ways in which wisdom is operationalized. The ways in which wisdom has been measured differ widely, including both typical-performance and maximal-performance measures. To understand how wisdom develops, one must understand how measurement operations affect the data.

In the end, the data seem consistent with a picture of the ability of the individual to continue to develop wisdom until the latter days in which health problems impair thinking. But whether wisdom actually will develop depends not so much on age as upon cognitive variables, personality variables, and life experiences. Most important, the person has to utilize life experience in a way that is consistent with the development of wisdom. There is a joke about how many psychologists it takes to change a lightbulb. The answer is it doesn't matter, so long as the lightbulb wants to change. Similarly, people must want to develop their wisdom-related skills in order for them actually to develop, and then must adopt the attitudes toward life – openness to experience, reflectivity upon experience, and willingness to profit from experience – that will enable this development to occur.

An important part of wisdom is positive ethical values. In this section, we discuss this particular aspect of giftedness, and in particular, whether there is a form of ethical giftedness.

"I am very proud of myself," the senior author of this book told the 17 students in his seminar, Psychology 60, the Nature of Leadership. He had just returned from a trip, he told them, and felt that the honorarium he was paid for his consulting on ethical leadership was less than he deserved. He felt bad that he had decided to accept such a consulting engagement for so little compensation. He then told the class that he was about to fill out the reimbursement forms when he discovered that he could actually get reimbursed twice. The first reimbursement would come from the organization that had invited him, which required him merely to fill out a form listing his expenses. The second reimbursement would come from his university, which required him to submit the receipts from the trip. He explained to the class that he had worked really hard on the trip consulting about ethical leadership, and so he was pleased that by getting reimbursed twice, he could justify to himself the amount of work he had put into the trip.

He waited for the firestorm. Would the class – which had already studied leadership for several months – rise up in a mass protest against what he had done? Or would only a half-dozen brave souls raise their hands and roundly criticize him for what was obviously patently unethical behavior? He waited, and waited, and waited. Nothing happened. He then decided to move on to the main topic of the day, which was ethical leadership! All the time he was speaking about that main topic, he expected some of the students to raise their hands and demand to return to the topic of his double reimbursement. It didn't happen.

Finally, he stopped talking about whatever the topic was, and flat-out asked the class whether any of them thought there was something off-the-mark with his desiring to obtain double reimbursement. If so, he told them, why had no one challenged him? He figured that, to a person, they would be embarrassed for not having challenged him. Quite a few of them were embarrassed. Others thought he must have been kidding. Others thought that as he was the professor and a dean to boot, whatever he did he must have had a good reason for. What he did not expect, though – especially after having taught them for several months about ethical leadership – was that some of the students would commend him on his clever idea and argue that, if he could get away with it, he was entitled to receive the money – more power to him!

This experience reminded him of how hard it is to translate theories of ethics, and even case studies, into one's own practice. The students had read about ethics in leadership, heard about ethics in leadership from a variety of real-world leaders, discussed ethics in leadership, and then apparently totally failed to recognize unethical behavior when it stared them in the face. Moreover, these were students who by conventional definitions would be classified as gifted. (Full disclosure: He did *not* really seek double reimbursement!) Why is it so hard to translate theory into practice, even after one has studied ethical leadership for several months?

Latané and Darley (1970) opened up a new field of research on bystander intervention. They showed that, contrary to expectations, bystanders intervene when someone is in trouble only in very limited circumstances. For example, if they think that someone else might intervene, the bystanders tend to stay out of the situation. Latané and Darley even showed that divinity students who were about to lecture on the parable of *The Good Samaritan* were no more likely than other bystanders to help a person in distress who was in need of – a good Samaritan! Drawing upon their model of bystander intervention, we propose here a model of ethical behavior that would seem to apply to a variety of ethical problems (see Sternberg, 2009).

The basic premise of the model is that ethical behavior is far harder to emit than one would expect simply on the basis of what we learn from our parents, from school, and from our religious training. To intervene, individuals must go through a series of steps, and unless all of the steps are completed, they are not likely to behave in an ethical way, regardless of the amount of training they have received in ethics, and regardless of their levels of gifts in other types of skills.

A MULTIPHASE MODEL FOR ETHICAL BEHAVIOR

According to the proposed model, enacting ethical behavior is much harder than it would appear to be because it involves multiple, largely sequential, steps. To behave ethically, the individual has to

1. recognize that there is an event to which to react;

2. define the event as having an ethical dimension;
3. decide that the ethical dimension is of sufficient significance to merit an ethics-guided response;
4. take personal responsibility for generating an ethical solution to the problem;
5. figure out what abstract ethical rule(s) might apply to the problem;
6. decide how these abstract ethical rules actually apply to the problem so as to suggest a concrete solution;
7. enact the ethical solution, meanwhile possibly counteracting contextual forces that might lead one not to act in an ethical manner;
8. deal with possible repercussions of having acted in what one considers an ethical manner.

Seen from this standpoint, it is rather challenging to respond to problems in an ethical manner. Consider the example of the supposed double reimbursement.

1. Recognize that there is an event to which to react.

The students were sitting in a class on leadership, expecting to be educated by an expert on leadership about leadership. In this case, he did not present the problem as one to which he expected them to react. He was simply telling them about something he had done. They had no a priori reason to expect that something an authority figure did would require any particular kind of reaction, perhaps, except for taking notes. So for some students, the whole narrative may have been a nonevent.

This, of course, is a problem that extends beyond this mere classroom situation. When people hear their political, educational, or religious leaders talk, they may not believe there is any reason to question what they hear. After all, they are listening to authority figures. In this way, leaders, including cynical and corrupt leaders, may lead their flocks to accept and even commit unethical acts.

2. Define the event as having an ethical dimension.

Not all students in the class defined the problem as an ethical one. It became clear in the discussion that some students saw the problem as utilitarian: He had worked hard, had been underpaid, and was trying to figure out a way to attain adequate compensation for his hard work. In this definition of the problem, he had come up with a clever way to make the compensation better fit the work he had done.

Cynical leaders may flaunt their unethical behavior – one is reminded today of Robert Mugabe of Zimbabwe, but there are other world leaders who might equally be relevant here. When Mugabe and his henchmen seized the farms of white farmers, the seizure was presented as one of compensating alleged war heroes for their accomplishments. Why should it be unethical to compensate war heroes?

The Chinese government attempted to manipulate media to downplay the dimensions of an event with a huge ethical component (Atlas, 2008). On May 12, 2008, an earthquake in Sichuan province killed an estimated 10,000 school children. Earthquakes are natural disasters but there was an irregularity in the buildings that imploded during the earthquake. Schools for children of well-connected party leaders as well as government buildings withstood the earthquake with no problem. In contrast, schools housing poor children crumbled to dust. It turned out that the schools had been built in ways that could only poorly withstand an earthquake. Presumably, the money that was supposed to have supported better construction went to line the pockets of Party functionaries (Atlas, 2008). The government is doing what it can to suppress these basic facts.

3. Decide that the ethical dimension is significant.

In the case of the professor having sought double reimbursement, some of the students may have felt that his behavior was suspect or questionable, but not sufficiently so to make an issue of it. Perhaps they had themselves asked for money twice for the same cause. Or perhaps they had sometimes taken what was not theirs – say, something small like a newspaper or even money they found on the ground – and saw what he was doing as no more serious than what they had done. So they may recognize an ethical dimension but not see it as sufficiently significant to create a fuss.

Politicians seem to specialize in trying to downplay the ethical dimension of their behavior. The shenanigans and subsequent lies of Bill Clinton regarding his behavior are well known. A few years ago, a state senator in Massachusetts was arrested for attempting to grope a woman on the street ("Senator faces list of assault allegations," http://www.boston.com/news/local/massachusetts/articles/2008/06/05/senator_faces_list_of_assault_allegations/, 2008, retrieved June 5, 2008). He apparently had a record of harassing other women over a period of years. What is more amazing than his pleading innocent after being caught red-handed is that, when asked his name, he gave the name of a colleague in the state senate as his own! He thereby sought to duck responsibility for his own unethical behavior.

4. Take personal responsibility for generating an ethical solution to the problem.

The students may have felt that they are, after all, merely students. Is it their responsibility, or even their right, to tell a professor in a course on leadership how to act, especially if the professor is a dean? From their point of view, it was perhaps his responsibility to determine the ethical dimensions of the situation, if any.

Similarly, people may allow leaders to commit wretched acts because they figure it is the leaders' responsibility to determine the ethical dimensions of their actions. Isn't that why they are leaders in the first place? Or people may assume that the leaders, especially if they are religious leaders, are in a uniquely good position to determine what is ethical. If a religious leader encourages someone to become a suicide bomber, that "someone" may feel that being such a bomber must be ethical. Why else would a religious leader suggest it?

5. Figure out what abstract ethical rule(s) might apply to the problem.

Perhaps some of the students recognized the problem the professor created for them as an ethical one. But what rule applies? Have they ever had to figure out reimbursements? Perhaps not. So it may not be obvious what rule would apply. Or even if they have, might there be some circumstances in which it is ethical to be dually reimbursed? Maybe the university supplements outside reimbursements, as they sometimes do fellowships. Or maybe the university does not care who else pays, so long as they get original receipts. Or maybe what he meant to say was that he had some expenses paid by the university and others by the sponsoring organization, and he had actually misspoken. Especially in new kinds of situations with which one has little familiarity, it may not be clear what constitutes ethical behavior.

Most of us have learned, in one way or another, ethical rules that we are supposed to apply to our lives. For example, we are supposed to be honest. But who among us can say he or she has not lied at some time, perhaps with the excuse that we were protecting someone else's feelings? By doing so, we insulate ourselves from the effects of our behavior. Perhaps, we can argue, that the principle that we should not hurt someone else's feelings takes precedence over not lying. Of course, as the lies grow larger, we can continue to use the same excuse. Or politicians may argue that they should provide generous tax cuts to the ultra-wealthy, on the theory that the benefits will "trickle down" to the rest of the population. So perhaps one is treating all people well, as we learn to do – just some people are treated better than others with the rationalization that eventually the effects will reach all the others.

6. Decide how these abstract ethical rules actually apply to the problem so as to suggest a concrete solution.

Perhaps the students had ethical rules available and even accessible to them but did not see how to apply them. Suppose they have the rule that one should only expect from others what one deserves. Well, what did he deserve? Maybe, in application, they saw him as deserving more because he said he did. Or suppose they had the rule that one should not expect something for nothing. Well, he did something, so he was only trying to get something back that adequately reflected his work. In the end, they may have had trouble translating abstract principles into concrete behavior.

This kind of translation is, we believe, nontrivial. In our work on practical intelligence, some of which was summarized in Sternberg et al. (2000), we found that there is, at best, a modest correlation between the more academic and abstract aspects of intelligence and its more practical and concrete aspects. Both aspects, though, predicted behavior in everyday life. People may have skills that shine brightly in a classroom but that they are unable to translate into real-world consequential behavior. For example, someone may be able to pass a written driver's test with flying colors but not be able to drive. Or someone may be able to get an A in a French class, but not speak French to passersby in Paris. Or a teacher may get an A in a classroom management course but be unable to manage a classroom. Translation of abstracted skills into concrete ones is difficult and may leave people knowing a lot of ethical rules that they are nevertheless unable to translate into their everyday lives.

If one follows reports in the media, there are any number of instances in which pastors who are highly trained in religion and ethics act in unethical and unscrupulous ways. They may be able to teach lessons on ethics, but they fail to translate what they teach into their own behavior. One may tend to be quick to blame them, but as psychologists, we know that there are many competent psychologists who are unable to apply what they do in therapy to their own lives. Being a psychologist is no protection against personal strife, any more than being an ethicist is protection against unethical behavior.

7. Enact the ethical solution, meanwhile possibly counteracting contextual forces that might lead one not to act in an ethical manner.

You sit in a classroom and hear your teacher brag about what you perhaps consider to be unethical behavior. You look around you. No one else is saying anything. As far as you can tell, no one else has even been fazed. Perhaps you are simply out of line. In the Latané and Darley (1970) work, the more bystanders there were, the less likely one was to take action to intervene. Why? Because one figured that if something is really wrong, then someone among all the others witnessing the event will take responsibility. You are better off having a breakdown on a somewhat lonely country road than on a busy highway, because a driver passing by on the country road may feel that he or she is your only hope.

Sometimes, the problem is not that other people seem oblivious to the ethical implications of the situation but that they actively encourage you to behave in ways you define as unethical. In the Rwandan genocides, Hutus were encouraged to hate Tutsis and to kill them, even if they were within their own family (see discussion in Sternberg & Sternberg, 2008). Those who were not willing to participate in the massacres risked becoming victims themselves (Gourevitch, 1998). The same applied in Hitler's Germany. Those who tried to save Jews from concentration camps themselves risked going to such camps (Totten, Parsons, & Charny, 2004).

8. Deal with possible repercussions of having acted in what one considers an ethical manner.

One may hesitate to act because of possible repercussions. Perhaps students in his class saw the professor as grossly unethical but did not want to risk challenging him openly and thereby potentially lowering their grade. In genocides, opposing the perpetrators may make one a victim. Or one may look foolish acting in an ethical way when others are taking advantage of a situation in a way to foster their personal good. Even before one acts, one may be hesitant because of the aftermath one anticipates, whether real or merely imagined.

We would like to think that the pressure to behave ethically will lead people to resist internal temptations to act less than admirably. But often, exactly the opposite is the case. In the Enron case, when Sherron Watkins blew the whistle on unethical behavior, she was punished and made to feel like an "outcast" ("Person of the Week: Enron Whistleblower Sherron Watkins," 2002, http://www.time.com/time/pow/

article/0,8599,194927,00.html, retrieved June 5, 2008). In general, whistle-blowers are treated poorly, despite the protections they are supposed to receive.

IS THERE AN ETHICAL GIFTEDNESS?

Gardner (1999b) has wrestled with the question of whether there is some kind of existential or even spiritual intelligence that guides people through challenging life dilemmas. Coles (1998) is one of many who have argued for a moral intelligence in children as well as adults. Is there some kind of moral or spiritual intelligence in which some children are inherently superior to others? Kohlberg (1984) believed that there are stages of moral reasoning, and that as children grow older, they advance in these stages. Some will advance faster and further than others, creating individual differences in levels of moral development.

Our perspective is perhaps a bit different. People can certainly differ in their moral reasoning and moral development, but we can teach children as well as adults to enhance their ethical reasoning and behavior simply by instructing them regarding the challenges of thinking and acting in an ethical way. It is not enough to teach religion or values or ethics. One needs to teach children about the steps leading to ethical behavior, as described in the earlier listing, so that they can recognize for and in themselves how and why ethical behavior presents such a challenge. They need education and they need inoculation against the forces that are likely to lead them to fail to behave ethically because they do not make it through all eight of the steps listed earlier.

From this point of view, ethical giftedness is not some kind of inherent characteristic but something we can develop in virtually all children (assuming they are not psychopathic). But such development is difficult because, as we have seen, thinking and acting ethically is more of a challenge than would appear. Merely going to religion or ethics classes will not, in and of itself, produce ethical behavior.

In speaking of the challenges of leadership, and particularly of leaders who become foolish, we have spoken of the risk of ethical disengagement (Sternberg, 2008b). Ethical disengagement (based on Bandura, 1999) is the dissociation of oneself from ethical values. One may believe that ethical values should apply to the actions of others, but one becomes disengaged from them as they apply to oneself. One may believe that one is above or beyond ethics, or simply not see its relevance to one's own life.

There are six fallacies, mentioned earlier, that lead people to be foolish (Sternberg, 2008a). They include:

1. *unrealistic optimism.* The person thinks he or she is so bright, or so powerful, that anything he or she does will turn out all right, regardless of how foolish or unethical it may be.
2. *egocentrism.* The person comes to believe that his or her leadership or power is for purposes of self-aggrandizement. Tyco CEO Dennis Kozlowski, currently in prison for tax evasion, ran the company as though it was his own personal piggybank ("Timeline of the Tyco International Scandal," 2005; http://www.usatoday.com/money/industries/manufacturing/2005–06-17-tyco-timeline_x.htm, retrieved June 5, 2008). Ethics took the backseat to Kozlowski's desire to enrich himself and his family.
3. *false omniscience.* Some people come to believe themselves as all-knowing. The surprising thing about the behavior of a Bill Clinton or a George W. Bush, in quite different domains, is not that they made mistakes, but rather, that they kept making the same mistakes over and over again. Clinton correctly viewed himself as very intelligent, and perhaps thought that his intelligence and excellent education gave him levels of knowledge that he did not have.
4. *false omnipotence.* Napoleon's failed invasion of Russia stands as one of the great historical monuments to false feelings of power. Napoleon believed himself to be extremely powerful. His invasion of Russia was politically pointless and strategically flawed; but he wanted the prize nevertheless. The invasion was the beginning of the end for Napoleon. Like so many other powerful leaders, he overreached, and his feelings of omnipotence led to his doom.
5. *false invulnerability.* Perhaps Eliot Spitzer, as governor of New York, felt himself not only extremely powerful but invulnerable. He must have felt pretty close to invulnerable, because as a former prosecutor, he must have known that police agencies had multiple ways of tracking patrons of prostitutes. He nevertheless engaged in a pattern of repeated reckless behavior ("Spitzer is linked to prostitution ring," 2008; http://www.nytimes.com/2008/03/10/nyregion/10cnd-spitzer.html?_r=1&oref=slogin, retrieved June 5, 2008), which eventually cost him the governorship.
6. *ethical disengagement.* How did Jimmy Swaggert go wrong? Or Jim Bakker? Or Ted Haggard? Or any of the countless men of the cloth who, when given the chance, acted in their own lives precisely the

way they told their listeners not to act in their lives. They exhibited ethical disengagement, whereby they came to believe that ethics are important for others, but not for them. They came to believe that they were, somehow, above acting ethically – until society decided they weren't.

THE ROLE OF WISDOM

If we want to nurture ethical giftedness, or at least behavior that is ethically gifted, then we have to value wisdom. Tests created to measure factual knowledge and analysis of such knowledge often bypass wisdom altogether.

In our own theory, WICS, wisdom is viewed according to a proposed balance theory of wisdom (Sternberg, 2003d), according to which an individual is wise to the extent he or she uses successful intelligence, creativity, and knowledge as moderated by positive ethical values to (a) seek to reach a common good, (b) by balancing intrapersonal (one's own), interpersonal (others'), and extrapersonal (organizational/institutional/spiritual) interests, (c) over the short and long term, to (d) adapt to, shape, and select environments. Wisdom is in large part a decision to use one's intelligence, creativity, and experience for a common good.

Wise individuals do not look out just for their own interests, nor do they ignore these interests. Rather, they skillfully balance interests of varying kinds, including their own, those of others, and those of the communities of which they are a part. They also recognize that they need to align the interests of their group or organization with those of other groups or organizations because no group operates within a vacuum. Wise people realize that what may appear to be a prudent course of action over the short term does not necessarily appear so over the long term.

Our society has made the mistake of heavily emphasizing traditional cognitive abilities and knowledge at the expense of wisdom and ethical reasoning. The economic crash of 2008 was the work of financiers who were smart but not wise. Lehman Brothers, Bear-Stearns, and other firms fell as smart people made foolish gambles. The Deepwater Horizon fiasco of 2010, perhaps the worst environmental disaster in the history of the United States, was wholly avoidable, but smart people foolishly cut corners. In a world with technologies as powerful as those available today, can we afford to educate students to be smart but not wise? Can we afford, in some cases, to produce "smart" terrorists with warped ethical compasses? We think not.

People may differ in their ability to behave ethically, but, to our knowledge, there is no evidence of intrinsic differences in "ethical giftedness" or "moral intelligence." The difference in people's behavior appears rather to be in their skill in completing a set of eight steps that, conjointly, produce ethical behavior. Failure of an earlier step is likely to lead to failure to execute the later steps. Teaching children abstract principles of ethical behavior or ethical rules is unlikely, in itself, to produce ethical behavior. Rather, children need to be taught the sequence of processes leading to ethical thinking and to inoculate themselves against pressures – both external and internal – to behave in unethical ways. If we want to produce ethical giftedness, we have to develop it, not hope it will be a given in some group of intrinsically gifted children.

7

Giftedness as Developing Expertise

There are two basic kinds of views of abilities and how they contribute to giftedness (see Heller, Monks, Sternberg, & Subotnik, 2000). One view is that giftedness is some relatively stable attribute of individuals that develops as an interaction between heredity and environment. This idea is based on conventional views of abilities (e.g., Guilford, 1967; Spearman, 1927; Thurstone, 1938), which see intelligence as a relatively static entity. Even modern theories often take this position, whether they suggest one kind of ability or many kinds (e.g., Carroll, 1993; Ceci, 1996; Gallagher & Courtright, 1986; Gardner, 2000; Jensen, 1998; Reis & Renzulli, in press; Renzulli, 1978, 1986; Sternberg, 1985a; see essays in Sternberg & Davidson, 1986). An alternative view is that giftedness is to be found within a zone of proximal development – that it can advance from abilities that are ready to be developed to those that are developed (Feuerstein, 1979; Vygotsky, 1978; see also Kanevsky, 1992; Morelock, 2000, for descriptions of how this view applies to giftedness, and Grigorenko & Sternberg, 1998; Lidz, 1987, 1991, for discussions of issues of assessment).

The argument of this chapter is that a particular construct, *developing expertise*, can integrate these two views of giftedness – one static, the other dynamic. This view is based on that of Sternberg (1998a, 1999a), according to which abilities can be viewed as forms of developing expertise. Ackerman (in press) has pointed out that in one sense, an advantage of intelligence is that it enables people to acquire expertise. In our view, intelligence tests and related tests can be viewed as measuring not some prior existing set of abilities but, rather, developing expertise. Developing expertise is defined here as the ongoing process of the acquisition and consolidation of a set of skills needed for a high level of mastery in one or more domains of life performance. Good performance on any kinds of tests requires a certain kind of expertise, and to the extent this expertise overlaps with that required by schooling or by the workplace, there will be a correlation between the tests and performance in school or in the workplace. But such correlations represent no intrinsic relation between abilities and other kinds of performance; rather, they represent overlaps in the kinds of expertise needed to perform well under different kinds of circumstances.

There is nothing privileged about ability tests. One could as easily use, say, academic achievement to predict ability-related scores. For example, it is as simple to use the SAT-II (the subject-matter tests used as measures of achievement) to predict the SAT-I (also called the SAT Reasoning Test, but formerly called the Scholastic Assessment Test and before that the Scholastic Aptitude Test) as vice versa, and of course, the levels of prediction will be the same. Both tests measure achievement, although the kinds of achievements they measure are different. Indeed, verbal skills tests that are called measures of achievement on some tests (e.g., the Kaufman Assessment Battery for Children) are called measures of ability on other tests (e.g., the Wechsler Intelligence Scale for Children).

According to this view, although ability tests may have temporal priority relative to various criteria in their administration (i.e., ability tests are administered first, and later, criterion indices of performance, such as grades or achievement test scores, are collected), they have no psychological priority. All of the various kinds of assessments are of the same kind psychologically. What distinguishes ability tests from other kinds of assessments is how the ability tests are used (usually predictively) rather than what they measure. There is no qualitative distinction among the various kinds of assessments. All tests measure various kinds of developing expertise.

Conventional tests of intelligence and related abilities measure achievement that individuals should have accomplished several years back (see also Anastasi & Urbina, 1997). Tests such as vocabulary, reading comprehension, verbal analogies, arithmetic problem solving, and the like are all, in part, tests of achievement. Even abstract-reasoning tests measure achievement in dealing with geometric symbols, skills taught in Western schools (Laboratory of Comparative Human Cognition, 1982; Serpell, 2000; Sternberg, 2004a). One might as well use academic performance to predict ability test scores. The problem regarding the traditional model is not in its statement of a correlation between ability tests and other forms of achievement but in its proposal of a causal relation whereby the tests reflect a construct that is somehow causal of, rather than merely temporally antecedent to, later success.

The developing-expertise view in no way rules out the contribution of genetic factors as a source of individual differences in who will be able to develop a given amount of expertise. Many human attributes, including intelligence, reflect the covariation and interaction of genetic and environmental factors (Grigorenko, 2000). But the contribution of genes to an individual's intelligence cannot be directly measured or even directly estimated. Rather, what is measured is a portion of what is expressed, namely, manifestations of developing expertise, the kind of expertise that potentially leads to reflective practitioners in a variety of fields (Schon, 1983). This approach to measurement is used explicitly by Royer, Carlo, Dufresne, and Mestre (1996), who have shown that it is possible to develop measurements of reading skill reflecting varying levels of developing expertise. In such assessments, outcome measures reflect not simply quantitative assessments of skill, but qualitative differences in the types of developing expertise that have emerged (e.g., ability to understand technical text material, ability to draw inferences from this material, or ability to draw out "big ideas" in technical text).

According to this view, measures of abilities *should* be correlated with later success because both measures of intelligence and various measures of success require developing expertise of related types. For example, both typically require what we have referred to as *metacomponents* of thinking: recognition of problems, definition of problems, formulation of strategies to solve problems, representation of information, allocation of resources, and monitoring and evaluation of problem solutions (Sternberg, Kaufman, & Grigorenko, 2008). These skills develop as results of gene-environment covariation and interaction. If we wish to call them *intelligence,* that is certainly fine, so long as we recognize that what we are calling intelligence and related abilities represent a form of developing expertise.

Gifted individuals, then, are those who develop expertise at a more rapid rate, or to a higher degree or deeper level, or to a qualitatively different kind of level than do nongifted individuals. Gifted individuals show greater promise for the development of expertise than do nongifted individuals, but they show such promise by means of assessment that are themselves measures of developing expertise. We can view such measures as predictive of later gifted performance, but they are themselves assessments of kinds of gifted performance. The predictors do not differ qualitatively from the criteria, except, perhaps, in our minds as a form of wishful thinking.

A major goal of work under the point of view presented here is to integrate the study of intelligence and related abilities (see reviews in Sternberg,

1990b, 1994, 2000b) with the study of expertise (Chi, Glaser, & Farr, 1988; Ericsson, 1996; Ericsson & Smith, 1991; Hoffman, 1992; Shore, 2000). These literatures, typically viewed as distinct, are here viewed as ultimately involved with the same psychological mechanisms. According to this view, then, abilities and expertise are two different faces of the same coin.

THE SPECIFICS OF THE DEVELOPING-EXPERTISE MODEL

At the heart of the model is the notion of *developing expertise* – that individuals are constantly in a process of developing expertise when they work within a given domain. They may and do, of course, differ in rate and asymptote of development. Gifted individuals show faster rates or higher asymptotes of development. The main constraint in achieving expertise is not some fixed prior level of capacity, but purposeful engagement involving direct instruction, active participation, role modeling, and reward.

Elements of the Model

The model of developing expertise has five key elements (although certainly they do not constitute an exhaustive list of elements in the development of expertise): metacognitive skills, learning skills, thinking skills, knowledge, and motivation. Gifted individuals excel in the development of expertise in some combination of these elements, and, at high levels of giftedness, in all of them. They influence each other, both directly and indirectly. For example, learning leads to knowledge, but knowledge facilitates further learning.

These elements are, to a large extent, domain specific. The development of expertise in one area does not necessarily lead to the development of expertise in another area, although there may be some transfer, depending upon the relationship of the areas, a point that has been made with regard to intelligence by others as well (e.g., Gardner, 1983, 1999a, 2000; Sternberg, 1997a, 1999a).

In the theory of successful intelligence (Sternberg, 1985a, 1997a, 1999c), described earlier, intelligence is viewed as having three aspects: analytical, creative, and practical. Our research suggests that the development of expertise in one creative domain (Sternberg & Lubart, 1995) or in one practical domain (Sternberg et al., 2000; Sternberg, Wagner, Williams, & Horvath, 1995) shows modest correlations with the development of expertise in other such domains. Psychometric research suggests more domain generality for the analytical domain (Jensen, 1998). Moreover, people can show analytical, creative, or practical expertise in one domain without showing all three of these kinds of expertise, or even two of the three.

1. *Metacognitive skills.* Metacognitive skills (or metacomponents – Sternberg, 1985a) refer to people's understanding and control of their own cognition. For example, such skills would encompass what an individual knows about writing papers or solving arithmetic word problems, both with regard to the steps that are involved and with regard to how these steps can be executed effectively. Seven metacognitive skills are particularly important: problem recognition, problem definition, problem representation, strategy formulation, resource allocation, monitoring of problem solving, and evaluation of problem solving (Sternberg, 1985a, 1986). All of these skills are modifiable (Sternberg, 1986, 1988b; Sternberg & Grigorenko, 2000; Sternberg & Spear-Swerling, 1996). Gifted individuals excel in metacognitive skills (Borkowski & Peck, 1986; Jackson & Butterfield, 1986; Shore, 2000).

2. *Learning skills.* Learning skills (knowledge-acquisition components) are essential to the model (Sternberg, 1985a, 1986), although they are certainly not the only learning skills that individuals use. Learning skills are sometimes divided into explicit and implicit ones. Explicit learning is what occurs when we make an effort to learn; implicit learning is what occurs when we pick up information incidentally, without any systematic effort. Examples of learning skills are selective encoding, which involves distinguishing relevant from irrelevant information; selective combination, which involves putting together the relevant information; and selective comparison, which involves relating new information to information already stored in memory (Sternberg, 1985a).

3. *Thinking skills.* There are three main kinds of thinking skills (or performance components) that individuals need to master (Sternberg, 1985a, 1986, 1994). It is important to note that these are sets of, rather than individual, thinking skills. Critical (analytical) thinking skills include analyzing, critiquing, judging, evaluating, comparing and contrasting, and assessing. Creative thinking skills include creating, discovering, inventing, imagining, supposing, and hypothesizing. Practical thinking skills include applying, using, utilizing, and practicing (Sternberg, 1997a; Sternberg & Grigorenko, 2000). They are the first step in the translation of thought into real-world action.

4. *Knowledge.* Two main kinds of knowledge are relevant in academic situations. Declarative knowledge is of facts, concepts, principles, laws,

and the like. It is "knowing that." Procedural knowledge is of procedures and strategies. It is "knowing how." Of particular importance is
procedural tacit knowledge, which involves knowing how the system
functions in which one is operating (Sternberg et al., 2000; Sternberg,
Wagner, Williams & Horvath, 1995).

5. *Motivation.* One can distinguish among several different kinds of
   motivation. A first kind of motivation is achievement motivation
   (McClelland, 1985; McClelland, Atkinson, Clark, & Lowell, 1976).
   People who are high in achievement motivation seek moderate challenges and risks. They are attracted to tasks that are neither very
   easy nor very hard. They are strivers – constantly trying to better
   themselves and their accomplishments.

   A second kind of motivation is competence (self-efficacy) motivation, which refers to persons' beliefs in their own ability to solve
   the problem at hand (Bandura, 1977, 1996). Experts need to develop
   a sense of their own efficacy to solve difficult tasks in their domain
   of expertise. This kind of self-efficacy can result both from intrinsic
   and extrinsic rewards (Amabile, 1996; Sternberg & Lubart, 1996). Of
   course, other kinds of motivation are important too. Indeed, motivation is perhaps the indispensable element needed for school success.
   Without it, the student never even tries to learn.

   A third kind of motivation is motivation to develop one's own
   intellectual skills. Dweck (Carr & Dweck, in press; Dweck, 1999) has
   distinguished between "entity" and "incremental" theorists among
   children. The former believe intelligence largely to be fixed; the latter
   believe it to be modifiable. Those who believe that intelligence is modifiable are more likely to make the effort to improve their skills simply
   because they believe that these skills are subject to improvement.

6. *Context.* All of the elements discussed here are characteristics of the
   learner. Returning to the issues raised in a previous chapter, a problem with conventional intelligence tests is their assumption that individuals operate in a more or less decontextualized environment. A
   test score is interpreted largely in terms of the individual's internal
   attributes. But a test measures much more, and the assumption of
   a fixed or uniform context across test-takers is not realistic. Contextual factors that can affect test performance include native language,
   emphasis of test on speedy performance, importance to the test-taker
   of success on the test, and familiarity with the kinds of material on
   the test (Barnett, Rindermann, Williams, & Ceci, in press; Ceci, 1996;
   Sternberg, 1997a).

Interactions of Elements

The novice works toward expertise through deliberate practice. But this practice requires an interaction of all five of the key elements. At the center, driving the elements, is motivation. Without it, the elements remain inert. Eventually, one reaches a kind of expertise, at which one becomes a reflective practitioner of a certain set of skills. But expertise occurs at many levels. The expert first-year graduate or law student, for example, is still far removed from the expert professional. People thus cycle through many times, on the way to successively higher levels of expertise. Those who are able to combine the elements in a particularly effective way so as to advance more quickly to expertise, or to a quantitatively higher level of expertise, or to a qualitatively superior kind of expertise, are called gifted. Those who merely show up as gifted on tests when they are young, but not in more consequential kinds of performance when they are older, often are viewed as gifted individuals who failed to fulfill their potential. This explanation may be correct, or it may simply be that the main expertise of these individuals was in taking tests of the kinds used to label young people as gifted. As we discussed when we presented some of our research results in Chapter 3, it seems that different types of skills contribute differently to identifying a person as gifted in different stages of life.

Motivation drives metacognitive skills, which in turn activate learning and thinking skills, which then provide feedback to the metacognitive skills, enabling one's level of expertise to increase (see also Sternberg, 1985a). The declarative and procedural knowledge acquired through the extension of the thinking and learning skills also results in these skills being used more effectively in the future.

All of these processes are affected by, and can in turn affect, the context in which they operate. For example, if a learning experience is in English but the learner has only limited English proficiency, his or her learning will be inferior to that of someone with more advanced English-language skills. Or if material is presented orally to someone who is a better visual learner, that individual's performance will be reduced.

How does this model of developing expertise relate to the construct of intelligence and to other abilities as well?

THE g FACTOR AND THE STRUCTURE OF ABILITIES

Some intelligence theorists point to the stability of the alleged general factor of human intelligence as evidence for the existence of some kind of stable and overriding structure of human intelligence. Theorists of giftedness might then view gifted individuals as those who excel in this general ability (e.g., Gallagher & Courtright, 1986; Robinson, 2005). But the existence of a *g* factor may reflect little more than an interaction between whatever latent (and not directly measurable) abilities individuals may have and the kinds of expertise that are developed in school. With different forms of schooling, *g* could be made either stronger or weaker. In effect, Western forms and related forms of schooling may, in part, create the *g* phenomenon by providing a kind of schooling that teaches in conjunction the various kinds of skills measured by tests of intellectual abilities. Individuals may be identified as "gifted" because they possess abilities that are key to performance only in somewhat limited spheres of human endeavor.

Suppose, for example, that children were selected from an early age to be schooled for a certain trade. Throughout most of human history, this is in fact the way most children were schooled. Boys, at least, were apprenticed at an early age to a master who would teach them a trade. There was no point in their learning skills that would be irrelevant to their lives.

To bring the example into the present, imagine we decided that certain students, from an early age, would study English (or some other native language) to develop language expertise; other students would study mathematics to develop their mathematical expertise. Still other students might specialize in developing spatial expertise to be used in flying airplanes or doing shop work or whatever. Instead of specialization beginning at the university level, it would begin from the age of first schooling.

This point of view is related to, but different from, that typically associated with the theory of crystallized and fluid intelligence (Cattell, 1971; Horn, 1994). In that theory, fluid ability is viewed as an ability to acquire and reason with information whereas crystallized ability is viewed as the information so acquired. According to this view, schooling primarily develops crystallized ability, based in part upon the fluid ability the individual brings to bear upon school-like tasks. In the theory proposed here, however, both fluid and crystallized ability are roughly equally susceptible to development through schooling or other means societies create for developing expertise. One could argue that the greater validity of the position presented here is shown by the near-ubiquitous Flynn effect (Flynn, 1987; Neisser, 1998), which documents massive gains in IQ around the world throughout most of the 20th century. The effect must be due to environment, because large genetic changes worldwide in such a short time frame are virtually impossible. Interestingly, gains are substantially larger in fluid abilities than in crystallized abilities, suggesting that fluid abilities are likely to be as susceptible as or probably more susceptible than crystallized abilities to environmental influences. Clearly, the notion of fluid abilities as some basic genetic potential one brings into the world, whose development is expressed in crystallized abilities, does not work.

The students who would have received specialized schooling from an early age then would be given an omnibus test of intelligence or any broad-ranging measure of intelligence. There would be no general factor because people schooled in one form of expertise would not have been schooled in others. One can imagine even negative correlations between subscores on the so-called intelligence test. The reason for the negative correlations would be that developing expertise in one area might preclude developing expertise in another because of the form of schooling (Sternberg et al., 2001a).

Thus, conventional tests may unduly favor a small segment of the population by virtue of the narrow kind of developing expertise they measure. When one measures a broader range of developing expertise, the results look quite different. Moreover, the broader range of expertise includes kinds of skills that will be important in the world of work and in the world of the family. Who is identified as gifted, then, will depend upon the range of abilities assessed.

Analytical, creative, and practical abilities, as measured by our tests or anyone else's, are simply forms of developing expertise. All are useful in various kinds of life tasks. But conventional tests may unfairly disadvantage those students who do not do well in a fairly narrow range of kinds of expertise. By expanding the range of developing expertise we measure, we discover that many children not now identified as able have, in fact, developed important kinds of expertise. The abilities conventional tests measure are important for school and life performance, but they are not the only abilities that are important.

Teaching in a way that departs from notions of abilities based on a general factor also pays dividends. In a set of studies, we have shown that generally lower socioeconomic class third-grade and generally middle-class eighth-grade students who are taught social studies (a unit on communities) or science (a unit on psychology) for successful intelligence (analytically, creative, and practically, as well as for memory) outperform students who are taught just for analytical (critical) thinking or just for memory (Sternberg, Torff, & Grigorenko, 1998a, 1998b). The students taught "triarchically" outperform the other students not only on performance assessments that look at analytical, creative, and practical kinds of achievements, but even on tests that measure straight memory (multiple-choice tests already being used in the courses). None of this is to say that analytical abilities are not important in school and life – obviously, they are. Rather, what our data suggest is that other types of abilities – creative and practical ones – are important as well and that students need to learn how to use all three kinds of abilities together.

Another study, looking specifically at middle school and high school students' reading comprehension, showed similar results – that is, students taught in a manner that addressed both their areas of strength and the abilities in which they were relatively weaker fared better than students who were taught to just focus on memory and analytical abilities (Grigorenko, Jarvin, & Sternberg, 2000).

Thus, teaching students in a way that takes into account their more highly developed expertise and that also enables them to develop other kinds of expertise results in superior learning outcomes, regardless of how these learning outcomes are measured. When children are taught in a way that lets them use expertise other than memory, they actually remember better, on average, than do children taught for memory.

We have also done studies in which we measured informal procedural knowledge in children and adults. We have done such studies with business managers, college professors, elementary-school students, salespeople, college students, and general populations. This important aspect of practical intelligence, in study after study, has been found to be uncorrelated with academic intelligence as measured by conventional tests, in a variety of populations, occupations, and at a variety of age levels (Cianciolo et al., 2006; Sternberg et al., 2000; Sternberg, Wagner, Williams, & Horvath, 1995). Moreover, the tests predict job performance as well as, or better than, do tests of IQ. The lack of correlation of the two kinds of ability tests suggests that the best prediction of job performance will result when both academic and practical intelligence tests are used as predictors. We have also developed a test of common sense for the workplace – for example, how to handle oneself in a job interview – that predicts self-ratings of common sense but not self-ratings of various kinds of academic abilities (Cianciolo et al., 2006).

Although the kinds of informal procedural expertise we measure in these tests does not correlate with academic expertise, it does correlate across work domains. For example, we found that subscores (for managing oneself, managing others, and managing tasks) on measures of informal procedural knowledge are correlated with each other and that scores on the test for academic psychology are moderately correlated with scores on the test for business managers (Sternberg et al., 2000; Sternberg, Wagner, Williams, & Horvath, 1995). In general, there is a modest to moderate correlation of tacit knowledge with work-related performance (Hedlund et al., 2006; Sternberg & Hedlund, 2002). So the kinds of developing expertise that matter in the world of work may show certain correlations with each other that are not shown with the kinds of developing expertise that matter in the world of primary and secondary school.

Both conventional academic tests and our tests of practical intelligence measure forms of developing expertise that matter in school and on the job. The two kinds of tests are not qualitatively distinct. The reason the correlations are essentially null is that the kinds of developing expertise they measure are quite different. The people who are good at abstract, academic kinds of expertise are often people who have not emphasized learning practical, everyday kinds of expertise, and vice versa, as we found in our Kenya study (Sternberg et al., 2001a). Indeed, children who grow up in challenging environments such as certain U.S. inner cities may need to develop practical over academic expertise as a matter of survival. As in Kenya, this practical expertise may better predict their survival than do academic kinds of expertise. The same applies in business, where tacit knowledge about how to perform on the job is as likely or more likely to lead to job success than is the academic expertise that in school seems so important.

The practical kinds of expertise matter in school too. In a study at Yale, Wendy Williams and Sternberg (cited in Sternberg, Wagner, & Okagaki, 1993) found that a test of tacit knowledge for college predicted grade-point average as well as did an academic-ability test. But a test of tacit knowledge for college life better predicted adjustment to the college environment than did the academic test.

TAKING TESTS

Developing expertise applies not only to the constructs measured by conventional intelligence tests, but also to the very act of taking the tests.

Sometimes the expertise children learn that is relevant for in-school tests may actually hurt them on conventional ability tests. In one example, we studied the development of children's analogical reasoning in a country day school where teachers taught in English in the morning and in Hebrew in the afternoon (Sternberg & Rifkin, 1979). We found a number of second-grade students who got no problems right on our test. They would have seemed, on the surface, to be rather stupid. We discovered the reason for this, however. We had tested in the afternoon, and in the afternoon, the children always read in Hebrew. So they read our problems from right to left, and got them all wrong. The expertise that served them so well in their normal environment utterly failed them on the test.

Our sample was of upper middle-class children who, in a year or two, would know better. But imagine what happens with other children in less supportive environments who develop kinds of expertise that may serve them well in their family or community lives or even school life, but not on the tests. They will appear to be stupid rather than lacking the kinds of expertise the tests measure.

Assessments of abilities measure developing expertise. Static views of abilities isolate a slice of performance in time. Dynamic views of abilities isolate a region of performance in time. Both views, though, represent only slices in the long-term continuum of developing expertise. Gifted individuals who excel in static or dynamic assessments, or both kinds of assessments, excel in developing expertise. The kinds of developing expertise assessed to identify gifted children may or may not correspond well to the kinds of developing expertise that are rewarded in adults. Often, the two kinds of developing expertise do not correspond well.

Tests can be created that favor the kinds of developing expertise formed in any kind of cultural or subcultural milieu (Serpell, 2000; Sternberg & Grigorenko, 2007a). Those who have created conventional tests of abilities have tended to value the kinds of skills most valued by Western schools. This system of valuing is understandable, given that Binet and Simon (1905) first developed intelligence tests for the purpose of predicting school performance. Moreover, these skills are important in school and in life. But in the modern world, the conception of abilities as fixed or even as predetermined is an anachronism. Moreover, our research and that of others (reviewed more extensively in Sternberg, 1997a) shows that the set of abilities assessed by conventional tests measures only a small portion of the kinds of developing expertise relevant for life success. It is for this reason that conventional tests predict only about 10% of individual-difference variation in various measures of success in adult life (Herrnstein & Murray, 1994; Jensen, 1998).

Of course, cognitive expertise matters in school and in life, but so does social and emotional expertise (Mayer, Salovey, Caruso, & Cherkasskiy, in press). Both need to be taught in the school and the home to all children. This latter kind of expertise may become even more important in the workplace. Until we expand our notions of abilities and recognize that when we measure them, we are measuring developing forms of expertise, we will risk consigning many potentially excellent contributors to our society to bleak futures. We will also be potentially overvaluing students with expertise for success in a certain kind of schooling but not necessarily with equal expertise for success later in life.

8

Giftedness and Culture

The study of culture and intelligence is based in part on the notion that behavior that in one cultural context is viewed as smart or even gifted may, in another cultural context, be stupid (Cole, Gay, Glick, & Sharp, 1971; Sternberg, 2004a; Sternberg & Grigorenko, 2007a). Stating one's political views honestly and openly, for example, may win one the top political job, such as the presidency, in one culture, and the gallows in another. Not all scholars believe that giftedness has any relativity at all: Herrnstein and Murray (1994), Lynn (2002, 2006, 2008), and Rushton (2000), for example, are among those who believe that IQs mean largely the same thing, regardless of the culture in which one resides. In this chapter, we will disagree with this view.

One reason to study culture and intelligence is because they are so inextricably interlinked. Indeed, Tomasello (2001) has argued that culture is what, in large part, separates human from animal intelligence. Humans have evolved as they have, he believes, in part because of their cultural adaptations, which in turn develop from their ability, even in infancy from about 9 months onward, to understand others as intentional agents.

The conceptualization, assessment, and development of intelligence cannot be fully or even meaningfully understood outside their cultural context. Work that seeks to study intelligence acontextually may impose an (often Western) investigator's view of the world on the rest of the planet, frequently attempting to show that individuals who are more similar to the investigator are smarter than individuals who are less similar. For example, a test of intelligence developed and validated in one culture may or may not be equally valid, or even be valid at all, in another culture.

WHAT IS CULTURE?

Because the topic of this chapter is culture and intelligence, it is necessary to define culture.

There have been many definitions of culture (e.g., Brislin, Lonner, & Thorndike, 1973; Kroeber & Kluckhohn, 1952), but it is defined here as "the set of attitudes, values, beliefs and behaviors shared by a group of people, communicated from one generation to the next via language or some other means of communication (Barnouw, 1985)" (Matsumoto, 1994, p. 4). The term *culture* can be used in many ways and has a long history (Benedict, 1946; Boas, 1911; Mead, 1928; see Matsumoto, 1996). Berry, Poortinga, Segall, and Dasen (1992) described six uses of the term: descriptively to characterize a group, historically to describe the traditions of a group, normatively to express rules and norms of a group, psychologically to emphasize how a group learns and solves problems, structurally to emphasize the organizational elements of a collectivity, and genetically to describe collective origins.

WHAT IS INTELLIGENCE ACROSS CULTURES?

How is intelligence defined? Earlier, we spoke of the definition of intelligence proposed by Edwin Boring (1923), who was content to define intelligence as whatever it is that tests of intelligence measure. This definition is circular because, according to it, the nature of intelligence determines what is tested, but what is tested must necessarily be determined by the nature of intelligence. In this definition, intellectual giftedness would be based on a definition that has no meaning outside what IQ tests happen to test. Moreover, what different tests of intelligence test is not always the same thing. Different tests measure somewhat different constructs (Daniel, 1997, 2000; Embretson & McCollam, 2000; Kaufman, 2000; Kaufman & Lichtenberger, 1998), so it is not feasible to define intelligence by what tests test, as though they all measured the same thing.

Moreover, if intelligence were to turn out to be not quite the same thing from one culture to another, the definition would become totally vacuous, meaning as many different things as there are cultures. Intellectual giftedness would then have no unique meaning cross-culturally. Tests, of course, can be translated. But what is to be translated? A test of English vocabulary would not work well with children in Dholuo-speaking rural Kenya, such as in the town of Busia. So the words would, at least, need to be translated. But are the translated words that would be optimal on a test in English the same ones that would be optimal on a test in Dholuo? Are there even exact translations, given that the roots of the two languages are so different? Perhaps not. But then, is vocabulary for low-frequency words itself of equal importance to village residents in rural Busia, Kenya, as it is to residents of, say, Cambridge, Massachusetts? The residents of the town will probably never use any of the complex words typical for vocabulary tests in the United States in their lives, and they may not even exist in their language. But, to survive, those residents need to know how to farm under very difficult conditions, and a test of farming knowledge would be quite appropriate to them as a measure of their adaptive skills. Most of the readers of this chapter would have difficulty answering the farming vocabulary questions that would be relevant to their lives, even in translation. Boring's definition simply does not hold up well under close cultural scrutiny.

Historically, there are many different definitions of intelligence ("Intelligence and Its Measurement," 1921; Sternberg, 2000b; Sternberg & Detterman, 1986). Over time, a consensus definition has tended to emphasize two important skills: adaptation to the environment and the ability to think and learn. In more recent times, a third component has been added to the definition, namely, understanding of oneself and one's own skills, often referred to as *metacognition*. Broadly speaking, metacognition also includes theory of mind, in general, or one's understanding of how other people's minds work as well.

Intelligence may be conceived in different ways in different cultures (see reviews in Berry, 1991; Nisbett, 2003, 2009; Serpell, 2000; and Sternberg & Kaufman, 1998). Such differences are important because cultures evaluate their members, as well as members of other cultures, in terms of their own conceptions of intelligence.

In some cases, Western notions about intelligence are not shared by other cultures. For example, at the mental level, the Western emphasis on speed of mental processing (Sternberg, Conway, Ketron, & Bernstein, 1981) is not shared in many cultures. Other cultures may even be suspicious of the quality of work that is done very quickly. Indeed, other cultures emphasize depth rather than speed of processing. They are not alone: Some prominent Western theorists have pointed out the importance of depth of processing for full command of material (e.g., Craik & Lockhart, 1972).

In some cases the conception of intelligence within a given culture depends on the language in which the respondent is schooled. Chen and Chen (1988) explicitly compared the concepts of intelligence of Chinese graduates from Chinese-language versus English-language schools in Hong Kong. Participants had all grown up in Hong Kong; only their language of schooling varied. The researchers found that both groups considered non-verbal reasoning skills the most relevant ones for measuring intelligence. Verbal reasoning and social skills came next, and then numerical skill. Memory was seen as least important. The Chinese-language-schooled group, however, tended to rate verbal skills as less important than did the English-language-schooled group. Moreover, in an earlier study, Chen, Braithwaite, and Huang (1982) found that Chinese students viewed memory for facts as important for intelligence, whereas Australian students viewed these skills as of only trivial importance.

Das (1994), also reviewing Eastern notions of intelligence, has suggested that in Buddhist and Hindu philosophies, intelligence involves waking up, noticing, recognizing, understanding, and comprehending, but also includes such things as determination, mental effort, and even feelings and opinions in addition to more intellectual elements. These views are similar to those observed by Nisbett (2003) in Asian cultures: A gifted individual is not born smart but rather works much harder than others to develop and, in some sense, to create his or her gifts.

In another study comparing Western and Eastern conceptions of intelligence, Gill and Keats (1980) noted that Australian University students value academic skills and the ability to adapt to new events as critical to intelligence, whereas Malay students value practical skills, as well as speed and creativity. Dasen (1984) found Malay students to emphasize both social and cognitive attributes in their conceptions of intelligence.

The differences between East and West, or South and West, may be due to differences in the kinds of skills valued by the two kinds of cultures (Srivastava & Misra, 1996). Western cultures and their schools emphasize what might be called "technological intelligence" (Mundy-Castle, 1974), and so things like artificial intelligence and so-called smart bombs are viewed, in some sense, as intelligent, or smart. African cultures place greater emphasis on "social intelligence" (Mundy-Castle, 1974).

Western schooling also emphasizes generalization more than do other cultures (Srivastava & Misra, 1996), or going beyond the information given (Connolly & Bruner, 1974; Goodnow, 1976), speed (Sternberg, 1985a), minimal moves to a solution (Newell & Simon, 1972), and creative thinking (Goodnow, 1976). Moreover, silence is interpreted as a lack of knowledge (Irvine, 1978). In contrast, the Wolof tribe in Africa views people of higher social class and distinction as speaking less (Irvine, 1978). In the United

States, giftedness is often associated with high levels of verbal fluency; among the Wolof, the opposite would be true.

Similar emphasis on social aspects of intelligence has been found as well among two other African groups – the Songhay of Mali and the Samia of Kenya (Putnam & Kilbride, 1980). The Yoruba, another African tribe, emphasize the importance of depth – of listening rather than just talking – to intelligence, and of being able to see all aspects of an issue and of being able to place the issue in its proper overall context (Durojaiye, 1993).

Ruzgis and Grigorenko (1994) argued that in Africa, conceptions of intelligence revolve largely around skills that help to facilitate and maintain harmonious and stable intergroup relations; intragroup relations are probably equally important, and at times even more important. For example, Serpell (1974, 1996) found that Chewa adults in Zambia emphasize social responsibilities, cooperativeness, and obedience as important to intelligence; intelligent children are expected to be respectful of adults. Kenyan parents also emphasize responsible participation in family and social life as important aspects of intelligence (Super & Harkness, 1982, 1986, 1993).

Among the Baoule in Ivory Coast, service to the family and community and politeness toward, and respect for, elders are also seen as key to intelligence (Dasen, 1984). In Zimbabwe, the word for intelligence in different local languages (*ngware*, in the Shona language; *njere*, in the Pokomo language; and *ukaliphile*, in the Ndebele language) actually means to be prudent and cautious; particularly in social relationships, it refers to behavior that is deliberate, socially responsible, positive public-spirited, and altruistic (Chimhundu, 2001; Hadebe, 2001; Irvine, 1988; Mpofu, 1993, 2004), as well as wise. Behavior is considered intelligent to the extent that it benefits the community as a whole (Mpofu, 2004).

The emphasis on the social aspects of intelligence is not limited to African cultures. Notions of intelligence in many Asian cultures also emphasize the social aspect of intelligence more than does the conventional Western or IQ-based notion (Azuma & Kashiwagi, 1987; Lutz, 1985; Poole, 1985; White, 1985).

In China, the Confucian perspective emphasizes the characteristic of benevolence and of doing what is right (Shi, 2004; Yang, 2001; Yang & Sternberg, 1997a). As in the Western notion, the intelligent person spends a great deal of effort in learning, enjoys learning, and persists in lifelong learning with a great deal of enthusiasm. The Taoist tradition, in contrast, emphasizes the importance of humility, freedom from conventional standards of judgment, and full knowledge of oneself as well as of external conditions.

China is believed to be the first nation to have employed tests of intelligence widely (Shi, 2004). Tests were used in ancient China for employment purposes. The tangram, which requires an individual to construct shapes, was first developed in the Song dynasty (Lin, 1980). Even young children were tested for their developmental skills, such as in placing objects where they belong (Yan, 2001).

The difference between Eastern and Western conceptions of intelligence may persist even in the present day. Yang and Sternberg (1997a; see also Yang & Sternberg, 1997b) studied contemporary Taiwanese Chinese conceptions of intelligence, and found five factors underlying these conceptions: (a) a general cognitive factor, much like the *g* factor in conventional Western tests; (b) interpersonal intelligence (i.e., social competence); (c) intrapersonal intelligence; (d) intellectual self-assertion; and (e) intellectual self-effacement. In a related study but with different results, Chen (1994) found three factors underlying Chinese conceptualizations of intelligence: (a) nonverbal reasoning ability, (b) verbal reasoning ability, and (c) rote memory. The difference may be due to different subpopulations of Chinese, to differences in methodology, or to differences in when the studies were done.

The factors uncovered in Taiwan differ substantially from those identified in U.S. people's conceptions of intelligence by Sternberg, et al. (1981) – (a) practical problem solving, (b) verbal ability, and (c) social competence – although in both cases, people's implicit theories of intelligence seem to go quite far beyond what conventional psychometric intelligence tests measure.

Neither African nor Asian notions emphasize exclusively social notions of intelligence. These conceptions of intelligence emphasize social skills much more than do conventional U.S. conceptions of intelligence, at the same time that they recognize the importance of cognitive aspects of intelligence. In a study of Kenyan conceptions of intelligence (Grigorenko et al., 2001), researchers found that there are four distinct terms constituting conceptions of intelligence among rural Kenyans – *rieko* (knowledge and skills), *luoro* (respect), *winjo* (comprehension of how to handle real-life problems), and *paro* (initiative) – with only the first directly referring to knowledge-based skills (including but not limited to the academic).

In India, words related to intelligence include *buddhi* (Sanskrit), which refers to awareness or consciousness (Baral & Das, 2004). Intelligence has been treated as a state, process, or entity in Indian philosophical literature (Srivastava & Misra, 2000). Das (1994) has referred to intelligence in Indian philosophy as pertaining to waking up, noticing, understanding, and comprehending.

In Latin America, implicit theories of teachers tend to emphasize academic skills as the main basis of intelligence (Kaplan, 1997). For example, a study in Argentina found that teachers emphasized as important to intelligence good discipline, interest in learning, learning and thinking ability, and also coming from a stable home (Kaplan, 1997). Many teachers in this study also believed in the concept of a "bad head," that is, a head not suited to studying.

It is difficult to separate linguistic differences from conceptual differences in cross-cultural comparisons of notions of intelligence. Converging operations can be used to achieve some separation between what is merely linguistic and what is also conceptual. That is, different and diverse empirical operations can be employed to ascertain notions of intelligence. So one may ask in one study that people identify aspects of competence; in another study, that they identify competent people; in a third study, that they characterize the meaning of "intelligence," and so forth.

Intelligence is viewed as being of great importance in many Western and some other cultures. This emphasis is not shared throughout the world, however. In Japan, for example, people rarely refer to an individual's level of intelligence at all (Sato, Namiki, Ando, & Hatano, 2004). Rather, there is much more emphasis on a person's motivation and diligence. Success is viewed as much more dependent on motivation than on intelligence (Sato et al., 2004). When participants are given a task followed by success or failure feedback, Japanese students are more likely than American students to attribute success to effort, good luck, or various situational factors, whereas the Americans are more likely to attribute their success to their ability. In contrast, the Japanese students are likely to attribute failure to lack of effort, the Americans to lack of ability (Miyamoto, 1985). Nevertheless, Japanese people do have a conception of intelligence. Factors emerging from a study of implicit theories were active social competence, processing efficiency, and receptive social competence (Azuma & Kashiwagi, 1987). None of the factors were considered to be innate.

It is important to realize, again, that there is no one overall U.S. conception of intelligence. Indeed, Okagaki and Sternberg (1993) found that different ethnic groups in San Jose, California, had rather different conceptions of what it means to be intelligent. For example, Latino parents of schoolchildren tended to emphasize the importance of social competence skills in their conceptions of intelligence, whereas Asian parents tended to emphasize rather heavily the importance of cognitive skills. Anglo parents also emphasized cognitive skills. Teachers, representing the dominant culture, emphasized cognitive skills more than social competence skills.

The rank order of children of various groups' performance (including subgroups within the Latino and Asian groups) could be perfectly predicted by the extent to which their parents shared the teachers' conception of intelligence. In other words, teachers tended to reward those children who were socialized into a view of intelligence that happened to correspond to the teachers' own.

Although researchers mostly emphasize lay implicit theories of intelligence in cultural studies, it is important to realize that expert implicit theories also differ. For example, Continental European thinking about intelligence, especially in French-speaking countries, was very heavily influenced by Piaget in the latter half of the 20th century, and this influence continues to be felt today (Lautrey & de Ribaupierre, 2004). Russian thinking was very heavily influenced by Vygotsky and Luria (Grigorenko, 2004). English thinking was very heavily influenced by Spearman (Deary & Smith, 2004), and North American thinking by Thurstone as well as by Spearman (Sternberg, 2004b). Indian thinking was very heavily influenced by Eastern philosophy (Baral & Das, 2004).

These varying conceptions of what it means to be smart suggest that giftedness is not a single thing across cultures. What might be considered gifted in one culture might, in another culture, be viewed as irrelevant. Many cultures around the world emphasize social and practical skills much more in their definitions of intelligence than do Western cultures. In these cultures, socially skilled individuals might be viewed as gifted, whereas cognitively skilled individuals might be passed over simply because Western schooling is hard to find or even nonexistent. Even in Western culture, after schooling, social and practical skills probably play at least as important a role as cognitive ones – and may be even more important. If we ignore social and practical skills, we risk having definitions of intelligence only poorly connected to the world in which we live.

WHAT IS GIFTEDNESS ACROSS CULTURES?

Conceptions of giftedness also differ across cultures (Phillipson & McCann, 2007). We consider some of these conceptions here. They are taken from the Phillipson and McCann (2007) book, which is, we believe, the best single compendium of views of conceptions of giftedness around the world.

Chan (2007) points out that although Chinese believe that aspects of giftedness are inborn, they also believe that many people can become gifted through industriousness, perseverance, and learning (p. 42). Ziegler and Stoeger (2007; Ziegler, 2005), discussing the German view of giftedness, view aptitude for high performance, individuality, creativity and innovation, and uniqueness to be aspects of giftedness (pp. 75–76). Anuruthwong (2002, 2007) has studied Thai conceptions of giftedness and has found that some of the attributes important to giftedness are being a fast learner, being a good problem solver, being a sharp thinker, and being able to respond well spontaneously.

Begay and Maker (2007) studied giftedness in the Navajo. They found that there were different categories, but that gifted individuals were seen as having remarkable ability to cause things to happen and to do things in a good way (p. 142). Wong-Fernandez and Bustos-Orosa (2007) studied the notion of giftedness of Tagalog-speaking Filipinos. They found that the gifted were considered to be intelligent, good in academics, knowledge-able in many things, possessing many inherent skills and talents, different from others, and able to learn easily (p. 186). Gibson and Vialle (2007) researched giftedness among Australian Aborigines. They found an emphasis on independence and helpfulness, bush skills, sporting ability, cognitive skills, school-related skills, and specific skills such as drawing, painting, and singing (p. 209).

Mpofu, Ngara, and Gudyanga (2007) investigated the notion of giftedness among the Shona of Central-Southern Africa. Everyone was seen as having latent giftedness, which was supposed to serve the collective good. Giftedness could be shown in different domains but involved consistency, creativity, cognitive ability, and eminence among the group (p. 235). Phillipson (2007) studied giftedness among Malay people and found cunningness, mastery, natural ability, and creativity to be critical to the notion of giftedness (p. 277). Conceptions of giftedness among other groups can be found in Sak (2007), Šefer (2007), Matsumura (2007), Kaufman and Sternberg (2007), McCann (2007), and Campbell and Eyre (2007).

MODELS OF THE RELATIONSHIP OF CULTURE TO INTELLIGENCE

Consider four basic models of the relationship of culture to intelligence (Sternberg, 2004a; see also Sternberg, 1988c, 1990a). They are shown in Table 8.1.

The models presented here differ in two key respects: whether there are cross-cultural differences in the nature of the mental processes and representations involved in adaptation that constitute intelligence, and whether there are differences in the instruments needed to measure intelligence (beyond simple translation or adaptation), as a result of cultural differences in the content required for adaptation.

TABLE 8.1. *Models of the Relationship of Culture to Intelligence*

	Dimensions of Intelligence		
Tests of Intelligence	*Relation*	Same	Different
	Same	Model I	Model II
	Different	Model III	Model IV

In Model I, the nature of intelligence is the same across cultures, as are the tests used to measure intelligence. The theoretical positions of Jensen (1982a, 1982b, 1998) and Eysenck (1986) represent Model I types of positions. The argument is that the nature of intelligence is precisely the same cross-culturally and that this nature can be assessed identically (using appropriate translations of text, where necessary) without regard to culture. For example, Jensen (1998) believes that general intelligence, or g (Spearman, 1927), is the same across time and place. What varies across time and place are its levels.

Model I is what is sometimes referred to as an "etic" approach to intelligence. One devises a measure or set of measures of a construct. One then uses the measures in various cultures, sometimes doing minor adaptations to fit the measures to the culture (Carlstedt, Gustafsson, & Hautamäki, 2004; Deary & Smith, 2004; Demetriou & Papadopolous, 2004; Fernández-Ballesteros & Colom, 2004; Gulgoz & Kagitcibasi, 2004; Rosas, 2004; Stankov, 2004; see, in general, essays in Sternberg, 2004b).

Model II represents a difference in the nature of intelligence but no difference in the instruments used to measure it. The measures used to assess intelligence are the same across cultures, but the outcomes obtained from using those measures are structurally different as a function of the culture being investigated. This approach is close to that taken by Nisbett (2003), who found that the same tests given in different cultures suggested that, across cultures, people think about problems in different ways.

In Model III, the dimensions of intelligence are the same, but the instruments of measurement are not. In this view, measurement processes for a given attribute must be emic, that is, derived from within the context of the culture being studied rather than from outside it. This is not to say that the same instruments cannot be used across cultures; but when they are, the psychological meanings to be assigned to the scores will differ from one culture to another. This is the position taken in this chapter and in some earlier work (e.g., Sternberg, 1990a).

According to this position, the components of intelligence and the mental representations on which they act are universal – that is, they are required for mental functioning in all cultures. For example, people in all cultures need to execute executive processes – to (a) recognize the existence of problems, (b) define what the problems are, (c) mentally represent the problems, (d) formulate one or more strategies for solving the problems, (e) allocate resources to solving the problems, (f) monitor solution of the problems, and (g) evaluate problem solving after it is done. What varies across cultures are the mental contents (i.e., types and items of knowledge) to which processes such as these are applied, and the judgments as to what are considered "intelligent" applications of the processes to these contents (Sternberg, 1997a).

Thus, a wholly relativistic view of intelligence and culture would be inadequate. Some things are constant across cultures (mental representations and processes) whereas others are not (the contents to which they are applied and how their application is judged). Tests must be modified if they are to measure the same basic processes as they apply from one culture to another.

As a result, one can translate a particular test of intelligence, but there is no guarantee it will measure the same thing in one culture as in another. For example, a test that is highly novel in one culture or subculture may be quite familiar in the next. Even if the components of information processing are the same, the experiential novelty to which they are applied may be different. Moreover, the extent to which the given task is practically relevant to adaptation, shaping, and selection may differ. Hence, the components may be universal, but not necessarily the relative novelty or adaptive practicality of the components as applied to particular contents.

In Model IV, both the instruments and the ensuing dimensions of intelligence are different as a function of the culture under investigation. This position embraces the radical cultural-relativist position (Berry, 1974) that intelligence can be understood and measured only as an indigenous construct within a given cultural context. It also embraces the position of Sarason and Doris (1979), who viewed intelligence largely as a cultural invention. In other words, nothing about intelligence is necessarily common across cultures.

Berry and Irvine (1986) have proposed four nested levels of the cultural context (in which intelligence and other hypothetical constructs reside). The broadest, ecological level comprises the permanent or almost permanent characteristics that provide the backdrop for human action. The experiential context refers to the pattern of recurrent experiences within the ecological context that provides a basis for learning and development. The performance context comprises the limited set of environmental circumstances that account for particular behaviors at specific points in space and time. The narrowest, experimental context comprises the environmental characteristics manipulated by psychologists and others to elicit particular responses or test scores.

STUDIES OF INTELLIGENCE AND GIFTEDNESS
IN THEIR CULTURAL CONTEXTS

The discussion above suggests that intelligence, understood wholly outside its cultural context, is a mythological construct. There are some aspects of intelligence that transcend cultures, namely, the mental processes underlying intelligence and the mental representations upon which they act. But these operations play themselves out in performance differently from one culture to another. As soon as one assesses performance, then one is assessing mental processes and representations in a cultural context (Model III).

Most psychological research is done within a single culture. But single-cultural studies whose results are implicitly or even explicitly generalized across cultures potentially deprive the field in several ways. In particular, they may (a) introduce limited definitions of psychological phenomena and problems, (b) engender risks of unwarranted assumptions about the phenomena under investigation, (c) raise questions about cultural generalizability of findings, (d) engender risks of cultural imperialism, and (e) represent lost opportunities to collaborate and develop psychology around the world.

Many research programs demonstrate the potential hazards of single-culture research. For example, Greenfield (1997) found that it means a different thing to take a test among Mayan children than it does among most children in the United States. The Mayan expectation is that collaboration is permissible, and that it is rather unnatural *not* to collaborate. Such a finding is consistent with the work of Markus and Kitayama (1991), suggesting different cultural constructions of the self in individualistic versus collectivistic cultures. Indeed, Nisbett (2003) has found that some cultures, especially Asian ones, tend to be more dialectical in their thinking, whereas other cultures, such as European and North American ones, tend to be more linear. And individuals in different cultures may construct concepts in quite different ways, rendering results of concept-formation or identification studies in a single culture suspect (Atran, 1999; Coley, Medin, Proffitt, Lynch, & Atran, 1999; Medin & Atran, 1999). Thus, groups may think about what appears superficially to be the same phenomenon – whether a concept or the taking of a test – differently. What appear to be differences in general intelligence may in fact be differences in cultural properties (Helms-Lorenz, Van de Vijver, & Poortinga, 2003). Helms-Lorenz et al. (2003) have argued that measured differences in intellectual performance may result from differences in cultural complexity; but complexity of a culture is extremely hard to define, and what appears to be simple or complex from the point of view of one culture may appear differently from the point of view of another.

Many investigators have realized the importance of cultural context for the psychology of intelligence and cognition. These realizations have taken diverse forms. Indeed, Berry (1974) reviewed concepts of intelligence across a wide variety of cultural contexts, showing major differences across cultures.

Cole (1998) and Shweder (1991) have helped define cultural psychology as a field, distinguishing it from cross-cultural psychology (e.g., Irvine, 1979; Irvine & Berry, 1983; Marsella, Tharp, & Cibrorowski, 1979), which they believe tends to be somewhat less sensitive to differences among cultures. The studies described in this chapter represent both approaches, although our own studies are generally more in the "cultural" rather than "cross-cultural" tradition. Cole's overview of the field builds on his earlier work (Cole, Gay, Glick, & Sharp, 1971; Cole & Means, 1981; Cole & Scribner, 1974; Laboratory of Comparative Human Cognition, 1982), which showed how cognitive performance among populations, such as the Kpelle in Africa, can be qualitatively as well as quantitatively different from that of the North Americans who typically are tested in lab experiments on thinking and reasoning. Bruner, Olver, and Greenfield (1966) found that among members of the Wolof tribe of Senegal, increasingly greater Western-style schooling was associated with greater use of taxonomic classification.

Cole's work built, in turn, upon earlier work, such as that of Luria (1931, 1976), which showed that Asian peasants in the Soviet Union might not perform well on cognitive tasks because of their refusal to accept the tasks as they were presented. Indeed, people in diverse cultures are presented with very diverse tasks in their lives. In related work, Serpell (1974) designed a study to distinguish between a generalized perceptual-deficit hypothesis and a more context-specific hypothesis for the reasons that children in certain cultures may show inferior perceptual abilities. He found that English children did better on a drawing task, but that Zambian children did better on a wire-shaping task. Thus, children performed better on materials that were more familiar to them from their own environments.

Kearins (1981) found that when asked to remember visuospatial displays, Anglo-Australians used verbal (school-appropriate) strategies whereas aboriginals used visual (desert nomad-appropriate) strategies. Goodnow (1962) found that for tasks using combinations and permutations, Chinese children with English schooling performed as well as, or better than, Europeans, whereas children with Chinese schooling or of very low-income families did somewhat worse than did the European children. These results suggested that form of schooling primes children to excel in certain ways and not others (see also Goodnow, 1969).

Children from non-European or non–North American cultures do not always do worse on tests. Super (1976) found evidence that African infants sit and walk earlier than do their counterparts in the United States and Europe. But Super also found that mothers in the African cultures he studied made a self-conscious effort to teach their babies to sit and walk as early as possible. At more advanced levels of development, Stigler, Lee, Lucker, and Stevenson (1982; see also Stevenson & Stigler, 1994) found that Japanese and Chinese children do better in developed mathematical skills than do North American children.

Carraher, Carraher, and Schliemann (1985) studied a group of children with an assessment methodology that is especially relevant for assessing intelligence as adaptation to the environment. The group comprised Brazilian street children, who are under great contextual pressure to form a successful street business. If they do not, they risk death at the hands of so-called death squads, which may murder children who, unable to earn money, resort to robbing stores (or who are suspected of robbing stores). Hence, if they are not intelligent in the sense of adapting to their environment, they risk death. The investigators found that the same children who are able to do the mathematics needed to run their street businesses are often little able or unable to do school mathematics. In fact, the more abstracted and removed from real-world contexts the problems are in their form of presentation, the worse the children typically do on the problems. For children in school, the street context would be more removed from their lives. These results suggest that differences in context can have a powerful effect on performance. (See also Ceci & Roazzi, 1994; Nuñes, 1994; Saxe, 1990, for related work.)

Such differences are not limited to Brazilian street children. Lave (1988) showed that Berkeley housewives who successfully could do the mathematics needed for comparison-shopping in the supermarket were unable to do the same mathematics when they were placed in a classroom and given isomorphic problems presented in an abstract form. In other words, their problem was not at the level of mental processes but at the level of applying the processes in specific environmental contexts.

In sum, a variety of researchers have done studies that suggest that how one tests abilities, competencies, and expertise can have a major effect on how "intelligent" students appear to be. Street children in Brazil, for example, need the same mathematical skills to solve problems involving discounts as do children in the United States about to take a high-stakes paper-and-pencil test of mathematical achievement. But the contexts in which they express these skills, and hence the contexts in which they can best display their knowledge on tests, are different (as in Model III described above). We have also done research suggesting that cultural context needs to be taken into account in testing for intelligence and its outcomes.

The measurement of intelligence may be viewed as occurring on a continuum from abilities to competencies to expertise (Sternberg, 1999a, 2003b). All tests of intelligence, even ones once believed to be culture-free, such as tests of abstract reasoning, measure skills that are, at least in part, acquired through the covariance and interaction of genes with environment. For example, a test of vocabulary, found on intelligence tests, is clearly a test of achievement. But so is a test of abstract reasoning, as shown by the Flynn effect, by which abstract-reasoning skills showed substantial secular increases over the 20th century in diverse cultures around the world (Flynn, 1984, 1987). Hence, one can test knowledge as part of intelligence, but all tests of intelligence require knowledge, even if it is only in how to take the tests and maximize one's score on them.

Children May Develop Contextually Important Skills at the Expense of Academic Ones

Many times, investigations of intelligence conducted in settings outside the developed world can yield a picture of intelligence that is quite at variance with the picture one would obtain from studies conducted only in the developed world. In a study in Usenge, Kenya, near the town of Kisumu, investigators devised a test of practical intelligence to assess school-age children's ability to adapt to their indigenous environment (see Sternberg & Grigorenko, 1997a; Sternberg et al., 2001). The test of practical intelligence measured children's informal tacit knowledge of natural herbal medicines that the villagers believe can be used to fight various types of infections. Tacit knowledge is, roughly speaking, knowledge that one needs to know to succeed in an environment, that is usually not explicitly taught, and that often is not even verbalized (Sternberg et al., 2000). Children in the villages use their tacit knowledge of these medicines on average once a week in medicating themselves and others. More than 95% of the children suffer from parasitic illnesses. Thus, tests of how to use these medicines constitute effective measures of one aspect of practical intelligence as defined by the villagers as well as their life circumstances in their environmental contexts. Note that the processes of intelligence are not different in Kenya. Children must still recognize the existence of an illness, define what it is, devise a strategy to combat it, and so forth. But the content to which the processes are applied, and hence appropriate ways of testing these processes, may be quite different (as per Model III, described above).

Westerners might have trouble with assessments relevant to Kenyans, but the Westerners also might have difficulties with assessments relevant to life even fairly close to their homes. Middle-class Westerners might find it quite a challenge to thrive or even survive in these contexts, or, for that matter, in the contexts of urban ghettos often not distant from their comfortable homes. They would certainly not know how to use any of the natural herbal medicines to combat the diverse and abundant parasitic illnesses they might acquire in rural Kenya.

The investigators measured the Kenyan children's ability to identify the medicines, where they come from, what they are used for, and how they are dosed. They also administered to the children of the study the Raven Colored Progressive Matrices Test (Raven, Court, & Raven, 1992), which is a measure of fluid or abstract-reasoning-based abilities, as well as the Mill Hill Vocabulary Scale (Raven et al., 1992), which is a measure of crystallized or formal-knowledge-based abilities. In addition, they gave the children a comparable test of vocabulary in their own Dholuo language. The Dholuo language is spoken in the home, English in the schools.

All correlations between the test of indigenous tacit knowledge and scores on fluid-ability and crystallized-ability tests were *negative*. The correlations with the tests of crystallized abilities were significantly so. In other words, the higher the children scored on the test of tacit knowledge, the lower they scored, on average, on the tests of crystallized abilities (vocabulary).

This surprising result can be interpreted in various ways, but based on the ethnographic observations of the anthropologists on the team, Prince and Geissler (see Prince & Geissler, 2001), the researchers concluded that a plausible scenario takes into account the expectations of families for their children. Many children drop out of school before graduation, for financial or other reasons, and many families in the village do not see the advantages of formal Western schooling. There is no reason they should, as the children of many families will for the most part spend their lives farming or engaged in other occupations that make little or no use of Western schooling. These families emphasize teaching their children the indigenous informal knowledge that will lead to their successful adaptation in the environments in which they will really live. Children who spend their time learning the indigenous practical knowledge of the community may not always invest themselves heavily in doing well in school, whereas children who do well in school generally may invest themselves less heavily in learning the indigenous knowledge – hence the negative correlations.

The Kenya study suggests that the identification of a general factor of human intelligence may tell us more about how abilities interact with cultural patterns of schooling and society and especially Western patterns of schooling and society than it does about the structure of human abilities. In Western schooling, children typically study a variety of subject matters from an early age and thus develop skills in a variety of skill areas. This kind of schooling prepares the children to take a test of intelligence, which typically measures skills in a variety of areas. Often intelligence tests measure skills that children were expected to acquire a few years before taking the intelligence test. But as Rogoff (1990, 2003) and others have noted, this pattern of schooling is not universal and has not even been common for much of the history of humankind. Throughout history and in many places still, schooling, especially for boys, takes the form of apprenticeships in which children learn a craft from an early age. They learn what they will need to know to succeed in a trade, but not a lot more. They are not simultaneously engaged in tasks that require the development of the particular blend of skills measured by conventional intelligence tests. Hence it is less likely that one would observe a general factor in their scores, much as was discovered in Kenya.

What does a general factor mean anyway? Some years back, Vernon (1971) pointed out that the axes of a factor analysis do not necessarily reveal a latent structure of the mind but rather represent a convenient way of characterizing the organization of mental abilities. Vernon believed that there was no one "right" orientation of axes, and indeed, mathematically, an infinite number of orientations of axes can be fit to any solution in an exploratory factor analysis. Vernon's point seems perhaps to have been forgotten or at least ignored by later theorists.

Just as it is argued here that the so-called *g* factor may partly reflect human interactions with cultural patterns, so has Tomasello (2001) argued that so-called modularity of mind may reflect, in part, human interactions with cultural patterns. This is not to dismiss the importance of biology. Rather, it is to emphasize its importance as it interacts with culture, rather than simply viewing it as some kind of immutable effect that operates independently and outside of a cultural context.

The partial context-specificity of intellectual performance does not apply only to countries far removed from North America or Europe. One can find the same on these continents, as was done in the studies of Yup'ik Eskimo children in southwestern Alaska.

Children May Have Substantial Practical Skills That Go Unrecognized in Academic Tests

Related although certainly not identical results appear in a study done among Yup'ik Eskimo children in southwestern Alaska (Grigorenko, Meier, Lipka, Mohatt, Yanez, & Sternberg, 2004). The investigators assessed the importance of academic and practical intelligence in rural and semi-urban Alaskan communities. They measured academic intelligence with conventional measures of fluid (the Cattell Culture Fair Test of *g*) and crystallized intelligence (the Mill-Hill Vocabulary Scale). They measured practical intelligence with a test of tacit knowledge of skills (hunting, fishing, dealing with weather conditions, picking and preserving plants, and so on) as acquired in rural Alaskan Yup'ik communities (the Yup'ik Scale of Practical Intelligence, YSPI). The semi-urban children statistically significantly outperformed the rural children on the measure of crystallized intelligence, but the rural children statistically significantly outperformed the semi-urban children on the measure of the YSPI. The test of tacit knowledge skills was superior to the tests of academic intelligence in predicting practical skills as evaluated by adults and peers of the rural children (for whom the test was created), but not of the semi-urban ones. This study, like the Kenya study, suggests the importance of practical intellectual skills for predicting adaptation to everyday environments. Can one find similar results in cultures that are urban and somewhat less remote from the kinds of cultures familiar to many readers?

Practical Intellectual Skills May Be Better Predictors of Health Than Academic Ones

In a study in Russia (Grigorenko & Sternberg, 2001a), entirely distinct measures of analytical, creative, and practical intelligence, with at least two summative indicators for each construct, were administered to participants. Principal-component analysis, with both varimax and oblimin rotations, yielded clear-cut analytical, creative, and practical factors for the tests.

The main objective of this study was to predict, using the analytical, creative, and practical tests, mental and physical health among the

Russian adults. Mental health was measured by widely used paper-and-pencil tests of depression and anxiety, and physical health was measured by self-report. The best predictor of mental and physical health was the practical-intelligence measure for mental and physical health. (Or, because the data are correlational, it may be that health predicts practical intelligence, although the connection here is less clear). Analytical intelligence came second and creative intelligence came third. All three contributed to prediction, however.

The results in Russia emphasized the importance of studying health-related outcomes as one measure of successful adaptation to the environment. Health-related variables can affect one's ability to achieve one's goals in life, or even to perform well on tests, as was found in Jamaica.

Physical Health May Moderate Performance on Assessments

In interpreting results, whether from developed or developing cultures, it is always important to take into account the physical health of the participants one is testing. In a study in Jamaica (Sternberg, Powell, McGrane, & McGregor, 1997), the investigators found that Jamaican schoolchildren who suffered from parasitic illnesses (for the most part, whipworm or Ascaris) did more poorly on higher level cognitive tests (such as of working memory and reasoning) than did children who did not suffer from these illnesses, even after controlling for socioeconomic status. The children with parasitic illnesses did better on fine-motor tasks, for reasons unknown to us. Anti-parasitic medications failed to improve their cognitive functioning as measured by conventional ability tests.

Thus, many children were poor achievers not because they lacked innate abilities but because they lacked the good health necessary to develop and display such abilities. If you are moderately to seriously ill, you probably find it more difficult to concentrate on what you read or what you hear than if you are well. Children in developing countries are ill much, and even most, of the time. They simply cannot devote the same attentional and learning resources to schoolwork that well children have to devote. Here, as in Kenya, their health knowledge would be crucial for their adaptation to the environment (although our group did not explicitly test the Jamaicans for their health knowledge). Testing that does not take into account health status is likely to give false impressions.

Do conventional tests, such as of working memory or of reasoning, measure all the skills that children in developing countries can bring to the table? Work done in Tanzania suggests they do not.

Dynamic Testing May Reveal Cognitive Skills Not Revealed by Static Testing

A study done in Tanzania (see Sternberg & Grigorenko, 1997a, 2002a; Sternberg et al., 2002) points out the risks of giving tests, scoring them, and interpreting the results as measures of some latent intellectual ability or abilities. Schoolchildren between the ages of 11 and 13 years near Bagamoyo, Tanzania, were given tests including a form-board classification test (a sorting task), a linear syllogisms test, and a Twenty Questions Test ("Find a Figure"), which measure the kinds of skills required on conventional tests of intelligence. Of course, the investigators obtained scores that they could analyze and evaluate, ranking the children in terms of their supposed general or other abilities. However, they administered the tests dynamically rather than statically (Brown & Ferrara, 1985; Feuerstein, 1979; Grigorenko & Sternberg, 1998; Guthke, 1993; Haywood & Tzuriel, 1992; Lidz, 1991; Sternberg & Grigorenko, 2002a; Tzuriel, 1995; Vygotsky, 1978).

Dynamic testing is like conventional static testing in that individuals are tested and inferences are made about their abilities. But dynamic tests differ in that children are given some kind of feedback to help them improve their performance. Vygotsky (1978) suggested that the children's ability to profit from the guided instruction they received during the testing session could serve as a measure of children's zone of proximal development (ZPD), or the difference between their developed abilities and their latent capacities. In other words, testing and instruction are treated as being of one piece rather than as being distinct processes. This integration makes sense in terms of traditional definitions of intelligence as the ability to learn ("Intelligence and Its Measurement," 1921; Sternberg & Detterman, 1986). What a dynamic test does is directly measure processes of learning in the context of testing rather than measuring these processes indirectly as the product of past learning. Such measurement is especially important when not all children have had equal opportunities to learn in the past.

In the dynamic assessments in Tanzania, children were first given the ability tests. Experimental-group children were then given an intervention. Control-group children were not. The intervention consisted of a brief period of instruction in which children were able to learn skills that would potentially enable them to improve their scores. For example, in the Twenty Questions tasks, children would be taught how a single true-false question could cut the space of possible correct solutions by half. Then all children – experimental and control – were tested again. Because the total time for instruction was less than an hour, one would not expect dramatic gains. Yet, on average, the gains from pretest to posttest in the experimental group were statistically significant and significantly greater than those in the control group.

In the control group, the correlations between pretest and posttest scores were generally high. One would expect a high correlation because there was no intervention and hence the retesting was largely a measure of alternate-forms reliability. More important, scores on the pretest in the experimental group showed only weak although significant correlations with scores on the posttest. These correlations, which were significantly and substantially less than those in the control group, suggested that when tests are administered statically to children in developing countries, the correlations may be rather unstable and easily subject to influences of training. The reason could be that the children are not accustomed to taking Western-style tests, and so they profit quickly from even small amounts of instruction as to what is expected from them.

Of course, the more important question is not whether the scores changed or even correlated with each other, but rather, how they correlated with other cognitive measures. In other words, which test was a better predictor of transfer to other cognitive performances on tests of working memory: the pretest score or the posttest score? The investigators found the posttest score to be the better predictor of working memory in the experimental group. Children in the dynamic-testing group improved significantly more than those in the control group (who did not receive intervening dynamic instruction between pre- and posttests).

In the Jamaica study, described earlier, the investigators had failed to find effects of an antiparasitic medication, albendazole, on cognitive functioning. Might this have been because the testing was static rather than dynamic? Static testing tends to emphasize skills developed in the past. Children who suffer from parasitic illnesses often feel too ill to profit from instruction and acquire skills that well children do. Dynamic testing emphasizes skills developed at the time of test. Indeed, the skills or knowledge are specifically taught at the time of test. Would dynamic testing show effects of medication (in this case, albendazole for hookworm and praziquantel for schistosomiasis) not shown by static testing?

The answer was yes. Over time, treated children showed an advantage over children who did not receive treatment, and were closer after time had passed to the control (uninfected) group than were the untreated children. In other words, conventional static tests of intelligence may fail fully to reveal children's intellectual potentials. Thus, when tests are modified in different environments, as per Model III, one may wish to modify not only their content, but the form in which they are administered, as was done in the dynamic testing.

CULTURE-FAIR AND CULTURE-RELEVANT TESTING

A culture-fair test is equally appropriate for members of all cultures and comprises items that are equally fair to everyone. Believers in culture-fair tests generally follow Model I, described earlier, for the relation between culture and intelligence. This approach is illustrated by Zeidner, Matthews, and Roberts (2004), who state:

> As in other multicultural nations [besides Israel], research has been directed toward sociocultural differences in test scores. Because the tests are translated from English, any comparison of groups rests on the assumption that test adaptation is "culture-fair." ... The basic principal [*sic*] guiding the development of all major Hebrew standardized test versions was to stay as close to the English original as possible, unless items lacked compatibility with Israeli culture or the psychometric attributes of the items in the Israeli samples needed upgrading. (p. 220)

In this approach, minor adaptations are made. For example, Israel uses a different calendar (the Jewish one) from the one used in the United States, and hence an adaptation was made for the proper year and time references. But these differences are quite minor.

Researchers compared the performance of Jewish examinees of Western and Eastern (Asian/African) backgrounds and found that on the Wechsler Preschool and Primary Scale of Intelligence and Wechsler Intelligence Scale for Children, the children of Western origins outperformed the children of Eastern origins. The difference tended to increase with age (Lieblich, 1983; Minkowitch, Davis, & Bashi, 1982; Zeidner, 1985). Ethnic group had a larger effect than socioeconomic group, although both mattered.

Comparisons of Israeli Jewish children with Israeli Arab children showed an advantage for the Jewish children of approximately one standard deviation (Kugelmass & Lieblich, 1975; Kugelmass, Lieblich, & Bossi, 1974; Lieblich, 1983; Lieblich & Kugelmass, 1981). Christian Arab children tend to outscore Muslim and Druze students on Raven's Matrices (Bashi, 1976). Differences tend to be larger on nonverbal than on verbal tests.

Similar results have been shown elsewhere. Savasir and Sahin (1995) found that Turkish children score about 12 points lower on the WISC-R than do American children. On the Gesell Developmental Schedules, Cantez and Girgin (1992) found Turkish children generally lagging behind in the norms created for American children. In general, children in the educational systems in rural Turkey, which are less Westernized, produce scores on translated Western intelligence and educational tests that are lower than those of students in the educational systems in urbanized Turkey, which are closer to the Western systems (Kagitcibasi, 1996; Kagitcibasi, Sunar, & Bekman, 2001).

The etic approach is at least somewhat open to question. Because members of different cultures define intelligence differently, the very behaviors that may be considered intelligent in one culture may be viewed as unintelligent in another, as discussed earlier in this chapter. Consider the concept of mental quickness, generally considered in mainstream U.S. culture as a sign of intelligence. Indeed, most group tests of intelligence are strictly timed. We have found this out the hard way when we have failed to answer all the items on some of them.

Performance on tests that have been labeled "culture fair" seems to be influenced by cultural factors. Examples are years of schooling and academic achievements (e.g., Ceci, 1996). In sum, one must be careful when drawing conclusions about group differences in intelligence (Greenfield, 1997; Loehlin, 2000). The conclusions may appear to be justified on the surface but represent only a superficial analysis of group differences.

In the proposed model of culture and intelligence, Model III, tests are adapted in form and content to take into account the differences in adaptive tasks that individuals confront in diverse cultures, within and across countries. Individuals in other cultures often do not do well on our tests, nor would we do well on theirs. The processes of intelligence are universal, but their manifestations are not. If investigators want best to understand, assess, and develop intelligence, they need to take into account the cultural contexts in which it operates. We cannot now create culture-free or culture-fair tests, given our present state of knowledge. But we can create *culture-relevant tests*, and that should be our goal. Culture-relevant tests require skills and knowledge that are relevant to the cultural experiences of the test-takers. The content and procedures are appropriate to the cultural norms of the test-takers.

CONCLUSION

When cultural context is taken into account, (a) individuals are better recognized for and are better able to make use of their talents, (b) schools teach and assess children better, and (c) society utilizes rather than wastes the talents of its members. Giftedness is viewed differently in different cultures, and the behaviors that are needed to excel also differ from one culture to the next. We can pretend to measure intelligence and to identify the gifted across cultures simply by translating Western tests and giving them to individuals in a variety of cultures. But such measurement is only pretense. We need to be careful even when we try to measure the intelligence of various cultural groups *within* a society.

What counts as gifted varies widely across cultures. Although theories of intelligence can be presented as cross-cultural constructs, people's implicit theories, as well as the behavior that is adaptive, vary widely. So we are best off considering giftedness as something whose nature can vary from one place to another. The fundamental skills may be the same – ability to recognize and define problems, ability to develop strategies and represent information, and so forth – but how they are manifested can differ drastically from one culture to the next, along the lines of Model III discussed earlier in the chapter.

9

Learning Disabilities, Giftedness, and Gifted/LD

Ellen is a superb musician but has trouble reading the newspaper. Mario can read the newspaper easily, but has difficulties with even the simplest mathematical problems. Ernest, a marvelous poet, can read and do mathematical computation problems, but he has great difficulty with mathematical reasoning problems. These hypothetical individuals are gifted and yet have a learning disability (LD). To understand the nature of such individuals, sometimes referred to as being "Gifted-LD," one must understand both the nature of giftedness and the nature of learning disabilities separately, and then in combination (see Newman & Sternberg, 2004).

Various theories characterize gifted children in different ways (Sternberg & Davidson, 1986, 2005). We view giftedness and learning disabilities in terms of excellence in various forms of developing competencies and, ultimately, expertise (Sternberg, 2001a).

The model of developing expertise, described in Chapter 7, has five key elements (although certainly they do not constitute an exhaustive list of elements in the development of expertise): metacognitive skills, learning skills, thinking skills, knowledge, and motivation. Gifted individuals excel in the development of expertise in some combination of these elements, and, at high levels of giftedness, in all of them. Although it is convenient to separate these five elements, they are fully interactive. They influence each other, both directly and indirectly. For example, learning leads to knowledge, but knowledge facilitates further learning.

These elements are, to a large extent, domain specific. The development of expertise in one area does not necessarily lead to the development of expertise in another area, although there may be some transfer, depending upon the relationship of the areas, a point that has been made with regard to intelligence by others as well (e.g., Gardner, 1983, 1999a, 2000; Sternberg, 1997a, 1999c).

In terms of the model of developing expertise presented earlier, gifted individuals excel in metacognitive skills (Borkowski & Peck, 1986; Jackson & Butterfield, 1986; Shore, 2000). Gifted-LD students tend to be high in general metacognitive processes. Gifted-LD students tend to excel in the use of learning skills in many domains but have one or more domains in which they exhibit a clear weakness. Gifted-LD students further have strong general thinking skills but often have difficulties in applying them to their domain of weakness because they have not learned well in this domain. One needs to have learned about an area in order to think about it well. Gifted-LD children tend to have a strong knowledge base, except in their area or areas of weakness because their reduced learning skills in that area have reduced their chances of acquiring knowledge in that area. Gifted-LD children tend, on average, to be highly motivated. But they may be only poorly motivated in their area of weakness because it is the one thing, or one of the few things, that frustrates them. When they can do so many things well, why dwell on what they do poorly? They may also find ways of compensating for their weakness so that they can get by without correcting the weakness, a strategy that may cost them in later life if they then need the skill for which they have compensated.

Ultimately, the label of *gifted-LD* is highly contextually determined; it depends on the society in which the individual lives and what that society considers to be appropriate domains both for gifts and for learning disabilities.

UNDERSTANDING GIFTEDNESS, LEARNING DISABILITIES, AND GIFTED-LD IN TERMS OF THE MODEL OF GIFTEDNESS AS DEVELOPING EXPERTISE

Gifted individuals excel in the elements of the model of developing expertise. They may not be outstanding in all elements – although some are – but they excel in at least some combination, in some way that allows them to produce exceptional work.

Individuals with learning disabilities fall short, at least relatively speaking, in at least one element of the model. Their learning skills in one domain are likely to be impaired, with the result that their achievement suffers in that domain as well. Their gifts may actually, in some ways, put them at a disadvantage because they may be able to use these gifts to mask their learning disability. For example, someone who performs poorly in the spatial domain may nevertheless get by through solving spatial problems verbally, to the extent he or she can.

Our views of giftedness and learning disabilities diverge somewhat from the standard views. Consider each in turn.

The situation with learning disabilities is complex. Although specific learning disabilities can be and have been defined in a number of different ways, a consensus view has emerged that is based loosely on the point of view represented in the *Diagnostic and Statistical Manual* (4th ed., 1995) of the American Psychiatric Association. According to this consensus view, learning disabilities are marked impairments in the development of specific skills, such as reading skills, mathematical skills, or writing skills, relative to the level of skills expected on the basis of an individual's education and intelligence. These impairments interfere with daily life and academic achievement. However, they are not due to physical deficits, such as visual or hearing deficits, or acquired neurological conditions such as those caused by brain trauma. Learning disabilities seldom can be diagnosed before the end of kindergarten or the beginning of first grade.

We view learning disabilities in a way that goes beyond this kind of standard definition. The thesis of this chapter is that *virtually everyone has a learning disability in something but society chooses to recognize only some individuals as having an LD. Whether someone is labeled as having a learning disability in many respects resembles the result of a lottery* (Sternberg & Grigorenko, 1999b). This means that many gifted students have some kind of "LD."

Many theorists of abilities agree that abilities are multiple – that there are many of them (see Sternberg, 2000b), although they may be correlated. These theorists may disagree as to exactly what the abilities are or how they are structured, but they agree that the abilities are distinguishable from each other. For example, the skills that constitute reading ability are different from the skills that constitute artistic ability, which are in turn different from the skills that constitute musical ability. Thus, someone could be an able reader but a poor musician, or vice versa.

If one were to make a list of the many abilities people can have, one would find that virtually no one is proficient in all the skills constituting all of these abilities, and virtually no one is hopelessly inept in all these skills. Rather, almost everyone is more proficient in some skills and less proficient in others. Some people may be proficient in more skills, or more proficient in particular skills, but virtually everyone shows a pattern of multiple strengths and multiple weaknesses.

Put another way, virtually everyone shows a complex pattern of abilities and disabilities. For example, even the straight-A student in school may be inept in certain aspects of interpersonal relations. Even the straight-F student in school may be able in many aspects of dealing with other people. This intuition is captured in modern theories of intelligence, which argue on the basis of plentiful and diverse data that interpersonal and practical skills actually are distinct from traditional academic skills (Gardner, 1999b; Sternberg, 1999c, 2003d). High and even gifted levels of these different kinds of skill may or may not be found in the same persons.

Given that everyone has a pattern of abilities and disabilities, how does it happen that some people get labeled as gifted learners or as having learning disabilities whereas other people do not? The reason is that learning abilities and disabilities reside neither totally in the individual nor totally in the society. *Labeling someone as being gifted or as having a learning disability is the result of an interaction between the individual and the society.* Labeling is a function of societal context.

How does the society make this selection? It selects on the basis of the set of skills that it values in school and on the job. If the society views a certain set of skills (such as reading skills) as essential, and as constituting a "specific" rather than a general ability, then individuals with low levels of proficiency in these skills are labeled as having a specific disability. People with high levels of proficiency are labeled as gifted, often regardless of whether the abilities are general or specific. One has a set of abilities and disabilities and metaphorically enters a lottery that determines whether the particular pattern will result in a label of *giftedness* or *learning disability*. We are not saying that the labeling process is arbitrary. Rather, we are saying that there are many different possible labeling processes that can yield totally different results.

U.S. society currently defines seven areas of learning disabilities: (a) listening, (b) speaking, (c) basic reading skills, (d) reading comprehension skills, (e) written expression, (f) arithmetic calculation skills, and (g) mathematics reasoning skills. These disabilities are viewed as specific. But in fact, there are no completely general abilities or disabilities. For example, IQ tests are sometimes seen as measuring "general ability," but in fact, a high score on an IQ test is no guarantee of a high level of creative ability, practical (commonsense) ability, athletic ability, musical ability, or any of a number of other abilities. So all abilities and disabilities are specific in greater or lesser degree. In the United States, the society invests much less in the gifted than it does in the learning disabled, and it does not have a corresponding societal (i.e., federally legislated) definition of giftedness. The most frequently used bases for assessing giftedness, at least in schoolchildren, are IQ and school achievement. Someone who has societally recognized gifts and who also has recognized deficits may be labeled as Gifted-LD.

Where and when an individual is born has a tremendous impact on whether that individual will be labeled as being gifted, as having a learning disability, or as Gifted-LD. In a preliterate society, for example, there are no individuals labeled as having a reading disability. There are no gifted readers either. One society might label someone with minimal musical skills as having a musical disability, whereas another society might not, just as whether musical precocity counts as a gift depends on whether the society values music. In effect, each individual becomes a mandatory participant in a lottery that determines whether the particular pattern of abilities and disabilities he or she has will lead to the individual's being labeled as having a learning disability. But the lottery applies only to the labeling process. Everyone has a pattern of both abilities and disabilities. The lottery represents how society chooses to label that pattern.

STRENGTHS OF GIFTED STUDENTS WITH LEARNING DISABILITIES

Given that all individuals have both strengths and weaknesses, individuals labeled as having learning disabilities have many strengths to offer society. Individuals who are labeled as gifted also have strengths but may also have weaknesses. Our society often inadvertently positions individuals with LDs to view themselves as potential victims rather than as potential victors, and does the reverse for the gifted. In this regard, we have three main contentions:

1. Individuals with specific learning disabilities often have considerable strengths in other abilities. Individuals with gifts often have weaknesses that need to be dealt with rather than ignored.
2. All these individuals should be encouraged to be successful in capitalizing on strengths and compensating for or correcting weaknesses.
3. Modifications of curriculum that excuse individuals with LDs from learning important skills or from the normal experiences of schooling may be well intentioned, but they often (but certainly not always) end up hurting these individuals more than helping them. The reason is that for the society to have labeled the individuals as having a learning disability in the first place, the ability for which they were labeled as lacking (i.e., as having a disability) must be one that the society views as important for adaptive living in that society. Modifications of curriculum that leave gifted children *only* to capitalize on strengths, without addressing weaknesses (such as specialized schools for young children) also are nonoptimal. For example, overlooking the social weaknesses of students gifted in academic areas may seem defensible when the children are in school but will prepare them poorly for life.

DOING BETTER

We challenge a system that, in meaning to do well, is often doing the opposite. We believe that society can do better, and that science can play a role. Here are some crucial points toward doing better.

1. The "LD" and "giftedness" labels can be and often are misunderstood.

Virtually everyone has a learning disability of some kind. Many people have gifts of one kind or another. What differs is whether the society chooses to label that way or those ways as recognized "gifts" or "learning disabilities." For example, U.S. society labels certain poor readers as having a learning disability but does not label certain people who are poor in shooting a bow and arrow as having a learning disability. Similarly, in today's developed world, an expert archer would be labeled as gifted only by a narrow segment of the population. Another society might choose the opposite path, labeling only the poor archers (who are unable to feed themselves or their families) as having a learning disability and the gifted archers as very valuable because of their superior hunting skills.

2. The "LD" label can be costly both to the individual and to society.

Once children are labeled as LD, a complex set of mechanisms is put into effect that renders it likely that the label will become a self-fulfilling prophecy, whether it was originally correct or not. A well-intentioned labeling procedure thus can become harmful to our young people.

3. Genuine LD and giftedness arise through interactions between the individual and the environment.

Certain biological predispositions can render an individual susceptible to the development of specific kinds of learning disabilities or gifts. These biological predispositions do not determine whether the individual will actually have a learning disability or gift. For example, as we mentioned, in a preliterate society, no one manifests reading disabilities or precocious reading. Even among literate societies, some orthographic (writing) systems impose challenges that others do not impose, challenges that affect the probability of individuals manifesting reading disabilities or reading gifts. For instance, Spanish is pronounced exactly the same way it is written; English is not. Chinese uses a logographic (picture-based) writing system whereas Indo-European languages such as English, French, German, and Russian use alphabetic writing systems. Whether a child will have a reading disability or excel in reading will be affected not only by that child's biological makeup but also by where and when the child grows up.

4. Biological does NOT imply immutable.

Even to the extent that the origins of learning disabilities are biological, these biological origins have nothing at all to do with whether the symptoms of learning disabilities are modifiable. Put another way, the partially biological origins of learning disabilities in no way preclude successful educational interventions. Contrary to a popular misconception, "biological" is not synonymous with "fixed."

5. Pedagogical programs for Gifted-LD students should enhance their strengths and help them compensate for their weaknesses.

This statement appears to be rather obvious, but it is not universally accepted. In fact, currently, multiple types of Gifted-LD programs can be classified into three groups. First, some are designed to address specific weaknesses these students possess. Second, other programs address areas of weakness but are primarily designed to develop areas of strength through enrichment activities. Finally, a number of programs are designed to develop areas of strength while remediating weaknesses. We argue that it is the programs of this last type that are needed for working with children with both gifts and disabilities. We have developed such a program for elementary school children. The program, *The Leonardo Laboratory*, is designed for children with coexisting learning disabilities and spatial gifts. Although not formally evaluated yet, it has shown some promising initial results (Newman et al., 2009).

The remedies used to improve performance of individuals with learning disabilities always should depend on the specific deficits that individual people experience, not on how these people are labeled. Similarly, instruction for gifted children should reflect the kinds of gifts they have. Lumping together all of the labeled children into one global category such as "LD" or "gifted," and then giving them what usually amounts to a single form of remediation or enrichment, may harm more students than it helps.

To sum up, the labels produce many effects. But we need to remember that the label is only a label. Everyone has learning abilities and disabilities. The label is not only about whether people have unusual abilities or disabilities, but about whether the disabilities they have are ones the society chooses, for reasons of its own, to label as such. Whether one is labeled is the result of a lottery into which one is automatically entered, like it or not.

In the recent past, more and more children have been labeled every successive year as having a learning disability. Although there are many motivations to label children as having a learning disability, it is important to remember that the LD label in the United States means different things to different populations. For children of parents who are of high socioeconomic status, the label can provide a means to maintain for the children the benefits of the society that the parents have enjoyed. To such parents, the thought that their children may be downwardly mobile, for whatever reason, may be distressing.

For children of parents of low socioeconomic status, the LD label also may help to ensure that the children stay where they are. Ironically, when these children are identified, they too may end up being assured a stable socioeconomic environment for the rest of their lives. What happens to these children is that they, too, often get special attention, but it often comes in the form of a warehousing phenomenon where the children are given ineffective educational gruel labeled as "interventions." These interventions sometimes ensure only that the children will fall further and further behind.

For children with rich parents, a label of giftedness accelerates the benefits they may have gotten anyway, or enhances their already existing advantages. For children with poor parents, a label of giftedness may be one of the few ways of saving the child from an inferior education or placement in unchallenging classes that will serve the child poorly.

There has been an increase in the labeling of children in a positive way, but it is more subtle than the increase in the labeling of children with LDs. It has occurred in several ways. First is grade inflation. Once a C was a respectable grade. It is no longer. Today there are not very many students who are not A or B students. A second way is in letters of recommendation, which educators find to be highly inflated and, as a result, difficult to interpret. Third, the recentering of SAT scores (to reposition the means at 500) has even raised SAT scores, which previously had been declining. Finally, people are afraid to label anyone as "below average." Garrison Keillor suggested that the Lake Wobegon norm is for everyone to be above the 50th percentile. In our society, we actively seek to realize this impossible dream.

The Gifted-LD label is, in some ways, a potentially risky one. We believe that it is often appropriate. But it may be misused. It could become a way for affluent parents to get the best of both worlds – to have their child labeled as gifted, which is advantageous in our society, and labeled as having an LD as well, which has also come to be advantageous. We think that this "game" is not at the present time being widely played. That could change as parents and those who do assessments realize that the label is not strange, that it is not pejorative, and that it may benefit children in their school careers. The solution is to have a clear notion of what gifted-LD is, and apply it assiduously. In this chapter, we have proposed such a notion based on the model of abilities as developing into competencies, and competencies, into expertise.

10

Identifying the Gifted

How are the gifted identified? In Chapter 1 we presented the pentagonal theory for identifying the gifted (Sternberg & Zhang, 1995). In this chapter we will review the methods most frequently used in the United States. There are many different techniques, but one of the most widespread is through the use of standardized tests. We will then present in some detail three studies in which we used alternate methods of assessment.

STANDARDIZED TESTS

A standardized test is a test given to many individuals, often across the nation, to develop appropriate content and scoring comparisons. It is administered and scored according to uniform procedures. Uniform, or standardized procedures are the key to the definition of a standardized test. Constructors of these tests try to assure that every student taking the test has a similar experience. Standardized tests are usually purchased from test publishers. They sell the tests only to those qualified to use them. Not all tests purchased from publishers are standardized. For example, textbook publishers often offer banks of test questions. The publisher, in this case, does not try to standardize the experience of every student who is tested. Teacher-made tests are not standardized. Instead, they are created by, or for, individual teachers who use them on only a limited number of students. Each teacher scores the tests he or she creates in an individual way. Ideally, all tests of achievement should be closely tied to the learning that students have done (Dochy & McDowell, 1997). This is important, in part, because the way you test can affect the way students decide to learn (Airasian, 1997).

Standardized tests are of two types: norm referenced and criterion referenced. Norm-referenced tests compare each test-taker's scores with the performance of all the test-takers (Haynes & O'Brien, 2000). Remember that standardized tests are given to large numbers of students to establish standards for scoring and content. Giving a test to many students allows test developers to develop norms, or normative scores, test scores that reflect the performance of individuals in the population of interest. Typically, students, teachers, administrators, and parents are interested in finding out how test scores in their school compare with the national norms for the test. Norms are often based on national samples. But they do not have to be. Sometimes, they are based on scores across a state (as in a statewide mastery test), across a school district, or even a classroom. It is important to know who constituted the normative sample.

Criterion-referenced tests measure a student's performance relative to what the student should know rather than to the performance of other students (Haynes & O'Brien, 2000). In an arithmetic test on fractions, for example, it is helpful for a teacher to know how well a student has done in comparison to others. But it is also important to know exactly which operations the child does and does not understand. Criterion-referenced tests are developed differently from norm-referenced tests. The goal is not simply to be able to compare students' scores to each other. Instead, emphasis is placed on being able to compare students' understanding of the knowledge required by a given curriculum. Publishers of some tests provide both normative and criterion-based information as part of their score reports.

Tests used to identify the gifted are typically norm referenced rather than criterion referenced. The goal is to place students in some kind of rank order so that a prespecified percentage of them can be labeled as gifted. Ironically, it is the criterion-referenced test that is, in the long run, more useful educationally, because it is this kind of test that better indicates to the test user what the student does and does not know or what the student can and cannot do. An alternative to conventional current means of identifying the gifted would be to identify in terms of knowledge or skills that typical students have, and the more advanced or sophisticated knowledge and skills that gifted students have. In this way, one would get away from identifying arbitrary percentages and tie identification to the knowledge and skills that matter.

There is also a difference between maximal-performance and typical-performance tests. Maximal-performance tests measure the very best you can perform under optimal circumstances. Typical-performance tests measure how well you perform under ordinary, everyday circumstances. Most of the standardized tests students take in school are designed to elicit maximal performance. To do well, students typically have to work as quickly and as hard as they can. Only in this way can they finish some fairly difficult problems within a limited time period. In other words, they have to work their fastest and be at their best. For example, students might be asked to do a difficult arithmetic problem or to read a passage. Then they would answer challenging questions on the material in the passage.

Many factors can prevent a student from giving a maximal performance. Several factors might lead a student who wants to give a maximal performance not to be able to do so. For example, a student might have a cold or be distracted in the testing room. Some students simply may not be interested in performing at their maximal level. Perhaps they do not regard the test as important or as worthy of their attention.

People's maximal performance is not necessarily a good predictor of their typical performance, and vice versa. Some students perform phenomenally well when they set their minds to doing well. On ordinary school tasks, such as homework, however, these same students might not put in much effort and not do well. Other students might not do well on maximal-performance tests. Yet they may give each task in school their all. As a result, their performance may actually be better on a day-to-day basis than that of the student who excelled in the maximal-performance test.

A reasonable question to ask is whether gifted identification should depend, as it usually does, on maximal-performance tests or whether it should depend as well on typical-performance tests. The risk of typical-performance tests is that they are easier to fake. The advantage is that they may give a better indication of how students function in more typical situations. Students are not always performing at their maximal level of performance. Indeed, they perform at such maximal levels only a small percentage of the time. So supplementing maximal-performance with typical-performance measures provides a better way to simulate how people function in their everyday lives.

Types of Standardized Tests

Examples of standardized tests are reading tests, math tests, general ability tests, general achievement tests, and even occupational-preference tests. It is important that a particular standardized test be the most appropriate test for the purpose for which it is being used. For example, a test of reading comprehension may not be the most appropriate test for helping some high school students determine their career direction. Consider the major types of tests so you will know what standardized tests you can use to assess students in a range of situations and for a range of purposes.

Tests of Intelligence

Conventional tests of intelligence were first developed by Frenchman Alfred Binet in the early 1900s to distinguish children who needed special education from those who were simply having behavior problems in school (for more on Binet, see Jarvin & Sternberg, 2002). Binet's test was very successful in making this distinction. A version of the test is still in use, along with many other intelligence tests.

Today, there are two basic types of intelligence tests: individual tests and group tests (Gregory, 2000). Like Binet's original test, intelligence tests are used as diagnostic tools to help determine whether children should receive special education. They can also be used as predictive tools, to suggest how students are likely to perform in school.

INDIVIDUAL TESTS. The Stanford-Binet Intelligence Scales (DiStefano & Dombrowski, 2006; Roid, 2003) are the modern version of Alfred Binet's original intelligence test (Binet & Simon, 1905, 1916). These scales can be used for children as young as 2 years up to adults of 90 and over to measure intelligence according to Binet's conception. The test, consisting of 10 subtests, is given individually and must be administered by a trained psychologist. In its current version, it offers an overall IQ score, verbal and nonverbal IQs, plus five factor scores: Fluid Reasoning, Knowledge, Quantitative Reasoning, Visual-Spatial Processing, and Working Memory. Each factor is measured by both verbal and nonverbal subtests.

A similar set of tests prepared by David Wechsler is also used (see Matarazzo, 1992; Wechsler, 1939, 1974/1991, 1967/2002, 2003). Rather than developing a single, multiaged scale, Wechsler used different but related scales for different age ranges. These scales, with different names at different levels, are the Wechsler Adult Intelligence Scale (WAIS-IV), the Wechsler Intelligence Scale for Children (WISC-IV), and the Wechsler Preschool and Primary Scale of Intelligence (WPPSI-III). The Wechsler scales yield an overall score, as well as separate verbal and performance scores.

Other kinds of individual intelligence tests are used as well (Kaufman, 2000), such as the second edition of Kaufman and Kaufman's (2004; Kaufman, Lichtenberger, Fletcher-Janzen, & Kaufman, 2005) Kaufman Assessment Battery for Children (K-ABC II), which is loosely based on a biological theory of intelligence (Luria, 1966). The Kaufman Brief Intelligence Test (K-BIT) is a short intelligence test that aims to measure intelligence with an abbreviated scale. Another test, the Differential Abilities Scales, provides a large number of subtests as options, from which the examiner decides which tests to administer. An innovative kind of individual intelligence test is Reuven Feuerstein's (1979) Learning Potential Assessment Device, or LPAD. This test measures not children's developed potential but rather their zone of proximal development (Vygotsky, 1978) – that is, the difference between their underlying capacity and their developed ability, as measured by their ability to profit from guided instruction.

GROUP TESTS. It is sometimes not practical to test each student individually. In these cases, schools may decide to use group tests of intelligence. Group tests typically are paper-and-pencil measures of intelligence that can be administered in an hour or two. These tests, unlike individual tests, do not require extensive professional training to administer. The main functions of the examiner are to read directions and to enforce time limits. Because they do not require each student to meet with a trained psychologist, group tests of intelligence tend to be faster and less costly to administer. However, the results of individual tests are often more accurate. In some states, use of group tests is restricted. For example, the state of California does not allow use of group tests of intelligence in schools. In general, group tests of intelligence are used quite a bit less in schools than they once were.

Group tests of intelligence generally are of two main kinds. In the first kind, an omnibus test, multiple kinds of test items are intermixed. For example, a series-completion item may follow immediately after a vocabulary item. Examples of omnibus tests are the Otis-Lennon School Ability Test (OLSAT 8) and the Henmon-Nelson Test of Mental Abilities. In the second kind, tests are divided into parts, or subtests, in which each part is typically timed separately. Each item in a part is the same kind (e.g., vocabulary). An example is the Cognitive Abilities Test (CogAT Form 6), divided into verbal, quantitative, and figural sets of subtests.

Intelligence Test Scores

What kinds of scores are used to interpret the results of intelligence tests? Here, we discuss two possibilities.

One possibility is mental age. Binet suggested that we can assess children's intelligence on the basis of their mental age, or MA – their level of intelligence compared to an average person of the same physical age (also called chronological age, or CA). Suppose, for example, a person performs on a test at a level comparable to that of an average 10-year-old. We say the person's mental age is 10. People with very different chronological ages can all have the same mental age. Thus consider the case in which an

8-year-old, a 10-year-old, and a 12-year-old all have the same score on a test of intelligence. Their mental ages are the same, despite the differences in their chronological, or physical, ages.

There are several problems with the concept of mental age. First, chronological age increases indefinitely throughout a person's lifetime. Mental age does not. Usually, people's mental age stops increasing, or starts to increase only slowly, at a chronological age of roughly 16. In old age, mental age often actually starts to decline. This decline typically is due to decreases in scores on tests of rapid and flexible abstract thinking. These facts suggest that the ratio of mental age to chronological age takes on a meaning different for adults than for children. It can even mean different things for adults of varying ages. For example, an average adult of 40 would have a mental age not of 40, but of around 16 to 17 or so. Although compensations in scoring systems have been made to account for this fact, the problem has never been resolved in a fully satisfactory way.

A second problem is that although mental age implies a continuous distribution of intellectual development, we know that intellectual development is not wholly continuous. Whether we see it as occurring in stages or in relation to the acquisition of domain-specific knowledge at certain ages, the fits and starts of mental development are not reflected in the mental-age construct.

The German psychologist William Stern (1912) suggested that mental age is a problematical measure because comparing scores of people of different ages is difficult. How do you compare the mental age of 10 achieved by an 8-year-old with that achieved by a 12-year-old? In order to deal with this difficulty, Stern suggested the intelligence quotient (IQ), a measure of intelligence comparing mental age (MA) to chronological age (CA) times 100. Because of the use of a ratio of MA to CA in calculating the IQ, an IQ calculated in this way is sometimes referred to as a ratio IQ. Thus:

$$\text{ratio IQ} = (\text{MA/CA}) \times 100.$$

Ratio IQs are rarely used today, because a weak link was discovered in their calculation, namely, the construct of mental age.

Today, therefore, people generally use a second possibility for computing IQs, what are called deviation IQ scores. Deviation IQs are calculated on the basis of how high a person's score is relative to that of other people of his or her age. The average score for either a ratio or deviation IQ is 100. Scores below 100 are "below average." Scores above 100 are "above average." Using common statistical calculations, roughly two-thirds of all IQ scores fall between 85 and 115. Roughly 19 out of 20 scores fall between 70 and 130. In the remainder of the chapter, we will be referring to deviation IQs.

Tests of Aptitudes and Interests

Aptitudes are abilities developed over a period of years that predict success in particular areas of endeavor. Examples are music, writing, or reading. Among the most widely used aptitude tests are the Differential Aptitude Tests (Bennett, Seashore, & Wesman, 1990). They are designed to measure such aptitudes as verbal reasoning, numerical ability, abstract reasoning, clerical speed and accuracy, mechanical reasoning, space relations, spelling, and language usage. Such tests are used to help students with curriculum or vocational planning.

Tests of specific aptitudes are used for narrower purposes, such as selection or vocational placement. They include, among others, the Bennett Mechanical Comprehension Test (BMCT) and the Seashore Tests of Musical Aptitudes (Seashore, 1960). For example, a student who wishes to be in the vocal music program at a performing arts high school might be given the Seashore tests as part of the admissions process.

Counselors and teachers often recommend that students engaged in career planning take not only an aptitude test but also a vocational interest test, such as the Strong Vocational Interest Inventory (originally the Strong Vocational Interest Blank). The goal of such tests is to help students decide where their vocational interests lie. The tests do not indicate ability for these vocations. For this reason, teachers often recommend taking both an interest test and an aptitude test. Unlike most of the other tests mentioned here, interest tests are designed to measure typical rather than maximal performance. Students are asked to describe or behave in ways that exemplify how they usually think or behave. For example, students are asked to rate statements such as "I enjoy working with others" and "I like to travel." A person rating each of these statements high might be encouraged to become a travel agent, tour guide, or scientific field researcher. The recommendation would depend on the person's other interests, skills, and abilities.

Tests of Achievement

An achievement test measures accomplishments in either single or multiple areas of endeavor. Areas include reading comprehension, mathematics, social studies, and science (Cohen & Swerdlik, 2001; Gregory, 2000). Five of the most commonly administered achievement tests are the Iowa Tests of Basic Skills, the SRA Achievement Series, the California Achievement Test, the Metropolitan Achievement Test, and the Stanford Achievement Test. All of these tests contain measures of achievement in multiple academic subjects. Consider, for example, the California Achievement Test. It contains measures of achievement in vocabulary, reading comprehension, language mechanics, language expression, mathematical computation, mathematical concepts and applications, spelling, study skills, science, and social studies. In all cases, these tests can be used at multiple levels throughout the elementary and secondary grade levels.

Some tests, such as the SAT, were originally conceived of as aptitude tests (the initials originally stood for "Scholastic Aptitude Test"). Today, however, they are conceived of as closer to achievement tests. There are two SATs. The SAT-I measures basic skills that are important for college. It is divided into verbal and mathematical sections. The SAT-II measures achievement in specific areas, such as mathematics, biology, various foreign languages, and so forth.

Over the years, there have been various changes in the SAT. For example, until 1995, the tests were based on a normative scale established in 1941. The mean was set to 500 and the standard deviation to 100 for each test (verbal and mathematical) in that year. Subsequently, scores were based on that normative sample. But as the years went by, the nature of the population of students taking the SAT changed. Far more students of much more diverse backgrounds started taking the test. As the years went by, the number of high scores decreased and the number of low scores increased. As a result, scores became lopsided. There was a preponderance of scores at the lower end of the distribution. For this reason, the scales were recentered in April 1995 so that the sample of students who took the test in that month became the basis for a new set of norms with a mean of 500 and a standard deviation of 100. Of course, old scores can be converted into new scores, and vice versa.

Beginning in 2005, the SAT-I took a new form. Indeed, the new form has been referred to as the "New SAT" (www.collegeboard.com/newsat/index. html, retrieved September 13, 2009). The goal of the College Board, the organization that creates the test, is to align the test more closely with current curriculum in high school and college. This change reflects not the scale by which the test is scored but the content. There is a new writing section, which is scored separately on the same 200 to 800 scale as the other two sections. It includes both an essay section and multiple-choice grammar and usage items. A "perfect" score (obtained by adding up part scores) therefore will increase from 1600 to 2400. What was previously called the verbal test became the critical-reading test. It has both short and long reading passages. The new quantitative section has more difficult mathematical items, extending as far as Algebra 2. Analogies and quantitative comparison were dropped from the verbal and quantitative sections, respectively.

Assessing Test Quality

Most of the standardized tests that teachers give their students are mandated by the school, school district, or state in which the school is located. Teachers may even encounter nationally mandated standardized tests. In such cases, teachers have little or no say over what tests are given or whether the tests are to be given at all. Sometimes, however, teachers and administrators have the opportunity to choose the standardized tests their students will take. After deciding what type of test they need, a group assigned to choose a standardized test must determine the quality of the various tests available. How do teachers and administrators pick a high-quality test?

Assessing the quality of a standardized test is a fairly involved procedure. It usually is done by school psychologists or others with advanced training in assessment. These professionals assess the test in a number of ways. For example, they look at whether the test predicts what it is supposed to predict. They also consider the appropriateness of the test for the students who will be taking it. To assess the fit of the test, professionals must understand the population to which test results are intended to apply. They also examine the samples, or members of the population on which the test was normed.

Populations and Samples

For a test to be good, the sample on which it is standardized needs to match the population of interest. The population is the complete set of individuals to which a set of results will be generalized (Rosnow & Rosenthal, 1999). For example, suppose test constructors are interested in constructing a test for third graders, the (imaginary) Whiz-Bang Intelligence Scale. Would the population be all third graders to which they wish to generalize their results? It is important that they think carefully about this group. Are they talking about all third graders in a school, a school district, a state, a country, or even the world? There is a difference in how one interprets the results. Countries vary drastically in the educational expectations they hold for schoolchildren, and even the typical age of a third grader.

When state departments of education construct tests for pupils in their state, they are usually interested in generalizing only to pupils in their state. The goal is to understand what pupils in that state have learned. Typically, they also wish to compare pupils and school districts within that state to each other. When a test publisher creates a standardized test, the publisher is usually concerned with national comparisons. But if the test is used in another country, the population will change. The standardization that held for the one country will almost certainly not apply to the other country.

A sample is a subset of a population. Test constructors are almost never able to try out their test on all the members of the population of interest. For example, it is not feasible to try out a test for third graders on every third grader in the United States. Thus test constructors have to content themselves with a sample, or portion of the population.

Suppose test constructors want to standardize the Whiz-Bang test for third graders in the United States. They can sample in two basic ways. In the first, called a random sample, every member of the population has an equal chance of being drawn for the sample. Thus, for the Whiz-Bang test, a truly random sample is one in which any third grader in the country has an equal chance of being included in the tryout. Such sampling is not practical. Test constructors do not have complete access to every third grader in the country that they would need to generate a truly random sample.

In the second way of sampling, called a stratified random sample, the test constructors make sure they proportionately take into account, in the group on which they try out the test, all of the characteristics that might be relevant to the scores that people receive. The sample is random within each stratified group (Rosnow & Rosenthal, 1999). What are some of the likely characteristics along which a test constructor might want to stratify the Whiz-Bang test? One is likely to be gender. Assuming the population consists of roughly one-half boys and one-half girls, they will want their sample to reflect this distribution of boys and girls. A second characteristic may be ethnic group. The test constructors will want to sample members of diverse ethnic groups. The sampling should be roughly in proportion to their appearance in the third-grade population of the country. A third characteristic may be type of community, such as urban, suburban, and rural. A fourth characteristic may be socioeconomic level. The goal is to ensure that the sample on which the test constructors build their test adequately reflects the population to which they wish to generalize.

A good stratified sample – in which the balance of relevant attributes in the sample is the same as that in the population – is called a representative sample. A representative sample is one that takes into account the distribution of relevant characteristics of the population as a whole. Test publishers generally stratify their samples, although they do not always achieve fully representative samples.

If the population and sampling of a test seem appropriate, teachers and administrators must then assess two other important measures of test quality: reliability and validity.

Reliability

Reliability is the consistency of test results (Anastasi & Urbina, 1997; Cook & Beckman, 2006; Fekken, 2000; Johnson & Christensen, 2007; Megargee, 2000). Suppose, for example, that Jolene Johnson's student Joe takes the Whiz-Bang test repeatedly. He (assuming the student's ability remains the same) keeps getting exactly the same score. Jolene can conclude that the test measurements are highly reliable. However, if the student's scores are very different each time he takes the test, Jolene will conclude that the test measurements are not very reliable. Reliability is usually expressed as a proportion, on a scale that ranges from 0 to 1. Decimal numbers near 0 indicate low reliability; numbers nearer 1 indicate high reliability.

There are several different ways to measure reliability. Each relies on a somewhat different aspect of consistency (Gliner & Morgan, 2000). For example, test constructors may give the same test to the same group of students more than one time, to determine test-retest reliability. Test constructors may also wish to determine alternate-forms reliability – whether measurements from two or more slightly different versions of the same test are consistent with one another. To determine this, they administer the different versions to a group of students and compare the results on each version.

Another way to calculate reliability is to compare students' performance on one part of the test with their performance on another part. This kind of internal-consistency reliability is often determined by split-halves reliability – dividing the test questions in half and comparing the two halves of the test. Finally, consider tests such as essay tests, in which a subjective judgment is required by graders. Test constructors try to determine interrater reliability, or the extent to which two or more evaluators of a given response (such as an essay) rate the response in the same way.

The reliability of standardized tests varies according to the method used, but it is generally high. One team of researchers suggested that well-constructed standardized tests used to make decisions about individuals should have a test-retest reliability of about .90 or above and an alternate-forms reliability of about .85 or above. Split-half reliability should be about .95 or above. Across standardized tests, there is somewhat more variation in internal-consistency reliabilities, such as split-half reliability, than there is in test-retest and alternate-forms reliabilities. Standardized tests divided into subtests generally have high split-half reliability for the test as a whole, but not necessarily for each of the subtests.

On average, longer tests tend to be more reliable in the measurement they provide than do shorter tests. The reason is that more items generally allow a better estimate of the level at which a person scores on the construct or attribute being assessed. To pick an extreme example, suppose you attempted to measure a person's achievement in the sciences with a 5-item test. You would not expect much consistency across different forms of 5-item tests. They are just too short to provide any kind of adequate measurement. If even one single item were a bad item susceptible to error of measurement, it would have a substantial effect on reliability. On the other hand, with 500 items, you would expect the errors of measurement to cancel each other out. So you would get a fairly consistent measure of science knowledge. One bad item would have little effect.

Relevant variation among individuals being tested also affects reliability. Here, too, test results from a large range of people in terms of the construct being measured also tend to be more reliable than those from a small range. To take an extreme example, suppose everyone you plan to test has almost the same level of achievement. It will be extremely difficult to develop a test that consistently distinguishes among them because they are hardly different at all. For example, try consistently measuring differences in height among people when they are all between 5 feet 6 inches and 5 feet 6 1/2 inches! It is difficult to distinguish among people within such a narrow range. It is not hard to construct a test that consistently distinguishes among people with broad ranges of abilities or achievements – in our example, analogous to heights ranging from 5 feet to 6 feet.

Validity

Validity refers to the degree to which a test provides measurements that are appropriate for its intended purpose (Anastasi & Urbina, 1997; Cook & Beckman, 2006; Krueger & Kling, 2000; Megargee, 2000). There are several different kinds of validity. We discuss three that are especially important to teaching and learning.

PREDICTIVE VALIDITY. Predictive validity refers to the extent to which a test predicts a performance that will be demonstrated after the test has been taken (Gliner & Morgan, 2000). When such a prediction is made, the test is referred to as the predictor. A predictor is the thing doing the forecasting of future results. The outcome to be predicted is referred to as the criterion. For example, tests of intelligence are often used as predictors of later school achievement. Tests of readiness for reading are used as predictors of how well a child will be able to learn how to read. School achievement and reading ability are the criteria being predicted in these two examples.

Predictive validities are expressed using a correlation coefficient. Correlations range from -1 (perfect inverse relation) to 0 (no relation) to 1 (perfect positive relation). A perfectly predictive test has a predictive validity of 1 (or -1) with respect to the criterion. For example, suppose you have a perfectly valid test for predicting a measure of school achievement, such as grades, as the criterion. You then will be able to forecast with absolute accuracy the grades each student will achieve. The correlation coefficient in this example is 1. Such tests, of course, do not really exist. A test with no predictive value at all in its measurements has a predictive validity of 0 with respect to the criterion. In this case, knowing the test score will tell you absolutely nothing about what grades students will achieve. A test for which higher scores are perfectly predictive of lower scores on the criterion has a predictive validity of -1. For example, a high score on a particular test might accurately predict a poor grade in the class.

Realistically, most predictive validities are greater than 0 but less than 1. What constitutes a good validity coefficient is largely a measure of subjective judgment. Anything significantly greater than 0 indicates some level of prediction. Typical ability tests predict school grades with validity coefficients ranging from about .3 to .6. But many tests fall outside this range.

The closer in time one measurement is to another, the higher is the probability that the two measurements are likely to correlate. For example, achievement in fourth grade is likely to be a better predictor of achievement in fifth grade than it is to be a predictor of achievement in 11th grade.

Predictive validities are lowered when there is restriction of range, the difference between the highest and lowest scores. Consider the case of students applying to a competitive college. If only students with SAT scores of 2000 or higher are admitted, by definition most students admitted will have SATs that are roughly comparable. The reason is that the SAT score goes up to only 2400. However, some of the students at the competitive college are bound to get poor grades. It is difficult to use the SAT to predict who these students will be because the SAT scores are all roughly comparable. Even though the SAT might predict freshman-year college grades for a wide range of students, the SAT will not be able to predict college grades as well for students at this school.

CONTENT VALIDITY. Content validity is the extent to which the content of a test actually measures the knowledge or skills the test is supposed to measure (Gliner & Morgan, 2000). Suppose, for example, that a general test of mathematical achievement for high school juniors were to include only plane geometry items. It would be seen as having relatively low content validity. A more valid test would include algebra as well, and probably arithmetical operations, too. Content validity is typically judged by a panel of experts. It is not expressed in terms of a single number. Rather, it represents a consensus judgment of how appropriate a test's content is.

Content validity must also be considered in terms of the particular curriculum used in a classroom, school, or district. Teachers should play an important role in evaluating the content validity of an achievement test. They are the ones who best know what they teach (or should be teaching). Teachers should also assess the content validity of the tests they develop themselves. Thus we return to the issue of how the test fits the students who will be taking it. Consider, for example, teachers and administrators in a school that embraces a curriculum emphasizing expressiveness and creativity in writing. They at the same time deemphasize the mechanical skills of writing, such as spelling and punctuation. These teachers and administrators might decide that an English achievement test composed primarily of multiple-choice questions about writing mechanics lacks content validity for evaluating their students.

CONSTRUCT-RELATED VALIDITY. All the kinds of validity just discussed are subsets of construct-related validity. Construct-related validity, sometimes called simply construct validity, is the extent to which a test completely and accurately captures the theoretical construct or attribute it is designed to measure (Cohen & Swerdlik, 1999; Gliner & Morgan, 2000; Westen & Rosenthal, 2003).

Suppose, for example, you want to develop a test of memory abilities. Your test will be construct valid to the extent that it fully and fairly measures the various aspects of memory. These aspects will depend on the theory of memory you accept. Whatever the theory, you will almost certainly want to use a variety of memory items in your test. For example, you might include items requiring students to recall lists of words. Or the students might have to recognize which items of a set of words were presented earlier. The goal is to ensure that you have captured your particular idea of memory as completely as possible.

Once an appropriate test has been chosen and administered to students, teachers and other professionals such as guidance counselors and school psychologists are faced with the task of deciding what the test scores mean to them and their students.

STATISTICAL CONCEPTS UNDERLYING TEST SCORES

To understand standardized tests and to use and interpret these tests effectively, expert teachers must also understand several basic statistical concepts that underlie these tests. These concepts include frequency distributions, measures of central tendency and dispersion, the relationship of scores to the normal distribution, and the statistical significance of scores.

Types of Scores

Many different types of scores are used to describe students' performance. Expert teachers are aware of how these scores compare to one another in terms of the information they provide.

Raw Scores
The first score to understand is the raw score, typically the number of items correctly answered.

Percentile Scores
Sometimes we wish to have a direct comparison of a person's performance with that of other people – to make a normative comparison. A useful kind of score for this purpose is the percentile score. The percentile score is the proportion of other students' scores that equal or fall below a given student's score, multiplied by 100.

Note the difference between raw scores, especially when they are expressed in percentages, and percentile scores. The percentage score pertains to the proportion of items on a test that are answered correctly. The percentile score pertains to an individual's standing on a given test relative to other individuals. Thus percentile scores are a measure of comparison against other students rather than of direct performance. Expressed in terms used earlier in the chapter, percentile scores are based on norms rather than criteria.

True Scores
A useful distinction to make is that between two different kinds of scores: observed scores and true scores (Cohen & Swerdlik, 2001; Gregory, 2000).

An observed score is the score someone actually receives on a test. Test constructors differentiate between the observed score and the true score. The true score is the hypothetical score someone would get if he or she took a test an infinite number of times with no practice effects in taking the test. Earlier in the chapter we described some of the factors that can keep an observed score from being a measure of a student's true abilities. The student can get a cold or be unmotivated to try hard on the test. A student might also receive a higher observed score than his or her true score. For example, the student may have just finished studying a book that includes the passage that tests reading comprehension.

You might want to determine the true score by giving a test many times. In reality, when people take a test multiple times, they begin to show practice effects. Practice effects are changes in score that occur as a result of increasing familiarity with the particular items, the test as a whole, and the experience of taking the test. For the purposes of thinking about true scores, we ignore practice effects.

A true score is obviously a hypothetical construct: We can never know what a person's true score would be because no one is able to take a test an infinite number of times. However, it is possible to estimate how likely it is that a student's observed score is similar to his or her true score. Whenever a person gets a score, it actually represents a range of scores that the person might plausibly receive. Sometimes teachers and test developers use the concept of a confidence interval to determine the likely range of scores within which a person's true score lies. A confidence interval is the probability that a person's true score falls within a certain range of the observed score. The measure used to express a confidence interval is called the standard error of measurement.

LET'S BE A BIT MORE PRECISE

If we assume a normal distribution of test scores, the chances that a person's true score will lie within plus or minus one standard error of measurement of the observed score are about 68%. The chances that the score will lie within plus or minus two standard errors are about 95%.

Standard Scores

Standard scores, also called z-scores, derive from converting a raw score into units of standard deviation. Standard scores are arbitrarily defined to have a mean of 0 and a standard deviation of 1. If the scores fall into a normal distribution, roughly 68% of the scores will be between -1 and 1. Roughly 95% of the scores will be between -2 and 2.

Standard scores are useful because they make it possible to compare results that initially are on different scales. For example, a teacher using standard scores can compare a student's scores for two tests, one on a 100-point scale and one on a 30-point scale. Suppose the mean on the first test is 75 points and the mean on the second test is 20 points. Both of these scores will correspond to a z score of 0, the mean value for z scores. To compute a standard score for a student, you need to know the mean and the standard deviation of the distribution of raw scores. Then, you calculate as follows:

1. Subtract the mean raw score from the student's raw score.
2. Divide the difference (the number found in step 1) by the standard deviation of the distribution of raw scores.

Thus, the formula for a z score is

$$(\text{observed score} - \text{mean raw score})/\text{standard deviation}$$

The z score tells teachers how many standard deviations above or below the mean a raw score is. For example, a raw score that is one standard deviation above the mean yields a z score of 1. A raw score that is two standard deviations below the mean translates into a z score of -2. Even if one test is harder than another test, translating two raw scores from two tests into standard scores is comparable because the scores are phrased in common terms: standard deviations from the mean.

Many standardized tests use variants on standard scores. For example, the College Board scores many of its tests, such as the SAT, on a scale that has a range of 200 to 800, with a mean of 500 and a standard deviation of 100. Thus a z score of 0 corresponds to an SAT score of 500, a z score of 1 corresponds to an SAT score of 600, and so on. A variant of the College Board–type score is the T score. The T score has a mean of 50 and a standard deviation of 10. Unfortunately, these two kinds of scores can lead users falsely to interpret small and insubstantial differences as meaningful.

Another type of standard score is the stanine. The stanine has a range of 1 to 9, a mean of 5, and a standard deviation of 2. The advantage of stanines is that they are relatively simple and make no pretense of being highly precise. The disadvantage of stanines is that their imprecision may blur meaningful differences in scores. The Terra Nova California Achievement Test uses stanine scores. Note that all the kinds of scores derived from z scores are interchangeable through mathematical formulas.

Grade Equivalent Scores

Achievement tests also can be scored using the grade equivalent score, a measure of grade-level achievement compared with the normative sample for a given test. Say a student in the second month of the third grade scores at the same level on a test of mathematical computation as an average student in the sixth month of the fifth grade is expected to score on that test. Her grade equivalent will be 5 years, 6 months, sometimes abbreviated 5–6.

Teachers often like grade equivalents because they are used to thinking in terms of grade levels. Grade equivalents are often misleading, however (Goodman & Hambleton, 2004). Use them cautiously. Even avoid them when possible. Keep in mind, though, that the fact that a fourth grader receives a grade equivalent of sixth to seventh grade on a fourth-grade test does not mean the fourth grader can do sixth to seventh grade math. In fact, many of the tests for elementary school have grade equivalents going up to high school for tests that cover none of the algebra, geometry, or trigonometry covered in high school math classes. The same problem applies across the curriculum. These grade equivalents refer to how well students at these grades would be expected to do on the elementary school test, were they given this test. Because students in the higher grades typically take grade-appropriate tests but do not usually take elementary school tests, the grade equivalents are often misleading.

Issues and Concerns in Standardized Testing

As the discussion of the challenges involved in presenting test scores points out, there are several potential pitfalls in using standardized tests. But some new developments in standardized testing show promise for overcoming some of the pitfalls. What are some of the larger issues involved in standardized testing?

Standardized tests, like most technology, can be helpful to teachers and students alike if they are used properly. But standardized tests can also be harmful if they are misused. For example, they will be harmful if they are biased in favor of one group of students at the expense of another group or if they do not work for students of certain cultural backgrounds. Even high-quality tests can be harmful if they are used for invalid purposes.

Test Bias

Test bias refers to a test's being unfair for members of some groups but not for others. Whether a test is considered biased or not, however, depends in large part on exactly how bias is defined (Anastasi & Urbina, 1997; Cronbach, 1990).

The most naive way of defining test bias is to state that a test is biased if there is a difference between groups in scores. For example, some groups have challenged the use of standardized college entrance examinations on the basis that African American and Hispanic American students often score lower on these tests than do white and Asian American students. Courts have occasionally ruled in favor of such challenges. But such legal views can be based on a false assumption that groups will not differ in the construct being measured. For instance, as different ethnic groups differ in average height, weight, hair color, eye color, and many other features, there is no reason to assume in principle that they could not differ in whatever is being tested.

A second way to define test bias is to view a test as biased if the content is judged by a panel of experts to favor certain groups over others. Most test publishers have panels of experts read test items carefully to search for bias against women, minorities, and members of other groups. The problem here is that the experts may be wrong. For instance, saying an item will discriminate against women does not necessarily make it so. And, of course, the experts may miss items that actually are discriminatory.

A third and more sophisticated view of test bias is that a test is biased if it either overpredicts or underpredicts some criterion or set of criteria for members of one group versus members of another. In overprediction, the test predicts a higher level of performance than a student actually achieves. In underprediction, the test predicts a lower level of performance than the student actually achieves. In other words, the predictive validity of the test varies between groups. Suppose scores on the fictional Whiz-Bang intelligence test described earlier predict school grades quite well for girls. But it consistently underestimates the grades of boys. The test is therefore biased in favor of girls (or, equivalently, against boys). As a result of the biased results, boys with low scores might not be admitted to advanced classes or other special programs in school. Their failure in admission would be despite the fact that they can probably do as well as girls who had higher test scores.

By this definition of test bias, the tests most frequently used to measure abilities typically are not statistically biased (Jensen, 1998). In other words, when members of a given group score lower on the tests – for example, tests of various abilities – their performance on the criteria to be predicted, such as school grades, is generally lower. Not everyone accepts this definition, however. Some people believe we need to view bias as part of a larger system, in which it is possible for the criteria (e.g., school grades) as well as the predictor test to be biased.

For roughly 100 years, since the work of Alfred Binet and Theodore Simon, testing to identify children's abilities has changed relatively little (see Binet & Simon, 1916). If any other technology had stayed about the same for 100 years, people would be amazed. Imagine if we had only telegraphs operated by Morse code, primitive telephones, no televisions, no computers, and no serious electrical appliances. That is a world hard to imagine. It is the world in which we live in the field of testing the abilities of the gifted.

It would not be fair to say that there have been no new developments. As noted earlier, Joseph Renzulli, Howard Gardner, and others (see Sternberg & Davidson, 2005) have proposed new models of identification that have been used to identify gifted children in ways that go beyond conventional IQ. But the tests used to measure IQ have not changed much. They still measure the same basic construct of so-called general ability that Charles Spearman identified early in the 20th century (Spearman, 1927). Our efforts have been addressed toward developing new kinds of tests to assess intelligence in broader ways than has been possible in the past. The rest of this chapter describes three of our efforts.

We have been involved in three related projects exploring whether broader quantitatively based assessments might be helpful in the university admissions process. The first of these projects is the Rainbow Project, the second, the Kaleidoscope Project, and the third, the Aurora Project. Our goal here is not to present the projects in detail, which is done elsewhere, but rather to explain their use in identifying the gifted.

THE RAINBOW PROJECT

One of the primary venues for identifying the gifted is university admissions. When universities make decisions about selective admissions, the main quantitative information they have available to them typically is grade-point average in high school or its equivalent and scores on standardized tests (Lemann, 1999). Is it possible to create assessments that are psychometrically sound and that provide incremental validity over existing measures, without destroying the cultural and ethnic diversity that makes a university environment a place in which students can interact with and learn from others who are different from themselves? Can one create assessments recognizing that people's gifts differ and that many of the variety of gifts they possess are potentially relevant to university and life success (Sternberg & Davidson, 2005)? And can one do so in a way that is not a mere proxy for socioeconomic class (Golden, 2006; Kabaservice, 2004; Karabel, 2006; Lemann, 1999; McDonough, 1997) or for IQ (Frey & Detterman, 2004)?

The Rainbow Project (for details, see Sternberg & the Rainbow Project Collaborators, 2006; see also Sternberg, 2005a, 2006a; Sternberg & the Rainbow Project Collaborators, 2005; Sternberg, the Rainbow Project Collaborators, & the University of Michigan Business School Collaborators, 2004) was a first project designed to enhance university admissions procedures at the undergraduate level. The Rainbow measures were intended, in the United States, to supplement the SAT, but they can supplement any conventional standardized test of abilities or achievement. In the theory of successful intelligence, abilities and achievement are viewed as being on a continuum – abilities are largely achieved (Sternberg, 1998a, 1999a) – so it is not clear that it matters greatly exactly what test is used, given that most of the tests that are used are highly g-loaded.

A wide variety of studies have shown the utility of the SAT and similar tests as predictors of university and job success, with success in college typically measured by GPA (grade-point average) (Hezlett et al., 2001; Kobrin et al., 2002; Schmidt & Hunter, 1998). Taken together, these data suggest reasonable predictive validity for the SAT in predicting undergraduate performance. Indeed, traditional intelligence or aptitude tests have been shown to predict performance across a wide variety of settings. But as is always the case for a single test or type of test, there is room for improvement. The theory of successful intelligence provides one basis for improving prediction and possibly for establishing greater equity and diversity, which is a goal of most higher educational institutions (Bowen, Kurzweil, & Tobin, 2006). It suggests that broadening the range of skills tested to go beyond analytic skills, to include practical and creative skills as well, might significantly enhance the prediction of undergraduate performance beyond current levels. Thus, the theory does not suggest *replacing* but rather *augmenting* the SAT and similar tests such as the ACT or the A-Levels in the undergraduate-admissions process. A collaborative team of investigators sought to study how successful such an augmentation could be. Even if we did not use the SAT, ACT, or A-Levels, in particular, we still would need some kind of assessment of the memory and analytical abilities the tests assess.

Methodological Considerations

In the Rainbow Project, data were collected at 15 schools across the United States, including 8 four-year undergraduate institutions, 5 community colleges, and 2 high schools.

The participants were 1,013 students predominantly in their first year as undergraduates or their final year of high school. Here we discuss analyses for only undergraduate students because they were the only ones for whom the authors had data available regarding undergraduate academic performance. The final number of participants included in these analyses was 793.

Baseline measures of standardized test scores and high school grade-point average were collected to evaluate the predictive validity of current tools used for undergraduate admission criteria, and to provide a contrast for the current measures. Students' scores on standardized university entrance exams were obtained from the College Board.

The measure of analytical skills was provided by the SAT (pre-2005 version) plus multiple-choice analytical items we added measuring inference of meanings of words from context, number series completions, and figural matrix completions.

Creative skills were measured by multiple-choice items and by performance-based items. The multiple-choice items were of three kinds. In one, students are presented with verbal analogies preceded by counterfactual premises (e.g., money falls off trees). They have to solve the analogies as though the counterfactual premises were true. In a second, students are presented with rules for novel number operations, for example, "flix," which involves numerical manipulations that differ as a function of whether the first of two operands is greater than, equal to, or less than the second. Participants have to use the novel number operations to solve presented math problems. In a third, participants are first presented with a figural series that involves one or more transformations; they then have to apply the rule of the series to a new figure with a different appearance, and complete the new series. These measures are not typical of assessments of creativity and were included for relative quickness of participants' responses and relative ease of scoring.

Creative skills also were measured using open-ended measures. One measure required writing two short stories with a selection from among unusual titles, such as "The Octopus's Sneakers"; one required orally telling two stories based upon choices of picture collages; and the third required captioning cartoons from among various options. Open-ended performance-based answers were rated by trained raters for novelty, quality, and task appropriateness. Multiple judges were used for each task and satisfactory reliability was achieved (Sternberg & the Rainbow Project Collaborators, 2006).

Multiple-choice measures of practical skills were of three kinds. In one, students are presented with a set of everyday problems in the life of an adolescent and have to select the option that best solves each problem. In another, students are presented with scenarios requiring the use of math in everyday life (e.g., buying tickets for a ballgame) and have to solve math problems based on the scenarios. In a third, students are presented with a map of an area (e.g., an entertainment park) and have to answer questions about navigating effectively through the area depicted by the map.

Practical skills also were assessed using three situational-judgment inventories: the Everyday Situational Judgment Inventory (Movies), the Common Sense Questionnaire, and the College Life Questionnaire, each of which taps different types of tacit knowledge. The general format of tacit-knowledge inventories has been described in Sternberg et al. (2000), so only the content of the inventories used in this study will be described here. The movies presented everyday situations that confront undergraduate students, such as asking for a letter of recommendation from a professor who shows, through nonverbal cues, that he does not recognize you very well. One then has to rate various options for how well they would work in response to each situation. The Common Sense Questionnaire provided everyday business problems, such as being assigned to work with a coworker whom one cannot stand, and the College Life Questionnaire provided everyday university situations for which a solution was required.

Unlike the creativity performance tasks, in the practical performance tasks the participants were not given a choice of situations to rate. For each task, participants were told that there was no "right" answer, and that the options described in each situation represented variations on how different people approach different situations.

All materials were administered in either of two formats. A total of 325 of the university students took the test in paper-and-pencil format, whereas a total of 468 students took the test on the computer via the World Wide Web.

No strict time limits were set for completing the tests, although the instructors were given rough guidelines of about 70 minutes per session. The time taken to complete the battery of tests ranged from 2 to 4 hours.

As a result of the lengthy nature of the complete battery of assessments, participants were administered parts of the battery using an intentional incomplete overlapping design. The participants were randomly assigned to the test sections they were to complete. Details of the use of the procedure are in Sternberg and the Rainbow Project Collaborators (2006).

Creativity in this (and the subsequent Kaleidoscope) project was assessed on the basis of the novelty and quality of responses. Practicality was assessed on the basis of the feasibility of the products with respect to human, temporal, and material resources, and with respect to persuasiveness.

Findings

The analysis described below is a conservative one that does not correct for differences in the selectivity of the institutions at which the study took place. In a study across so many undergraduate institutions differing in selectivity, validity coefficients will seem to be lower than is typical, because an A at a less selective institution counts the same as an A at a more selective institution. When the authors corrected for institutional selectivity, the results described below became stronger. But correcting for selectivity has its own problems (e.g., on what basis does one evaluate selectivity?), and so uncorrected data are used here. We also did not control for university major: Different universities may have different majors, and the exact course offerings, grading, and populations of students entering different majors may vary from one university to another, rendering control difficult.

When examining undergraduate students alone, the sample showed a slightly higher mean level of SAT than that found in undergraduate institutions across the United States. The standard deviation was above the normal 100-point standard deviation, meaning we did not suffer from restriction of range. Our means, although slightly higher than typical, are within the range of average undergraduate students.

Another potential concern is pooling data from different institutions. We pooled data because in some institutions we simply did not have large enough numbers of cases for the data to be meaningful.

Some scholars believe that there is only one set of skills that is highly relevant to school performance, what is sometimes called "general ability," or *g* (e.g., Jensen, 1998). These scholars believe that tests may appear to measure different skills, but when statistically analyzed, show themselves just to be measuring the single general ability. Does the test actually measure distinct analytical, creative, and practical skill groupings? Factor analysis addresses this question. Three meaningful factors were extracted from the data: practical performance tests, creative performance tests, and multiple-choice tests (including analytical, creative, and practical). In other words, multiple-choice tests, regardless of what they were supposed to measure, clustered together (see also Sternberg, Castejón, Prieto, Hautamäki, & Grigorenko, 2001, for similar findings). Thus, method variance proved to be very important. The results show the importance of measuring skills using multiple formats, precisely because method is so important in determining factorial structure. The results show the limitations of exploratory factor analysis in analyzing such data, and also of dependence on multiple-choice items outside the analytical domain. In the ideal, one wishes to ensure that one controls for method of testing in designing aptitude and other test batteries.

Undergraduate admissions offices are not interested, exactly, in whether these tests predict undergraduate academic success. Rather, they are interested in the extent to which these tests predict school success beyond those measures currently in use, such as the SAT and high school grade-point average (GPA). In order to test the incremental validity provided by Rainbow measures above and beyond the SAT in predicting GPA, a series of statistical analyses (called hierarchical regressions) was conducted that included the items analyzed above in the analytical, creative, and practical assessments.

If one looks at the simple correlations, the SAT-V, SAT-M, high school GPA, and the Rainbow measures all predict first-year GPA. But how do the Rainbow measures fare on incremental validity? In one set of analyses, the SAT-V, SAT-M, and high school GPA were included in the first step of the prediction equation because these are the standard measures used today to predict undergraduate performance. Only high school GPA contributed uniquely to prediction of undergraduate GPA. Inclusion of the Rainbow measures roughly doubled prediction (percentage of variance accounted for in the criterion) versus the SAT alone.

These results suggest that the Rainbow tests add considerably to the prediction yielded by SATs alone. They also suggest the power of high school GPA in prediction, particularly because it is an atheoretical composite that includes within it many variables, including motivation and conscientiousness.

Studying group differences requires careful attention to methodology and sometimes has led to erroneous conclusions (Hunt & Carlson, 2007). Although one important goal of the present study was to predict success in the undergraduate years, another important goal involved developing measures that reduce ethnic group differences in mean levels. There has been a lively debate as to why there are socially defined racial group differences, and as to whether scores for members of underrepresented minority groups are over- or underpredicted by SATs and related tests (see, e.g., Bowen & Bok, 2000; Camara & Schmidt, 1999; Rowe, 2005; Rushton & Jensen, 2005; Sternberg, Grigorenko, & Kidd, 2005; Turkheimer, Haley, Waldron, d'Onofrio, & Gottesman, 2003). There are a number of ways one can test for group differences in these measures, each of which involves a test of the size of the effect of ethnic group. Two different measures were chosen: ω^2 – omega squared – and Cohen's D.

There were two general findings. First, in terms of overall differences, the Rainbow tests appeared to reduce ethnic-group differences relative to traditional assessments of abilities like the SAT. Second, in terms of specific differences, it appears that the Latino students benefited the most from the reduction of group differences. The Black students, too, seemed to show a reduction in difference from the white mean for most of the Rainbow tests, although a substantial difference appeared to be maintained with the practical performance measures.

Although the group differences are not perfectly reduced, these findings suggest that measures can be designed that reduce ethnic and racial group differences on standardized tests, particularly for historically disadvantaged groups like Black and Latino students. These findings have important implications for reducing adverse impact in undergraduate admissions.

The SAT is based on a conventional psychometric notion of cognitive skills. Using this notion, it has had substantial success in predicting undergraduate academic performance. The Rainbow measures alone roughly doubled the predictive power of undergraduate GPA when compared to the SAT alone. Additionally, the Rainbow measures predict substantially beyond the contributions of the SAT and high school GPA. These findings, combined with encouraging results regarding the reduction of between-ethnicity differences, make a compelling case for furthering the study of the measurement of analytic, creative, and practical skills for predicting success in the university.

One important goal for the current study, and future studies, is the creation of standardized assessments that reduce the different outcomes between different groups as much as possible to maintain test validity. The measures described here suggest results toward this end. Although the group differences in the tests were not reduced to zero, the tests did substantially attenuate group differences relative to other measures such as the SAT. This finding could be an important step toward ultimately ensuring fair and equal treatment for members of diverse groups in the academic domain.

The principles behind the Rainbow Project apply at other levels of admissions as well. For example, Hedlund, Wilt, Nebel, Ashford, and Sternberg (2006) have shown that the same principles can be applied in admissions to business schools, also with the result of increasing prediction and decreasing ethnic- (as well as gender-) group differences. Stemler, Grigorenko, Jarvin, and Sternberg (2006) have found that including creative and practical items in augmented psychology and statistics Advanced Placement Examinations can reduce ethnic-group differences on the tests. And the same principles are being employed in a test for identification of gifted students in elementary school described further on in this chapter (see also Chart, Grigorenko, & Sternberg, 2008).

It is one thing to have a successful research project, and another actually to implement the procedures in a high-stakes situation. We have had the opportunity to do so. The results of a second project, Project Kaleidoscope, are reviewed here.

THE KALEIDOSCOPE PROJECT

Tufts University in Medford, Massachusetts, has strongly emphasized the role of active citizenship in education. It has put into practice some of the ideas from the Rainbow Project. In collaboration with Dean of Admissions Lee Coffin, we instituted Project Kaleidoscope, which represents an implementation of the ideas of Rainbow, but goes beyond that project to include in its assessment the construct of wisdom (for more details, see Sternberg, 2007a, 2007b, 2010; Sternberg & Coffin, 2010).

In the 2006–07 application for all of the more than 15,000 students applying to Arts, Sciences, and Engineering at Tufts, we placed questions designed to assess wisdom, analytical and practical intelligence, and creativity synthesized (WICS, described in Chapter 3). The program has been continued, but the data reported here are for the first year (Sternberg, 2009a; Sternberg, Bonney, Gabora, Jarvin, Karelitz, & Coffin, in press; Sternberg & Coffin, 2009).

The questions were optional in the first 2 years. Whereas the Rainbow Project was done as a separate high-stakes test administered with a proctor, the Kaleidoscope Project was done as a section of the Tufts-specific supplement to the Common Application. It just was not practical to administer a separate high-stakes test such as the Rainbow assessment for admission to one university. Moreover, the advantage of Kaleidoscope is that it got us away from the high-stakes testing situation in which students must answer complex questions in very short amounts of time under incredible pressure.

Students were encouraged to answer just a single question so as not overly to burden them. Tufts University competes for applications with many other universities, and if our application was substantially more burdensome than those of our competitor schools, it would put us at a real-world disadvantage in attracting applicants. In the theory of successful intelligence, successful intelligent individuals capitalize on strengths and compensate for or correct weaknesses. Our format gave students a chance to capitalize on a strength.

As examples of items, a creative question asked students to write stories with titles such as "The End of MTV" or "Confessions of a Middle-School

Bully." Another creative question asked students what the world would be like if some historical event had come out differently, for example, if Rosa Parks had given up her seat on the bus. Yet another creative question, a nonverbal one, gave students an opportunity to design a new product or an advertisement for a new product. A practical question queried how students had persuaded friends of an unpopular idea they held. A wisdom question asked students how a passion they had could be applied toward a common good.

Creativity and practicality were assessed in the same way as in the Rainbow Project. Analytical quality was assessed by the organization, logic, and balance of the essay. Wisdom was assessed by the extent to which the response represented the use of abilities and knowledge for a common good by balancing one's own, others', and institutional interests over the long and short terms through the infusion of positive ethical values.

Note that the goal is not to replace SAT and other traditional admissions measurements like grade-point averages and class rank with some new test. Rather, it is to reconceptualize applicants in terms of academic/analytical, creative, practical, and wisdom-based abilities, using the essays as one but not the only source of information. For example, highly creative work submitted in a portfolio also could be entered into the creativity rating, or evidence of creativity through winning of prizes or awards. The essays were major sources of information, but if other information was available, the trained admissions officers used it.

Among the applicants who were evaluated as being academically qualified for admission, approximately half completed an optional essay in the first year and roughly two-thirds in subsequent years. Merely doing these essays had no meaningful effect on chances of admission. However, *quality* of essays or other evidence of creative, practical, or wisdom-based abilities did have an effect. For those rated as an "A" (top rating) by a trained admissions officer in any of these three categories, average rates of acceptance were roughly double those for applicants not getting an A.

Many measures do not look like conventional standardized tests but have statistical properties that mimic them. We were therefore interested in convergent-discriminant validation of our measures. The correlation of our measures with a rated academic composite that included SAT scores and high school GPA were modest but significant for creative, practical, and wise thinking. The correlations with a rating of quality of high school extracurricular participation and leadership were moderate for creative, practical, and wise thinking. Thus, the pattern of convergent-discriminant validation was what we had hoped for.

The average academic quality of applicants in Arts and Sciences rose slightly in 2006–07, again in 2007–08, and yet again in 2008–09, in terms of both SAT and high school grade-point average. In addition, there were notably fewer students in what before had been the bottom third of the pool in terms of academic quality than in previous years. Many of those students, seeing the new application, seem to have decided not to bother to apply. More strong applicants applied.

Thus, adopting these new methods does not result in applicants who are less qualified applying to the institution and being admitted. Rather, the applicants who are admitted are *more* qualified, but in a broader way. Perhaps most rewarding were the positive comments from large numbers of applicants that they felt our application gave them a chance to show themselves for who they are. Of course, many factors are involved in admissions decisions, and Kaleidoscope ratings were only one small part of the overall picture.

The early results at Tufts illustrate that a highly selective college can introduce an "unconventional" exercise into its undergraduate admissions process without disrupting the quality of the entering class. It is important to underscore the point that academic achievement has always been and remains the most important dimension of Tufts' undergraduate admissions process. Since we introduced the Kaleidoscope pilot in 2006, applications have remained roughly steady or increased slightly, and, as noted above, the mean SAT scores of accepted and enrolling students increased to new highs. In addition, we have not detected statistically meaningful ethnic group differences on the Kaleidoscope measures. Controlling for the academic rating given to applicants by admissions officers (which combines information from the transcript and standardized tests), students rated for Kaleidoscope achieved significantly higher academic averages in their undergraduate work than students who were not so rated by the admissions staff. In addition, research found that students with higher Kaleidoscope ratings were more involved in, and reported getting more out of, extracurricular, active-citizenship, and leadership activities in their first year at Tufts.

The positive effects of Kaleidoscope on the university's undergraduate applicant pool and enrolled class should not be disentangled from the effects of other initiatives, especially increased undergraduate financial aid – which at Tufts is always need-based. Initiatives like Kaleidoscope can help identify an able, diverse group of students but, without adequate financial aid and university commitment, the effects of the program will not be fully shown in actual matriculation figures.

In sum, as Tufts seeks to identify and develop new leaders for a changing world, Kaleidoscope provides a vehicle to help identify the potential leaders who may be best positioned to make a positive and meaningful difference to the world in the future. In the fast-paced, data-driven atmosphere of highly competitive college admissions, Kaleidoscope validates the role of qualitative measures of student ability and excellence.

THE AURORA PROJECT

Aurora is a battery for identifying gifted children roughly in the age range of 8–12. Two parts comprise the Aurora battery: a newly designed, augmented part (Aurora-*a* or Aurora-*a* battery) and a more conventional, intelligence-based part (Aurora-*g* or Aurora-*g* battery). Both are paper-and-pencil assessments intended for group administration to mainstreamed students at the elementary to middle school levels at which gifted programming is most prevalent. The augmented assessment is more substantial and is grounded in the theory of successful intelligence as presented earlier. The conventional assessment of general intellectual ability has been developed as a supplement. Of greatest importance and significance is the former, which, accordingly, we discuss more extensively here. More detail can be found in Chart, Grigorenko, and Sternberg (2008).

In designing the augmented assessment, we used a basic grid structure to depict graphically the broad range of item types to be developed. Analytical, creative, and practical domains are depicted as columns and figural, verbal, and quantitative modes as rows (see Table 10.1). Subtests were created such that their dominant properties fulfilled the criteria of each cell of the grid (see, for another example of such item development, Sternberg & Clinkenbeard, 1995). Resulting are nine different types of subtests that together assess each combination of domain and modal specificity. This design is implemented for three reasons: to anchor the assessment securely in the theory of successful intelligence, to allow students balanced opportunities to demonstrate multiple and varied abilities, and to serve as a clear guide for assessing abilities across and between domains and modes.

Augmented assessment items differ in ways beyond the categorical properties of the grid. Difficulty varies from subtest to subtest, and from item to item within these. A central goal of task creation is the elimination of ceilings on each subtest to the extent possible (and reasonable) without compromising the capacity of the assessment to be given not only to students already thought to be gifted but to whole student populations without generating

TABLE 10.1. *Aurora-a grid: The Aurora Subtests Grouped by Target Ability and Domain*

	Analytical	Creative	Practical
Images (visual/spatial)	Shapes (Abstract Tangrams): Complete shapes with missing pieces. (10 items)(MC) Floating Boats: Identify matching patterns among connected boats. (5 items)(MC)	Book Covers: Interpret an abstract picture and invent a story to accompany it. (5 items) (OE) Multiple Uses: Devise three new uses for each of several household items. (5 items)(OE)	Paper Cutting: Identify the proper unfolded version of a cut piece of paper. (10 items)(MC) Toy Shadows: Identify the shadow that will be cast by a toy in a specific orientation. (8 items)(MC)
Words (verbal)	Words That Sound the Same (Homophone Blanks): Complete a sentence with two missing words using homonyms. (20 items) (RW) (Limited) Metaphors: Explain how two somewhat unrelated things are alike. (10 items)(OE)	(Inanimate) Conversations: Create dialogues between objects that cannot typically talk. (10 items) (OE) Interesting (Figurative) Language: Interpret what sentence logically comes next after one containing figurative language. (12 items)(MC)	(Silly) Headlines: Identify and explain an alternative "silly" meaning of actual headlines. (11 items) (RW)
Numbers (numerical)	Number Cards (Letter Math): Find the single-digit number that letters represent in equations. (5 items) (RW) Story Problems (Algebra): (before any algebra training) Devise ways to solve logical math problems with two or more missing variables. (5 items) (RW)	Number Talk: Imagine reasons for various described social interactions between numbers. (7 items)(OE) Money (Exchange): Divide complicated "bills" appropriately between friends. (5 items) (RW)	Decisions: List elements given in a scenario on either "good" or "bad" side of a list in order to make a decision. (3 items) (RW) Maps (Logistics Mapping): Trace the best carpooling routes to take between friends' houses and destinations. (10 items) (RW)

Notes:

MC: Multiple Choice

OE: Open-ended items that need to be scored by an individual using a rating scale

RW: Answers are either Right or Wrong

() in subtest titles: Subtest titles or portions of titles no longer in use undue distress or anxiety. Both subtests and tasks range in length, and individual questions take many forms. Some items require receptive answers, those chosen from a discrete set of options, and others ask for productive answers, generated by the student with varying degrees of constraint. Among other variations, there are multiple-choice and fill-in-the-blank questions answered, math problems solved, lists generated, short selections written, pieces of information classified and ordered, money allocated, paths drawn, and subjective decisions made. A glance at the assessment reveals photographs, arrangements of numbers, drawings, short paragraphs, and computer-generated images.

Progressing across the grid of the Aurora-*a* battery as if reading cells from left to right and then top to bottom, let's describe some example subtests. *Floating Boats* allows students to match patterns of connected toys whose arrangement changes from one photograph to another. *Book Covers* allows students to generate a brief story plot to describe somewhat abstract pictures portrayed as children's book covers. *Toy Shadows* allows students to choose the shadow that is made by a toy oriented in a particular way in relation to a light. *Limited Metaphors* allows students to generate a link between two somewhat unrelated nouns. *Inanimate Conversations* allows students to imagine what certain objects might say to each other if they could speak. *Tough Decisions* allows students to categorize given information in pro – or con – lists to make an everyday choice. *Letter Math* allows students to find numerical solutions to math problems with letters in place of some "missing" values. *Number Talk* allows students to explain the reason for a social interaction briefly described and illustrated between two cartoon-like drawings of numbers. *Logistics Mapping* allows students to compare different routes to destinations based on incremental distances provided. This selection offers a sample of the range of tasks developed for the augmented assessment.

As a supplement to the analytical, creative, and practical measures described above, a *g*-factor assessment has also been developed (the so-called Aurora-*g* battery). Its design is likewise guided by a grid structure with identical modes, but with task types rather than skill areas informing the second axis. These are analogy, series completion, and classification tasks – all typical traditional measures of general intelligence. Analogy requires students to analyze a relationship between a pair of stimuli (images, words, or numbers) and extend this relationship to a second, unfinished pair by choosing the correct stimulus from choices. Series completion requires students to evaluate the logic of a progressive series of stimuli (images, words, or numbers) and choose the next stimulus in the series from choices. Finally, classification tasks require students to compare and contrast the properties of a list of stimuli (images, words, or numbers) and select the one that conforms least to the others. Exactly nine subtests were developed such that the criteria of each cell of the design grid are met.

The two sections that make up the Aurora battery are intended to complement each other by reserving a place for traditionally valued g-factor skills while expanding the scope of identification methods to recognize less formally appreciated creative and practical skills with the augmented assessment. The inclusion of both tests grants schools the ability to demonstrate the relative effectiveness of each for assessing the abilities valued in their stated definitions of giftedness and fostered through their programming. Educators are also given the opportunity to consider how the augmented assessment compares with a more traditional one in identifying students in the school's particular context without employing multiple test batteries. This single battery might therefore be uniquely applied in accordance with the needs and goals of particular schools.

As Robinson (2005) reminds us, psychometric instruments can be particularly effective tools for gifted identification when educators capitalize on the flexibility offered by different types of assessments. Depending on the variable definitions of giftedness adopted, types of programs offered, and particular concerns of gifted educators, the Aurora battery may be viewed as a series of assessments and therefore employed in several ways. Because the g-factor assessment (g-battery) is intended as a supplement, the use of only this portion of the battery is likely to offer schools little beyond what is already available. Conversely, the augmented assessment is designed to allow for several alternative uses. First, schools that are uninterested in, or discouraged by, the performance of traditional instruments with their population might use the a-battery independent of the g-battery. Alternatively, schools seeking to better identify only a particular skill, either as a complement to existing identification measures or for selection for more specialized gifted programming, might use only part of the Aurora-a assessment. For example, creativity subtests, or only those dealing with figures as opposed to verbal and numerical modes, might be administered alone. Particularly with employment of the entire augmented assessment, educators may better meet a number of goals and enhance their gifted identification possibilities in important ways.

LIMITATIONS

There are many limitations of these studies that circumscribe the conclusions that can be drawn from them.

A first limitation is that socioeconomic class is confounded with ethnicity. So ethnicity differences may be attributable, in unknown measure, to socioeconomic class differences. The differences are unlikely to be solely a function of socioeconomic class, in that, where we obtained differences, others have obtained similar patterns of differences (see, e.g., Loehlin, Lindzey, & Spuhler, 1975). For example, in a study we did in 2001, Asian Americans did better on quantitative analytical measures than did White Americans and worse on the creative measures than did White Americans, and in a result with Chinese and American college students in comparably selective universities, we obtained the same result regarding creativity, regardless of whether we used Chinese or American university professors as raters (Niu & Sternberg, 2001). Moreover, Asian Americans are generally not at a higher socioeconomic level than are Whites but performed better on the quantitative analytical tests, such as the math SAT, here and in other studies (Lynn, 2006). The reason we did not control for socioeconomic class is that we were unable to obtain the data that would have enabled us to do so.

A second limitation is that there were problematical methodological issues in both the Rainbow and Kaleidoscope Projects. In Rainbow, we used an incomplete design, meaning that not all students took all tests. This made the statistical analysis complex to the point that we would not recommend the use of this design by others. In Kaleidoscope, unlike in Rainbow, assessments were done without proctoring. Thus, we cannot be certain of the conditions under which the assessments were taken, or even that it was the applicant who took the assessment. The nature of the assessments, though, makes it questionable whether parents or others who might take the assessment would do better than the applicants (for example, to cite one of the essays, many parents know far less about MTV than do their children). Moreover, an advantage of doing the assessment at home is that students have more time to think carefully and deeply than they do in a timed proctored test; often it is hard to think creatively, practically, or wisely when there is not sufficient time to do so.

A third limitation is that the new assessments require more time, resources, and money for scoring. We had to hire raters and train them. Although reliability was good, it could be achieved only with training. Schools would therefore have to decide that the additional information was worth the cost. In the Rainbow Project, we got substantially better prediction than with SAT alone (double) or with SAT plus high school GPA (roughly 50% increase) and decreased ethnic-group differences. In the Kaleidoscope Project, we did not see academic differences between groups, but these results were considered excellent, given the absence of ethnic-group differences in Kaleidoscope. So to the extent one wishes to increase diversity and maintain academic standards, these measures seem promising.

A fourth limitation is that our follow-up data at this time are limited. For Rainbow, we had only first-year university grades. For Kaleidoscope, the project has been in effect only for 4 years. For this project, we will be following up by measuring progress broadly – including nonacademic measures – during the 4 years the students are at the university.

A fifth limitation, in Kaleidoscope, is selection bias. Students who completed the essays were not a random sample of applicants: They chose to do extra work. However, because admission probabilities were not related to the fact of completing the essays, only to the quality of essays for those who did complete them, the bias may not have been an important factor in the results.

In sum, WICS (*w*isdom, *i*ntelligence, *c*reativity, *s*ynthesized) appears to provide a strong theoretical basis for augmented assessment of the skills needed for undergraduate success. There is evidence to indicate that it has good incremental predictive power and serves to increase equity. As teaching improves and university teachers emphasize more the creative and practical skills needed for success in school and life, the predictive power of the test may increase. Cosmetic changes in testing over the last century have made relatively little difference to the construct validity of assessment procedures. The theory of successful intelligence could provide a new opportunity to increase construct validity at the same time that it reduces differences in test performance between groups. It may indeed be possible to accomplish the goals of affirmative action through tests such as the Rainbow assessments, either as supplements to traditional affirmative action programs or as substitutes for them.

Other modern theories of intelligence, such as those mentioned earlier in the book, may also serve to improve prediction and increase diversity. Moreover, additional approaches to supplementing the SAT may be called for. For example, Oswald, Schmitt, Kim, Ramsay, and Gillespie (2004) have found biodata and situational-judgment tests (the latter of which we also used) to provide incremental validity to the SAT. Sedlacek (2004) has developed noncognitive measures that appear to have had success in enhancing the university admissions process.

The theory and principles of assessment used in the Rainbow, Kaleidoscope, and Aurora projects can be extended beyond the United States (Sternberg, 2004a, 2007c). At present, we are in the midst of a collaboration with psychologists in Germany to determine whether the instruments we have used in the United States might, in suitable form, be useful there as well.

There is no question but that the methods used in the Rainbow Project, the Kaleidoscope Project, and related projects are at early stages of development. They do not have 100 years – and more – of experience behind them, as do traditional methods. What the results suggest is that an argument is to be made for broader assessments – that broader assessments are not synonymous with fuzzy-headed assessments. Such assessments can improve prediction and increase diversity, rather than trading off the one for the other. Broader assessments do not replace conventional ones: They supplement them. Our results show an important role for traditional analytical abilities in university success. But these are not the only abilities that matter, and should not be the only abilities we measure.

11

Educating the Gifted

More and more, educators are recognizing that many children, including gifted children, fail to live up to their potential. There can be a number of reasons for this failure, but one reason is that the way students are taught and often assessed in school does not enable them to learn and perform in an optimal way. We have developed the WICS theory (wisdom, intelligence, creativity, synthesized) to understand these children (Sternberg, 1997a, 1999c), and have developed a set of methods of teaching for successful intelligence to help these students reach their full potential (Sternberg & Grigorenko, 2000, 2007b; Sternberg, Grigorenko, & Zhang, 2008; Sternberg, Jarvin, & Grigorenko, 2009).

TEACHING AND ASSESSING THE GIFTED FOR WICS

We have developed several principles for teaching:

1. Because students have different life goals and hence different outcomes that, for them, are successful, student success needs to be defined in terms that are meaningful to the students as well as to the institution.

Students take courses for many reasons. How can teachers translate such a wide range of needs into effective teaching and assessment strategies?

(a) *Provide numerous examples of concepts that cover a wide range of applications*. In almost any course, examples can be narrowly or broadly conceived. Broadly conceived examples – and lots of them – help more students relate to the material. For example, historical events have implications for helping students understand literature, current news events, notions of science and scientific progress; spot sources

213

of future political unrest; and so forth. By giving multiple and diverse concrete examples, teachers meet the needs of more students. Teachers may make the mistake of believing that because children are gifted, they can automatically provide their own concrete examples. On the contrary, gifted students sometimes are extremely strong in abstract thinking but may have the same problems as anyone else in translating what they learn into concrete specifics.

(b) *Give students multiple and diverse options in assessment.* Gifted students can be gifted in very diverse ways, and assessments should reflect this diversity. Options can take various forms. For example, students can have a term-project/paper assignment (which itself may be optional) that enables them to write about any topic of interest to them so long as it falls within the purview of the course. In this way, students are invited to find a way to relate a given course to their own current or potential future personal or professional interests. Usually, it is a good idea to have students submit a proposal or précis for comments before they start on the full-fledged project or paper. As an example, a test may have options built into it. Students might have, for instance, a common multiple-choice section followed by a selection of essays that involve application of concepts in diverse ways to different fields. A test on a novel, for example, might have a choice of essays such as on (i) an analysis of the plot of the novel, (ii) a comparison of two characters, (iii) the application of the themes of the novel to everyday life, and so forth.

(c) *Grade student work in a way that preserves the integrity of the course as well as the integrity of the students' varied life goals.* Diverse forms of assessment will succeed only if the teachers are able to understand and, to some extent, identify with student goals in preparation of projects or essays. If students learn that certain types of projects or essays or even points of view consistently receive higher grades than do others, the students quickly will learn that the teacher is letting a thousand flowers bloom in theory but not in practice (much as happened when Mao Tse-tung encouraged dissent and then punished the dissenters). Some gifted students are very quick to pick up what teachers expect – that is part of their giftedness. Unless the teacher gives them the freedom to explore, they may be quicker than other students merely to dish out what they think a teacher wants.

2. Help students to capitalize on strengths and at the same time help them correct or compensate for weaknesses.

Think back to your three or four best teachers. Were they identical in their methods of instruction and assessment? Did they all achieve their success in the same way? Almost certainly they did not. People succeed (and fail) for different reasons. One teacher might stand out for the lectures she gave, another for her facilitation of group discussions, a third for his serving as a role model to emulate. Just as professionals (in all fields) succeed (and fail) in different ways, so do students. In order to maximize students' opportunities for success, it is important to enable them to capitalize on their strengths and to correct or compensate for weaknesses. Teaching in this way maximizes students' achievement (Sternberg, Grigorenko, Ferrari, & Clinkenbeard, 1999a, 1999b; Sternberg, Grigorenko, & Jarvin, 2001). Gifted students, as noted in this book, can be gifted in multiple ways; even the best of them will have weaknesses as well as strengths. These facts have several implications.

(a) *There is no one right way of teaching and learning.* Different students learn and think in different ways (Sternberg, 1997a, 1997b). Some students may learn better from lectures, others from class discussions. Some may learn better via oral presentation, others by reading. Some may prefer verbal presentation of material; others may want pictorial representation. Some may love to delve into details; others may prefer to concentrate on the big picture. By varying teaching techniques, a teacher is likely to reach more students more successfully.

(b) *There is no one right way of assessing students' achievement.* Experience suggests that some students excel in multiple-choice tests, others in essays. Some students do well so long as the questions are limited to factual recall whereas others do better if they are allowed to show their deeper understanding, perhaps of fewer facts. Unidimensional assessments (e.g., tests that are all multiple-choice, all short-answer, or all essay) often fail to enable students to capitalize on strengths. The same students may repeatedly excel and others repeatedly do poorly not for lack of ability or even achievement, but for lack of variety in the way their knowledge and skills are assessed.

(c) *Teach and assess to weaknesses as well as to strengths.* Some teachers might misunderstand the message here as a plea for extreme indi-vidualization – an individualized program for each student. Such a program is usually impractical, especially at the introductory level, and often is counterproductive. Students need to learn to correct or compensate for weaknesses as well as to capitalize on strengths. Thus it is important that students be intellectually uncomfortable some of the time, just as it is important for them to be intellectually comfortable and secure some of the time. The students need to learn to deal with more challenging methods of instruction and assessment as well as with ones that challenge them less. By varying methods of instruction and assessment for all students, you automatically provide an environment in which, at a given time, some students will be more, and others less, comfortable. Fortunately, different students will be at different comfort levels at different times.

3. Students need to learn to balance adaptation to, shaping of, and selection of environments.

The balance of these three responses to the environment has certain implications for teaching:

(a) *Students, like teachers, need to develop flexibility.* A rigid classroom or institutional environment is likely to foster rigidity in the thinking of the students in it. Given the amazingly rapid rate of development today – the rapidly changing environment of the Internet, the changing nature of jobs and the requirements of those jobs, the rapidly changing social structures that render behavior that is socially acceptable one year, socially unacceptable the next – schools are obliged to develop flexibility in their students. The rapid accumulation of knowledge may render much of the knowledge students acquire in school obsolete, but it will never render obsolete the facility they acquire in coping with novel environments. As a result, teachers need not only to encourage students by challenging them but also to encourage students to challenge themselves. For example, the school environment should be structured in a way that encourages students to take difficult courses or courses that challenge the boundaries students may previously have set for themselves.

The environment should also encourage students to understand and be able to represent points of view other than their own. At the same time, students need to learn to critique in a thoughtful and systematic manner beliefs that they may have held dear throughout their lives, whatever these beliefs may be.

(b) *Students need to be allowed and even encouraged to take risks and to make mistakes.* People often learn more from their mistakes and failures than from their successes. An environment that does not allow students to make mistakes or ever to fail in their endeavors deprives the students of important learning opportunities. Environmental selection means choosing a new environment over an old one. It can apply to changing one's term paper topic after discovering that one's first choice did not work out, or changing one's course schedule after deciding that the selection of a particular course was a mistake. Students often view the decisions to make such changes as implying that they have wasted time in their former choices (e.g., of paper topics or courses). Quite the contrary, the students have learned a lesson they will need in life – to have a sense of when and how to cut losses and to recognize that there is a need to change one's direction or even one's goals. Put succinctly, they need to learn that nothing ventured, nothing gained.

(c) *Students need to learn how to overcome obstacles.* When the environment of the classroom, the institution, or even the society is less than ideal, it often requires guts to try to change (shape) it. Outmoded and often counterproductive practices continue in all institutions and even classroom settings simply because no one, including the faculty, wants to challenge authority and cut through the red tape needed to improve the learning or working environment. Often when students or their teachers try to make changes, they encounter opposition and even outright defiance. Yet the world would be a much worse place to live if no one had had the courage to stand up to opposition and fight for change – to shape the environment.

At the same time, students need to learn to balance adaptation with shaping. Someone who initiates and then fights one battle after another is likely to lose considerable time, as well as credibility, in the resulting skirmishes. Students and faculty alike need to learn to pick their battles carefully, and then to stand up for the causes that truly are meaningful to them. As teachers, we might find numerous aspects of our institutions in need of change. We cannot change them all. We, just like our students, therefore need to develop a taste for which battles are worth fighting and which are not. But when we choose, we must then be willing to stand up for our beliefs and show persuasively why others should adopt them.

4. Teaching and assessment should balance use of analytical, creative, practical, and wise thinking.

All teaching and assessment should be balanced in terms of the thinking skills they require. At the same time, as teachers, we need to put behind us the false dichotomy between "teaching for thinking" and "teaching for the facts," or between emphases on thinking and emphases on memory.

Thinking always requires memory and the knowledge base that is accessed through the use of our memories. One cannot analyze what one knows if one knows nothing. One cannot creatively go beyond the existing boundaries of knowledge if one does not know what those boundaries are. And one cannot apply what one knows in a practical manner if one does not know anything to apply.

At the same time, memory for facts without the ability to use those facts is really useless. A story appeared in the news about a man who entered a truck on which an electrical wire had fallen during a continuing storm. A second man, observing the first man's imminent entrance into the truck, shouted at him to stop, but too late. The first man was electrocuted. The first man had master's degrees in physics and engineering; the second man had no such degrees. Who was gifted? Without doubt, the first man's educational achievements gave him the declarative (factual) knowledge that he could have used to save his life. But he was unable to apply this knowledge (turn it into procedures) in a way that would have ensured his survival.

It is for this reason that we encourage teachers to teach and assess achievement in ways that enable students to analyze, create with, and apply their knowledge. When students think to learn, they also learn to think. And there is an added benefit: Students who are taught analytically, creatively, and practically perform better on assessments, apparently without regard to the form the assessments take. That is, they outperform students instructed in conventional ways, even if the assessments are for straight factual memory (Sternberg, Torff, & Grigorenko, 1998a, 1998b). Moreover, our research shows that these techniques succeed, regardless of subject-matter area. But what, exactly, are the techniques used to teach analytically, creatively, and practically (see Table 11.1 for a summary)? We shall discuss these first, and then the skills involved in teaching for wisdom later.

1. Teaching analytically means encouraging students to (a) analyze, (b) critique, (c) judge, (d) compare and contrast, (e) evaluate, and (f) assess. When teachers refer to teaching for "critical thinking," they typically mean teaching for analytical thinking. How does such teaching translate into instructional and assessment activities? Consider various examples across the school curriculum:

   (a) *Analyze* the development of the character of Heathcliff in *Wuthering Heights*. [Literature]

TABLE 11.1 *Summary of Selected Prompts for Analytical, Creative, and Practical Instruction and Assessment*

Analytical
(a) analyze
(b) critique
(c) judge
(d) compare and contrast
(e) evaluate
(f) assess

Creative
(a) create
(b) invent
(c) discover
(d) imagine if...
(e) suppose that...
(f) predict

Practical
(a) apply
(b) use
(c) put into practice
(d) implement
(e) employ
(f) render practical

(b) *Critique* the design of the experiment (just gone over in class or in a reading) showing that certain plants grew better in dim light than in bright sunlight. [Biology]

(c) *Judge* the artistic merits of Roy Lichtenstein's "comic-book art," discussing its strengths as well as its weaknesses as fine art. [Art]

(d) *Compare and contrast* the respective natures of the American Revolution and the French Revolution, pointing out ways in which they were similar and those in which they were different. [History]

(e) *Evaluate* the validity of the following solution to a mathematical problem, and discuss weaknesses in the solution, if there are any. [Mathematics]

(f) *Assess* the strategy used by the winning player in the tennis match you just observed, stating what techniques she used to defeat her opponent. [Physical Education]

2. Teaching creatively means encouraging students to (a) create, (b) invent, (c) discover, (d) imagine if..., (e) suppose that...,

(f) predict. Teaching for creativity requires teachers not only to support and encourage creativity but also to role-model it and to reward it when it is displayed (Sternberg & Lubart, 1995; Sternberg & Williams, 1996). In other words, teachers need not only to talk the talk, but also to walk the walk. Consider some examples of instructional or assessment activities that encourage students to think creatively.

(a) *Create* an alternative ending to the short story you just read that represents a different way things might have gone for the main characters in the story. [Literature]

(b) *Invent* a dialogue between an American tourist in Paris and a French man he encounters on the street from whom he is asking directions on how to get to the Rue Pigalle. [French]

(c) *Discover* the fundamental physical principle that underlies all of the following problems, each of which differs from the others in the "surface structure" of the problem but not in its "deep structure." [Physics]

(d) *Imagine if* the government of China keeps evolving over the course of the next 20 years in much the same way it has been evolving. What do you believe the government of China will be like in 20 years? [Government/Political Science]

(e) *Suppose that* you were to design one additional instrument to be played in a symphony orchestra for future compositions. What might that instrument be like, and why? [Music]

(f) *Predict* changes that are likely to occur in the vocabulary or grammar of spoken Spanish in the border areas of the Rio Grande over the next 100 years as a result of continuous interactions between Spanish and English speakers. [Linguistics]

3. Teaching practically means encouraging students to (a) apply, (b) use, (c) put into practice, (d) implement, (e) employ, (f) render practical what they know. Such teaching must relate to the real practical needs of the students, not just to what would be practical for individuals other than the students (Sternberg et al., 2000). Consider some examples:

(a) *Apply* the formula for computing compound interest to a problem people are likely to face when planning for retirement. [Economics, Math]

(b) *Use* your knowledge of German to greet a new acquaintance in Berlin. [German]

(c) *Put into practice* what you have learned from teamwork in football to making a classroom team project succeed. [Athletics]

(d) *Implement* a business plan you have written in a simulated business environment. [Business]

(e) *Employ* the formula for distance, rate, and time, to compute a distance. [Math]

(f) *Render practical* a proposed design for a new building so that it will work in the aesthetic context of the surrounding buildings, all of which are at least 100 years old. [Architecture]

Clearly, it is possible to implement teaching for successful intelligence in a wide variety of academic contexts. But there are potential problems with any new methodology. What are the potential problems for this one?

POTENTIAL OBJECTIONS TO TEACHING FOR SUCCESSFUL INTELLIGENCE WITH REPLIES

Here are common objections and replies with respect to the implementation of the techniques described in this chapter.

1. *Teaching for successful intelligence requires individualization to many patterns of abilities, which is impractical, because one cannot know all students' abilities, and in a large class one even may not know any students' patterns of abilities.*

This objection is based on a misunderstanding. As noted above, teaching for successful intelligence actually is largely uniform across students because all students need to learn both how to capitalize on strengths and how to correct or compensate for weaknesses. At a given time, instruction may be favoring some students and not others. But over time, it should roughly equally favor all students.

Teaching for successful intelligence stresses maximizing, not equalizing, all students' outcomes. This type of teaching neither assumes equal achievement of students nor aims at eliminating individual differences. Teaching for successful intelligence is a tool devised to ensure content presentation in a number of ways, all of which engage students' diverse patterns of abilities.

2. *Teaching for successful intelligence means teaching everything in three ways and that is impractical.*

It *is* impractical to teach everything in three ways, and few if any concepts should be taught all three ways. Rather, teachers should vary their use of analytical, creative, and practical techniques over concepts and over time.

On average, a roughly equal amount of time should be devoted to each kind of teaching. But it is not necessary or desirable to teach every concept in three ways. Thus teaching for successful intelligence does not mean that the school year must somehow magically be extended. The amount of teaching is not different, but rather, the quality of the teaching. The teacher needs to gauge students' needs and understanding and then teach in the ways that are appropriate.

   3. *Teaching for successful intelligence is too novel for most teachers and requires too much effort to implement.*

When we give workshops on teaching for successful intelligence, one of the first things we emphasize is that *all* teachers will have used the large majority of the techniques at least some of the time. There is relatively little, and for some teachers, nothing new in teaching for successful intelligence. Good teachers do these things spontaneously or learn how to do them in short order. Rather, good teachers are often out of balance: They emphasize certain kinds of teaching and assessment techniques at the expense of others. Thus the main thing many teachers have to work on is balance rather than learning how to teach in totally novel ways.

   4. *Exams tend to stress memory for material and so it really does not make sense to teach in a way that encourages thinking that will prove to be at best irrelevant and at worst detrimental to exam performance.*

As noted above, this objection simply is wrong. Teaching for successful intelligence seems to raise student achievement, on average, regardless of subject matter or means of assessment (Grigorenko, Jarvin, & Sternberg, 2000; Sternberg, Torff, & Grigorenko, 1998a, 1998b).

   5. *Teaching for successful intelligence seems applicable to higher level but not lower level courses.*

This misconception is common but incorrect. Students should learn to think analytically, creatively, and practically at all levels. The techniques can be and have been applied at all levels, including the introductory level (e.g., Sternberg, 1995). Even the most basic material can be taught in any of the three ways.

An additional reason to teach for successful intelligence is precisely that the kinds of thinking required more closely resemble those required for the real-world work for which school is preparatory. In a conventional course, a student who is a poor memorizer using conventional memory learning may conclude that he or she lacks the skills needed to be a successful historian, biologist, psychologist, geographer, language interpreter, or whatever, when in fact the skills in which he or she is weak may apply largely only to achieving success in introductory-level courses. Students may thus drop out of subject-matter areas in which they actually have the skills needed to succeed on the job, but not to succeed especially well in the first-level courses that prepare for the job. Teaching for successful intelligence thus may enable many students to pursue their dreams when they might otherwise give up in despair, falsely believing themselves to be incompetent.

6. *Teaching for successful intelligence is applicable to small courses but not to large ones.*

In fact, teaching for successful intelligence may be done, at least at some level, in courses of any size. In extreme cases, it may be feasible only to give multiple-choice or short-answer exams if the number of students is extremely large and the resources for grading the students' work extremely small. But having students analyze ideas, come up with their own ideas, and learn how to apply ideas can be done in any course. Teachers can encourage students to think in these ways, and can role-model these kinds of thinking for the students.

Large classes may mean that a teacher can only use certain aspects of teaching for successful intelligence. But approximating full teaching for successful intelligence is better than giving up on it altogether. Even if one is limited to multiple-choice exams, it still is possible to design questions that require at least some amount of analytical, creative, and practical thinking in addition to questions that require only pure factual recall.

7. *Teaching for successful intelligence is applicable only to certain subject areas.*

As the preceding examples show, teaching for successful intelligence is applicable to all subject-matter areas. This interpretation of the role of the teacher is designed to make teaching easier rather than more effective. The problem is that students often take only a few introductory courses, and perhaps just one. In elementary education, students may just have one teacher for the entire year, and in secondary education there is often just one teacher per subject area in any given year. Thus the students may never even get to view the thinking of the other teachers. If they find that they do not excel in learning the way the teacher prefers to teach, chances are the students (as well as the teachers) will not attribute their failure to succeed to a mismatch between teaching and learning preferences. Rather, they will attribute their failure to sheer incompetence and never even get the chance to find out that they could have succeeded with another teacher and another method of teaching. Teachers thus have a responsibility to make sure that they maximize the conditions of learning for all students, not just for those whose strengths happen to match the teachers' own.

8. *As a teacher, I already do all these things anyway, so I can do what I have been doing without applying a fancy name to it.*

If you are already doing all these things, that's wonderful! But our research has shown that there frequently is a discrepancy between what teachers think they are doing and what they are actually doing, as revealed by classroom observations (Spear & Sternberg, 1987). Thus the teacher needs to make sure he or she truly is doing these things, rather than merely thinking he or she is doing them.

9. *Students won't like learning analytically, creatively, or practically, or will find it too hard.*

There are always some students who do not like any particular method of teaching. But on average, you will reach more students teaching for successful intelligence. Outside the classroom, students learn in these ways. Now they can learn in these ways inside the classroom as well. There may be an adjustment at first on the part of students. But our data show that, once they are familiar with the proposed methods of teaching and assessment, students like them more, not less, than traditional methods (Sternberg, Torff, & Grigorenko, 1998a).

SOME INSTRUCTIONAL DATA

We have sought to test the theory of successful intelligence in the classroom. In a first set of studies, we explored the question of whether conventional education in school systematically discriminates against children with creative and practical strengths (Sternberg & Clinkenbeard, 1995; Sternberg, Ferrari, Clinkenbeard, & Grigorenko, 1996; Sternberg, Grigorenko, Ferrari, & Clinkenbeard, 1999a). Motivating this work was the belief that the systems in most schools tend to favor strongly those children with strengths in memory and analytical abilities. However, schools can be unbalanced in other directions as well. One school we visited in Russia in 2000 placed a heavy emphasis on the development of creative abilities – much more so than on the development of analytical and practical abilities. While on this trip, we were told of yet another school – catering to the children of Russian businessman – that strongly emphasized practical abilities, and in which children who were not practically oriented were told that, eventually, they would be working for their classmates who were practically oriented.

To validate the relevance of the theory of successful intelligence in class-rooms, we have carried out a number of instructional studies.

Aptitude-Treatment Interaction Study

In one study (Sternberg, Ferrari, Clinkenbeard, & Grigorenko, 1996), we used the Sternberg Triarchic Abilities Test. The test was administered around the United States and in some other countries to 326 children who were identified by their schools as gifted by any standard whatsoever. Children were selected for a summer program in (college-level) psychology if they fell into one of five ability groupings: high analytical, high creative, high practical, high balanced (high in all three abilities), or low balanced (low in all three abilities). Thus, all students were identified as gifted except those in the last group. Students came to Yale for the instruction and then were divided into four instructional groups.

Students in all four instructional groups used the same introductory psychology textbook and listened to the same psychology lectures. What differed among them was the type of afternoon discussion section to which they were assigned. These were instructional conditions that emphasized memory, analytical, creative, or practical instruction. For example, in the memory condition, they might be asked to describe the main tenets of a major theory of depression. In the analytical condition, they might be asked to compare and contrast two theories of depression. In the creative condition, they might be asked to formulate their own theory of depression. In the practical condition, they might be asked how they could use what they had learned about depression to help a friend who was depressed.

Students in all four instructional conditions were evaluated in terms of their performance on homework, a mid-term exam, a final exam, and an independent project. Each type of work was evaluated for memory, analytical, creative, and practical quality. Thus, all students were evaluated in exactly the same way.

Our results suggested the utility of the theory of successful intelligence. This utility showed itself in several ways.

First, we observed when the students arrived at Yale that the students in the high-creative and high-practical groups were much more diverse in racial, ethnic, socioeconomic, and educational backgrounds than were the students in the high-analytical group, suggesting that correlations of measured intelligence with status variables such as these may be reduced by using a broader conception of intelligence. Thus, the kinds of students identified as strong differed in terms of populations from which they were drawn in comparison with students identified as strong solely by analytical measures. More important, just by expanding the range of abilities measured, we discovered intellectual strengths that might not have been apparent through a conventional test.

Second, we found that all three ability tests – analytical, creative, and practical – significantly predicted course performance. When multiple-regression analysis was used, at least two of these ability measures contributed significantly to the prediction of each of the measures of achievement. Perhaps as a reflection of the difficulty of deemphasizing the analytical way of teaching, one of the significant predictors was always the analytical score.

Third and most important, there was an aptitude-treatment interaction whereby students who were placed in instructional conditions that better matched their pattern of abilities outperformed students who were mismatched. In other words, when students are taught in a way that fits how they think, they do better in school. Children with creative and practical abilities, who are almost never taught or assessed in a way that matches their pattern of abilities, may be at a disadvantage in course after course, year after year.

Social Studies and Science Study

A follow-up study (Sternberg, Torff, & Grigorenko, 1998a, 1998b) examined learning of social studies and science by third graders and eighth graders. The 225 third graders were students in a very low-income neighborhood in Raleigh, North Carolina. The 142 eighth graders were students who were largely middle to upper-middle class studying in Baltimore, Maryland, and Fresno, California. In this study, students were assigned to one of three instructional conditions. In the first condition, they were taught the course that basically they would have learned had there been no intervention. The emphasis in the course was on memory. In a second condition, students were taught in a way that emphasized critical (analytical) thinking. In the third condition, they were taught in a way that emphasized analytical, creative, and practical thinking. All students' performance was assessed for memory learning (through multiple-choice assessments) as well as for analytical, creative, and practical learning (through performance assessments).

As expected, students in the successful-intelligence (analytical, creative, practical) condition outperformed the other students in terms of the performance assessments. One could argue that this result merely reflected the way they were taught. Nevertheless, the result suggested that teaching for these kinds of thinking succeeded. More important, however, was the result that children in the successful-intelligence condition outperformed the other children even on the multiple-choice memory tests. In other words, to the extent that one's goal is just to maximize children's memory for information, teaching for successful intelligence is still superior. It enables children to capitalize on their strengths and to correct or to compensate for their weaknesses, and it allows children to encode material in a variety of interesting ways.

Reading Study

We extended these results to reading curricula at the middle school and the high school level (Sternberg, Grigorenko, & Jarvin, 2001; Grigorenko, Jarvin, & Sternberg, 2002). In a study of 871 middle school students and 432 high school students, we taught reading either triarchically or through the regular curriculum. At the middle school level, reading was taught explicitly. At the high school level, reading was infused into instruction in mathematics, physical sciences, social sciences, English, history, foreign languages, and the arts. In all settings, students who were taught triarchically substantially outperformed students who were taught in standard ways.

Study on Teaching for Successful Intelligence in Language Arts, Mathematics, and Science in Grade 4

The pattern of results indicating the advantage of teaching for successful intelligence has been replicated in yet another study, the largest so far (Sternberg, Grigorenko, & Zhang, 2008). This study was carried out on a national scale and involved thousands of fourth-grade students. We report the study in somewhat more detail because there is only one previously published article to which the reader might refer.

In this study, a group of educators and psychologists collaborated to develop and improve instructional materials and assessments in three subject areas for students in fourth-grade language arts, mathematics, and science. In addition, this study was also characterized by a conservative experimental design; specifically, curricula based on ideas of teaching for successful intelligence were compared with curricula based on modern theories of memory and critical thinking.

In each of these subject-matter areas, we developed several curriculum units, covering approximately a 12-week classroom intervention period. There were fewer science units than mathematics and language-arts units, but each one of these units covered a longer period. Each unit was composed of a preintervention assessment, a teacher guide, a set of activities and materials for students, and a postintervention assessment.

Each of the units in each subject area was developed in three versions, corresponding to the three educational methods (successful intelligence, critical thinking, and memory) being compared in this study. The three versions were parallel and shared the same knowledge content, but adopted different theoretical foci to teach the content.

The pre- and postintervention assessments consisted of a set of 30 items (half multiple-choice and half open-ended) related to the unit's content. These assessments were identical for students in all three conditions. In addition to the unit-specific assessments, a general baseline assessment was administered to all students participating in the program (either the Woodcock-Johnson III Test of Achievement, a normed test of academic achievement, or the Ohio Department of Education Proficiency Test for Grade 4).

The instructional materials consisted of a teacher guide containing background content information and instructional guidelines and an activity workbook for students. The activities were labeled according to their level of difficulty (from less challenging to more challenging), and teachers selected those activities they judged best fit the abilities of their students. Particular care was exercised to ensure that the content taught in the three versions of a unit was comparable. The content of the materials was carefully aligned with national and state (for states participating in this study) standards.

Overall, 196 teachers and 7,702 students participated in the study. The study spanned 4 years, 9 states, 14 school districts, and 110 schools. The sample included primarily fourth graders, but also third and fifth graders who were taught by teachers participating in the study with their fourth graders. The number of participants was approximately equal in all experimental groups.

The analyses generally proceeded in two phases. First, multifacet Rasch analysis was employed to determine scale and item characteristics, interrater reliability, and student ability estimates. Second, student ability estimates were subjected to hierarchical-linear modeling analyses to compare performance for each student in each condition.

Each pre- and postinstructional assessment contained a mix of multiple-choice and open-ended items assessing creative, practical, analytic, and memory abilities specific to each unit. Open-ended items were scored by trained raters using test-specific rubrics. In addition to the *total test* ability score, subscale scores for the *creative–practical* and *analytical–memory* components were also derived for each participating student. The first score represents ability-based styles proposed in particular by the theory of successful intelligence, whereas the second score represents ability-based styles proposed by conventional theories of intelligence (Sternberg, 1997a).

When considered across multiple units and the three academic domains (language arts, mathematics, and sciences), the *total test* scores of students in the successful-intelligence group were higher than those in the critical-thinking group and the memory group. When considered separately for *creative–practical* and *analytical–memory* scores, however, the patterns of results were different across experimental conditions. Specifically, children in the successful-intelligence group did better on creative and practical items than did students in the critical-thinking or memory groups. Yet, when performance on analytical and memory items was considered, although the students in the successful-intelligence group differed from their peers in the critical-thinking group, they did not differ significantly from participants in the memory group. The abilities thus once again met our definition of ability-based styles.

Overall, all three instructional conditions demonstrated substantial gain from pretest to posttest. Yet, the results indicate that students from the successful-intelligence group overall tended to have consistently higher gain scores than did students in the control conditions. Thus the results of these sets of studies suggest that children learn and think with different ability-based styles. Teaching in ways that recognize these individual differences improves learning.

On the whole, the results of the four sets of studies suggest that the theory of successful intelligence is valid as a whole. Moreover, the results suggest that the theory can make a difference not only in laboratory tests but also in school classrooms and even the everyday life of adults as well.

WHY TEACHING FOR SUCCESSFUL INTELLIGENCE WORKS

Why should teaching for successful intelligence improve performance relative to standard (or critical-thinking) instruction, even when performance is assessed for straightforward memory-based recall? There are at least four reasons. First, teaching for successful intelligence encourages deeper and more elaborated encoding of material than does traditional teaching, so that students learn the material in a way that enhances probability of retrieval at time of test. Second, teaching for successful intelligence encourages more diverse forms of encoding material, so that there are more retrieval paths to the material and hence there is greater likelihood of recall at time of test. Third, teaching for successful intelligence enables students to capitalize on strengths and to correct or compensate for weaknesses. Fourth, teaching for successful intelligence is more motivating to both teachers and students, so that the teachers are likely to teach more effectively and the students are likely to learn more. Ideally, of course, exams should *not* assess only static memory learning. Further guidelines and examples of how teachers can adapt a balanced approach to teaching for successful intelligence can be found in Sternberg, Jarvin, and Grigorenko (2009).

TEACHING FOR WISDOM

The Role of Wisdom in Education and Society

WICS involves wisdom as well as the elements of successful intelligence (analytical, creative, practical). Some time ago, one of us was on his way to an important meeting but got stuck in a maddening traffic jam. As he approached an exit along the slow, bumpy, and obstacle-laden route, he noted that the highway that extended out from the exit, which was perpendicular to the direction in which he was going, was wonderfully paved and the traffic was moving rapidly with no obstacles along its course. He actually considered taking that route. There was only one problem: The route led nowhere he wanted or needed to go, nor that he should have gone. Nevertheless, it was just so tempting!

Although he did not take that route, the U.S. educational system has. We believe it is going rapidly and relatively smoothly – in the wrong direction. That wrong direction is illustrated by the high-stakes system of testing that has come to dominate the country. It is not that high-stakes testing is, in itself, necessarily bad. It is that what the tests measure, to a large extent, doesn't matter in the long run. What matters is not *only* how much knowledge you have, but how you use that knowledge – whether for good ends (as for Mahatma Gandhi or Martin Luther King, Jr.) or for bad ones (as for Adolph Hitler and Joseph Stalin). What has distinguished wise leaders from foolish ones is not how much they know, but how they used what they know – whether they used it to foster a democratic ideal and a common good, or a totalitarian society good only for the dictator and his cronies.

Many societies today are preoccupied with the development of knowledge and basic cognitive skills in schoolchildren. But are knowledge and basic cognitive skills – the essential ingredients of intelligence as classically defined – enough? Consider the following.

As noted earlier, Flynn (1998) has pointed out that in more than a dozen other countries for which records have been available, IQs were rising in the twentieth century at a rate of roughly 9 points per generation (30 years). This increase went on for at least several generations (see also Neisser, 1998). With IQs going up and IQ-related abilities counting more and more for success in the society, one can only conclude that the IQ-like abilities of those at the top of the socioeconomic spectrum are higher than ever before – even higher than would be predicted merely by the Flynn effect, because IQs have become more important for gaining access to higher education and premium jobs. But again, the rise in IQs among the socioeconomic elite does not seem to have created a happier or more harmonious society, and one only has to read the daily newspapers to see the poor uses to which high IQ can be put. Judging by the amount, seriousness, and sheer scale of global conflict, perhaps not much of the increase in IQ is going to creating a common good.

There is no reason to believe that increasing IQs have improved people's or nations' relations with each other. Indeed, today there is more terrorism than at any time in recent memory. In the 1990s, there were more genocides and massacres than at any time since World War II. As people became smarter, they became, if anything, less wise and moved further from rather than closer to the pursuit of a common good. Indeed, there seems to be more hate in the world now than ever before (Sternberg, 2003a).

The memory and analytical skills that are so central to intelligence are certainly important for school and life success, but perhaps they are not sufficient. One can be smart but foolish. We all are susceptible to foolish thinking. Indeed, the "smarter" we are, the more we may think ourselves immune. And it is this fantasy that we are immune that makes us all the more susceptible!

It seems as if increases in intelligence – at least as measured by IQ – have not been matched by comparable increases in wisdom. Indeed, to the extent that our society has increasingly stressed the use of IQ to maximize one's own chances of admission to and success in the "cognitive elite" posited by Herrnstein and Murray (1994), increases in IQ may have been concomitant with decreases in wisdom. High IQ with a scarcity of wisdom has bought us a world with the power to finish itself off many times over.

Wisdom might bring us a world that would seek instead to better itself and the conditions of all the people in it. At some level, we as a society have a choice. What do we wish to maximize through our schooling? Is it only knowledge? Is it only intelligence? Or is it knowledge, intelligence, and wisdom too? If it is wisdom too, then we need to put our students on a much different course. We need to value not only how they use their outstanding individual abilities to maximize their attainments but also how they use their individual abilities to maximize the attainments of others as well. We need, in short, to value wisdom.

What would education look like that valued wisdom? Consider these principles of teaching for wisdom derived from the balance theory of wisdom (Sternberg, 1998b).

Teachers who teach for wisdom will explore with students the notion that conventional abilities and achievements are not enough for a satisfying life. Many people become trapped in their lives and, despite feeling conventionally successful, feel that their lives lack fulfillment. Fulfillment is not an alternative to success, but rather, is an aspect of it that, for most people, goes beyond money, promotions, large houses, and so forth. The teacher will further demonstrate how wisdom is critical for a satisfying life. In the long run, wise decisions benefit people in ways that foolish decisions never do. The teacher must teach students the usefulness of interdependence – a rising tide raises all ships; a falling tide can sink them.

It is also important to role-model wisdom, because what you do is more important than what you say. Wisdom is in what you do, not just in what you say. So students should read about wise judgments and decision making in the context of the actions that followed so that the students understand that such means of judging and decision making exist. Teachers need to help students to learn to recognize their own interests, those of other people, and those of institutions. They need further to help students learn to balance their own interests, those of other people, and those of institutions. They need to teach students that the "means" by which the end is obtained matters, not just the end. Students need to be encouraged to form, critique, and integrate their own values in their thinking. They further need to learn to think dialectically (Hegel, 1931), realizing that both questions and their answers evolve over time, and that the answer to an important life question can differ at different times in one's life (such as whether to marry). Wisdom further requires them to learn to think dialogically, whereby they understand interests and ideas from multiple points of view. For example, what one group views as a "settler," another may view as an "invader." Most important, students need to learn to search for and then try to reach the common good – a good where everyone wins and not only those with whom one identifies.

Teaching for wisdom will succeed only if teachers encourage and reward wisdom. Teachers must make wisdom real for students' lives. They should teach students to monitor events in their lives and their own thought processes about these events. One way to learn to recognize others' interests is to begin to identify your own. Teachers also should help students understand the importance of inoculating themselves against the pressures of unbalanced self-interest and small-group interest.

Students will develop wisdom by becoming engaged in class discussions, projects, and essays that encourage them to discuss the lessons they have learned from both classical and modern works and how these lessons can be applied to their own lives and the lives of others. They need to study not only "truth," as we know it, but values. The idea is not to force-feed a set of values, but to encourage students reflectively to develop their own pro-social ones.

Students should be encouraged to think about how almost everything they study might be used for better or worse ends, and to realize that the ends to which knowledge is put *do* matter. Teachers need to realize that the only way they can develop wisdom in their students is to serve as role models of wisdom themselves. A role model of wisdom will, we believe, take a much more Socratic approach to teaching than what teachers customarily do. Students often want large quantities of information spoon-fed or even force-fed to them. They then attempt to memorize this material for exams, only to forget it soon thereafter. In a wisdom-based approach to teaching, students will need to take a more active role in constructing their learning. But a wisdom-based approach is not, in my view, tantamount to a constructivist approach to learning. Students have not achieved or even come close to achieving wisdom when they merely have constructed their own learning. Rather, they must be able to construct knowledge not only from their own point of view, but to construct and sometimes reconstruct it from the point of view of others. Constructivism from only a single point of view can lead to egocentric rather than balanced understanding.

Lessons taught to emphasize wisdom would have a rather different character from lessons as they are often taught today. Consider examples.

Implications of Teaching for Wisdom

First, social studies and especially history lessons would look very different. For example, high school American history books typically teach American history from only one point of view, that of the new Americans. Thus Columbus is referred to as having "discovered" America, a strange notion from the standpoint of the many occupants who already lived there when it was "discovered." The conquest of the southwest and the Alamo also are presented only from the point of view of the new settlers, not also from the standpoint of, say, the Mexicans who lost roughly half their territory. This kind of ethnocentric and frankly propagandistic teaching would have no place in a curriculum that sought to develop wisdom and an appreciation of the need to balance interests.

Second, science teaching would no longer be about facts presented as though they are the final word. Science is often presented as though it represents the end point of a process of evolution of thought rather than one of many midpoints (Sternberg, 1998d). Students could scarcely realize from this kind of teaching that the paradigms of today, and thus the theories and findings that emanate from them, will eventually be superseded, much as the paradigms, theories, and findings of yesterday were replaced by those of today. Students further need to learn that, contrary to the way many textbooks are written, the classical "scientific method" is largely a fantasy rather than a reality and that scientists are as susceptible to fads as are members of other groups.

Third, teaching of literature needs to reflect a kind of balance that right now is frequently absent. Literature is often taught in terms of the standards and context of the contemporary U.S. scene. Characters often are judged in terms of our contemporary standards rather than in terms of the standards of the time and place in which the events took place. From the proposed standpoint, the study of literature must, to some extent, be done in the context of the study of history. The banning of books often reflects the application of certain contemporary standards to literature, standards of which an author from the past never could have been aware.

Fourth, foreign languages always would be taught in the cultural context in which they are embedded. We suggest that American students have so much more difficulty learning foreign languages than do children in much of Europe not because they lack the ability but because they lack the motivation. They do not see the need to learn another language whereas, say, a Flemish-speaking child in Belgium (where Flemish co-exists with French) does. Americans would be better off, we suggest, if they made more of an attempt wisely to understand other cultures rather than just to expect people from other cultures to understand them. And learning the language of a culture is a key to understanding. Americans might be less quick to impose their cultural values on others if they understood the others' cultural values. It is also interesting to speculate why Esperanto, a language that was to provide a common medium of communication across cultures, has been a notable failure. We suggest it is because Esperanto is embedded in no culture at all. It is the language of no one.

Culture cannot be taught, in the context of foreign-language learning, in the way it now often is – as an aside divorced from the actual learning of the language. It should be taught as an integral part of the language – as a primary context in which the language is embedded. The vituperative fights we see about bilingual education and about the use of Spanish in the United States or French in Canada are not just or even primarily fights about language. They are fights about culture, and they are fights in need of wise resolutions.

Finally, as implied throughout these examples, the curriculum needs to be far more integrated. Literature needs to be integrated with history, science with history, and social-policy studies and foreign language with culture. Even within disciplines, far more integration is needed.

The road to this new approach is bound to be a rocky one. First, entrenched structures, whatever they may be, are difficult to change, and wisdom is neither taught in schools nor, in general, is it even discussed. Second, many people will not see the value of teaching something that shows no promise of raising conventional test scores. These scores, which formerly were predictors of more interesting criteria, have now become criteria, or ends in themselves. The society has lost track of why they ever mattered in the first place and they have engendered the same kind of mindless competition we see in people who relentlessly compare their economic achievements with those of others. Third, wisdom is much more difficult to develop than is the kind of achievement that can be developed and then readily tested via multiple-choice tests. Finally, people who have gained influence and power in a society via one means are unlikely to want either to give up that power or to see a new criterion be established on which they do not rank as favorably.

There is no easy road to wisdom. There never was, and probably never will be. As an educational system, we have turned on to the easy road, but the wrong road. It is not too late to turn back. By ratcheting up our emphasis on a narrow conception of what it means to be a "good student," we are ignoring the broader conception that will make a difference to individuals and society. It is not merely what we know, but how we use it, that will determine the fate of our society and of others. We need to teach for WICS, so we use our knowledge for the positive ends we all seek.

REFERENCES

Ackerman, P. L. (1996). A theory of adult intellectual development: Process, personality, interests, and knowledge. *Intelligence, 22,* 229–259.

Ackerman, P. L. (in press). Intelligence and expertise. In R. J. Sternberg & S. B. Kaufman (Eds.), *Cambridge handbook of intelligence.* New York: Cambridge University Press.

Adams, C. M. (2009). Myth 14: Waiting for Santa Claus. *Gifted Child Quarterly, 53,* 272–273.

Adams, J. L. (1974). *Conceptual blockbusting: A guide to better ideas.* San Francisco: Freeman.

Adams, J. L. (1986). *The care and feeding of ideas: A guide to encouraging creativity.* Reading, MA: Addison-Wesley.

Aging and life span. http://www.bookrags.com/research/aging-and-life-span-gen-01/, retrieved 8/23/09.

Airasian, P. W. (1997). *Classroom assessment* (3rd ed.). New York: McGraw-Hill.

Alcock, K. J., & Bundy, D. A. P. (2001). The impact of infectious disease on cognitive development. In R. J. Sternberg & E. L. Grigorenko (Eds.), *Environmental effects on cognitive abilities* (pp. 221–253). Mahwah, NJ: Erlbaum.

Amabile, T. M. (1983). *The social psychology of creativity.* New York: Springer.

Amabile, T. M. (1996). *Creativity in context.* Boulder, CO: Westview.

Anastasi, A., & Urbina, S. (1997). *Psychological testing* (7th ed.). Upper Saddle River, NJ: Prentice-Hall.

Anderson, B. J. (1998). *Development of wisdom-related knowledge in adolescence and young adulthood* (Doctoral dissertation, University of Toronto).

Andrews, F. M. (1975). Social and psychological factors which influence the creative process. In I. A. Taylor & J. W. Getzels (Eds.), *Perspectives in creativity* (pp. 117–145). Chicago: Aldine.

Ang, S., & Van Dyne, L. (in press). Cultural intelligence. In R. J. Sternberg & S. B. Kaufman (Eds.), *Cambridge handbook of intelligence.* New York: Cambridge University Press.

Anuruthwong, U. (2002, December). Gifted education policy in Thailand. *Sanpati-loop Magazine,* 102–104.

237

Anuruthwong, U. (2007). Thai conceptions of giftedness. In S. N. Phillipson & M. McCann (Eds.), *Conceptions of giftedness: Sociocultural perspectives* (pp. 99–126). Mahwah, NJ: Erlbaum.

Ardelt, M. (1997). Wisdom and life satisfaction in old age. *Journal of Gerontology, 52,* 15–27.

Ardelt, M. (2000a). Antecedents and effects of wisdom in old age. *Research on Aging, 22*(4), 360–394.

Ardelt, M. (2000b). Intellectual versus wisdom-related knowledge: The case for a different kind of learning in the later years of life. *Educational Gerontology, 26,* 771–789.

Arlin, P. K. (1990). Wisdom: The art of problem finding. In R. J. Sternberg (Ed.), *Wisdom: Its nature, origins, and development* (pp. 230–243). New York: Cambridge University Press.

Atlas, T. (2008, June 9). The cost of corruption. *US News & World Report, 144,* 8–9.

Atran, S. (1999). Itzaj Maya folkbiological taxonomy: Cognitive universals and cultural particulars. In D. L. Medin & S. Atran (Eds.), *Folkbiology* (pp. 119–213). Cambridge, MA: MIT Press.

Average life span at birth by race and sex, 1930–2005. http://www.infoplease.com/ipa/A0005148.html, retrieved August 23, 2009.

Azuma, H., & Kashiwagi, K. (1987). Descriptions for an intelligent person: A Japanese study. *Japanese Psychological Research, 29,* 17–26.

Baer, J. (in press). Is creativity domain specific? In J. C. Kaufman & R. J. Sternberg (Eds.), *Cambridge handbook of creativity.* New York: Cambridge University Press.

Baltes, P. B. (1997). *Wolfgang Edelstein: Über ein Wissenschaftlerleben in konstruktivistischer Melancholie [Wolfgang Edelstein: A scientific life in constructive melancholy]. Reden zur Emeritierung von Wolfgang Edelstein.* Berlin, Germany: Max Planck Institute for Human Development.

Baltes, P. B., Dittmann-Kohli, F., & Dixon, R. A. (1984). New perspectives on the development of intelligence in adulthood: Toward a dual-process conception and a model of selective optimization with compensation. In P. B. Baltes, & O. G. Brim, Jr. (Eds.), *Life-span development and behavior* (Vol. 6, pp. 33–76). New York: Academic Press.

Baltes, P. B., & Smith, J. (1987, August). *Toward a psychology of wisdom and its ontogenesis.* Paper presented at the Ninety-Fifth Annual Convention of the American Psychological Association, New York City.

Baltes, P., & Smith, J. (1990). Toward a psychology of wisdom and its ontogenesis. In R. Sternberg (Ed.), *Wisdom, its nature, origins and developmen* (pp. 87–120). Cambridge: Cambridge University Press.

Baltes, P. B., Smith, J., & Staudinger, U. M. (1992). Wisdom and successful aging. In T. Sonderegger (Ed.), *Nebraska Symposium on Motivation* (Vol. 39, pp. 123–167). Lincoln: University of Nebraska Press.

Baltes, P. B., & Staudinger, U. M. (1993). The search for a psychology of wisdom. *Current Directions in Psychological Science, 2,* 75–80.

Baltes, P. B., & Staudinger, U. M. (2000). Wisdom: A metaheuristic (pragmatic) to orchestrate mind and virtue toward excellence. *American Psychologist, 55,* 122–136.

Baltes, P. B., Staudinger, U. M., Maercker, A., & Smith, J. (1995). People nominated as wise: A comparative study of wisdom-related knowledge. *Psychology and Aging, 10,* 155–166.

Bandura, A. (1977). Self-efficacy: Toward a unifying theory of behavioral change. *Psychological Review, 84,* 181–215.

Bandura, A. (1996). *Self-efficacy: The exercise of control.* New York: Freeman.

Bandura, A. (1999). Moral disengagement in the perpetration of inhumanities. *Personality and Social Psychology Review, 3,* 193–209.

Baral, B. D., & Das, J. P. (2004). Intelligence: What is indigenous to India and what is shared? In R. J. Sternberg (Ed.), *International handbook of intelligence* (pp. 270–301). New York: Cambridge University Press.

Barnett, S. M., Rindermann, H., Williams, W. M., & Ceci, S. J. (in press). The relevance of intelligence for society: Predictiveness and relevance of IQ for societal outcomes. In R. J. Sternberg & S. J. Kaufman (Eds.), *Cambridge handbook of intelligence.* New York: Cambridge University Press.

Barnouw, V. (1985). *Culture and personality.* Chicago: Dorsey Press.

Barrett, P. T., & Eysenck, H. J. (1992). Brain evoked potentials and intelligence: The Hendrickson Paradigm. *Intelligence, 16,* 361–381.

Barron, F. (1963). *Creativity and psychological health.* Princeton, NJ: D. Van Nostrand.

Barron, F. (1968). *Creativity and personal freedom.* New York: Van Nostrand.

Barron, F. (1969). *Creative person and creative process.* New York: Holt, Rinehart & Winston.

Barron, F. (1988). Putting creativity to work. In R. J. Sternberg (Ed.), *The nature of creativity* (pp. 76–98). New York: Cambridge University Press.

Barron, F., & Harrington, D. M. (1981). Creativity, intelligence, and personality. *Annual Review of Psychology, 32,* 439–476.

Bashi, Y. (1976). *Verbal and nonverbal abilities of students in grades four, six, and eight in the Arab sector.* Jerusalem: School of Education, Hebrew University.

Basseches, M. (1984a). *Dialectical thinking and adult development.* Norwood, NJ: Ablex.

Basseches, M. A. (1984b). Dialectic thinking as a metasystematic form of cognitive orientation. In M. L. Commons, F. A. Richards, & C. Armon (Eds.), *Beyond formal operations* (pp. 216–328). New York: Praeger.

Bateson, G. (1979). *Mind and nature.* London: Wildwood House.

Begay, H., & Maker, C. J. (2007). When geniuses fail: Na-Dene' (Navajo) conception of giftedness in the eyes of the holy deities. In S. N. Phillipson & M. McCann (Eds.), *Conceptions of giftedness: Sociocultural perspectives* (pp. 127–168). Mahwah, NJ: Erlbaum.

Beghetto, R. A. (in press). Creativity in the classroom. In J. C. Kaufman & R. J. Sternberg (Eds.), *Cambridge handbook of creativity.* New York: Cambridge University Press.

Bellinger, D. C., & Adams, H. F. (2001). Environmental pollutant exposures and children's cognitive ability. In R. J. Sternberg & E. L. Grigorenko (Eds.), *Environmental effects on cognitive abilities* (pp. 157–188). Mahwah, NJ: Erlbaum.

Benbow, C. P., Lubinski, D., & Suchy, B. (1996). Impact of the SMPY model and programs from the perspective of the participant. In C. P. Benbow & D. Lubinski

(Eds.), *Intellectual talent: Psychometric and social issues* (pp. 206–300). Baltimore, MD: Johns Hopkins University Press.

Benedict, R. (1946). *The crysanthemum and the sword*. Boston: Houghton Mifflin.

Bennett, G. K., Seashore, H. G., & Wesman, A. G. (1990). *Differential aptitude tests* (5th ed.). Upper Saddle River, NJ: Pearson.

Berry, J. W. (1974). Radical cultural relativism and the concept of intelligence. In J. W. Berry, & P. R. Dasen (Eds.), *Culture and cognition: Readings in cross-cultural psychology* (pp. 225–229). London: Methuen.

Berry, J. W. (1991). Cultural variations in cognitive style. In S. Wapner (Ed.), *Biological, social and cultural factors in cognitive style* (pp. 289–308). Hillsdale, N.J.: Erlbaum.

Berry, J. W., & Irvine, S. H. (1986). Bricolage: Savages do it daily. In R. J. Sternberg & R. K. Wagner (Eds.), *Practical intelligence: Nature and origins of competence in the everyday world* (pp. 271–306). New York: Cambridge University Press.

Berry, J. W., Poortinga, Y. H., Segall, M. H., & Dasen, P. R. (1992). *Cross-cultural psychology: Research and applications*. New York: Cambridge University Press.

Binet, A., & Simon, T. (1905). Méthodes nouvelles pour le diagnostic du niveau intellectuel des anormaux. *L'Année Psychologique, 11,* 191–336.

Binet, A., & Simon, T. (1916). *The development of intelligence in children* (E. S. Kite, Trans.). Baltimore: Williams & Wilkins. (Original work published in 1905)

Birren, J. E., & Fisher, L. M. (1990). Conceptualizing wisdom: The primacy of affect-cognition relations. In R. J. Sternberg (Ed.), *Wisdom: Its nature, origins, and development* (pp. 317–332). New York: Cambridge University Press.

Birren, J. E., & Svensson, C. M. (2005). Wisdom in history. In R. J. Sternberg & J. Jordan (Eds.), *A handbook of wisdom: Psychological perspectives*. New York: Cambridge University Press.

Bjorklund, D. F., & Kipp, K. (2002). Social cognition, inhibition, and theory of mind: The evolution of human intelligence. In R. J. Sternberg & J. C. Kaufman (Eds.), *The evolution of intelligence* (pp. 27–54). Mahwah, NJ: Erlbaum.

Blanchard-Fields, F. C. (1986). Reasoning on social dilemmas varying in emotional saliency: An adult development perspective. *Psychology and Aging, 1,* 325–332

Bloom, B. S. (1964). *Stability and change in human characteristics*. New York: Wiley.

Bluck, S., & Glück, J. (2005). From the inside out: People's implicit theories of wisdom. In R. J. Sternberg & J. Jordan (Eds.), *A handbook of wisdom: Psychological perspectives*. New York: Cambridge University Press.

Boas, F. (1911). *The mind of primitive man*. New York: Macmillan.

Boden, M. (1992). *The creative mind: Myths and mechanisms*. New York: Basic Books.

Boden, M. A. (1999). Computer models of creativity. In R. J. Sternberg (Ed.), *Handbook of creativity* (pp. 351–372). New York: Cambridge University Press.

Boring, E. G. (1923, June 6). Intelligence as the tests test it. *New Republic, 35*–37.

Borland, J. H. (2003). The death of giftedness. In J. H. Borland (Ed.), *Rethinking gifted education* (pp. 105–124). New York: Teachers College Press.

Borland, J. H. (2005). Gifted education without gifted children. In R. J. Sternberg & J. E. Davidson (Eds.), *Conceptions of giftedness* (2nd ed., pp. 1–19). New York: Cambridge University Press.

Borland, J. H. (2009a). Gifted education without gifted programs or gifted students: An anti-model. In J. S. Renzulli, E. J. Gubbins, K. S. McMillen, R. D. Eckert, & C. A. Little (Eds.), *Systems and models for developing the gifted and talented* (2nd ed., pp. 105–118). Mansfield Center, CT: Creative Learning Press.

Borland, J. H. (2009b). Myth 2: The gifted constitute 3% to 5% of the population. Moreover, giftedness equals high IQ, which is a stable measure of aptitude: Spinal tap psychometrics in gifted education. *Gifted Child Quarterly, 53,* 236–238.

Borkowski, J. G., & Peck, V. A. (1986). Causes and consequences of metamemory in gifted children. In R. J. Sternberg & J. E. Davidson (Eds.), *Conceptions of giftedness* (pp. 182–200). New York: Cambridge University Press.

Bors, D. A., & Forrin, B. (1995). Age, speed of information processing, recall, and fluid intelligence. *Intelligence, 20*(3), 229–248.

Bors, D. A., MacLeod, C. M., & Forrin, B. (1993). Eliminating the IQ-RT correlation by eliminating an experimental confound. *Intelligence, 17*(4), 475–500.

Bowen, W. G., & Bok, D. (2000). *The shape of the river: Long-term consequences of considering race in college and university admissions.* Princeton, NJ: Princeton University Press.

Bowen, W. G., Kurzweil, M. A., & Tobin, E. M. (2006). *Equity and excellence in American higher education.* Charlottesville: University of Virginia Press.

Bowers, K. S., Regehr, G., Balthazard, C., & Parker, K. (1990). Intuition in the context of discovery. *Cognitive Psychology, 22,* 72–109.

Bradley, R. H., & Caldwell, B. M. (1984). 174 children: A study of the relationship between home environment and cognitive development during the first 5 years. In A. W. Gottfried (Ed.), *Home environment and early cognitive development: Longitudinal research.* San Diego, CA: Academic Press.

Bradshaw, J. L. (2002). The evolution of intellect: Cognitive, neurological, and primatological aspects and hominid culture. In R. J. Sternberg & J. C. Kaufman (Eds.), *The evolution of intelligence* (pp. 57–58). Mahwah, NJ: Erlbaum.

Bransford, J. D., & Stein, B. (1984). *The IDEAL problem solver.* New York: Freeman.

Brislin, R. W., Lonner, W. J., & Thorndike, R. M. (Eds.). (1973). *Cross-cultural research methods.* New York: Wiley.

Brody, L. E., & Stanley, J. C. (2005). Youths who reason exceptionally well mathematically and/or verbally: Using the MVT:D4 model to develop their talents. In R. J. Sternberg & J. E. Davidson (Eds.), *Conceptions of giftedness* (2nd ed., pp. 20–37). New York: Cambridge University Press.

Brody, N. (2000). History of theories and measurements of intelligence. In R. J. Sternberg (Ed.), *Handbook of intelligence* (pp. 16–33). New York: Cambridge University Press.

Brown, A. L., & DeLoache, J. S. (1978). Skills, plans, and self-regulation. In R. Siegler (Ed.), *Children's thinking: What develops?* Hillsdale, NJ: Erlbaum.

Brown, A. L., & Ferrara, R. A. (1985). Diagnosing zones of proximal development. In J. V. Wertsch (Ed.). *Culture, communication, and cognition: Vygotskian perspectives* (pp. 273–305). New York: Cambridge University Press.

Brugman, G. (2000). *Wisdom: Source of narrative coherence and eudaimonia.* Published doctoral dissertation, University of Utrecht. Delft, The Netherlands.

Bruner, J. S., Olver, R. R., & Greenfield, P. M. (1966). *Studies in cognitive growth.* New York: Wiley.

Byrne, R. W. (2002). The primate origins of human intelligence. In R. J. Sternberg & J. C. Kaufman (Eds.), *The evolution of intelligence* (pp. 79–96). Mahwah, NJ: Erlbaum.

Callahan, C. M. (2009). Myth 3: A family of identification myths: Your sample must be the same as the population. There is a "silver bullet" in identification. There must be "winners" and "losers" in identification and programming. *Gifted Child Quarterly, 53*(4), 239–241.

Calvin, W. H. (2002). Pumping up intelligence: Abrupt climate jumps and the evolution of higher intellectual functions during the Ice Ages. In R. J. Sternberg & J. C. Kaufman (Eds.), *The evolution of intelligence* (pp. 97–116). Mahwah, NJ: Erlbaum.

Camara, W. J., & Schmidt, A. E. (1999). Group differences in standardized testing and social stratification (College Board Research Rep. No. 99–5). New York: College Board. http://www.collegeboard.com/research/home/, retrieved 12/21/2006.

Campbell, D. T. (1960). Blind variation and selective retention in creative thought and other knowledge processes. *Psychological Review, 67*, 380–400.

Campbell, J., & Eyre, D. (2007). The English model of gifted and talented education: Policy, context, and challenges. In S. N. Phillipson & M. McCann (Eds.), *Conceptions of giftedness: Sociocultural perspectives* (pp. 459–475). Mahwah, NJ: Erlbaum.

Cantez, E., & Girgin, Y. (1992). *Istanbul'da yasayan 3–11 yas grubundaki kiz va erkek cocuklara Gesell Gelisim Testi'nin uygulanmiasindan elde edilen sonuclarin Gesell Gelisim Testi Normlari ile karsilastirilmasi ve normlara uygunlugunun arastirilmasi ile ilgili bir calisma. [A study about the comparison of the results obtained from the application of Gesell Development Schedules to 3–11-year-old male and female children living in Istanbul with the norms of the Gesell Developmental Schedules].* In *VIII. Ulusal Psikoloji Kongresi Bilimsel Calismalari.* Ankara, Turkey: Turkish Psychological Association.

Cantor, N., & Kihlstrom, J. F. (1987). *Personality and social intelligence.* Englewood Cliffs, NJ: Prentice-Hall.

Carlstedt, B., Gustafsson, J.-E., & Hautamäki, J. (2004). Intelligence–Theory, research, and testing in the Nordic countries. In R. J. Sternberg (Ed.), *International handbook of intelligence* (pp. 49–78). New York: Cambridge University Press.

Carr, P. B., & Dweck, C. S. (in press). Motivation and intelligence. In R. J. Sternberg & S. B. Kaufman (Eds.), *Cambridge handbook of intelligence.* New York: Cambridge University Press.

Carraher, T. N., Carraher, D., & Schliemann, A. D. (1985). Mathematics in the streets and in schools. *British Journal of Developmental Psychology, 3*, 21–29.

Carroll, J. B. (1993). *Human cognitive abilities: A survey of factor-analytic studies.* New York: Cambridge University Press.

Carstensen, L. L. (1995). Evidence for a life-span theory of socioemotional selectivity. *Current Directions in Psychological Science, 4*(5), 151–156.

Caruso, D. R., Mayer, J. D., & Salovey, P. (2002). Emotional intelligence and emotional leadership. In R. E. Riggio, S. E. Murphy, & F. J. Pirozzolo, *Multiple intelligences and leadership* (pp. 55–74). Mahwah, NJ: Erlbaum.

Cattell, R. B. (1971). *Abilities: Their structure, growth, and action.* Boston: Houghton Mifflin.

Ceci, S. J. (1996). *On intelligence: A bioecological treatise on intellectual development* (2nd ed.). Cambridge, MA: Harvard University Press.

Ceci, S. J., & Bronfenbrenner, U. (1985). Don't forget to take the cupcakes out of the oven: Strategic time-monitoring, prospective memory and context. *Child Development, 56,* 175–190.

Ceci, S. J., Nightingale, N. N., & Baker, J. G. (1992). The ecologies of intelligence: Challenges to traditional views. In D. K. Detterman (Ed.), *Current topics in human intelligence: Vol. 2. Is mind modular or unitary?* (pp. 61– 82). Norwood, NJ: Ablex.

Ceci, S. J., & Roazzi, A. (1994). The effects of context on cognition: Postcards from Brazil. In R. J. Sternberg & R. K. Wagner (Eds.), *Mind in context: Interactionist perspectives on human intelligence* (pp. 74–101). New York: Cambridge University Press.

Chan, J. (2007). Giftedness and China's Confucian heritage. In S. N., Phillipson & M. McCann (Eds.), *Conceptions of giftedness: Sociocultural perspectives* (pp. 35–64). Mahwah, NJ: Erlbaum.

Chart, H., Grigorenko, E. L., & Sternberg, R. J. (2008). Identification: The Aurora Battery. In J. A. Plucker & C. M. Callahan (Eds.), *Critical issues and practices in gifted education* (pp. 281–301). Waco, TX: Prufrock.

Chen, M. J. (1994). Chinese and Australian concepts of intelligence. *Psychology and Developing Societies, 6,* 101–117.

Chen, M. J., Braithwaite, V., & Huang, J. T. (1982). Attributes of intelligent behaviour: Perceived relevance and difficulty by Australian and Chinese students. *Journal of Cross-Cultural Psychology, 13,* 139–156.

Chen, M. J., & Chen, H-C. (1988). Concepts of intelligence: A comparison of Chinese graduates from Chinese and English schools in Hong Kong. *International Journal of Psychology,* 471–487.

Chi, M. T. H., Glaser, R., & Farr, M. J. (Eds.). (1988). *The nature of expertise.* Hillsdale, NJ: Erlbaum.

Chimhundu, H. (Ed.). (2001). *Dura manzwi guru rechiShona.* Harare, Zimbabwe: College Press.

Christian, K., Bachnan, H. J., & Morrison, F. J. (2001). Schooling and cognitive development. In R. J. Sternberg & E. L. Grigorenko (Eds.), *Environmental effects on cognitive abilities* (pp. 287–335). Mahwah, NJ: Erlbaum.

Cianciolo, A.T., Grigorenko, E. L., Jarvin, L., Gil, G., Drebot, M. E., & Sternberg, R. J. (2006). Practical intelligence and tacit knowledge: Advancements in the measurement of developing expertise. *Learning and Individual Differences, 16*(3), 235–253.

Ciarrochi, J., Forgas, J. P., & Mayer, J. D. (Eds.). (2001). *Emotional intelligence in everyday life: A scientific inquiry.* Philadelphia, PA: Psychology Press.

Clayton, V. P. (1975). Erikson's theory of human development as it applies to the aged: Wisdom as contradictory cognition. *Human Development, 18,* 119–128.

Clayton, V. P. (1976). *A multidimensional scaling analysis of the concept of wisdom* (Doctoral dissertation, University of Southern California, Los Angeles).

Clayton, V. P. (1982). Wisdom and intelligence: The nature and function of knowledge in the later years. *International Journal of Aging and Development, 15,* 315–321.

Clayton, V. P., & Birren, J. E. (1980). The development of wisdom across the lifespan: A reexamination of an ancient topic. In P. B. Baltes & O. G. Brim, Jr. (Eds.), *Life-span development and behavior* (pp. 103–135). New York: Academic Press.

Clement, J. (1989). Learning via model construction and criticism: Protocol evidence on sources of creativity in science. In G. Glover, R. Ronning, & C. Reynolds (Eds.), *Handbook of creativity* (pp. 341–381). New York: Plenum.

Cohen, R. J., & Swerdlik, M. (2001). *Psychological testing and assessment: An introduction to tests and measurements.* New York: McGraw-Hill.

Cole, M. (1998). *Cultural psychology: A once and future discipline.* Cambridge, MA: Harvard University Press.

Cole, M., Gay, J., Glick, J., & Sharp, D. W. (1971). *The cultural context of learning and thinking.* New York: Basic Books.

Cole, M., & Means, B. (1981). *Comparative studies of how people think.* Cambridge, MA: Harvard University Press.

Cole, M., & Scribner, S. (1974). *Culture and thought.* New York: Wiley.

Coles, R. (1998). *The moral intelligence of children: How to raise a moral child.* New York: Plume.

Coley, J. D., Medin, D. L., Proffitt, J. B., Lynch, E., & Atran, S. (1999). Inductive reasoning in folkbiological thought. In D. L. Medin & S. Atran (Eds.), *Folkbiology* (pp. 205–232). Cambridge, MA: MIT Press.

Collier, G. (1994). *Social origins of mental ability.* New York: Wiley.

Collins, M. A., & Amabile, T. M. (1999). Motivation and creativity. In R. J. Sternberg (Ed.), *Handbook of creativity* (pp. 297–312). New York: Cambridge University Press.

Connolly, H., & Bruner, J. (1974). Competence: Its nature and nurture. In K. Connolly & J. Bruner (Eds.), *The growth of competence.* New York: Academic Press.

Conway, A. R. A., Getz, S., Macnamara, B., & Engel, P. (in press). Working memory and fluid intelligence: A multi-mechanism view. In R. J. Sternberg & S. B. Kaufman (Eds.), *Cambridge handbook of intelligence.* New York: Cambridge University Press.

Cook, D. A., & Beckman, T. J. (2006). Current concepts in validity and reliability for psychometric instruments: Theory and application. *American Journal of Medicine, 119*(2), 166.e7–16.

Coon, H., Carey, G., & Fulker, D. W. (1992). Community influences on cognitive ability. *Intelligence, 16*(2), 169–188.

Corballis, M. C. (2002). Evolution of the generative mind. In R. J. Sternberg & J. C. Kaufman (Eds.), *The evolution of intelligence* (pp. 117–144). Mahwah, NJ: Erlbaum.

Cosmides, L., & Tooby, J. (2002). Unraveling the enigma of human intelligence: Evolutionary psychology and the multimodular mind. In R. J. Sternberg & J. C. Kaufman (Eds.), *The evolution of intelligence* (pp. 145–198). Mahwah, NJ: Erlbaum.

Cox, C. M. (1926). *The early mental traits of three hundred geniuses.* Stanford, CA: Stanford University Press.

Craik, F. I. M., & Lockhart R. S. (1972). Levels of processing: A framework for memory research. *Journal of Verbal Learning and Verbal Behavior, 11,* 671–684.

Cronbach, L. J. (1990). *Essentials of psychological testing* (5th ed.). New York: Harper-Collins.

Cropley, D., & Cropley, A. (in press). Functional creativity: "Products" and the generation of effective novelty. In J. C. Kaufman & R. J. Sternberg (Eds.), *Cambridge handbook of creativity*. New York: Cambridge University Press.

Crutchfield, R. (1962). Conformity and creative thinking. In H. Bruber, G. Terrell, & M. Wertheimer (Eds.), *Contemporary approaches of creative thinking* (pp. 120–140). New York: Atherton.

Csikszentmihalyi, M. (1988). Society, culture, and person: A systems view of creativity. In R. J. Sternberg (Ed.), *The nature of creativity* (pp. 325–339). New York: Cambridge University Press.

Csikszentmihalyi, M. (1996). *Creativity*. New York: HarperCollins.

Csikszentmihalyi, M. (1999). Implications of a systems perspective for the study of creativity. In R. J. Sternberg (Ed.), *Handbook of creativity* (pp. 313–335). New York: Cambridge University Press.

Czikszentmihalyi, M., & Nakamura, J. (2005). The role of emotions in the development of wisdom. In R. J. Sternberg & J. Jordan (Eds.). *A handbook of wisdom: Psychological perspectives*. New York: Cambridge University Press.

Csikszentmihalyi, M., & Rathunde, K. (1990). The psychology of wisdom: An evolutionary interpretation. In R. Sternberg (Ed.), *Wisdom: Its nature, origins, and development* (pp. 25–51). New York: Cambridge University Press.

Csikszentmihalyi, M., & Robinson, R. E. (1986). Culture, time, and the development of talent. In R. J. Sternberg & J. E. Davidson (Eds.), *Conceptions of giftedness* (pp. 264–284). New York: Cambridge University Press.

Cziko, G. A. (1998). From blind to creative: In defense of Donald Campbell's selectionist theory of human creativity. *Journal of Creative Behavior, 32,* 192–208.

Daneman, M., & Carpenter, P. A. (1983). Individual differences in integrating information between and within sentences. *Journal of Experimental Psychology: Learning, Memory, & Cognition, 9*(4), 561–584.

Daniel, M. (1997). Intelligence testing: Status and trends. *American Psychologist, 52,* 1038–1045.

Daniel, M. (2000). Interpretation of intelligence test scores. In R. J. Sternberg (Ed.), *Handbook of intelligence* (pp. 477–491). New York: Cambridge University Press.

Das, J. P. (1994). Eastern views of intelligence. In R. J. Sternberg (Ed.), *Encyclopedia of intelligence* (pp. 91–97). New York: Macmillan.

Dasen, P. (1984). The cross-cultural study of intelligence: Piaget and the Baoule. *International Journal of Psychology, 19,* 407–434.

Davidson, J. E., & Kemp, I. A. (in press). Contemporary models of intelligence. In R. J. Sternberg & S. B. Kaufman (Eds.), *Cambridge handbook of intelligence*. New York: Cambridge University Press.

Davies, M., Stankov, L., & Roberts, R. D. (1998). Emotional intelligence: In search of an elusive construct. *Journal of Personality & Social Psychology, 75,* 989–1015.

Davis, K., Christodoulou, J., Seider, S., & Gardner, H. (in press). The theory of multiple intelligences. In R. J. Sternberg & S. B. Kaufman (Eds.), *Cambridge handbook of intelligence*. New York: Cambridge University Press.

De Bono, E. (1971). *Lateral thinking for management*. New York: McGraw-Hill.

De Bono, E. (1985). *Six thinking hats.* Boston: Little, Brown.

De Bono, E. (1992). *Serious creativity: Using the power of lateral thinking to create new ideas.* New York: HarperCollins.

De Vise, D. (2008, December 16). Montgomery erasing gifted label. http://www.washingtonpost.com/wp-dyn/content/article/2008/12/15/AR2008121503114_pf.html, retrieved 1/2/09.

Deary, I. J. (2000). Simple information processing. In R. J. Sternberg (Ed.), *Handbook of intelligence* (pp. 267–284). New York: Cambridge University Press.

Deary, I. J. (2002). g and cognitive elements of information processing: An agnostic view. In R. J. Sternberg, & E. L. Grigorenko (Eds.), *The general factor of intelligence: How general is it?* (pp. 151–181). Mahwah, NJ: Erlbaum.

Deary, I. J., & Batty, G. D. (in press). Intelligence as a predictor of health, illness, and death: "Cognitive epidemiology." In R. J. Sternberg & S. B. Kaufman (Eds.), *Cambridge handbook of intelligence.* New York: Cambridge University Press.

Deary, I. J., & Smith, P. (2004). Intelligence research and assessment in the United Kingdom. In R. J. Sternberg (Ed.), *International handbook of intelligence* (pp. 1–48). New York: Cambridge University Press.

Deary, I. J., & Stough, C. (1996). Intelligence and inspection time: Achievements, prospects, and problems. *American Psychologist, 51,* 599–608.

Deary, I. J., Whalley, L. J., & Starr, J. M. (2008). *A lifetime of intelligence: Follow-up studies of the Scottish Mental Surveys of 1932 and 1947.* Washington, DC: American Psychological Association.

Demetriou, A. (2002). Tracing psychology's invisible giant and its visible guards. In R. J. Sternberg & E. L. Grigorenko (Eds.), *The general factor of intelligence: How general is it?* (pp. 3–18). Mahwah, NJ: Erlbaum.

Demetriou, A., & Papadopoulos, T. C. (2004). Human intelligence: From local models to universal theory. In R. J. Sternberg (Ed.), *International handbook of intelligence* (pp. 445–474). New York: Cambridge University Press.

Dempster, F. N. (1991). Inhibitory processes: A neglected dimension of intelligence. *Intelligence, 15,* 157–173.

Detterman, D. K., & Sternberg, R. J. (Eds.). (1982). *How and how much can intelligence be increased?* Norwood, NJ: Erlbaum.

Diagnostic and Statistical Manual of the American Psychiatric Association (1995, 4th ed.). Washington, DC: American Psychiatric Association.

DiStefano, C., & Dombrowski, S. C. (2006). Investigating the theoretical structure of the Stanford-Binet, Fifth edition. *Journal of Psychoeducational Assessment, 24,* 123–136.

Dochy, F., & McDowell, L. (1997). Assessment as a tool for learning. *Studies in Educational Evaluation, 23,* 279–298.

Dunbar, K., & Fugelsang, J. (2005). Scientific thinking and reasoning. In K. Holyoak & R. G. Morrison (Eds.), *Cambridge handbook of thinking and reasoning* (pp. 705–729). Cambridge: Cambridge University Press.

Duncker, K. (1945). On problem solving. *Psychological Monographs, 58*(5, Whole No. 270).

Durojaiye, M. O. A. (1993). Indigenous psychology in Africa. In U. Kim & J. W. Berry (Eds.), *Indigenous psychologies: Research and experience in cultural context.* Newbury Park, CA: Sage.

Dweck, C. S. (1999). *Self-theories: Their role in motivation, personality, and development.* Philadelphia: Psychology Press.

Dyer, W. (1998). *Wisdom of the ages.* New York: HarperCollins.

Embretson, S., & McCollam, K. (2000). Psychometric approaches to the understanding and measurement of intelligence. In R. J. Sternberg (Ed.), *Handbook of intelligence* (pp. 423–444). New York: Cambridge University Press.

Ericsson, K. A. (Ed.). (1996). *The road to excellence: The acquisition of expert performance in the arts and sciences, sports and games.* Hillsdale, NJ: Erlbaum.

Ericsson, K. A., Krampe, R. T., & Tesch-Roemer, C. (1993). The role of deliberate practice in the acquisition of expert performance. *Psychological Review, 100,* 363–406.

Ericsson, K. A., & Smith, J. (Eds.). (1991). *Toward a general theory of expertise: Prospects and limits.* New York: Cambridge University Press.

Erikson, E. (1950). *Childhood and society.* New York: Norton.

Erikson, E. H. (1959). Identity and the life cycle. *Psychological Issues, 1,* 1–173.

Estes, W. K. (1982). Similarity-related channel interactions in visual processing. *Journal of Experimental Psychology: Human Perception & Performance, 8*(3), 353–382.

Eysenck, H. J. (1986). A theory of intelligence and the psychophysiology of cognition. In R. J. Sternberg (Ed.), *Advances in the psychology of human intelligence* (Vol. 3, pp. 1–34). Hillsdale, NJ: Erlbaum.

Eysenck, H. J. (1993). Creativity and personality: A theoretical perspective. *Psychological Inquiry, 4,* 147–178.

Feist, G. J. (1999). The influence of personality on artistic and scientific creativity. In R. J. Sternberg (Ed.), *Handbook of creativity* (pp. 273–296). New York: Cambridge University Press.

Feist, G. J. (in press). The function of personality in creativity: The nature and nurture of the creativity personality. In J. C. Kaufman & R. J. Sternberg (Eds.), *Cambridge handbook of creativity.* New York: Cambridge University Press.

Fekken, G. C. (2000). *Reliability.* In A.E. Kazdin (Ed.), *Encyclopedia of psychology* (Vol. 7, pp. 30–34). Washington, DC: American Psychological Association.

Feldhusen, J. F. (1986). A conception of giftedness. In R. J. Sternberg & J. E. Davidson (Eds.), *Conceptions of giftedness* (pp. 112–127). New York: Cambridge University Press.

Feldhusen, J. F. (2005). Giftedness, talent, expertise, and creative achievement. In R. J. Sternberg & J. E. Davidson (Eds.), *Conceptions of giftedness* (2nd ed., pp. 64–79). New York: Cambridge University Press.

Feldman, D. H. (1986). Giftedness as the developmentalist sees it. In R. J. Sternberg & J. E. Davidson (Eds.), *Conceptions of giftedness* (pp. 285–305). New York: Cambridge University Press.

Feldman, D. H. (1999). The development of creativity. In R. J. Sternberg (Ed.), *Handbook of creativity* (pp. 169–186). New York: Cambridge University Press.

Feldman, D. H., Csikszentmihalyi, M., & Gardner, H. (1994). *Changing the world: A framework for the study of creativity.* Westport, CT: Praeger.

Feldman, D. H., with Goldsmith, L. T. (1991). *Nature's gambit: Child prodigies and the development of human potential.* New York: Teachers College Press.

Fernández-Ballesteros, R., & Colom, R. (2004). The psychology of human intelligence in Spain. In R. J. Sternberg (Ed.), *International handbook of intelligence* (pp. 79–103). New York: Cambridge University Press.

Feuerstein, R. (1979). *The dynamic assessment of retarded performers: The learning potential assessment device, theory, instrument, and techniques.* Baltimore, MD: University Park Press.

Feuerstein, R. (1980). *Instrumental enrichment: An intervention program for cognitive modifiability.* Baltimore, MD: University Park Press.

Fiese, B. H. (2001). Family matters: A systems view of family effects on children's cognitive health. In R. J. Sternberg & E. L. Grigorenko (Eds.), *Environmental effects on cognitive abilities* (pp. 39–57). Mahwah, NJ: Erlbaum.

Findlay, C. S., & Lumsden, C. J. (1988). The creative mind: Toward an evolutionary theory of discovery and invention. *Journal of Social and Biological Structures, 11,* 3–55.

Finke, R. (1990). *Creative imagery: Discoveries and inventions in visualization.* Hillsdale, NJ: Erlbaum.

Finke, R. (1995). A. Creative insight and preinventive forms. In R. J. Sternberg & J. E. Davidson (Eds.), *The nature of insight* (pp. 255–280). Cambridge, MA: MIT Press.

Finke, R. A., & Slayton, K. (1988). Explorations of creative visual synthesis in mental imagery. *Memory & Cognition, 16*(3), 252–257.

Finke, R. A., Ward T. B. & Smith, S. M. (1992). *Creative cognition: Theory, research, and applications.* Cambridge, MA: MIT Press.

Flanagan, O., Hardcastle, V. G., & Nahmias, E. (2002). Is human intelligence an adaptation? Cautionary observations from the philosophy of biology. In R. J. Sternberg & J. C. Kaufman (Eds.), *The evolution of intelligence* (pp. 199–222). Mahwah, NJ: Erlbaum.

Flavell, J. H. (1981). Cognitive monitoring. In W. P. Dickson (Ed.), *Children's oral communication skills* (pp. 35–60). New York: Academic Press.

Flescher, I. (1963). Anxiety and achievement of intellectually gifted and creatively gifted children. *Journal of Psychology, 56,* 251–268.

Flynn, J. R. (1984). The mean IQ of Americans: Massive gains 1932 to 1978. *Psychological Bulletin, 95,* 29–51.

Flynn, J. R. (1987). Massive IQ gains in 14 nations: What IQ tests really measure. *Psychological Bulletin, 101,* 171–191.

Flynn, J. R. (1998). IQ gains over time: Toward finding the causes. In U. Neisser (Ed.), *The rising curve: Long-term gains in IQ and related measures* (pp. 25–66). Washington, DC: American Psychological Association.

Flynn, J. R. (in press). Secular changes in intelligence. In R. J. Sternberg & S. B. Kaufman (Eds.), *Cambridge handbook of intelligence.* New York: Cambridge University Press.

Freeman, J. (2005). Permission to be gifted: How conceptions of giftedness can change lives. In R. J. Sternberg & J. E. Davidson (Eds.), *Conceptions of giftedness* (2nd ed., pp. 80–97). New York: Cambridge University Press.

Frensch, P. A., & Sternberg, R. J. (1989). Expertise and intelligent thinking: When is it worse to know better? In R. J. Sternberg (Ed.), *Advances in the psychology of human intelligence.* Hillsdale, NJ: Erlbaum.

Freud, S. (1908/1959). The relation of the poet to day-dreaming. In S. Freud (Ed.), *Collected papers* (Vol. *4*, pp. 173–183). London: Hogarth Press.

Freud, S. (1910/1964). *Leonardo da Vinci and a memory of his childhood*. New York: Norton. (Original work published in 1910)

Frey, M. C., & Detterman, D. K. (2004). Scholastic assessment or g? The relationship between the Scholastic Assessment Test and general cognitive ability. *Psychological Science, 15*, 373–378.

Friedman-Nimz, R. (2009). Myth 6: Cosmetic use of multiple selection criteria. *Gifted Child Quarterly, 53*, 248–250.

Gabora, L., & Kaufman, S. B. (in press). Evolutionary approaches to creativity. In J. C. Kaufman & R. J. Sternberg (Eds.), *Cambridge handbook of creativity*. New York: Cambridge University Press.

Gabora, L., & Russon, A. (in press). The evolution of intelligence. In R. J. Sternberg & S. B. Kaufman (Eds.), *Cambridge handbook of intelligence*. New York: Cambridge University Press.

Gagné, F. (2000). Understanding the complex choreography of talent development through DMGT-based analysis. In K. A. Heller, F. J. Mönks, R. J. Sternberg, & R. Subotnik (Eds.), *International handbook for research on giftedness and talent* (2nd ed., pp. 67–79). Oxford, UK: Pergamon.

Gagné, F. (2005). From gifts to talents. In R. J. Sternberg & J. E. Davidson (Eds.), *Conceptions of giftedness* (2nd ed., pp. 98–119). New York: Cambridge University Press.

Gallagher, J. J. (1996). A critique of critiques of gifted education. *Journal for the Education of the Gifted, 19*, 234–249.

Gallagher, J. J. (2000). Changing paradigms for gifted education in the United States. In K. A. Heller, F. J. Mönks, R. J. Sternberg, & R. F. Subotnik (Eds.), *International handbook of giftedness and talent* (pp. 681–694). New York: Elsevier.

Gallagher, J. J., & Courtright, R. D. (1986). The educational definition of giftedness and its policy implications. In R. J. Sternberg & J. E. Davidson (Eds.), *Conceptions of giftedness* (pp. 93–111). New York: Cambridge University Press.

Gallagher, S. A. (2009). Myth 19: Is Advanced Placement an adequate program for gifted students? *Gifted Child Quarterly, 53*, 286–288.

Galton, F. (1869). *Hereditary genius*. New York: Macmillan.

Galton, F. (1883). *Inquiry into human faculty and its development*. London: Macmillan.

Gardner, H. (1983). *Frames of mind: The theory of multiple intelligences*. New York: Basic Books.

Gardner, H. (1993). *Multiple intelligences: The theory in practice*. New York: Basic Books.

Gardner, H. (1994). The stories of the right hemisphere. In W. D. Spaulding (Ed.), *Integrative views of motivation, cognition, and emotion. Nebraska symposium on motivation* (Vol. 41, pp. 57–69). Lincoln: University of Nebraska Press.

Gardner, H. (1995). *Leading minds*. New York: Basic Books.

Gardner, H. (1999a). Are there additional intelligences? The case for naturalist, spiritual, and existential intelligences. In J. Kane (Ed.), *Education, information, and transformation* (pp. 111–131). Upper Saddle River, NJ: Prentice-Hall.

Gardner, H. (1999b). *Intelligence reframed*. New York: Basic Books.

Gardner, H. (2000). The giftedness matrix: A developmental perspective. In R. C. Friedman & B. M. Shore (Eds.), *Talents unfolding: Cognition and development* (pp. 77–88). Washington, DC: American Psychological Association.

Gardner, H. (2006). *Multiple intelligences: New horizons in theory and practice.* New York: Basic.

Gardner, H., Feldman, D. H., Krechevsky, M., & Chen, J. Q. (1998). *Building on children's strengths: The experience of Project Spectrum (Project Zero Frameworks for Early Childhood Education)*, Vol. 1. New York: Teachers College Press.

Garrison Keillor quotes (2009). http://www.brainyquote.com/quotes/quotes/g/garrisonke137097.html, retrieved 1/2/09.

Gentry, M. (2009). Myth 11: Comprehensive continuum of gifted education and talent development services: Discovering, developing, and enhancing young people's gifts and talents. *Gifted Child Quarterly, 53*, 262–265.

Getzels, J., & Csikszentmihalyi, M. (1976). *The creative vision: A longitudinal study of problem finding in art.* New York: Wiley-Interscience.

Getzels, J. W., & Jackson, P. W. (1962). *Creativity and intelligence: Explorations with gifted students.* New York: Wiley.

Ghiselin, B. (Ed.). (1985). *The creative process: A symposium.* Berkeley: University of California Press.

Gibson, K., & Vialle, W. (2007). The Australian Aboriginal view of giftedness. In S. N. Phillipson & M. McCann (Eds.), *Conceptions of giftedness: Sociocultural perspectives* (pp. 197–224). Mahwah, NJ: Erlbaum.

Gill, R., & Keats, D. M. (1980). Elements of intellectual competence: Judgments by Australian and Malay university students. *Journal of Cross-Cultural Psychology, 11*, 233–243.

Gladwin, T. (1970). *East is a big bird.* Cambridge, MA: Harvard University Press.

Gliner, J. A., & Morgan, G. A. (2000). *Research methods in applied settings: An integrated approach to design and analysis.* Mahwah, NJ: Erlbaum.

Glück, J., Bluck, S., Baron, J., & McAdams, D. P. (2005). The wisdom of experience: Autobiographical narratives across adulthood. *International Journal of Behavioral Development, 29*(3), 197–208.

Golann, S. E. (1962). The creativity motive. *Journal of Personality, 30*, 588–600.

Golden, D. (2006). *The price of admission.* New York: Crown.

Goleman, D. (1998a, November–December). What makes a good leader? *Harvard Business Review, 93*–102.

Goleman, D. (1998b). *Working with emotional intelligence.* New York: Bantam.

Goodman, D. P., & Hambleton, R. K. (2004). Student test score reports and interpretive guides: Review of current practices and suggestions for future research. *Applied Measurement in Education, 172*, 145–220.

Goodnow, J. J. (1962). A test of milieu effects with some of Piaget's tasks. *Psychological Monographs, 76*, Whole No. 555.

Goodnow, J. J. (1969). Cultural variations in cognition skills. In D. R. Price-Williams (Ed.), *Cross-cultural studies* (pp. 246–264). Hardmondsworth, England: Penguin.

Goodnow, J. J. (1976). The nature of intelligent behavior: Questions raised by cross-cultural studies. In L. Resnick (Ed.), *The nature of intelligence* (pp. 169–188). Hillsdale, NJ: Erlbaum.

Gordon, E. W., & Bridglall, B. L. (2005). Nurturing talent in gifted students of color. In R. J. Sternberg & J. E. Davidson (Eds.), *Conceptions of giftedness* (2nd ed., pp. 120–146). New York: Cambridge University Press.

Gordon, W. J. J. (1961). *Synectics: The development of creative capacity.* New York: Harper & Row.

Gough, H. G. (1979). A creativity scale for the adjective check list. *Journal of Personality and Social Psychology, 37,* 1398–1405.

Gourevitch, P. (1998). *We wish to inform you that tomorrow we will be killed with our families: Stories from Rwanda.* New York: Farrar, Straus & Giroux.

Grantham-McGregor, S., Ani, C., & Fernald, L. (2002). The role of nutrition in intellectual development. In R. J. Sternberg, & E. L. Grigorenko (Eds.), *Environmental effects on cognitive abilities* (pp. 119–155). Mahwah, NJ: Erlbaum.

Greenfield, P. M. (1997). You can't take it with you: Why abilities assessments don't cross cultures. *American Psychologist, 52,* 1115–1124.

Gregory, R. J. (2000). *Psychological testing: History, principles, and applications* (3rd ed.), Boston, MA: Allyn & Bacon.

Grigorenko, E. L. (2000). Heritability and intelligence. In R. J. Sternberg (Ed.), *Handbook of intelligence* (pp. 53–91). New York: Cambridge University Press.

Grigorenko, E. L. (2001). The invisible danger: The impact of ionizing radiation on cognitive development and functioning. In R. J. Sternberg & E. L. Grigorenko (Eds.), *Environmental effects on intellectual functioning* (pp. 255–286). Mahwah, NJ: Erlbaum.

Grigorenko, E. L. (2002). Other than g: The value of persistence. In R. J. Sternberg & E. L. Grigorenko (Eds.), *The general factor of intelligence: Fact or fiction* (pp. 299–327). Mahwah, NJ: Erlbaum.

Grigorenko, E. L. (2004). Is it possible to study intelligence without using the concept of intelligence? An example from Soviet/Russian psychology. In R. J. Sternberg (Ed.), *International handbook of intelligence* (pp. 170–211). New York: Cambridge University Press.

Grigorenko, E. L., Geissler, P. W., Prince, R., Okatcha, F., Nokes, C., Kenny, D. A., Bundy, D. A., & Sternberg, R. J. (2001). The organization of Luo conceptions of intelligence: A study of implicit theories in a Kenyan village. *International Journal of Behavior Development, 25,* 367–378.

Grigorenko, E. L., Jarvin, L., & Sternberg, R. J. (2002). School-based tests of the triarchic theory of intelligence: Three settings, three samples, three syllabi. *Contemporary Educational Psychology, 27,* 167–208.

Grigorenko, E. L., Meier, E., Lipka, J., Mohatt, G., Yanez, E., & Sternberg, R. J. (2004). Academic and practical intelligence: A case study of the Yup'ik in Alaska. *Learning and Individual Differences, 14,* 183–207.

Grigorenko, E. L., & Sternberg, R. J. (1998). Dynamic testing. *Psychological Bulletin, 124,* 75–111.

Grigorenko, E. L., & Sternberg, R. J. (2001a). Analytical, creative, and practical intelligence as predictors of self-reported adaptive functioning: A case study in Russia. *Intelligence, 29,* 57–73.

Grigorenko, E. L., & Sternberg, R. J. (Eds.). (2001b). *Family environment and intellectual functioning: A life-span perspective.* Mahwah, NJ: Erlbaum.

Grossman, J. B., & Kaufman, J. C. (2002). Evolutionary psychology: Promise and perils. In R. J. Sternberg & J. C. Kaufman (Eds.), *The evolution of intelligence* (pp. 9–25). Mahwah, NJ: Erlbaum.

Grotzer, T. A., & Perkins, D. A. (2000). Teaching of intelligence: A performance conception. In R. J. Sternberg (Ed.), *Handbook of intelligence* (pp. 492–515). New York: Cambridge University Press.

Gruber, H. E. (1981). *Darwin on man: A psychological study of scientific creativity* (2nd ed.). Chicago: University of Chicago Press. (Original work published in 1974)

Gruber, H. E. (1986). Self-construction of the extraordinary. In R. J. Sternberg & J. E. Davidson (Eds.), *Conceptions of giftedness* (pp. 247–263). New York: Cambridge University Press.

Gruber, H. E. (1989). The evolving systems approach to creative work. In D. B. Wallace & H. E. Gruber (Eds.), *Creative people at work: Twelve cognitive case studies* (pp. 3–24). New York: Oxford University Press.

Gruber, H. E., & Davis, S. N. (1988). Inching our way up Mount Olympus: The evolving-systems approach to creative thinking. In R. J. Sternberg (Ed.), *The nature of creativity* (pp. 243–270). New York: Cambridge University Press.

Gruber, H. E., & Wallace, D. B. (1999). The case study method and evolving systems approach for understanding unique creative people at work. In R. J. Sternberg (Ed.), *Handbook of creativity* (pp. 93–115). New York: Cambridge University Press.

Guidubaldi, J., & Duckworth, J. (2001). Divorce and children's cognitive ability. In E. L. Grigorenko & R. J. Sternberg (Eds.), *Family environment and intellectual functioning* (pp. 97–118). Mahwah, NJ: Erlbaum.

Guilford, J. P. (1950). Creativity. *American Psychologist, 5*, 444–454.

Guilford, J. P. (1967). *The nature of human intelligence.* New York: McGraw-Hill.

Guilford, J. P. (1968). Intelligence has three facets. *Science, 60*(3828), 615–620.

Guilford, J. P. (1982). Cognitive psychology's ambiguities: Some suggested remedies. *Psychological Review, 89*, 48–59.

Guilford, J. P. (1988). Some changes in the structure-of-intellect model. *Educational & Psychological Measurement, 48*, 1–4.

Gulgoz, S., & Kagitcibasi, C. (2004). Intelligence and intelligence testing in Turkey. In R. J. Sternberg (Ed.), *International handbook of intelligence* (pp. 248–269). New York: Cambridge University Press.

Guthke, J. (1993). Current trends in theories and assessment of intelligence. In J. H. M. Hamers, K. Sijtsma, & A. J. J. M. Ruijssenaars (Eds.), *Learning potential assessment* (pp. 13–20). Amsterdam: Swets & Zeitlinger.

Hadebe, S. (Ed.). (2001). *Isichamazwi.* Harare, Zimbabwe: College Press.

Haensly, P., Reynolds, C. R., & Nash, W. R. (1986). Giftedness: Coalescence, context, conflict, and commitment. In R. J. Sternberg & J. E. Davidson (Eds.), *Conceptions of giftedness* (pp. 128–148). New York: Cambridge University Press.

Haier, R. J. (in press). Biological basis of intelligence: What does brain imaging show? In R. J. Sternberg & S. B. Kaufman (Eds.), *Cambridge handbook of intelligence.* New York: Cambridge University Press.

Haier, R. J., Chueh, D., Touchette, R., Lott, I., et al. (1995). Brain size and cerebral glucose metabolic rate in nonspecific mental retardation and Down syndrome. *Intelligence, 20*, 191–210.

Haier, R. J., Siegel, B., Tang, C., Abel, L., & Buchsbaum, M. S. (1992). Intelligence and changes in regional cerebral glucose metabolic rate following learning. *Intelligence, 16*, 415–426.

Hartman, P. S. (2000). *Women developing wisdom: Antecedents and correlates in a longitudinal sample* (Doctoral dissertation, University of Michigan).

Hayes, J. R. (1989). Cognitive processes in creativity. In J. A. Glover, R. R. Ronning, & C. J. Reynolds (Eds.), *Handbook of creativity* (pp. 135–145). New York: Plenum

Haynes, S. N., & O'Brien, W. H. (2000). *Principles and practice of behavioral assessment.* New York: Springer.

Haywood, H. C., &. Tzuriel, D. (Eds.). (1992). *Interactive assessment.* New York: Springer-Verlag.

Heckhausen J., Dixon, R., & Baltes, P. (1989). Gains and losses in development throughout adulthood as perceived by different adult age groups. *Developmental Psychology, 25*, 109–121.

Hedlund, J., Forsythe, G. B., Horvath, J. A., Williams, W. M., Snook, S., & Sternberg, R. J. (2003). Identifying and assessing tacit knowledge: Understanding the practical intelligence of military leaders. *Leadership Quarterly, 14*, 117–140.

Hedlund, J., Wilt, J. M., Nebel, K. R., Ashford, S. J., & Sternberg, R. J. (2006). Assessing practical intelligence in business school admissions: A supplement to the Graduate Management Admissions Test. *Learning and Individual Differences, 16*, 101–127.

Hegel, G. W. F. (1931). *The phenomenology of the mind* (2nd ed.; J. D. Baillie, Trans.). London: Allen & Unwin. (Original work published 1807)

Heller, K., Monks, F., Sternberg, R. J., & Subotnik, R. (Eds.). (2000). *International handbook of giftedness and talent.* Amsterdam: Elsevier.

Helms-Lorenz, M., Van de Vijver, F. J. R., & Poortinga, Y. H. (2003). Cross-cultural differences in cognitive performance and Spearman's hypothesis: g or c? *Intelligence, 31*, 9–29.

Hennessey, B. A., & Amabile, T. M. (1988). The conditions of creativity. In R. J. Sternberg (Ed.), *The nature of creativity* (pp. 1–38). New York: Cambridge University Press.

Herr, E. L., Moore, G. D., & Hasen, J. S. (1965). Creativity, intelligence, and values: A study of relationships. *Exceptional Children, 32*, 114–115.

Herrnstein, R. J., & Murray, C. (1994). *The bell curve.* New York: Free Press.

Hertzberg-Davis, H. (2009). Myth 7: Differentiation in the regular classroom is equivalent to gifted programs and is sufficient: Classroom teachers have the time, the skill, and the will to differentiate adequately. *Gifted Child Quarterly, 53*, 251–253.

Hezlett, S., Kuncel, N., Vey, A., Ones, D., Campbell, J., & Camara, W. J. (2001). *The effectiveness of the SAT in predicting success early and late in college: A comprehensive meta-analysis.* Paper presented at the annual meeting of the National Council of Measurement in Education, Seattle, WA.

Hira, F. J., & Faulkender, P. J. (1997). Perceiving wisdom: Do age and gender play a part? *International Journal of Aging and Human Development, 44*(2), 85–101.

Hoffman, R. R. (Ed.). (1992). *The psychology of expertise: Cognitive research and empirical AI.* New York: Springer-Verlag.

Holliday, S. G., & Chandler, M. J. (1986). Wisdom: Explorations in adult competence. In J. A. Meacham (Ed.), *Contributions to human development* (Vol. 17, pp. 1–96). Basel, Switzerland: Karger.

Horn, J. L. (1994). Fluid and crystallized intelligence, theory of. In R. J. Sternberg (Ed.), *Encyclopedia of human intelligence* (Vol. 1, pp. 443–451). New York: Macmillan.

Horn, J. L., & Cattell, R. B. (1966). Refinement and test of the theory of fluid and crystallized intelligence. *Journal of Educational Psychology, 57,* 253–270.

Horn, J. L., & Knapp, J. R. (1973). On the subjective character of the empirical base of Guilford's structure-of-intellect model. *Psychological Bulletin, 80,* 33–43.

Hui, H. C., & Yee, C. (1994). The shortened individualism and collectivism scale: Its relationship to demographic and work related variables. *Journal of Research in Personality, 28,* 409–424.

Hunt, E. B. (1978). Mechanics of verbal ability. *Psychological Review, 85,* 109–130.

Hunt, E. B., & Lansman, M. (1982). Individual differences in attention. In R. J. Sternberg (Ed.), *Advances in the psychology of human intelligence* (Vol. 1, pp. 207–254). Hillsdale, NJ: Erlbaum.

Hunt, E., & Carlson, J. (2007). Considerations relating to the study of group differences in intelligence. *Perspectives on Psychological Science, 2,* 194–213.

Intelligence and its measurement: A symposium (1921). Journal of Educational Psychology, 12, 123–147, 195–216, 271–275.

Irvine, J. T. (1978). "Wolof magical thinking": Culture and conservation revisited. *Journal of Cross-Cultural Psychology, 9,* 300–310.

Irvine, S. H. (1979). The place of factor analysis in cross-cultural methodology and its contribution to cognitive theory. In L. Eckensberger, W. Lonner, & Y. Poortinga (Eds.), *Cross-cultural contributions to psychology.* Amsterdam, The Netherlands: Swets & Zeitlinger.

Irvine, S. H. (1988). Constructing the intellect of the Shona: A taxonomic approach. In J. W. Berry, S. H. Irvine, & E. B. Hunt (Eds.), *Indigenous cognitive functioning in a cultural context* (pp. 3–59). New York: Cambridge University Press.

Irvine, S. H., & Berry, J. W. (Eds.). (1983). *Human abilities in cultural context.* New York: Cambridge University Press.

Jackson, N. E., & Butterfield, E. C. (1986). A conception of giftedness designed to promote research. In R. J. Sternberg & J. E. Davidson (Eds.), *Conceptions of giftedness* (pp. 151–181). New York: Cambridge University Press.

Jarvin, L., & Sternberg, R. J. (2002). Alfred Binet's contributions to educational psychology. In B. J. Zimmerman & D. H. Schunk (Eds.), *Educational psychology: A century of contributions* (pp. 65–79). Mahwah, NJ: Erlbaum.

Jason, L. A., Reichler, A., King, C., Madsen, D., Camacho, J., & Marchese, W. (2001). The measurement of wisdom: A preliminary effort. *Journal of Community Psychology, 29,* 585–598.

Jenkins, J. J. (1979). Four points to remember: A tetrahedral model of memory experiments. In L. S. Cermak, & F. I. M. Craik (Eds.), *Levels of processing in human memory* (pp. 429–446). Hillsdale, NJ: Erlbaum.

Jensen, A. R. (1979). g: Outmoded theory or unconquered frontier? *Creative Science and Technology, 2,* 16–29.

Jensen, A. R. (1982a). The chronometry of intelligence. In R. J. Sternberg (Ed.), *Advances in the psychology of human intelligence* (Vol. 1, pp. 255–310). Hillsdale, NJ: Erlbaum.

Jensen, A. R. (1982b). Reaction time and psychometric g. In H. J. Eysenck (Ed.), *A model for intelligence.* Heidelberg: Springer-Verlag.

Jensen, A. R. (1998). *The g factor: The science of mental ability.* Westport, CT: Praeger/Greenwood.

Jensen, A. R. (2002). Psychometric g: Definition and substantiation. In R. J. Sternberg & E. L. Grigorenko (Eds.), *The general factor of intelligence: How general is it?* (pp. 39–53). Mahwah, NJ: Erlbaum.

Jerison, H. J. (2000). The evolution of intelligence. In R. J. Sternberg (Ed.), *Handbook of intelligence* (pp. 216–244). New York: Cambridge University Press.

Johnson-Laird, P. N. (1988). Freedom and constraint in creativity. In R. J. Sternberg (Ed.), *The nature of creativity* (pp. 202–219). New York: Cambridge University Press.

Johnson, R. B., & Christensen, L. B. (2007). *Educational research: Quantitative, qualitative, and mixed approaches.* Thousand Oaks, CA: Sage.

Jordan, J. (2005). The quest for wisdom in adulthood: A psychological perspective. In R. J. Sternberg & J. Jordan, *A handbook of wisdom: Psychological perspectives.* New York: Cambridge University Press.

Jung, C. (1964). *Man and his symbols.* London: Aldus Books.

Kabaservice, G. (2004). *The guardians: Kingman Brewster, his circle, and the rise of the liberal establishment.* New York: Henry Holt.

Kagitcibasi, C. (1996). *Family and human development across cultures: A view from the other side.* Mahwah, NJ: Erlbaum.

Kagitcibasi, C., Sunar, D., & Bekman, S. (2001). Long-term effects of early intervention: Turkish low-income mothers and children. *Journal of Applied Developmental Psychology, 22,* 333–361.

Kanevsky, L. S. (1992). The learning game. In P. S. Klein & A. J. Tannenbaum (Eds.), *To be young and gifted* (pp. 204–241). Norwood, NJ: Ablex.

Kaplan, C. A., & Simon, H. A. (1990). In search of insight. *Cognitive Psychology, 22,* 374–419.

Kaplan, K. (1997). Inteligencia, escuela y sociedad. Las categories del juicio magisterial sbore la inteligencia. [Intelligence, school, and society. The categories of the teachers' judgment about intelligence.] *Propuesta Educativa, 16,* 24–32.

Kaplan, S. N. (2009). Myth 9: There is a single curriculum for the gifted. *Gifted Child Quarterly, 53,* 257–258.

Karabel, J. (2006). *The chosen: The hidden history of admission and exclusion at Harvard, Yale, and Princeton.* New York: Mariner.

Kaufman, A. (2000). Tests of intelligence. In R. J. Sternberg (Ed.), *Handbook of intelligence* (pp. 445–476). New York: Cambridge University Press.

Kaufman, A. S., & Kaufman, N. L. (2004). *Kaufman Assessment Battery for Children* (2nd ed.). Circle Pines, MN: American Guidance Service.

Kaufman, A. S., & Lichtenberger, E. O. (1998). Intellectual assessment. In C. R. Reynolds (Ed.), *Comprehensive clinical psychology*. Vol. 4: Assessment (pp. 203–238). Tarrytown, NY: Elsevier Science.

Kaufman, A. S., Lichtenberger, E. O., Fletcher-Janzen, E., & Kaufman, N. L. (2005). *Assessing adolescent and adult intelligence*. New York: Wiley.

Kaufman, J. C. (2001a). Genius, lunatics, and poets: Mental illness in prize-winning authors. *Imagination, Cognition, and Personality, 20*(4), 305–314.

Kaufman, J. C. (2001b). The Sylvia Plath effect: Mental illness in eminent creative writers. *Journal of Creative Behavior, 35*(1), 37–50.

Kaufman, J. C. (2002). Creativity and confidence: Price of achievement? *American Psychologist, 57*, 375–376.

Kaufman, J. C., & Baer, J. (2002). I bask in dreams of suicide: Mental illness and poetry. *Review of General Psychology, 6*(3), 271–286.

Kaufman, J. C., & Sternberg, R. J. (2000). Are there mental costs to creativity? *Bulletin of Psychology and the Arts, 1*(2), 38.

Kaufman, J. C., & Sternberg, R. J. (Eds.). (2006). *The international handbook of creativity*. New York: Cambridge University Press.

Kaufman, S. B., & Sternberg, R. J. (2007). Giftedness in the Euro-American culture. In S. N. Phillipson & M. McCann (Eds.), *Conceptions of giftedness: Sociocultural perspectives* (pp. 377–411). Mahwah, NJ: Erlbaum.

Kearins, J. M. (1981). Visual spatial memory in Australian Aboriginal children of desert regions. *Cognitive Psychology, 13*, 434–460.

Keating, D. P. (1984). The emperor's new clothes: The "new look" in intelligence research. In R. J. Sternberg (Ed.), *Advances in the psychology of human intelligence* (Vol. 2, pp. 1–45). Hillsdale, NJ: Erlbaum.

Kihlstrom, J., & Cantor, N. (2000). Social intelligence. In R. J. Sternberg (Ed.), *Handbook of intelligence* (pp. 359–379). New York: Cambridge University Press.

Kipling, R. (1985). Working-tools. In B. Ghiselin (Ed.), *The creative process: A symposium* (pp. 161–163). Berkeley: University of California Press. (Original work published in 1937)

Kim, K. H., Cramond, B., & VanTassel-Baska, J. (in press). The relationship between creativity and intelligence. In J. C. Kaufman & R. J. Sternberg (Eds.), *Cambridge handbook of creativity*. New York: Cambridge University Press.

Kitchener, K. S. (1986). Formal reasoning in adults: A review and critique. In R. A. Mines & K. S. Kitchener (Eds.), *Adult cognitive development*. New York: Praeger.

Kitchener, K. S., & Kitchener, R. F. (1981). The development of natural rationality: Can formal operations account for it? In J. Meacham & N. R. Santilli (Eds.), *Social development in youth: Structure and content*. Basel, Switzerland: Karger.

Kitchener, R. F. (1983). Changing conceptions of the philosophy of science and the foundations of developmental psychology. *Human Development, 8*, 1–30.

Kitchener, R. F., & Brenner, H. G. (1990). Wisdom and reflective judgment: Knowing in the face of uncertainty. In R. J. Sternberg (Ed.), *Wisdom: Its nature, origins, and development* (pp. 212–229). New York: Cambridge University Press.

Knight, A., & Parr, W. (1999). Age as a factor in judgements of wisdom and creativity. *New Zealand Journal of Psychology, 28*(1), 37–47.

Kobrin, J. L., Camara, W. J., & Milewski, G. B. (2002). *The utility of the SAT I and SAT II for admissions decisions in California and the nation*. (College Board Report No. 2002–6). New York: College Entrance Examination Board.

Koestler, A. (1964). *The act of creation.* New York: Dell.

Kohlberg, L. (1984). *The psychology of moral development: The nature and validity of moral stages.* New York: HarperCollins.

Kozbelt, A., Beghetto, R. A., & Runco, M. A. (in press). Theories of creativity. In J. C. Kaufman & R. J. Sternberg (Eds.), *Cambridge handbook of creativity.* New York: Cambridge University Press.

Kramer, D. A. (1990). Conceptualizing wisdom: The primacy of affect-cognition relations. In R. J. Sternberg (Ed.), *Wisdom: Its nature, origins, and development* (pp. 279–313). New York: Cambridge University Press.

Kramer, D. A. (2000). Wisdom as a classical source of human strength: Conceptualizing and empirical inquiry. *Journal of Social and Clinical Psychology, 19,* 83–101.

Kramer, D. A., Kahlbaugh, P. E., & Goldston, R. B. (1992). A measure of paradigm beliefs about the social world. *Journal of Gerontology, 47*(3), 180–189.

Kris, E. (1952). *Psychoanalytic exploration in art.* New York: International Universities Press.

Kroeber, A. L., & Kluckhohn, C. (1952). *Culture: A critical review of concepts and definitions.* Cambridge, MA: Peabody Museum.

Krueger, R. F. & Kling, K. C. (2000). Validity. In A. E. Kadzin (Ed.), *Encyclopedia of psychology* (Vol. *8,* pp. 149–153). New York: Oxford University Press.

Kubie, L. S. (1958). *The neurotic distortion of the creative process.* Lawrence: University of Kansas Press.

Kugelmass, S., & Lieblich, A. (1975). *A developmental study of the Arab child in Israel.* Scientific Report. Ford Foundation Grant 015.1261.

Kugelmass, S., Lieblich, A., & Bossik, D. (1974). Patterns of intellectual ability in Jewish and Arab children in Israel. *Journal of Cross-Cultural Psychology, 5,* 184–198.

Kuhn, T. S. (1970). *The structure of scientific revolutions* (2nd ed.). Chicago: University of Chicago Press.

Kunzmann, U., & Baltes, P. B. (2005). The psychology of wisdom: Theoretical and empirical challenges. In R. J. Sternberg, & J. Jordan (Eds.), *A handbook of wisdom: Psychological perspectives.* New York: Cambridge University Press.

Kupperman, J. J. (2005). Morality, ethics, and wisdom. In R. J. Sternberg & J. Jordan (Eds.), *A handbook of wisdom: Psychological perspectives.* New York: Cambridge University Press.

Kyllonen, P. C. (2002). g: Knowledge, speed, strategies, or working-memory capacity? A systems perspective. In R. J. Sternberg & E. L. Grigorenko (Eds.), *The general factor of intelligence: How general is it?* (pp. 415–445). Mahwah, NJ: Erlbaum.

Kyllonen, P., & Christal, R. (1990). Reasoning ability is (little more than) working-memory capacity? *Intelligence, 14,* 389–433.

Laboratory of Comparative Human Cognition. (1982). Culture and intelligence. In R. J. Sternberg (Ed.), *Handbook of human intelligence* (pp. 642–719). New York: Cambridge University Press.

Labouvie-Vief, G. (1980). Beyond formal operations: uses and limits of pure logic in life span development. *Human Development, 23,* 141–161.

Labouvie-Vief, G. (1982). Dynamic development and mature autonomy: A theoretical prologue. *Human Development, 25,* 161–191.

Labouvie-Vief, G. (1990). Wisdom as integrated thought: Historical and developmental perspectives. In R. J. Sternberg (Ed.), *Wisdom: Its nature origins, and development* (pp. 52–86). New York: Cambridge University Press.

Labouvie-Vief, G., Hakim-Larson, J., DeVoe, M., & Schoeberlein, S. (1989). Emotions and self-regulation: A life-span view. *Human Development, 32,* 279–299.

Langley, P., Simon, H. A., Bradshaw, G. L., & Zytkow, J. M. (1987). *Scientific discovery: Computational explorations of the creative processes.* Cambridge, MA: MIT Press.

Lapsley, D. K., & Murphy, M. N. (1985). Another look at the theoretical assumptions of adolescent egocentrism. *Developmental Review, 5,* 201–217.

Larkin, J. H., McDermott, J., Simon, D. P., & Simon, H. A. (1980). Expert and novice performance in solving physics problems. *Science, 208,* 1335–1342.

Larson, G. E., Haier, R. J., LaCasse, L., & Hazen, K. (1995). Evaluation of a "mental effort" hypothesis for correlation between cortical metabolism and intelligence. *Intelligence, 21,* 267–278.

Latané, B., & Darley, J. M. (1970). *Unresponsive bystander: Why doesn't he help?* Englewood Cliffs, NJ: Prentice-Hall.

Lautrey, J., & De Ribaupierre, A. (2004). Intelligence in France and French-speaking Switzerland. In R. J. Sternberg (Ed.), *International handbook of intelligence* (pp. 104–134). New York: Cambridge University Press.

Lave, J. (1988). *Cognition in practice.* New York: Cambridge University Press.

Lazar, I., & Darlington, R. (1982). Lasting effects of early education: A report from the consortium for longitudinal studies. *Monographs of the Society for Research in Child Development, 47* (Serial No. 195, 2–3).

Lemann, N. (1999). *The big test: The secret history of the American meritocracy.* New York: Farrar, Straus & Giroux.

Levy, B. R., Slade, M. D., Kunkel, S. R., & Kasl, S. V. (2002). Longevity increased by positive self-perceptions of aging. *Journal of Personality and Social Psychology, 83*(2), 261–270.

Lidz, C. S. (1991). *Practitioner's guide to dynamic assessment.* New York: Guilford Press.

Lidz, C. S. (Ed.). (1987). *Dynamic assessment: An interactional approach to evaluating learning potential.* New York: Guilford Press.

Lieblich, A. (1983). Intelligence patterns among ethnic and minority groups in Israel. In M. Nisan & U. Last (Eds.), *Between education and psychology* (pp. 335–357). Jerusalem: Magnes Press. (In Hebrew)

Lieblich, A., & Kugelmass, S. (1981). Patterns of intellectual ability of Arab school children in Israel. *Intelligence, 5,* 311–320.

Lin, C. T. (1980). A sketch on the methods of mental testing in ancient China. *Acta Psychological Sinica, 1,* 75–80. (In Chinese)

Locher, P. J. (in press). How does a visual artist create an artwork? In J. C. Kaufman & R. J. Sternberg (Eds.), *Cambridge handbook of creativity.* New York: Cambridge University Press.

Loehlin, J. C. (2000). Group differences in intelligence. In R. J. Sternberg (Ed.), *Handbook of intelligence* (pp. 176–193). New York: Cambridge University Press.

Loehlin, J. C., Horn, J. M., & Willerman, L. (1997). Heredity, environment, and IQ in the Texas adoption project. In R. J. Sternberg & E. L. Grigorenko (Eds.),

Intelligence, heredity, and environment (pp. 105–125). New York: Cambridge University Press.

Loehlin, J. C., Lindzey, G., & Spuhler, J. N. (1975). *Race differences in intelligence.* New York: Freeman.

Lohman, D. F. (2000). Complex information processing and intelligence. In R. J. Sternberg (Ed.), *Handbook of intelligence* (pp. 285–340). New York: Cambridge University Press.

Lohman, D. F., & Lakin, J. M. (in press). Reasoning and intelligence. In R. J. Sternberg & S. B. Kaufman (Eds.), *Cambridge handbook of intelligence.* New York: Cambridge University Press.

Lubart, T. I. (1990). Creativity and cross-cultural variation. *International Journal of Psychology, 25,* 39–59.

Lubart, T. I. (1994). Creativity. In R. J. Sternberg (Ed.), *Thinking and problem solving* (pp. 290–332). San Diego: Academic Press.

Lubart, T. I. (1999). Componential models of creativity. In M. A. Runco & S. Pritzer (Eds.), *Encyclopedia of creativity* (pp. 295–300). New York: Academic Press.

Lubart, T. I. (2000–2001). Models of the creative process: Past, present and future. *Creativity Research Journal, 13*(3–4), 295–308.

Lubart, T. I. (2003). In search of creative intelligence. In R. J. Sternberg, J. Lautrey, & T. I. Lubart (Eds.), *Models of intelligence for the next millennium* (pp. 279–292). Washington, DC: American Psychological Association.

Lubart, T. I., Mouchiroud, C., Tordjman, S., & Zenasni, F. (2003). Psychologie de la créativité [*Psychology of creativity*]. Paris: Colin.

Lubart, T. I., & Runco, M. A. (1999). Economic perspective on creativity. In M. A. Runco & S. Pritzer (Eds.), *Encyclopedia of creativity* (pp. 623–627). New York: Academic Press.

Lubart, T. I., & Sternberg, R. J. (1995). An investment approach to creativity: Theory and data. In S. M. Smith, T. B. Ward, & R.A. Finke (Eds.), *The creative cognition approach* (pp. 269–302). Cambridge, MA: MIT Press.

Ludwig, A. M. (1995). *Price of greatness.* New York: Guilford Press.

Luria, A. R. (1931). Psychological expedition to central Asia. *Science, 74,* 383–384.

Luria, A. R. (1966). *The human brain and psychological processes.* New York: Harper & Row.

Luria, A. R. (1976). *Cognitive development: Its cultural and social foundations.* Cambridge, MA: Harvard University Press.

Lutz, C. (1985). Ethnopsychology compared to what? Explaining behaviour and consciousness among the Ifaluk. In G. M. White & J. Kirkpatrick (Eds.), *Person, self, and experience: Exploring Pacific ethnopsychologies* (pp. 35–79). Berkeley: University of California Press.

Lynn, R. (2002). *IQ and the wealth of nations.* Santa Barbara, CA: Praeger.

Lynn, R. (2006). *Race differences in intelligence: An evolutionary analysis.* Augusta, GA: Washington Summit.

Lynn, R. (2008). *The global bell curve: Race, IQ, and inequality worldwide.* Augusta, GA: Washington Summit Publishers.

Mackintosh, N. (in press). History of theories and measurement of intelligence. In R. J. Sternberg & S. B. Kaufman (Eds.), *Cambridge handbook of intelligence.* New York: Cambridge University Press.

MacKinnon, D. W. (1965). Personality and the realization of creative potential. *American Psychologist, 20,* 273–281.

Maduro, R. (1976). Artistic creativity in a Brahmin painter community. *Research monograph 14.* Berkeley: Center for South and Southeast Asia Studies, University of California.

Mandelman, S. D., & Grigorenko, E. L. (in press). Intelligence: Genes, environment, and everything in between. In R. J. Sternberg & S. B. Kaufman (Eds.), *Cambridge handbook of intelligence.* New York: Cambridge University Press.

Markus, H. R., & Kitayama, S. (1991). Culture and the self: Implications for cognition, emotion, and motivation. *Psychological Review, 98,* 224–253.

Marsella, A. J., Tharp, R., & Ciborowski, T. (Eds.). *Perspectives on cross-cultural psychology.* New York: Academic Press.

Maslow, A. (1967). The creative attitude. In R. L. Mooney & T. A. Rasik (Eds.), *Explorations in creativity* (pp. 43–57). New York: Harper & Row.

Maslow, A. (1968). *Toward a psychology of being.* New York: Van Nostrand.

Matarazzo, J. D. (1992). Psychological testing and assessment in the 21st century. *American Psychologist, 47*(8), 1007–1018.

Matsumoto, D. (1994). *People: Psychology from a cultural perspective.* Pacific Grove, CA: Brooks-Cole.

Matsumoto, D. (1996). *Culture and psychology.* Pacific Grove, CA: Brooks-Cole.

Matsumura, N. (2007). Giftedness in the culture of Japan. In S. N. Phillipson & M. McCann (Eds.), *Conceptions of giftedness: Sociocultural perspectives* (pp. 349–376). Mahwah, NJ: Erlbaum.

Mayer, J. D., Brackett, M. A., & Salovey, P. (Eds.) (2004). *Emotional intelligence: Key readings on the Mayer and Salovey model.* Portchester, NY: Dude Publishing.

Mayer, J. D., & Salovey, P. (1997). What is emotional intelligence? In P. Salovey & D. J. Sluyter (Eds.), *Emotional development and emotional intelligence: Educational implications* (pp. 3–34). New York: Basic Books.

Mayer, J. D., Salovey, P., & Caruso, D. (2000). Emotional intelligence. In R. J. Sternberg (Ed.), *Handbook of intelligence* (pp. 396–421). New York: Cambridge University Press.

Mayer, J. D., Salovey, P., Caruso, D., & Cherkasskiy, L. (in press). Emotional intelligence at 20 years. In R. J. Sternberg & S. B. Kaufman (Eds.), *Cambridge handbook of intelligence.* New York: Cambridge University Press.

Mayer, R. E. (2000). Intelligence and education. In R. J. Sternberg (Ed.), *Handbook of intelligence* (pp. 519–533). New York: Cambridge University Press.

Mayer, R. E. (in press). Intelligence and achievement. In R. J. Sternberg & S. K. Kaufman (Eds.), *Cambridge handbook of intelligence.* New York: Cambridge University Press.

Mayes, L. C., & Fahy, T. (2001). Prenatal drug exposure and cognitive development. In R. J. Sternberg, & E. L. Grigorenko (Eds.), *Environmental effects on cognitive abilities* (pp. 189–219). Mahwah, NJ: Erlbaum.

McAdams, D. P., & de St. Aubin, E. (1992). A theory of generativity and its assessment through self-report, behavioral acts, and narrative themes in autobiography. *Journal of Personality & Social Psychology, 62,* 1003–1015.

McCann, M. (2007). Such is life – in the land down under: Conceptions of giftedness in Australia. In S. N. Phillipson & M. McCann (Eds.), *Conceptions of giftedness: Sociocultural perspectives* (pp. 413–458). Mahwah, NJ: Erlbaum.

McClellan, S. (2008). *What happened: Inside the Bush White House and Washington's culture of deception*. New York: PublicAffairs.

McClelland, D. C. (1973). Testing for competence rather than for intelligence. *American Psychologist, 28*, 1–14.

McClelland, D. C. (1985). *Human motivation*. New York: Scott Foresman.

McClelland, D. C., Atkinson, J. W., Clark, R. A., & Lowell, E. L. (1953). *The achievement motive*. New York: Irvington.

McCrae, R. R., & Costa, P. T. (1997). Personality trait structure as a human universal. *American Psychologist, 5*, 509–516.

McDonough, P. M. (1997). *Choosing colleges: How social class and schools structure opportunity*. Albany: State University of New York Press.

McGarry-Roberts, P. A., Stelmack, R. M., & Campbell, K. B. (1992). Intelligence, reaction time, and event-related potentials. *Intelligence, 16*(3, 4), 289–313.

McKee, P., & Barber, C. (1999). On defining wisdom. *International Journal of Aging and Human Development, 49*, 149–164.

McNemar, Q. (1964). Lost: Our intelligence? Why? *American Psychologist, 19*, 871–882.

Meacham, J. (1990). The loss of wisdom. In R. Sternberg (Ed.), *Wisdom: Its nature, origins, and development* (pp. 181–211). New York: Cambridge University Press.

Mead, M. (1928). *Coming of age in Samoa*. New York: Morrow.

Medin, D. L., & Atran, S. (Eds.). (1999). *Folkbiology*. Cambridge, MA: MIT Press.

Mednick, M. T., & Andrews, F. M. (1967). Creative thinking and level of intelligence. *Journal of Creative Behavior, 1*, 428–431.

Mednick, S. A. (1962). The associative basis of the creative process. *Psychological Review, 69*, 220–232.

Megargee, E. I. (2000). Testing. In A. E. Kazdin (Ed.), *Encyclopedia of psychology* (Vol. 8, pp. 47–52). New York: Macmillan.

Minkowitch, A., Davis, D., & Bashi, Y. (1982). *Success and failure in Israeli elementary education*. New Brunswick, NJ: Transaction Books.

Miyamoto, M. (1985). Parents' and children's beliefs and children's achievement and development. In R. Diaz-Guerrero (Ed.), *Cross-cultural and national studies in social psychology* (pp. 209–223). Amsterdam: Elsevier Science.

Mönks, F. J., & Katzko, M. W. (2005). Giftedness and gifted education. In R. J. Sternberg & J. E. Davidson (Eds.), *Conceptions of giftedness* (2nd ed., pp. 187–200). New York: Cambridge University Press.

Montgomery, A., Barber, C., & McKee, P. (2002). A phenomenological study of wisdom in later life. *International Journal of Aging and Human Development, 52*, 139–157.

Moon, S. M. (2009). Myth 15: High-ability students don't face problems and challenges. *Gifted Child Quarterly, 53*, 274–276.

Moon, T. R. (2009). Myth 16: High-stakes tests are synonymous with rigor and difficulty. *Gifted Child Quarterly, 53*, 277–279.

Moran, S. (in press). The roles of creativity in society. In J. C. Kaufman & R. J. Sternberg (Eds.), *Cambridge handbook of creativity*. New York: Cambridge University Press.

Morelock, M. J. (2000). A sociohistorical perspective on exceptionally high-IQ children. In R. C. Friedman & B. M. Shore (Eds.), *Talents unfolding: Cognition and development* (pp. 55–75). Washington, DC: American Psychological Association.

Morrison, R. G., & Wallace, B. (2002). Imagery vividness, creativity, and the visual arts. *Journal of Mental Imagery, 25*, 135–152.

Mpofu, E. (1993). The context of mental testing and implications for psychoeducational practice in modern Zimbabwe. In W. Su (Ed), *Proceedings of the second Afro-Asian psychological conference* (pp. 17–25). Beijing: University of Peking Press.

Mpofu, E. (2004). Intelligence in Zimbabwe. In R. J. Sternberg (Ed.), *International handbook of intelligence* (pp. 364–390). New York: Cambridge University Press.

Mpofu, E., Ngara, C., & Gudyanga, E. (2007). Constructions of giftedness among the Shona of Central-Southern Africa. In S. N. Phillipson & M. McCann (Eds.), *Conceptions of giftedness: Sociocultural perspectives* (pp. 225–252). Mahwah, NJ: Erlbaum.

Mumford, M. D., & Gustafson, S. B. (1988). Creativity syndrome: Integration, application, and innovation. *Psychological Bulletin, 103*, 27–43.

Mundy-Castle, A. C. (1974). Social and technological intelligence in Western or nonwestern cultures. *Universitas, 4*, 46–52.

Neisser, U. (1979). The concept of intelligence. In R. J. Sternberg & D. K. Detterman (Eds.), *Human intelligence: Perspectives on its theory and measurement* (pp. 179–189). Norwood, NJ: Ablex.

Neisser, U. (Ed.). (1998). *The rising curve.* Washington, DC: American Psychological Association.

Neisser, U., Boodoo, G., Bouchard T. J., Boykin, W. A., Brody, N., Ceci, S. J., et al. (1996). Intelligence: Knowns and unknowns. *American Psychologist, 51*(2), 77–101.

Nettelbeck, T. (1987). Inspection time and intelligence. In P. A. Vernon (Ed.), *Speed of information-processing and intelligence* (pp. 295–346). Norwood, New Jersey: Ablex.

Nettelbeck, T. (in press). Basic processes of intelligence. In R. J. Sternberg & S. B. Kaufman (Eds.), *Cambridge handbook of intelligence.* New York: Cambridge University Press.

Nettelbeck, T., & Lally, M. (1976). Inspection time and measured intelligence. *British Journal of Psychology, 67*(1), 17–22.

Nettelbeck, T., & Rabbitt, P. M. (1992). Aging, cognitive performance, and mental speed. *Intelligence, 16*(2), 189–205.

Nettelbeck, T., Rabbitt, P. M. A., Wilson, C., & Batt, R. (1996). Uncoupling learning from initial recall: The relationship between speed and memory deficits in old age. *British Journal of Psychology, 87*, 593–607.

Nettelbeck, T., & Young, R. (1996). Intelligence and savant syndrome: Is the whole greater than the sum of the fragments? *Intelligence, 22*, 49–67.

Newell, A., & Simon, H. A. (1972). *Human problem solving.* Englewood Cliffs, NJ: Prentice-Hall.

Newman, T. M., & Sternberg, R. J. (Eds.). (2004). *Students with both gifts and learning disabilities.* Boston: Kluwer Academic.

Newman, T. M., Brown, W., Hart, L., Macomber, D., Doyle, N., Kornilov, S. A., Jarvin, L., Sternberg, R. J., & Grigorenko, E. L. (2009). The Leonardo Laboratory: Developing targeted programs for academic underachievers with visual-spatial gifts. *Talent Development & Excellence, 1*, 67–78.

Nisbett, R. E. (2003). *The geography of thought: Why we think the way we do.* New York: Free Press.

Nisbett, R. E. (2009). *Intelligence and how to get it: Why schools and cultures count.* New York: Norton.

Niu, W., & Sternberg, R. J. (2001). Cultural influences on artistic creativity and its evaluation. *International Journal of Psychology, 36*(4), 225–241.

Noy, P. (1969). A revision of the psychoanalytic theory of the primary process. *International Journal of Psychoanalysis, 50,* 155–178.

Nuñes, T. (1994). Street intelligence. In R. J. Sternberg (Ed.), *Encyclopedia of human intelligence* (Vol. *2,* pp. 1045–1049). New York: Macmillan.

Ochse, R. (1990). *Before the gates of excellence.* New York: Cambridge University Press.

Ogbu, J. U. (1986). The consequences of the American caste system. In U. Neisser (Ed.), *The school achievement of minority children.* Hillsdale, NJ: Erlbaum.

Ogbu, J. U., & Stern, P. (2001). Caste status and intellectual development. In R. S. Sternberg, & E. L. Grigorenko (Eds.), *Environmental effects on intellectual functioning.* Hillsdale, NJ: Erlbaum.

Okagaki, L., & Sternberg, R. J. (1993). Parental beliefs and children's school performance. *Child Development, 64,* 36–56.

Olson, H. C. (1994). Fetal alcohol syndrome. In R. J. Sternberg (Ed.), *Encyclopedia of human intelligence* (Vol. *1,* pp. 439–443). New York: Macmillan.

Orwoll, L., & Perlmutter, M. (1990). The study of wise persons: Integrating a personality perspective. In R. J. Sternberg (Ed.), *Wisdom: Its nature, origins, and development* (pp.160–180). New York: Cambridge University Press.

Osbeck, L. M., & Robinson, D. N. (2005). Philosophical theories of wisdom. In R. J. Sternberg, & J. Jordan, *A handbook of wisdom: Psychological perspectives.* New York: Cambridge University Press.

Osborn, A. F. (1953). *Applied imagination* (rev. ed.). New York: Charles Scribner's Sons.

Oswald, F. L., Schmitt, N., Kim, B. H., Ramsay, L. J., & Gillespie, M. A. (2004). Developing a biodata measure and situational judgment inventory as predictors of college student performance. *Journal of Applied Psychology, 89,* 187–207.

Pascual-Leone, J. (1990). An essay on wisdom: toward organismic processes that make it possible. In R. J. Sternberg (Ed.), *Wisdom: Its nature, origins, and development* (pp. 244–278). New York: Cambridge University Press.

Pasupathi, M., & Staudinger, U. M. (2001). Do advanced moral reasoners also show wisdom? Linking moral reasoning and wisdom-related knowledge and judgment. *International Journal of Behavioral Development, 25,* 401–415.

Pasupathi, M., Staudinger, U. M., & Baltes, P. B. (2001). Seeds of wisdom: Adolescents' knowledge and judgment about difficult life problems. *Developmental Psychology, 37,* 351–361.

Paulhus, D. L., Wehr, P., Harms, P. D., & Strausser, D. I. (2002). Use of exemplar surveys to reveal implicit types of intelligence. *Personality and Social Psychology Bulletin, 28,* 1051–1062.

Perkins, D. N. (1981). *The mind's best work.* Cambridge, MA: Harvard University Press.

Perkins, D. N. (1995). Insight in minds and genes. In R. J. Sternberg, & J. E. Davidson (Eds.), *The nature of insight* (pp. 495–534). Cambridge, MA: MIT Press.

Perkins, D. N. (1998). In the country of the blind: An appreciation of Donald Campbell's vision of creative thought. *Journal of Creative Behavior, 32*(3), 177–191.

Perkins, D. N., & Grotzer, T. A. (1997). Teaching intelligence. *American Psychologist, 52,* 1125–1133.

Perlmutter, M., Adams, C., Nyquist, L., & Kaplan, C. (1988). *Beliefs about wisdom.* Unpublished data. (Cited in Orwoll & Perlmutter, 1990.)

"Person of the Week: 'Enron Whistleblower' Sherron Wilson" (2002). http://www.time.com/time/pow/article/0,8599,194927,00.html, retrieved June 5, 2008.

Peterson, J. S. (2009). Myth 17: Gifted and talented individuals do not have unique social and emotional needs. *Gifted Child Quarterly, 53,* 280–282.

Phillipson, S. (2007). Toward an understanding of a Malay conception of giftedness. In S. N. Phillipson & M. McCann (Eds.), *Conceptions of giftedness: Sociocultural perspectives* (pp. 253–282). Mahwah, NJ: Erlbaum.

Phillipson, S. N., & McCann, M. (Eds.). (2007). *Conceptions of giftedness: Sociocultural perspectives.* Mahwah, NJ: Erlbaum.

Piaget, J. (1972). Intellectual evolution from adolescence to adulthood. *Human Development, 15,* 1–12.

Pianta, R. C., & Egeland, B. (1994). Predictors of instability in children's mental test performance at 24, 48, and 96 months. *Intelligence, 18*(2), 145–163.

Pinker, S. (1997). *How the mind works.* New York: Norton.

Plomin, R. (1997). Identifying genes for cognitive abilities and disabilities. In R. J. Sternberg & E. L. Grigorenko (Eds.), *Intelligence, heredity, and environment* (pp. 89–104). New York: Cambridge University Press.

Plucker, J. A., & Makel, M. C. (in press). Assessment of creativity. In J. C. Kaufman & R. J. Sternberg (Eds.), *Cambridge handbook of creativity.* New York: Cambridge University Press.

Policastro, E., & Gardner, H. (1999). From case studies to robust generalizations: An approach to the study of creativity. In R. J. Sternberg (Ed.), *Handbook of creativity* (pp. 213–225). New York: Cambridge University Press.

Poole, F. J. P. (1985). Coming into social being: Cultural images of infants in Bimin-Kuskusmin folk psychology. In G. M. White & J. Kirkpatrick (Eds.), *Person, self, and experience: Exploring Pacific ethnopsychologies* (pp. 183–244). Berkeley: University of California Press.

Posner, M. I., & Mitchell, R. F. (1967). Chronometric analysis of classification. *Psychological Review, 74,* 392–409.

Postlethwaite, B., Robbins, S., Rickerson, J., & McKinniss, T. (2009). The moderation of conscientiousness by cognitive ability when predicting workplace safety behavior. *Personality and Individual Differences, 47,* 711–716.

Prince R. J. & Geissler P. W. (2001). Becoming "one who treats": A case study of a Luo healer and her grandson in western Kenya. *Educational Anthropology Quarterly, 32,* 447–471.

Puccio, G. J., & Cabra, J. F. (in press). Organizational creativity: A systems approach. In J. C. Kaufman & R. J. Sternberg (Eds.), *Cambridge handbook of creativity.* New York: Cambridge University Press.

Putnam, D. B., & Kilbride, P. L. (1980). *A relativistic understanding of social intelligence among the Songhay of Mali and Smaia of Kenya.* Paper presented at the meeting of the Society for Cross-Cultural Research, Philadelphia, PA.

Ramey, C. T., & Ramey, S. L. (2000). Intelligence and public policy. R. J. Sternberg (Ed.), *Handbook of intelligence* (pp. 534–548). New York: Cambridge University Press.

Raven, J. C., Court, J. H., & Raven, J. (1992). *Manual for Raven's Progressive Matrices and Mill Hill Vocabulary Scales.* Oxford: Oxford Psychologists Press.

Reed, T. E. (1993). Effect of enriched (complex) environment on nerve conduction velocity: New data and review of implications for the speed of information processing. *Intelligence, 17*(4), 533–540.

Reed, T. E., & Jensen, A. R. (1991). Arm nerve conduction velocity (NCV), brain NCV, reaction time, and intelligence. *Intelligence, 15*, 33–47.

Reed, T. E., & Jensen, R. (1993). A somatosensory latency between the thalamus and cortex also correlates with level of intelligence. *Intelligence, 17*, 443–450.

Reis, S. M. (2005). Feminist perspectives on talent development: A research-based conception of giftedness in women. In R. J. Sternberg & J. E. Davidson (Eds.), *Conceptions of giftedness* (2nd ed., pp. 217–245). New York: Cambridge University Press.

Reis, S. M., & Renzulli, J. S. (2009a). Myth 1: The gifted and talented constitute one single homogeneous group and giftedness is a way of being that stays in the person over time and experiences. *Gifted Child Quarterly, 53*, 229–232.

Reis, S. M., & Renzulli, J. S. (2009b). The schoolwide enrichment model: A focus on student strengths and interests. In J. S. Renzulli, E. J. Gubbins, K. S. McMillen, R. D. Eckert, & C. A. Little (Eds.), *Systems and models for developing the gifted and talented* (2nd ed., pp. 323–352). Mansfield Center, CT: Creative Learning Press.

Reis, S. M., & Renzulli, J. S. (in press). The development of intellectual giftedness: Searching for what remains after everything else has been explained. In R. J. Sternberg & S. B. Kaufman (Eds.), *Cambridge handbook of intelligence.* New York: Cambridge University Press.

Renzulli, J. S. (1977). *The enrichment triad model: A guide for developing defensible programs for the gifted and talented.* Mansfield Center, CT: Creative Learning Press.

Renzulli, J. S. (1978). What makes giftedness? Reexamining a definition. *Phi Delta Kappan, 60*, 18–24.

Renzulli, J. S. (1984). The triad/revolving door system: A research based approach to identification and programming for the gifted and talented. *Gifted Child Quarterly, 28*, 163–171.

Renzulli, J. S. (1986). The three-ring conception of giftedness: A developmental model for creative productivity. In R. J. Sternberg & J. E. Davidson (Eds.), *Conceptions of giftedness* (pp. 53–92). New York: Cambridge University Press.

Renzulli, J. S. (2005). The three-ring conception of giftedness: A developmental model for promoting creative productivity. In R. J. Sternberg & J. E. Davidson (Eds.), *Conceptions of giftedness* (2nd ed., pp. 246–279). New York: Cambridge University Press.

Renzulli, J. S. (2009). The multiple menu model for developing differentiated curriculum. In J. S. Renzulli, E. J. Gubbins, K. S. McMillen, R. D. Eckert, & C. A.

Little (Eds.), *Systems and models for developing the gifted and talented* (2nd ed., pp. 353–381). Mansfield Center, CT: Creative Learning Press.

Renzulli, J. S., Gubbins, E. J., McMillen, K. S., Eckert, R. D., & Little, C. A. (2009). *Systems and models for developing programs for the gifted and talented* (2nd ed.). Mansfield Center, CT: Creative Learning Press.

Richards, R. (in press). Everyday creativity: Process and way of life – five key issues. In J. C. Kaufman & R. J. Sternberg (Eds.), *Cambridge handbook of creativity*. New York: Cambridge University Press.

Richardson, M. J., & Pasupathi, M. (2005) Young and growing wiser: Wisdom during adolescence and young adulthood. In R. J. Sternberg & J. Jordan (Eds.), *A handbook of wisdom: Psychological perspectives*. New York: Cambridge University Press.

Riegel, K. F. (1973). Dialectic operation: The final period of cognitive development. *Human development, 16*, 346–370.

Ritchhart, R., & Perkins, D. N. (2005). Learning to think: The challenges of teaching thinking. In K. Holyoak & R. G. Morrison (Eds.), *Cambridge handbook of thinking and reasoning* (pp. 775–801). Cambridge, UK: Cambridge University Press.

Robinson, A. (2009). Myth 10: Examining the ostrich: Gifted services do not cure a sick regular program. *Gifted Child Quarterly, 53*, 259–261.

Robinson, D. N. (1989). *Aristotle's psychology*. New York: Columbia University Press.

Robinson, D. N. (1990). Wisdom through the ages. In R. J. Sternberg (Ed.), *Wisdom: Its nature, origins, and development* (pp. 13–24). New York: Cambridge University Press.

Robinson, F. (1992). *Love's story told: A life of Henry A. Murray*. Cambridge, MA: Harvard University Press.

Robinson, N. M. (2005). In defense of a psychometric approach to the definition of academic giftedness: A conservative view from a die-hard liberal. In R. J. Sternberg & J. E. Davidson (Eds.), *Conceptions of giftedness* (Vol. 2, pp. 280–294). New York: Cambridge University Press.

Roe, A. (1953). *The making of a scientist*. New York: Dodd, Mead.

Roe, A. (1972). Patterns of productivity of scientists. *Science, 176*, 940–941.

Rogers, C. R. (1954). Toward a theory of creativity. *ETC: A Review of General Semantics, 11*, 249–260.

Rogoff, B. (1990). *Apprenticeship in thinking: Cognitive development in social context*. New York: Oxford University Press.

Rogoff, B. (2003). *The cultural nature of human development*. London: Oxford University Press.

Roid, G. (2003). *Stanford-Binet Intelligence Scales* (5th ed.). Itasca, IL: Riverside.

Rosas, R. (2004). Intelligence research in Latin America. In R. J. Sternberg (Ed.), *International handbook of intelligence* (pp. 391–410). New York: Cambridge University Press.

Rosch, E. (1975). Cognitive representations of semantic categories. *Journal of Experimental Psychology: General, 104*, 192–233.

Rosnow, R. L., & Rosenthal, R. (1999). *Beginning behavioral research: A conceptual primer* (4th ed.). Englewood Cliffs, NJ: Prentice-Hall

Rothenberg, A. (1979). *The emerging goddess*. Chicago: University of Chicago Press.

Rothenberg, A., & Hausman, C. R. (Eds.). (1976). *The creativity question.* Durham, NC: Duke University Press.

Rowe, D. C. (2005). Under the skin: On the impartial treatment of genetic and environmental hypotheses of racial differences. *American Psychologist, 60*(1), 60–70.

Royer, J. M., Carlo, M. S., Dufresne, R., & Mestre, J. (1996). The assessment of levels of domain expertise while reading. *Cognition and Instruction, 14,* 373–408.

Rubenson, D. L., & Runco, M. A. (1992). The psychoeconomic approach to creativity. *New Ideas in Psychology, 10,* 131–147.

Rubin, D. C., & Schulkind, M. D. (1997). Distribution of important and word-cued autobiographical memories in 20-, 35-, and 70-year-old adults. *Psychology and Aging, 12,* 524–535.

Runco, M. A. (Ed.). (1994). *Problem finding, problem solving, and creativity.* Norwood, NJ: Ablex.

Runco, M. A. (2005). Creative giftedness. In R. J. Sternberg & J. E. Davidson (Eds.), *Conceptions of giftedness* (2nd ed., pp. 280–294). New York: Cambridge University Press.

Runco, M. A. (in press). Divergent thinking, creativity, and ideation. In J. C. Kaufman & R. J. Sternberg (Eds.), *Cambridge handbook of creativity.* New York: Cambridge University Press.

Rushton, J. P. (2000). *Race, evolution, and behavior: A life history perspective* (2nd abridged ed.). Port Huron, MI: Charles Darwin Research Institute.

Rushton, J. P., & Jensen, A. R. (2005). Thirty years of research on race differences in cognitive ability. *Psychology, Public Policy, and Law, 11,* 235–294.

Ruzgis, P. M., & Grigorenko, E. L. (1994). Cultural meaning systems, intelligence, and personality. In R. J. Sternberg and P. Ruzgis (Eds.), *Personality and intelligence* (pp. 248–270). New York: Cambridge.

Ryff, C. D. (1989). Happiness is everything, or is it? Explorations on the meaning of psychological well-being. *Journal of Personality and Social Psychology, 57,* 1069–1081.

Sak, U. (2007). Giftedness and the Turkish culture. In S. N. Phillipson & M. McCann (Eds.), *Conceptions of giftedness: Sociocultural perspectives* (pp. 283–310). Mahwah, NJ: Erlbaum.

Salovey, P., & Sluyter, D. J. (Eds.) (1997). *Emotional development and emotional intelligence: Educational implications.* New York: Basic Books.

Sarason, S. B., & Doris, J. (1979). *Educational handicap, public policy, and social history.* New York: Free Press.

Sato, T., Namiki, H., Ando, J., & Hatano, G. (2004). Japanese conception of and research on intelligence. In R. J. Sternberg (Ed.), *International handbook of intelligence* (pp. 302–324). New York: Cambridge University Press.

Savasir, L., & Sahin, N. (1995). *Wechsler Cocuklar icin Zeka Olcegi [Wechsler Intelligence Scale for Children].* Ankara, Turkey: Turkish Psychological Association.

Sawyer, R. K. (in press). Individual and group creativity. In J. C. Kaufman & R. J. Sternberg (Eds.), *Cambridge handbook of creativity.* New York: Cambridge University Press.

Saxe, G. B. (1990). *Culture and cognitive development: Studies in mathematical understanding.* Mahwah, NJ: Erlbaum.

Schaie, K.W. (1996). *Intellectual development in adulthood: The Seattle longitudinal study*. New York: Cambridge University Press.

Schliemann, A. D., & Magalhües, V. P. (1990). *Proportional reasoning: From shops, to kitchens, laboratories, and, hopefully, schools*. Proceedings of the Fourteenth International Conference for the Psychology of Mathematics Education, Oaxtepec, Mexico.

Schmidt, F. L., & Hunter, J. E. (1998). The validity and utility of selection methods in personnel psychology: Practical and theoretical implications of 85 years of research findings. *Psychological Bulletin, 124,* 262–274.

Schon, D. A. (1983). *The reflective practitioner*. New York: Basic Books.

Seashore, C.E. (1960). *Seashore Measures of Musical Talents*. New York: Psychological Corporation.

Sedlacek, W. E. (2004). *Beyond the big test: Noncognitive assessment in higher education*. San Francisco: Jossey-Bass.

Šefer, J. (2007). Slavic conceptions of giftedness and creativity. In S. N. Phillipson & M. McCann (Eds.), *Conceptions of giftedness: Sociocultural perspectives* (pp. 311–347). Mahwah, NJ: Erlbaum.

Seifer, R. (2001). Socioeconomic status, multiple risks, and development of intelligence. In R. J. Sternberg, & E. L. Grigorenko (Eds.), *Environmental effects on cognitive abilities* (pp. 59–81). Mahwah, NJ: Erlbaum.

"*Senator faces list of assault allegations*" (2008). http://www.boston.com/news/local/massachusetts/articles/2008/06/05/senator_faces_list_of_assault_allegations/, retrieved June 5, 2008.

Serpell, R. (1974). Aspects of intelligence in a developing country. *African Social Research, 17,* 576–96.

Serpell, R. (1996). Cultural models of childhood in indigenous socialization and formal schooling in Zambia. In C. P. Hwang & M. E. Lamb (Eds.), *Images of childhood.* (pp. 129–142). Mahwah, NJ: Erlbaum.

Serpell, R. (2000). Intelligence and culture. In R. J. Sternberg (Ed.), *Handbook of intelligence* (pp. 549–577). New York: Cambridge University Press.

Shi, J. (2004). Diligence makes people smart: Chinese perspectives on intelligence. In R. J. Sternberg (Ed.), *International handbook of intelligence* (pp. 325–343). New York: Cambridge University Press.

Shore, B. M. (2000). Metacognition and flexibility. In R. C. Friedman & B. M. Shore (Eds.), *Talents unfolding: Cognition and development* (pp. 167–187). Washington, DC: American Psychological Association.

Shweder, R. A. (1991). *Thinking through cultures: Expeditions in cultural psychology*. Cambridge, MA: Harvard University Press.

Silver, H. R. (1981). Calculating risks: The socioeconomic foundations of aesthetic innovation in an Ashanti carving community. *Ethnology, 20*(2), 101–114.

Simon, H. A. (1976). Identifying basic abilities underlying intelligent performance of complex tasks. In L. B. Resnick (Ed.), *The nature of intelligence* (pp. 65–98). Hillsdale, NJ: Erlbaum.

Simonton, D. K. (1984). *Genius, creativity, and leadership*. Cambridge, MA: Harvard University Press.

Simonton, D. K. (1988a). Creativity, leadership, and chance. In R. J. Sternberg (Ed.), *The nature of creativity* (pp. 386–426). New York: Cambridge University Press.

Simonton, D. K. (1988b). *Scientific genius.* New York: Cambridge University Press.

Simonton, D. K. (1994). *Greatness: Who makes history and why.* New York: Guilford Press.

Simonton, D. K. (1995). Foresight in insight: A Darwinian answer. In R. J. Sternberg & J. E. Davidson (Eds.), *The nature of insight* (pp. 495–534). Cambridge, MA: MIT Press.

Simonton, D. K. (1996). Creative expertise: A life-span developmental perspective. In K. A. Ericsson (Ed.), *The road to excellence* (pp. 227–253). Mahwah, NJ: Erlbaum.

Simonton, D. K. (1997). Creative productivity: A predictive and explanatory model of career trajectories and landmarks. *Psychological Review, 104,* 66–89.

Simonton, D. K. (1998). Donald Campbell's model of the creative process: Creativity as blind variation and selective retention. *Journal of Creative Behavior, 32,* 153–158.

Simonton, D. K. (1999). Talent and its development: An emergenic and epigenetic mode. *Psychological Review, 106,* 435–457.

Simonton, D. K. (in press). Creativity in highly eminent individuals. In J. C. Kaufman & R. J. Sternberg (Eds.), *Cambridge handbook of creativity.* New York: Cambridge University Press.

Sisk, D. (2009). Myth 13: The regular classroom teacher can "go it alone." *Gifted Child Quarterly, 53,* 269–271.

Slavin, R. E. (1990). Achievement effects of ability grouping in secondary schools: A best-evidence synthesis. *Review of Educational Research, 60,* 471–499.

Smith, J., & Baltes, P. B. (1990). Wisdom-related knowledge: Age/Cohort differences in response to life-planning problems. *Developmental Psychology, 26,* 494–505.

Smith, J. K., & Smith, L. F. (in press). Educational creativity. In J. C. Kaufman & R. J. Sternberg (Eds.), *Cambridge handbook of creativity.* New York: Cambridge University Press.

Smith, J., Staudinger, U. M., & Baltes, P. B. (1994). Occupational settings facilitative of wisdom-related knowledge: The sample case of clinical psychologists. *Journal of Consulting and Clinical Psychology, 64,* 989–1000.

Smith, S. M., Ward, T. B., & Finke, R. A. (Eds.). (1995). *The creative cognition approach.* Cambridge, MA: MIT Press.

Solomon, J. L., Marshall, P., & Gardner, H. (2005). Crossing boundaries to generative wisdom: An analysis of professional work. In R.J. Sternberg & J. Jordan (Eds.), *A handbook of wisdom: Psychological perspectives.* New York: Cambridge University Press.

Sowarka, D. (1989). Weisheit und weise Personen: Common-Sense-Konzepte älterer Menschen. [Wisdom and wise persons: Common-sense conceptions of older people.] *Zeitschrift für Entwicklungspsychologie und Paedagogische Psychologie, 21,* 87–109.

Spear, L. C., & Sternberg, R. J. (1987). Teaching styles: Staff development for teaching thinking. *Journal of Staff Development, 8*(3), 35–39.

Spearman, C. (1923). *The nature of intelligence and the principles of cognition.* London: Macmillan.

Spearman, C. (1927). *The abilities of man.* London: Macmillan.

"*Spitzer is linked to prostitution ring,*" 2008; http://www.nytimes.com/2008/03/10/nyregion/10cnd-spitzer.html?_r=1&oref=slogin, retrieved June 5, 2008.

Srivastava, S., & Misra, G. (1996). Changing perspectives on understanding intelligence: An appraisal. *Indian Psychological Abstracts and Reviews, 3.* New Delhi: Sage.

Srivastava, S., & Misra, G. (2000). *Culture and conceptualization of intelligence.* New Delhi: National Council of Educational Research and Training.

Stabley, M. (2008, December 16). *Montgomery County schools try scrapping the "gifted" label.* http://www.nbcwashington.com/news/local/Montgomery-County-Schools-Try-Scrapping-Gifted-Label.html, retrieved 1/2/09.

Stange, A., Kunzmann, U., & Baltes, P. B. (2003). *Perceived wisdom: The interplay of age, wisdom-related knowledge, and social behavior.* Poster presented at the Annual Convention of the American Psychological Association, Toronto, Canada.

Stankov, L. (2004). Similar thoughts under different stars: Conceptions of intelligence in Australia. In R. J. Sternberg (Ed.), *International handbook of intelligence* (pp. 344–363). New York: Cambridge University Press.

Stanley, J. C., & Benbow, C. P. (1986). Youths who reason exceptionally well mathematically. In R. J. Sternberg & J. E. Davidson (Eds.), *Conceptions of giftedness* (pp. 361–387). New York: Cambridge University Press.

Stanley, J. C., & Brody, L. E. (2001). History and philosophy of the talent search model. *Gifted and Talented International, 16,* 94–96.

Staudinger, U. M. (1999). Older and wiser? Integrating results on the relationship between age and wisdom-related performance. *International Journal of Behavioral Development, 23,* 641–664.

Staudinger, U. M., & Baltes, P. B. (1996). Interactive minds: A facilitative setting for wisdom-related performance? *Journal of Personality and Social Psychology, 71,* 746–762.

Staudinger, U. M., Dörner, J., & Mickler, C. (2003). *Self-insight: Operationalizations and plasticity.* Unpublished manuscript, International University Bremen, Bremen, Germany.

Staudinger, U. M., Dörner, J., & Mickler, C. (2005). Wisdom and personality. In R. J. Sternberg & J. Jordan (Eds.). *A handbook of wisdom: Psychological perspectives.* New York: Cambridge University Press.

Staudinger, U. M., & Glueck, J. (in press). Wisdom and intelligence. In R. J. Sternberg & S. B. Kaufman (Eds.), *Cambridge handbook of intelligence.* New York: Cambridge University Press.

Staudinger, U. M., Lopez, D. F., & Baltes, P. B. (1997). The psychometric location of wisdom-related performance: Intelligence, personality, and more? *Personality & Social Psychology Bulletin, 23,* 1200–1214.

Staudinger, U. M., Maciel, A. G., Smith, J., & Baltes, P. B. (1998). What predicts wisdom-related performance? A first look at personality, intelligence, and facilitative experiential contexts. *European Journal of Personality, 12,* 1–17.

Staudinger, U. M., Smith, J., & Baltes, P. B. (1992). Wisdom-related knowledge in life review task: Age differences and the role of professional specialization. *Psychology and Aging, 7,* 271–281.

Steele, C. (1990, May). A conversation with Claude Steele. *APS Observer,* pp. 1–17.

Stemler, S. E., Grigorenko, E. L., Jarvin, L., & Sternberg, R. J. (2006). Using the theory of successful intelligence as a basis for augmenting AP exams in psychology and statistics. *Contemporary Educational Psychology, 31*(2), 344–376.

Stern, W. (1912). *Psychologische Methoden der Intelligenz-Prüfung.* Leipzig, Germany: Barth.

Sternberg, R. J. (1977). *Intelligence, information processing, and analogical reasoning: The componential analysis of human abilities.* Hillsdale, NJ: Erlbaum.

Sternberg, R. J. (1979). Is absolute time relatively interesting? *Behavioral and Brain Sciences, 2,* 281–282.

Sternberg, R. J. (1981). Intelligence and nonentrenchment. *Journal of Educational Psychology, 73,* 1–16.

Sternberg, R. J. (1982). Natural, unnatural, and supernatural concepts. *Cognitive Psychology, 14,* 451–488.

Sternberg, R. J. (1983). Components of human intelligence. *Cognition, 15,* 1–48.

Sternberg, R. J. (1985a). *Beyond IQ: A triarchic theory of human intelligence.* New York: Cambridge University Press.

Sternberg, R. J. (1985b). Implicit theories of intelligence, creativity, and wisdom. *Journal of Personality and Social Psychology, 49,* 607–627.

Sternberg, R. J. (1986). *Intelligence applied.* Orlando, FL: Harcourt Brace College.

Sternberg, R. J. (1987). Teaching intelligence: The application of cognitive psychology to the improvement of intellectual skills. In J. B. Baron & R. J. Sternberg (Eds.), *Teaching thinking skills: Theory and practice* (pp. 182–218). New York: Freeman.

Sternberg, R. J. (1988a). *The triangle of love.* New York: Basic

Sternberg, R. J. (1988b). *The triarchic mind: A new theory of human intelligence.* New York: Viking.

Sternberg, R. J. (1988c). A triarchic view of intelligence in cross–cultural perspective. In S. H. Irvine & J. W. Berry (Eds.), *Human abilities in cultural context* (pp. 60–85). New York: Cambridge University Press.

Sternberg, R. J. (1988d). What's love got to do with it? *Omni, 10,* p. 27.

Sternberg, R. J. (1990a). Wisdom and its relations to intelligence and creativity. In R. J. Sternberg (Ed.), *Wisdom: Its nature, origins, and development* (pp. 142–159). New York: Cambridge University Press.

Sternberg, R. J. (Ed.). (1990b). *Wisdom: Its nature, origins, and development.* New York: Cambridge University Press.

Sternberg, R. J. (1993). The concept of "giftedness": A pentagonal implicit theory. *The origins and development of high ability* (pp. 5–21). United Kingdom: CIBA Foundation.

Sternberg, R. J. (1994). Cognitive conceptions of expertise. *International Journal of Expert Systems: Research and Application, 7,* 1–12.

Sternberg, R. J. (1995). *In search of the human mind.* Ft. Worth, TX: Harcourt.

Sternberg, R. J. (1996a). For whom does the bell curve toll? It tolls for you. *Journal of Quality Learning, 6*(1), 9–27.

Sternberg, R. J. (1996b). *Successful Intelligence.* New York: Simon & Schuster.

Sternberg, R. J. (1997a). *Successful intelligence.* New York: Plume.

Sternberg, R. J. (1997b). *Thinking styles.* New York: Cambridge University Press.

Sternberg, R. J. (1998a). Abilities are forms of developing expertise. *Educational Researcher, 27,* 11–20.

Sternberg, R. J. (1998b). A balance theory of wisdom. *Review of General Psychology, 2*(4), 347–365.

Sternberg, R. J. (1998c). Principles of teaching for successful intelligence. *Educational Psychologist, 33*, 65–72.

Sternberg, R. J. (1999a). Intelligence as developing expertise. *Contemporary Educational Psychology, 24*, 259–375.

Sternberg, R. J. (1999b). A propulsion model of types of creative contributions. *Review of General Psychology, 3*, 83–100.

Sternberg, R. J. (1999c). The theory of successful intelligence. *Review of General Psychology, 3*, 292–316.

Sternberg, R. J. (2000a). Creativity is a decision. In B. Z. Presseisen (Ed.), *Teaching for intelligence II: A collection of articles* (pp. 83–103). Arlington Heights, IL: Skylight Training.

Sternberg, R.J. (Ed.). (2000b). *Handbook of intelligence.* New York: Cambridge University Press.

Sternberg, R. J. (2000c). Intelligence and wisdom. In R. J. Sternberg (Ed.), *Handbook of intelligence* (pp. 629–647). New York: Cambridge University Press.

Sternberg, R. J. (2001a). Giftedness as developing expertise: A theory of the interface between high abilities and achieved excellence. *High Ability Studies, 12*(2), 159–179.

Sternberg, R. J. (2001b). Why schools should teach for wisdom: The balance theory of wisdom in educational settings. *Educational Psychologist, 36*(4), 227–245.

Sternberg, R. J. (2002a). Smart people are not stupid, but they sure can be foolish: The imbalance theory of foolishness. In R. J. Sternberg (Ed.), *Why smart people can be so stupid* (pp. 232–242). New Haven, CT: Yale University Press.

Sternberg, R. J. (2002b). Successful intelligence: A new approach to leadership. In R. E. Riggio, S. E. Murphy, & F. J. Pirozzolo (Eds.), *Multiple intelligences and leadership* (pp. 9–28). Mahwah, NJ: Erlbaum.

Sternberg, R. J. (2003a). A duplex theory of hate: Development and application to terrorism, massacres, and genocide. *Review of General Psychology, 7*(3), 299–328.

Sternberg, R. J. (2003b). What is an expert student? *Educational Researcher, 32*(8), 5–9.

Sternberg, R. J. (2003c). *WICS: A model of leadership in organizations.* Academy of Management Learning and Education.

Sternberg, R. J. (2003d). *Wisdom, intelligence, and creativity synthesized.* New York: Cambridge University Press.

Sternberg, R. J. (2004a). Culture and intelligence. *American Psychologist, 59*(5), 325–338.

Sternberg, R. J. (Ed.). (2004b). *International handbook of intelligence.* New York: Cambridge University Press.

Sternberg, R. J. (2005a). Accomplishing the goals of affirmative action – with or without affirmative action. *Change, 37*(1), 6–13.

Sternberg, R. J. (2005b). The theory of successful intelligence. *Interamerican Journal of Psychology, 39*(2), 189–202.

Sternberg, R. J. (2005c). WICS: A model of giftedness in leadership. *Roeper Review, 28*(1), 37–44.

Sternberg, R. J. (2005d). The WICS model of giftedness. In R. J. Sternberg & J. E. Davidson (Eds.), *Conceptions of giftedness* (2nd ed., pp. 327–342). New York: Cambridge University Press.

Sternberg, R. J. (2006). How can we simultaneously enhance both academic excellence and diversity? *College and University, 81*(1), 17–23.

Sternberg, R. J. (2007a). Culture, instruction, and assessment. *Comparative Education, 43*(1), 5–22.

Sternberg, R. J. (2007b). Finding students who are wise, practical, and creative. *Chronicle of Higher Education, 53*(44), B11.

Sternberg, R. J. (2007c). How higher education can produce the next generation of positive leaders. In M. E. Devlin (Ed.), *Futures Forum 2007* (pp. 33–36). Cambridge, MA: Forum for the Future of Higher Education.

Sternberg, R. J. (2008a, September/October). It's the foolishness, stupid. *American Interest,* 19–23.

Sternberg, R. J. (2008b). The WICS approach to leadership: Stories of leadership and the structures and processes that support them. *Leadership Quarterly, 19*(3), 360–371.

Sternberg, R. J. (2009a). The Rainbow and Kaleidoscope projects: A new psychological approach to undergraduate admissions. *European Psychologist, 14,* 279–287.

Sternberg, R. J. (2009b). Reflections on ethical leadership. In D. Ambrose & T. L. Cross (Eds.), *Morality, ethics, and gifted minds.* New York: Springer.

Sternberg, R. J. (2010). *College admissions for the 21st century.* Cambridge, MA: Harvard University Press.

Sternberg, R. J., & Arroyo, C. G. (2006). Beyond expectations: A new view of the gifted disadvantaged. In B. Wallace & G. Eriksson (Eds.), *Diversity in gifted education: International perspectives on global issues* (pp. 110–124). London: Routledge.

Sternberg, R. J., Bonney, C. R., Gabora, L., Jarvin, L., Karelitz, T. M., & Coffin, L. A. (in press). Broadening the spectrum of undergraduate admissions. *College and University.*

Sternberg, R. J., Castejón, J. L., Prieto, M. D., Hautamäki, J., & Grigorenko, E. L. (2001). Confirmatory factor analysis of the Sternberg triarchic abilities test in three international samples: An empirical test of the triarchic theory of intelligence. *European Journal of Psychological Assessment, 17*(1) 1–16.

Sternberg, R. J., & Clinkenbeard, P. R. (1995). The triarchic model applied to identifying, teaching, and assessing gifted children. *Roeper Review, 17*(4), 255–260.

Sternberg, R. J., & Coffin L. A. (2010). Admitting and developing "new leaders for a changing world." *New England Journal of Higher Education.*

Sternberg, R. J., Conway, B. E., Ketron, J. L., & Bernstein, M. (1981). People's conceptions of intelligence. *Journal of Personality and Social Psychology, 41,* 37–55.

Sternberg, R. J., & Davidson, J. E. (Eds.). (1986). *Conceptions of giftedness.* New York: Cambridge University Press.

Sternberg, R. J., & Davidson, J. E. (Eds.). (1994). *The nature of insight.* Cambridge, MA: MIT Press.

Sternberg, R. J., & Davidson, J. E. (Eds.). (2005). *Conceptions of giftedness* (2nd ed.). New York: Cambridge University Press.

Sternberg, R. J., & Detterman, D. K. (Eds.). (1986). *What is intelligence?* Norwood, NJ: Ablex.

Sternberg, R. J., Ferrari, M., Clinkenbeard, P. R., & Grigorenko, E. L. (1996). Identification, instruction, and assessment of gifted children: A construct validation of a triarchic model. *Gifted Child Quarterly, 40*(3), 129–137.

Sternberg, R. J., Forsythe, G. B., Hedlund, J., Horvath, J., Snook, S., Williams, W. M., Wagner, R. K., & Grigorenko, E. L. (2000). *Practical intelligence in everyday life*. New York: Cambridge University Press.

Sternberg, R. J., & Gastel, J. (1989a). Coping with novelty in human intelligence: An empirical investigation. *Intelligence, 13*, 187–197.

Sternberg, R. J., & Gastel, J. (1989b). If dancers ate their shoes: Inductive reasoning with factual and counterfactual premises. *Memory and Cognition, 17*, 1–10.

Sternberg, R. J., & Grigorenko, E. L. (1997a). The cognitive costs of physical and mental ill health: Applying the psychology of the developed world to the problems of the developing world. *Eye on Psi Chi, 2*, 20–27.

Sternberg, R. J., & Grigorenko, E. L. (Eds.). (1997b). *Intelligence, heredity, and environment*. New York: Cambridge University Press.

Sternberg, R. J., & Grigorenko, E. L. (1999a). Myths in psychology and education regarding the gene environment debate. *Teachers College Record, 100*, 536–553.

Sternberg, R. J., & Grigorenko, E. L. (1999b). *Our labeled children: What every parent and teacher needs to know about learning disabilities*. Cambridge, MA: Perseus.

Sternberg, R. J., & Grigorenko, E. L. (2000). *Teaching for successful intelligence*. Arlington Heights, IL: Skylight Training.

Sternberg, R. J., & Grigorenko, E. L. (2001a). All testing is dynamic testing. *Issues in Education, 7*(2), 137–170.

Sternberg, R. J., & Grigorenko, E. L. (Eds.). (2001b). *Environmental effects on cognitive abilities*. Mahwah, NJ: Erlbaum.

Sternberg, R. J., & Grigorenko, E. L. (2002a). *Dynamic testing*. New York: Cambridge University Press.

Sternberg, R. J., & Grigorenko E. L. (Eds.). (2002b). *The general factor of intelligence: How general is it?* Mahwah, NJ: Erlbaum.

Sternberg, R. J., & Grigorenko, E. L. (2007a). Ability testing across cultures. In L. Suzuki (Ed.), *Handbook of multicultural assessment* (3rd ed., pp. 449–470). New York: Jossey-Bass.

Sternberg, R. J., & Grigorenko, E. L. (2007b). *Teaching for successful intelligence* (2nd ed.). Thousand Oaks, CA: Corwin.

Sternberg, R. J., Grigorenko, E. L., Ferrari, M., & Clinkenbeard, P. (1999a). A triarchic analysis of an aptitude–treatment interaction. *European Journal of Psychological Assessment, 15*(1), 1–11.

Sternberg, R. J., Grigorenko, E. L., Ferrari, M., & Clinkenbeard, P. (1999b). The triarchic model applied to gifted identification, instruction, and assessment. In N. Colangelo & S. G. Assouline (Eds.), *Talent development III: Proceedings from the 1995 Henry B. and Jocelyn Wallace National Research Symposium on Talent Development* (pp. 71–80). Scottsdale, AZ: Gifted Psychology Press.

Sternberg, R. J., Grigorenko, E. L., & Jarvin, L. (2001). Improving reading instruction: The triarchic model. *Educational Leadership, 58*(6), 48–52.

Sternberg, R. J., Grigorenko, E. L., & Kidd, K. K. (2005). Intelligence, race, and genetics. *American Psychologist, 60*(1), 46–59.

Sternberg, R. J., Grigorenko, E. L., Ngorosho, D., Tantufuye, E., Mbise, A., Nokes, C., Jukes, M., & Bundy, D. A. (2002). Assessing intellectual potential in rural Tanzanian school children. *Intelligence, 30,* 141–162.

Sternberg, R. J., Grigorenko, E. L., & Zhang, L.-F. (2008). Styles of learning and thinking matter in instruction and assessment. *Perspectives on Psychological Science, 3*(6), 486–506.

Sternberg, R. J., & Hedlund, J. (2002). Practical intelligence, g, and work psychology. *Human Performance, 15,* 143–160.

Sternberg, R. J., Jarvin, L., & Grigorenko, E. L. (2009). *Teaching for wisdom, intelligence, creativity, and success.* Thousand Oaks, CA: Sage.

Sternberg, R. J., & Jordan, J. (Eds.). (2005). *A handbook of wisdom: Psychological perspectives.* New York: Cambridge University Press.

Sternberg, R. J., & Kaufman J. C. (1998). Human abilities. *Annual Review of Psychology, 49,* 479–502.

Sternberg, R. J., & Kaufman, S. (Eds.). (in press). *Cambridge handbook of intelligence.* New York: Cambridge University Press.

Sternberg, R. J., Kaufman, J. C., & Grigorenko, E. L. (2008). *Applied intelligence.* New York: Cambridge University Press.

Sternberg, R. J., Kaufman, J. C., & Pretz, J. E. (2002). *The creativity conundrum: A propulsion model of kinds of creative contributions.* Philadelphia: Psychology Press.

Sternberg, R. J., Kaufman, J. C., & Pretz, J. E. (2003). A propulsion model of creative leadership. *Leadership Quarterly, 14,* 453–473.

Sternberg, R. J., & Lubart, T. I. (1991). An investment theory of creativity and its development. *Human Development, 34*(1), 1–31.

Sternberg, R. J., & Lubart, T. I. (1995). *Defying the crowd: Cultivating creativity in a culture of conformity.* New York: Free Press.

Sternberg, R. J., & Lubart, T. I. (1996). Investing in creativity. *American Psychologist, 51*(7), 677–688.

Sternberg, R. J., & Lubart, T. I. (2001). Wisdom and creativity. In J. E. Birren, & K. W. Schaie (Eds.), *Handbook of the psychology of aging* (5th ed., pp. 500–522). San Diego, CA: Academic Press.

Sternberg, R. J., Nokes, K., Geissler, P. W., Prince, R., Okatcha, F., Bundy, D. A., & Grigorenko, E. L. (2001a). The relationship between academic and practical intelligence: A case study in Kenya. *Intelligence, 29,* 401–418.

Sternberg, R. J., & O'Hara, L. (1999). Creativity and intelligence. In R. J. Sternberg (Ed.), *Handbook of creativity* (pp. 251–272). New York: Cambridge University Press.

Sternberg, R. J., & O'Hara, L. A. (2000). Intelligence and creativity. In R. J. Sternberg (Ed.), *Handbook of intelligence* (pp. 609–628). New York: Cambridge University Press.

Sternberg, R. J., Powell, C., McGrane, P. A., & McGregor, S. (1997). Effects of a parasitic infection on cognitive functioning. *Journal of Experimental Psychology: Applied, 3,* 67–76.

Sternberg, R. J., & Rifkin, B. (1979). The development of analogical reasoning processes. *Journal of Experimental Child Psychology, 27,* 195–232.

Sternberg, R. J., & Ruzgis, P. (Eds.). (1994). *Personality and intelligence.* New York: Cambridge University Press.

Sternberg, R. J., & Spear-Swerling, L. (1996). *Teaching for thinking.* Washington, DC: APA Books.

Sternberg, R. J., & Sternberg, K. (2008). *The nature of hate.* New York: Cambridge University Press.

Sternberg, R. J., & The Rainbow Project Collaborators. (2005). Augmenting the SAT through assessments of analytical, practical, and creative skills. In W. Camara & E. Kimmel (Eds.), *Choosing students: Higher education admission tools for the 21st century* (pp. 159–176). Mahwah, NJ: Erlbaum.

Sternberg, R. J., & The Rainbow Project Collaborators. (2006). The Rainbow Project: Enhancing the SAT through assessments of analytical, practical, and creative skills. *Intelligence, 34*(4), 321–350.

Sternberg, R. J., The Rainbow Project Collaborators, & University of Michigan Business School Project Collaborators. (2004). Theory based university admissions testing for a new millennium. *Educational Psychologist, 39*(3), 185–198.

Sternberg, R. J., Torff, B., & Grigorenko, E. L. (1998a). Teaching for successful intelligence raises school achievement. *Phi Delta Kappan, 79,* 667–669.

Sternberg, R. J., Torff, B., & Grigorenko, E. L. (1998b). Teaching triarchically improves school achievement. *Journal of Educational Psychology, 90,* 1–11.

Sternberg, R. J., & Wagner, R. K. (1993). The g-ocentric view of intelligence and job performance is wrong. *Current Directions in Psychological Science, 2*(1), 1–4.

Sternberg, R. J., & Wagner, R. K. (Eds.). (1994). *Mind in context.* New York: Cambridge University Press.

Sternberg, R. J., Wagner, R. K., & Okagaki, L. (1993). Practical intelligence: The nature and role of tacit knowledge in work and at school. In H. Reese & J. Puckett (Eds.), *Advances in lifespan development* (pp. 205–227). Hillsdale, NJ: Erlbaum.

Sternberg, R. J., Wagner, R. K., Williams, W. M., & Horvath, J. A. (1995). Testing common sense. *American Psychologist, 50*(11), 912–927.

Sternberg, R. J., & Williams, W. M. (1996). *How to develop student creativity.* Alexandria, VA: Association for Supervision and Curriculum Development.

Sternberg, R. J., & Zhang, L. F. (1995). What do we mean by "giftedness"? A pentagonal implicit theory. *Gifted Child Quarterly, 39*(2), 88–94.

Stevenson, H. W., & Stigler, J. W. (1994). *The learning gap: Why our schools are failing and what we can learn from Japanese and Chinese education.* New York: Simon & Schuster.

Stigler, J. W., Lee, S., Lucker, G. W., & Stevenson, H. W. (1982). Curriculum and achievement in mathematics: A study of elementary school children in Japan, Taiwan, and the United States. *Journal of Educational Psychology, 74,* 315–322.

Subotnik, R. F., & Arnold, K. D. (Eds.) (1993). *Beyond Terman: Longitudinal studies in contemporary gifted education.* Norwood, NJ: Ablex

Subotnik, R. F., & Jarvin, L. (2005). Beyond expertise: Conceptions of giftedness as great performance. In R. J. Sternberg & J. E. Davidson (Eds.), *Conceptions of giftedness* (2nd ed., pp. 343–357). New York: Cambridge University Press.

Subotnik, R. F., Jarvin, L., Moga, E., & Sternberg, R. J. (2003) Wisdom from gatekeepers: Secrets of success in music performance. *Bulletin of Psychology and the Arts, 4*(1), 5–9.

Suler, J. R. (1980). Primary process thinking and creativity. *Psychological Bulletin*, *88*, 555–578.

Super, C. M. (1976). Environmental effects on motor development: The case of "African infant precocity." *Developmental Medicine and Child Neurology*, *8*(5), 561–567.

Super C. M., & Harkness, S. (1982). The development of affect in infancy and early childhood. In D. Wagner & H. Stevenson (Eds.), *Cultural perspectives on child development* (pp. 1–19). San Francisco: W. H. Freeman.

Super, C. M., & Harkness, S. (1986). The developmental niche: A conceptualization at the interface of child and culture. *International Journal of Behavioral Development*, *9*, 545–569.

Super, C. M., & Harkness, S. (1993). The developmental niche: A conceptualization at the interface of child and culture. In R. A. Pierce & M. A. Black (Eds.), *Life-span development: A diversity reader* (pp. 61–77). Dubuque, IA: Kendall/Hunt.

Takahashi, M., & Bordia, P. (2000). The concept of wisdom: A cross cultural comparison. *International Journal of Psychology*, *35*(1), 1–9.

Takahashi, M., & Overton, W. F. (2005). Cultural foundations of wisdom: An integrated developmental approach. In R. J. Sternberg & J. Jordan (Eds.). *A handbook of wisdom: Psychological perspectives*. New York: Cambridge University Press.

Takayama, M. (2002). *The concept of wisdom and wise people in Japan* (Doctoral dissertation, Tokyo University, Japan).

Tannenbaum, A. J. (1986). Giftedness: A psychosocial approach. In R. J. Sternberg & J. E. Davidson (Eds.), *Conceptions of giftedness* (pp. 21–52). New York: Cambridge University Press.

Taranto, M. A. (1989). Facets of wisdom: A theoretical synthesis. *International Journal of Aging and Human Development*, *29*, 1–21.

Terman, L. M. (1925). *Genetic studies of genius: Mental and physical traits of a thousand gifted children* (Vol. 1). Stanford, CA: Stanford University Press.

Terman, L. M., & Merrill, M. A. (1937). *Measuring intelligence*. Boston: Houghton Mifflin.

Terman, L. M., & Merrill, M. A. (1973). *Stanford–Binet Intelligence Scale: Manual for the third revision*. Boston: Houghton Mifflin.

Terman, L. M., & Oden, M. H. (1959). *Genetic studies of genius: The gifted group at midlife* (Vol. 4). Stanford, CA: Stanford University Press.

Tetewsky, S. J., & Sternberg, R. J. (1986). Conceptual and lexical determinants of nonentrenched thinking. *Journal of Memory and Language*, *25*, 202–225.

Therivel, W. A. (1999). Why Mozart and not Salieri? *Creativity Research Journal*, *12*, 67–76.

Thomason, T. C., & Qiong, X. (2008). Counseling psychology in China: Past and present. *International Journal for the Advancement of Counselling*, *30*, 213–219.

Thorndike, R. L., Hagen, E. P., & Sattler, J. M. (1986). *Technical manual for the Stanford-Binet Intelligence Scale: Fourth edition*. Chicago: Riverside.

Thurstone, L. L. (1924/1973). *The nature of intelligence*. London: Routledge.

Thurstone, L. L. (1938). *Primary mental abilities*. Chicago, IL: University of Chicago Press.

"*Timeline of the Tyco International Scandal*," 2005; http://www.usatoday.com/money/industries/manufacturing/2005–06–17-tyco-timeline_x.htm, retrieved June 5, 2008.

Tomasello, M. (2001). *The cultural origins of human cognition*. Cambridge, MA: Harvard University Press.

Tomlinson, C. A. (2009). Myth 8: The "patch-on" approach to programming is effective. *Gifted Child Quarterly, 53,* 254–256.

Torrance, E. P. (1962). *Guiding creative talent*. Englewood Cliffs, NJ: Prentice-Hall.

Torrance, E. P. (1974). *Torrance tests of creative thinking*. Lexington, MA: Personnel Press.

Torrance, E. P., & Wu, T. H. (1981). A comparative longitudinal study of the adult creative achievements of elementary school children identified as highly intelligent and as highly creative. *Creative Child and Adult Quarterly, 6,* 71–76.

Totten, S., Parsons, W. S., & Charny, I. W. (Eds.). (2004). *Century of genocide: Critical essays and eyewitness accounts* (2nd ed.). New York: Routledge.

Treffinger, D. J. (2009). Myth 5: Creativity is too difficult to measure. *Gifted Child Quarterly, 53,* 245–247.

Turkheimer, E., Haley, A., Waldron, M., D'Onofrio, B., & Gottesman, I. I. (2003). Socioeconomic status modifies heritability of IQ in young children. *Psychological Science, 14*(6), 623–628.

Turner, M. L., & Engle, R. W. (1989). Is working memory capacity task dependent? *Journal of Memory & Language, 28*(2), 127–154.

Tzuriel, D. (1995). *Dynamic-interactive assessment: The legacy of L. S. Vygotsky and current developments*. Unpublished manuscript.

VanTassel-Baska, J. (1998). *Excellence in educating the gifted* (3rd ed.). Denver: Love.

VanTassel-Baska, J. (2005). Domain-specific giftedness. In R. J. Sternberg & J. E. Davidson (Eds.), *Conceptions of giftedness* (pp. 358–376). New York: Cambridge University Press.

VanTassel-Baska, J. (2009). Myth 12: Gifted programs should stick out like a sore thumb. *Gifted Child Quarterly, 53,* 266–268.

Vernon, P. A., & Mori, M. (1992). Intelligence, reaction times, and peripheral nerve conduction velocity. *Intelligence, 8,* 273–288.

Vernon, P. A., Wickett, J. C., Bazana, P. G., & Stelmack, R. M. (2000). The neuropsychology and psychophysiology of human intelligence. In R. J. Sternberg (Ed.), *Handbook of intelligence* (pp. 245–264). New York: Cambridge University Press.

Vernon, P. E. (Ed.). (1970). *Creativity: Selected readings* (pp. 126–136). Baltimore: Penguin Books.

Vernon, P. E. (1971). *The structure of human abilities*. London: Methuen.

Von Károlyi, C., & Winner, E. (2005). Extreme giftedness. In R. J. Sternberg & J. E. Davidson (Eds.), *Conceptions of giftedness* (2nd ed., pp. 377–394). New York: Cambridge University Press.

von Oech, R. (1983). *A whack on the side of the head*. New York: Warner.

von Oech, R. (1986). *A kick in the seat of the pants*. New York: Harper & Row.

Vygotsky, L. S. (1978). *Mind in society: The development of higher psychological processes*. Cambridge, MA: Harvard University Press.

Wagner, D. A. (1978). Memories of Morocco: The influence of age, schooling, and environment on memory. *Cognitive Psychology, 10,* 1–28.

Wagner, R. K. (1987). Tacit knowledge in everyday intelligent behavior. *Journal of Personality and Social Psychology, 52,* 1236–1247.

Wagner, R. K. (2000). Practical intelligence. In R. J. Sternberg (Ed.), *Handbook of human intelligence* (pp. 380–395). New York: Cambridge University Press.

Wagner, D. A., & Sternberg, R. J. (1985). Practical intelligence in real-world pursuits: The role of tacit knowledge. *Journal of Personality and Social Psychology, 49,* 436–458.

Wahlsten, D., & Gottlieb, G. (1997). The invalid separation of effects of nature and nurture: Lessons from animal experimentation. In R. J. Sternberg & E. L. Grigorenko (Eds.), *Intelligence, heredity, and environment* (pp. 163–192). New York: Cambridge University Press.

Wallach, M., & Kogan, N. (1965). *Modes of thinking in young children.* New York: Holt, Rinehart, & Winston.

Walters, J., & Gardner, H. (1986). The crystallizing experience: Discovering an intellectual gift. In R. J. Sternberg & J. E. Davidson (Eds.), *Conceptions of giftedness* (pp. 306–331). New York: Cambridge University Press.

Ward, T. B. (1994). Structured imagination: The role of conceptual structure in exemplar generation. *Cognitive Psychology, 27,* 1–40.

Ward, T. B., & Kolomyts, Y. (in press). Cognition and creativity. In J. C. Kaufman & R. J. Sternberg (Eds.), *Cambridge handbook of creativity.* New York: Cambridge University Press.

Ward, T. B., Smith, S. M., & Finke, R. A. (1999). Creative cognition. In R. J. Sternberg (Ed.), *Handbook of creativity* (pp. 189–212). New York: Cambridge University Press.

Wechsler, D. (1939). *The measurement of adult intelligence.* Baltimore: Williams & Wilkins.

Wechsler, D. (1974/1991). *Manual for the Wechsler Intelligence Scales for Children* (3rd ed.). San Antonio, TX: Psychological Corporation.

Wechsler, D. (1967/2002). *Wechsler Primary and Preschool Scale of Intelligence* (3rd ed.). San Antonio, TX: Harcourt Brace.

Wechsler, D. (2003). *WISC-IV: Administration and scoring manual.* San Antonio: Psychological Corporation.

Wehner, L., Csikszentmihalyi, M., & Magyari-Beck, I. (1991). Current approaches used in studying creativity: An exploratory investigation. *Creativity Research Journal, 4*(3), 261– 271.

Weisberg, R. W. (1986). *Creativity, genius and other myths.* New York: Freeman.

Weisberg, R. W. (1988). Problem solving and creativity. In R. J. Sternberg (Ed.), *The nature of creativity* (pp. 148–176). New York: Cambridge University Press.

Weisberg, R. W. (1993). *Creativity: Beyond the myth of genius.* New York: Freeman.

Weisberg, R. W. (1999). Creativity and knowledge: A challenge to theories. In R. J. Sternberg (Ed.), *Handbook of creativity* (pp. 226–250). New York: Cambridge University.

Weisberg, R. W., & Alba, J. W. (1981). An examination of the alleged role of "fixation" in the solution of several "insight" problems. *Journal of Experimental Psychology: General, 110,* 169–192.

Werner, H., & Kaplan, B. (1963). *Symbol formation.* Hillsdale, NJ: Erlbaum.

Westen, D., & Rosenthal, R. (2003). Quantifying construct validity: Two simple measures. *Journal of Personality and Social Psychology, 84,* 608–618.

White, G. M. (1985). Premises and purposes in a Solomon Islands ethnopsychology. In G. M. White & J. Kirkpatrick (Eds.), *Person, self, and experience: Exploring Pacific ethnopsychologies* (pp. 328–366). Berkeley: University of California Press.

Wickett, J. C., & Vernon, P. A. (1994). Peripheral nerve conduction velocity, reaction time, and intelligence: An attempt to replicate Vernon and Mori. *Intelligence, 18,* 127–132.

Williams, W. M., Blythe, T., White, N., Li, J., Gardner, H., & Sternberg, R. J. (2002). Practical intelligence for school: Developing metacognitive sources of achievement in adolescence. *Developmental Review, 22*(2), 162–210.

Willis, J. O., Dumont, R., & Kaufman, A. S. (in press). Factor-analytic models of intelligence. In R. J. Sternberg & S. B. Kaufman (Eds.), *Cambridge handbook of intelligence.* New York: Cambridge University Press.

Wink, P., & Helson, R. (1997). Practical and transcendent wisdom: Their nature and some longitudinal findings. *Journal of Adult Development, 4,* 1–16.

Winner, E. (1996). *Gifted children: Myths and realities.* New York: Basic Books.

Wissler, C. (1901). The correlation of mental and physical tests. *Psychological Review, Monograph Supplement, 3*(6).

Wong-Fernandez, B., & Bustos-Orosa, Ma. A. (2007). Conceptions of giftedness among Tagalog-speaking Filipinos. In S. N. Phillipson & M. McCann (Eds.), *Conceptions of giftedness: Sociocultural perspectives* (pp. 169–196). Mahwah, NJ: Erlbaum.

Woodman, R. W., & Schoenfeldt, L. F. (1989). Individual differences in creativity: An interactionist perspective. In J. A. Glover, R. R. Ronning, & C. R. Reynolds (Eds.), *Handbook of creativity* (pp. 77–91). New York: Plenum.

Worrell, F. C. (2009). Myth 4: A single test score or indicator tells us all we need to know about giftedness. *Gifted Child Quarterly, 53,* 242–244.

Yamamoto, K. (1964). Creativity and sociometric choice among adolescents. *Journal of Social Psychology, 64,* 249–261.

Yan, Z. (2001). Yan's family rules – Piece of conduct. In *Chinese classic books series (multimedia version).* Beijing: Beijing Yinguan Electronic Publishing. (In Chinese)

Yang, S. (2001). Conceptions of wisdom among Taiwanese Chinese. *Journal of Cross-Cultural Psychology, 32*(6), 662–680.

Yang, S. Y., & Sternberg, R. J. (1997a). Conceptions of intelligence in ancient Chinese philosophy. *Journal of Theoretical and Philosophical Psychology, 17,* 101–119.

Yang, S. Y., & Sternberg, R. J. (1997b). Taiwanese Chinese people's conceptions of intelligence. *Intelligence, 25,* 21–36.

Zeidner, M. (1985). A cross-cultural test of the situational bias hypothesis – the Israeli scene. *Evaluation and Program Planning, 8,* 367–376.

Zeidner, M. (1990). Perceptions of ethnic group modal intelligence: Reflections of cultural stereotypes or intelligence test scores? *Journal of Cross-Cultural Psychology, 21*(2), 214–231.

Zeidner, M., Matthews G., & Roberts, R. (2004). Emotional intelligence in the workplace: A critical review. *Applied Psychology: An International Review, 53,* 371–399.

Zentall, T. R. (2000). Animal intelligence. In R. J. Sternberg (Ed.), *Handbook of intelligence* (pp. 197–215). New York: Cambridge University Press.

Ziegler, A. (2005). The Actiotype model of giftedness. In R. J. Sternberg & J. E. Davidson (Eds.), *Conceptions of giftedness* (pp. 411–436). New York: Cambridge University Press.

Ziegler, A., & Stoeger, H. (2007). The Germanic view of giftedness. In S. N. Phillipson & M. McCann (Eds.), *Conceptions of giftedness: Sociocultural perspectives* (pp. 65–98). Mahwah, NJ: Erlbaum.

Zigler, E., & Berman, W. (1983). Discerning the future of early childhood intervention. *American Psychologist, 38,* 894–906.

INDEX

Abecedarian Project, 78
abilities. *See also* developing-expertise
    model
  and disabilities, 170–171
  general versus specific, 171
  structure of, 137–141
ability tests, 132, 141–143
Aborigines, 152, 156–157
abstract ethical rules, 124–125
academic giftedness, 11
academic intelligence. *See also* IQ
    (intelligence quotient)
  versus contextually important skills,
    158–161
  in developing-expertise model,
    137–141
  overview, 43–44
  practical skills unrecognized in tests of,
    161
academic quality, and Kaleidoscope
    Project, 205
achievement, measures of, 132
achievement motivation, 136
achievement tests, 183–184, 194
Ackerman, P. L., 131
Adams, C., 112
Adams, J. L., 85
adaptability of IQ tests, 23–24
adaptation to environment, 217
adaptive regression, 86
admissions, 203–206. *See also* Rainbow
    Project

adolescence, development of wisdom
    during, 115
adult lifespan, trajectory of wisdom
    throughout, 116–118
advance forward incrementation, 40
Advanced Placement (AP) courses, 13
Africa. *See also specific African countries or*
    tribes by name
  concepts of intelligence in, 147–148,
    149
  intelligence in cultural context, 157
age. *See also* explicit theories of wisdom
  and IQ, 22
  mental, 181–182
  and wisdom, 102–103, 106, 110–114
Alaskan Eskimo children, 161
Alba, J. W., 90
alternate approaches to creativity,
    98–101
alternate-forms reliability, 187
Amabile, T. M., 93, 96
ambiguity, willingness to tolerate, 38
America
  conceptions of intelligence in, 149,
    150–151
  ethics of government,
  giftedness label in, 175
  implicit theories of wisdom in,
    105–106
  learning disability label in, 171, 175
analogy, in Aurora-*g* battery, 208
analysis, problem, 37

283

failure, helping students to learn from, 216–217

false invulnerability, 128

false omnipotence, 128

false omniscience, 128

familiarity, of IQ-based framework, 19–20

Faulkender, P. J., 113

Feldhusen, J. F., 27–28

Feldman, D. H., 29

field, 29, 96, 97

Filipinos, concept of giftedness among, 152

Finke, R. A., 91, 99–100

Fisher, L. M., 106, 109

flexibility
developing in students, 216
Torrance Tests of Creative Thinking, 87

Floating Boats subtest, Aurora Project, 208

fluency
Torrance Tests of Creative Thinking, 87
verbal, 59

fluid ability, 61

fluid intelligence, 110–111, 138–139

Flynn effect, 138–139, 158, 231

Flynn, J. R., 4, 80, 231

focusing, 99

follow-up data, Rainbow and Kaleidoscope Projects, 211

foreign languages, teaching for wisdom, 234–235

Forrin, B., 64

forward incrementation, 39–40

frameworks for giftedness. *See* IQ plus other qualities framework; IQ-based framework; no conceptual framework

Freud, Anna, 100

Freud, Sigmund, 51, 86, 100

fulfillment, teaching for, 232

functional magnetic resonance imaging, 70–71

Gagné, Francois, 31–32

Gallagher, J. J., 15, 35

Galton, F., 56–57

Gardner, H.
confluence approaches to creativity, 96–97
crystallizing experience, 31
ethical giftedness, 127
multiple intelligences, 35, 74–75
types of creative contributions, 99

Geissler P. W., 159–160

Geneplore model, 91

general abilities, 171

general factor of human intelligence. *See* *g*-factor (general factor of human intelligence)

generative phase of creativity, 91

genetic factors, 79–80, 133

Germany
Nazi, 126
view of giftedness in, 151–152

g-factor (general factor of human intelligence)
Aurora Project assessment of, 208–209
and culture, 160
developing-expertise model, 137–141
and IQ-based framework, 17
Rainbow Project, 200–201
Spearman's theory of, 58–59

Gibson, K., 152

Gifted Child Quarterly journal, 11–13

gifted leadership, 52–53

gifted-LD students. *See also* learning disabilities (LDs)
developing-expertise model, 168–169
label of, 175–176
pedagogical programs for, 174–176
strengths of, 172

giftedness
from interactions between individual and environment, 173–174
misunderstandings regarding label, 173
myths about, 11–13
need for label of, 10–11
overview, 1–2

Gill, R., 147

Gillespie, M. A., 211

Girgin, Y., 165–166

Gladwin, T., 156